Spectacle and Sacrifice

*The Ritual Foundations of Village Life
in North China*

Harvard East Asian Monographs 315

Spectacle and Sacrifice

The Ritual Foundations of Village Life in North China

David Johnson

Published by the Harvard University Asia Center
Distributed by Harvard University Press
Cambridge (Massachusetts) and London 2009

© 2009 by the President and Fellows of Harvard College

Printed in the United States of America

The Harvard University Asia Center publishes a monograph series and, in coordination with the Fairbank Center for Chinese Studies, the Korea Institute, the Reischauer Institute of Japanese Studies, and other faculties and institutes, administers research projects designed to further scholarly understanding of China, Japan, Vietnam, Korea, and other Asian countries. The Center also sponsors projects addressing multidisciplinary and regional issues in Asia.

Library of Congress Cataloging-in-Publication Data

Johnson, David G. (David George), 1938-
  Spectacle and sacrifice : the ritual foundations of village life in North China / David Johnson.
    p. cm. -- (Harvard East Asian monographs ; 315)
  Includes bibliographical references and index.
  ISBN 978-0-674-03304-7 (cloth : alk. paper)
    1. China--Religion. 2. Festivals--China. 3. Rites and ceremonies--China.
4. City and town life--China. I. Title.
  BL1803.J64 2009
  299.5′1136095117--dc22

                                                        2009033043

Index by Mary Mortensen

⊗ Printed on acid-free paper

Last figure below indicates year of this printing
19 18 17 16 15 14 13 12 11 10 09

To

Wu Xiaoling 吳曉鈴, in memoriam

and

Wang Ch'iu-kuei 王秋桂

Acknowledgments

No serious scholarly book can be written without substantial time free from teaching and administrative duties, and that free time costs money. I was fortunate to receive support from many sources during the years I worked on this book, more than once from some, and they deserve to be named first in this catalogue of appreciation. My deep thanks to the American Council of Learned Societies, the Chiang Ching-kuo Foundation, the Project on Chinese Ritual and Ritual Opera (funded by the Chiang Ching-kuo Foundation), the National Endowment for the Humanities, and the University of California President's Research Fellowship in the Humanities for major grants. Generous support was also received from the Committee on Research, the Department of History, and the Center for Chinese Studies, all of the University of California, Berkeley.

Many people have helped me over the years; I wish I could name them all here. The inimitable Wang Ch'iu-kuei was responsible for my plunge into the sea of village studies and provided introductions to scholars, copies of important documents and videotapes, and other support vital to the project (including vigorous goading). Liao Ben, whom I have known since his year with the Chinese Popular Culture Project here in Berkeley, accompanied me on an initial reconnaisance into Shanxi in the summer heat of 1992, during which we collected a body of valuable texts, met with scholars at Shanxi Shifan University in Linfen, and others based in Jincheng and Changzhi, and visited Renzhuang Village and other sites. In the fall of 1993 my friend Yang

Mengheng, the former director of the Shanxi Provincial Drama Research Institute, was my guide on an extended trip to southeastern Shanxi that included visits to villages and temples and interviews with numerous local scholars and villagers. In Shanxi I received invaluable help from local historians and theater scholars including Zhang Zhennan, Li Tiansheng, Li Shoutian, Yuan Shuangxi, and Han Sheng. In Beijing Bo Songnian was always the kindest of hosts.

It has been my good fortune to have had regular contacts over the years with John Lagerwey, Kenneth Dean, and David Holm, genuine fieldworkers, from whom I have learned much about what the village world is really like. I have also been fortunate to be able to discuss my work with Myron Cohen, Woody and Rubie Watson, Bob Hymes, Peter Bol, and David Cohen during the past decade and more. Their camaraderie and that of Evelyn Rawski, Susan Naquin, and Pauline Yu have meant much to me in the long years I worked on this project. My thanks also to Syd Wayman for her help with the maps and to Yvonne Tsang and Christine Taylor of Wilsted and Taylor, who made designing the cover what it should be, a pleasure. And for always supporting a husband and father who for many years was often absent in spirit though present in person, blessings on In Ja and Caroline.

D.J.

Contents

Part II
Shanxi Village Ritual Opera,
an Overview 145

Part III
The Great Temple Festivals of
Southeastern Shanxi 177

Maps, Figures, and Table

MAPS

FIGURES

TABLE

Spectacle and Sacrifice

The Ritual Foundations of Village Life
in North China

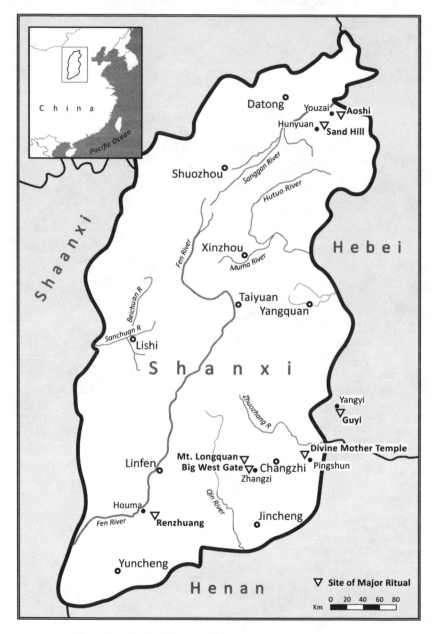

Map 1 Sites of major New Year and *Sai* rituals discussed in this book.

Introduction

DEFINITIONS AND ARGUMENT

This book is about village rituals. In southern Shanxi the festivals at which the most important rituals were performed were sponsored by territorial units called *shê*. *Shê* were frequently identical with natural villages, but especially in southeastern Shanxi some *shê* were made up of a number of villages and some large villages contained several *shê*. A festival might be sponsored by a single *shê*, or sponsorship might rotate among a group of them.[1] *Shê* were highly stable; when a *shê* was composed of several villages it therefore amounted to a long-lived village alliance. Alliances of villages (and of *shê*) may have been as significant a structuring factor in the countryside as Skinner's standard marketing areas or Kuhn's *tuanlian*.[2] *Shê* existed only to sponsor festivals and their associated rituals; it was villages that were the basic units of settlement in rural China. Therefore in this book I consistently speak of village festivals and village rituals, even though strictly speaking they often were *shê* festivals and *shê* rituals in southern Shanxi.

By "rituals" I mean the scripted performances through which villagers interacted with the Powers, natural and divine, nameless and

---

1. I use "festival" here to refer to the event in its entirety, including commercial activities, socializing, gambling, and so on, while "ritual" refers to those portions of a festival that had special symbolic importance. (For a general description of temple festivals, see Wu Cheng-han, "The Temple Fairs in Late Imperial China.") But a hard and fast distinction is not possible; for example, was a procession a ritual?

2. Skinner, "Marketing and Social Structure in Rural China: Part I"; Kuhn, *Rebellion and Its Enemies in Late Imperial China.*

named, malevolent and benign, that they believed had a certain degree of control over their fates. Although many rituals took place in the household—funerals, exorcisms, offerings to the stove god, and the like—rituals performed for the village as a whole had a particular importance. The residents of a village believed their fate was, in part, bound up with its rituals. Because the rituals were dense and complex and the entire community was actively involved in staging them, they had a powerful emotional impact. The people who grew up with them could never unlearn them.

Village rituals were of two basic types, seasonal and liturgical. Seasonal rituals belonged to the realm of custom; people did them because they had always done them, and the notion that they might have had authors was unimaginable: they may have changed, but they had always existed. They were performed almost exclusively in the village lanes and nearby fields and seldom required the guidance of specialists. They frequently featured exorcisms, of a kind that did not use priests or rely on textual authority. Seasonal rituals were embedded in seasonal festivals; by far the most important of these was Yuanxiao, which centered on the day of the first full moon of the first lunar month, the climax of the New Year celebrations. Liturgical rituals, by contrast, were focused on a temple and the temple's god; they took place during the annual festival celebrating the god's birthday, featured sacrifices rather than exorcisms, and used written liturgies and opera scripts, which necessarily had authors. Their most important segments were carefully scripted and performed on stages or in stage-like pavilions, with little room for spontaneity; they were performed by specially trained members of the community and directed by experts from outside the village.

Every village ritual, whether seasonal or liturgical, was a combination of spectacle and sacrifice. The spectacles tended to be public and filled with color and excitement, while the sacrifices or offerings were performed inside temples and were far more solemn. Seasonal rituals like New Year, in their communal aspect, were virtually all spectacle, sometimes entertaining but at other times frightening or horrific. Official rituals—which we will not consider in this book—had far more sacrifice than spectacle; indeed, they were deliberately unspectacular. Liturgical rituals, the most important of all village rituals, combined spectacle and sacrifice in roughly equal measure. Their central spectacle was the procession, their sacrifices a combination of food offerings and operas. In southeastern Shanxi, the largest and richest liturgical rituals were embedded in great festivals called *yingshen saihui*, or *sai*.

Part I of this book describes four village New Year celebrations, seasonal rituals; Part III describes three *sai*, liturgical rituals. Part II is a brief overview of the operas performed at liturgical rituals in southern Shanxi. This subject might seem irrelevant in a book about the ritual foundations of village life, but in fact operas were indispensable to temple festivals not only in southern Shanxi but all over north China from as early as the eleventh century.[3] Stages in southern Shanxi temples are the earliest physical evidence of opera in China. The oldest surviving one is dated 1157, but inscriptions prove that there was a temple stage in the Houtu Temple in Qiaoshang village, Wanrong county, in the first decade of the eleventh century, 150 years earlier. This is considerably earlier than the earliest non-epigraphic literary evidence.

In China, ritual and opera always went together. Even Daoist and Buddhist priests incorporated highly dramatic material into their rituals. Sometimes the ritual action itself was inherently theatrical, as in the exaggerated gestures of an exorcist; in other cases, drama was added to ritual, as when adaptations of scenes from operas were used as a sort of counterpoint to the more solemn parts of a ceremony. Real priests performed on stage in certain operas, and actors sometimes performed real exorcisms for villagers. In the remote valleys of northwest Hunan as recently as the early twentieth century, there were bands of spirit-mediums who traveled from village to village, first performing the rituals that were needed by the community and then changing costumes and staging the Buddho-Confucian opera about Mulian rescuing his mother from Hell, which was itself construed as a kind of communal exorcism.[4] Rather than thinking of village ritual and village opera as two

---

3. Since customary or seasonal village rituals were not temple-centered and were not focused on sacrifice, they did not employ ritual opera. They did make use of other kinds of performance, some very spectacular, as we shall see. I use "opera" in preference to "drama" because the latter can refer to many different kinds of performance while the former points specifically to stories enacted with music on stages.

4. Li Huaisun, "Chenhe xi 'Mulian' chutan," p. 44.

separate genres, we should view them as different facets of a single ritual-operatic performance complex.

Asserting that ritual and opera had much in common does not, however, explain why, virtually as soon as opera appeared, it began to be performed in rural temples. What about opera made it so attractive to country folk that they spent large sums of money constructing stages in quite adequate temples and made significant changes to time-honored rituals? A convincing explanation of why opera was adapted so quickly to ritual use in the countryside would illuminate much that is still obscure about the history of both opera and village ritual in China, and I return to this matter in the Concluding Observations. For the moment, it should be clear why a chapter on ritual opera occupies the center of this book.

After this brief survey of the main themes of the book, I turn to some questions that are likely to arise in the minds of readers. To put it baldly, why should we bother with village ritual? This is really two questions: Why bother with villages? And why bother with ritual? As for villages, at least two issues are in play. There are those—probably a large portion of the historians who study China—who feel that it is not important to study villages because the people who lived in them had no influence on events. But what events are we talking about? If the relevant arena is the abstraction we call "the state," then we must bid the farmers adieu except for those times when they rebelled or otherwise caught the attention of the mighty. But if the arena we are concerned with is a village, or even a county, then villagers obviously had an influence on the course of events. So it all depends on the kind of events we choose to study.

But why study a village when there is an entire country to work on? One reason is that to study an entire country one has to work at such a high level of generalization that the results are of little interest. Most historians will disagree with this: large generalizations are precisely what they—or at least reviewers and graduate seminars—find interesting. They prefer structure to texture, explanation to incident; after all, what can detail, no matter how fine-grained, tell us? From this perspective, understanding China means answering questions deemed to be important, developing large generalizations, and so on. This is what we were taught was the historian's prime task, and it is completely legitimate. But it is important to recognize that this conception of the historian's craft involves a commitment to a particular definition of understanding. Relying on abstractions like the state, social structure, or modernization estranges us from what is most human in our subject. Is the price worth paying? At a sufficiently high level of generalization apples and oranges are similar—both are round, grow on trees, and contain seeds—but in that rarefied atmosphere we can no longer taste the apple or smell the orange.

Village studies are also criticized by raising the problem of typicality: How can one or a few villages stand for many? The implication here is that understanding rural Chinese society and culture requires a survey of large numbers of villages. But this assumes precisely the definition of understanding that I just called into question, and obviously cannot be accepted uncritically.

There is another, blunter response to the typicality issue: in the present state of our knowledge of Chinese villages, especially before 1949, who is to say what is unique and what is typical? At the moment we know next to nothing about Chinese rural life, especially before the brutal simplifications of the twentieth century. In my research I have been surprised again and again by the striking differences in the ritual repertoires of villages in the same region. I agree with Philip Huang's conclusion that "even in the 1930's, all but the most highly commercialized villages of the North China plain were still relatively insular communities."[5] For a long time to come, every additional village that we study will force us to adjust our ideas about village culture to make room for new and unexpected information. Our studies will not necessarily enable us to make more powerful generalizations, but they will force us to recognize possibilities we had not previously imagined.

Another reason why many historians of China feel that villages are not worth studying is that virtually everything we know about village life, at least before the twentieth century, comes from tainted sources, sources written by men who for the most part knew next to nothing about the countryside or who, if they did, felt there was nothing of

---

5. Philip Huang, *The Peasant Economy and Social Change in North China*, p. 219. The insularity of north China villages is one of Huang's basic arguments in this book. He gives some remarkable examples on pp. 221–22.

value to be found there unless it had been appropriated and reinterpreted by people like themselves. This fundamental bias in our sources, the unquestioned assumption that villages and the people who lived in them did not matter, is so universal as to be virtually invisible. The result is a profoundly impoverished view of Chinese history and culture. For example, two of the three large *sai* discussed in Part III took place at temples in Zhangzi county dedicated to the ancient culture hero Hou Yi, the great archer who saved the world by shooting down nine suns when all ten appeared at the same time. The festivals were held on his birthday, the sixth day of the sixth lunar month, and were probably among the most splendid festivals in all of north China. But the only thing the sections on popular customs in the Qing dynasty Zhangzi county gazetteers say about the sixth of the sixth is: "The villagers vie to present offerings of animals at the San Zong Temple(s). They also present offerings to the god of livestock," and "On the sixth month, sixth day, the villagers offer *sai* in the San Zong Temple(s) and to the god of livestock."[6] These books do not even hint at the realities of village practice, yet they belong to a genre that many historians believe to be our best source for local history.

To my mind the best historians are those who see the people they are studying and thinking about as in some sense akin to them. They enter the world of their subjects by using concrete, specific, human-scale evidence such as biographies, diaries, and direct observation. What they write has the same characteristics. It is sometimes called "microhistory," and there are many celebrated practitioners of it among historians of Europe.[7] This sort of history partakes of a quality I call

---

6. Ding Shiliang and Zhao Fang, *Zhongguo difangzhi minsu ziliao: Huabei juan*, p. 622, quoting *Zhangzi xian zhi* 長子縣志 (1778), and p. 624, quoting *Zhangzi xian zhi* (1816).

7. They include Emmanuel Le Roy Ladurie, Natalie Davis, Robert Darnton, and Carlo Ginzburg. For modern China there are also some notable contributions, including two works jointly authored by Edward Friedman, Paul Pickowicz, and Mark Selden: *Chinese Village, Socialist State* and *Revolution, Resistance, and Reform in Village China*; Ralph Thaxton's *Catastrophe and Contention in Rural China*; and Huang Shu-min's *The Spiral Road*. These books cannot, however, be compared with microhistories by historians of Europe since they are so heavily concerned with political power and economic conditions in the very recent past. The books by Friedman and his coauthors draw lessons from the experience of a single village that seem intended to be relevant to rural China

anecdotal. The dictionary definition of anecdote is "a short account of an interesting event of some kind," but I use the term simply to refer to accounts of specific events or places or persons. Every such anecdote is embedded in a social, cultural, historical, and symbolic matrix from which it cannot be separated and without which it cannot be understood. Thinking about a particular event or state of affairs or person brings with it a consciousness, sometimes focused, sometimes vague, of the whole world within which it existed. It is one thing to read about the Industrial Revolution, for example, and quite a different thing to read biographies of James Watt or Matthew Boulton, or to turn from a history of navigation to an account of John Harrison's invention of a true marine chronometer. Full-scale accounts of particular events, such as Emmanuel Le Roy Ladurie's carnival in Romans in 1580 or Robert Darnton's massacre of cats in Paris in the late 1730s, have the same ability to reveal entire worlds.

Accounts of particular events or places or people, if reconstructed as completely as possible, confront us with a richer, more complex reality than conventional histories can. But what can a historian do with such material, with mere anecdotes, even defined in this generous way? This is like asking what is the point of studying a single village. My response is that the anecdote can lead to understanding, although not the sort of understanding sought by most historians. It is understanding achieved not through analysis but through empathy. Intellectuals tend to value empathy less than analysis because they assume that the most important kind of understanding comes from framing "interesting" questions and answering them, or developing large generalizations. But it is not obvious that analysis is superior to empathy in understanding human beings and the worlds they create. Is science a better way of understanding people than poetry?

A final variant of the objection to studying villages arises from impatience with studying villagers. There are after all many studies of kings

---

as a whole. (Note the shift from "Chinese Village" to "Village China" in the titles.) Whether they have found a solution to the "typicality" problem is an open question. *Catastrophe and Contention* and *The Spiral Road* are much more "anecdotal" in the sense developed in the following section.

and generals, poets and philosophers, and of specific events in which they played leading roles (which incidentally fit my definition of anecdotal history). This bias toward well-known individuals is understandable, since their careers and creations are far better documented than any peasant's—but it still is a bias. Are they really more worth studying? Who is more important, the official who decrees policies or the individuals who may or may not carry them out? Do we not assume that if we deal with leaders we will know better what actually happened? But is this in fact the case? We assume, for example, that the works of Zhu Xi have an importance incomparably superior to anything a villager might write. But who read Zhu Xi? Only a very small number of highly educated men. Most people came into contact with Zhu Xi's ideas, if at all, at second hand, in a myriad popularizations, or third hand, in oral interpretations of those popularizations, and so on. If we want to understand Zhu Xi's impact, obviously we should study the popularizations and their interpretations, and scholars have begun to do this. The point here is that Zhu Xi's works, or the poetry of Du Fu, or the essays of Chen Hongmou, monuments of Chinese philosophy, literature, and statecraft though they may be, have little to teach us about the attitudes and values of ordinary people. To assume that knowledge of Zhu Xi's works automatically brings an understanding of his influence is a fundamental error. We must start at the bottom and work up, which, outrageous as it may sound, means giving the villager's worldview priority over Zhu Xi's.

This is my very long answer to the question Why bother with villages (and villagers)? The second question was Why bother with ritual? The answer is very clear. Chinese culture was a performance culture: even in pre-Qin times Chinese philosophers were concerned more with how people should act, and what counted as good actions, than with using logic to prove propositions. Ritual was the highest form of action or performance; every significant life event, social, political, or religious, was embedded in and expressed through ritual. If we wish to understand how Chinese people thought and felt about the family, the community, the state, or the gods, we must study the rituals by which those thoughts and feelings were expressed and shaped. Of course, not all scholars are interested in attitudes and values; they may wish to study economic conditions, social formations, or the institutions of imperial rule; technology, art, geography, or food; power, prestige, or conflict. But if one is interested in the symbolic world of the broad population, educated and uneducated alike, then, in China, it is essential to study ritual.

The subtitle of this book was chosen very deliberately: I am interested in the ritual foundations of village life, not the religious foundations. Although I use the terms "religion" and, especially, "popular religion" from time to time, I do so only when there is no alternative. Adam Chau correctly suggests in his recent book that we "should question the very concept of 'belief' in the Chinese popular religious context, as the concept carries with it enormous Judeo-Christian theological baggage."[8] The term "religion" carries even more baggage, and it is important to make clear at the outset why I think so. I suspect that for most of my readers, as for me, "religion" implies an ecclesiastical organization, a church; and traditionally churches have been defined by their doctrines. One was not born into a religion; one became a member by means of formal rituals, such as baptism and confirmation. Conversion was possible: it involved acceptance of the doctrines of the church; denial of those doctrines brought expulsion from it.

China did not have religions in this sense of the word. This is what so frustrated the Protestant missionaries in particular, who insisted on asking the people they met what religion they believed in ("*Ni xin shenme jiao?*"); the question simply baffled those they were questioning.[9] Similarly, the term most frequently used today for (religious) beliefs—*xinyang*—grates on the ear like the neologism it is.[10] Buddhism is the

---

8. Adam Yuet Chau, *Miraculous Response*, p. 59.

9. Note that a Chinese word for "religion" (*zongjiao*) had to be invented as well. The traditional term, *jiao* (teaching), did not capture the full meaning of the word in European languages. I single out Protestants in the text, but, as is well known, Catholic missionaries also struggled with the question of whether Chinese beliefs were doctrinally acceptable.

10. I was fascinated to discover in Chau's *Miraculous Response* (p. 48) that villagers in northern Shaanxi use the word *jiang* 講—to discuss, to speak about—where we would use the term "believe," as for example in the phrase *jiang mixin* 講密信: "believe in superstition." (Of course, *mixin* is another neologism.)

closest the Chinese came to religion in the Judeo-Christian-Islamic sense, but it is not monotheistic, which puts it in a radically different category. My point is that the foundations of Christianity are complex structures of carefully formulated definitions and tightly argued conclusions created by medieval theologians using tools provided by Greek logic and metaphysics. The Christian church was virtually created out of centuries-long theological disputes about highly complex and abstract concepts such as Original Sin, the Trinity, the Real Presence, and so on,[11] and the same presumably can be said of Islam and Judaism.

Chinese philosophers, to say nothing of ordinary people, were simply not interested in that sort of thing. But tremendous debates concerning what we call "ritual" took place in every dynasty. How imperial rituals were to be performed, whether certain actions were ritually correct or not—issues such as these were as close to the heart of Chinese religion as theological disputes were to Christianity. The leaders of the Christian churches were intensely concerned with heresy—improper beliefs—and punished heretics mercilessly. By contrast, Chinese thinkers, following Xunzi, usually assumed that if people's actions conformed to the proper patterns, the beliefs could be left to take care of themselves. And ritual supplied the proper patterns. This was an idea that was shared by virtually all Chinese, of all classes and stations, from chief minister to farmer.

Communal rituals were thus the highest expression of the values and beliefs of ordinary people. At the same time, traditional Chinese village ritual practices were extremely heterogeneous. Villages literally within

---

11. For a taste of this, see Frend, *The Rise of Christianity*, chap. 18. Even laymen could be passionately engaged in these theological disputes; for a charming example from the fourth century, see ibid., p. 636. In the late thirteenth century, the archbishop of Canterbury ordered priests preaching to the simplest audiences to "expound to the people in the vulgar tongue, without any fantastic texture of subtlety, the fourteen articles of faith, the ten commandments, the two precepts of the gospel . . . the seven deadly sins . . . the seven chief virtues, and the seven sacraments of grace" (Homans, *English Villagers of the Thirteenth Century*, p. 391). What is notable here is the precedence given to the articles of faith, that is, the creed, the distilled essence of centuries of theological analysis and debate.

shouting distance of each other could have radically different ways of sacrificing to their deities or of driving away evil influences.[12] Since there was no ecclesiastical authority to enforce ritual conformity, and since officials had little interest in the customary practices of villagers as long as they did not disturb the peace or weaken the tax base, it was natural for a state of ritual autarky to develop. This is another reason for focusing on single villages or small regions.

This state of affairs is fatal to Maurice Freedman's argument that "a Chinese religion exists."[13] To anyone who has studied Chinese villages closely, it is obvious that there was no single system of beliefs and practices most ordinary Chinese followed. There were deities known to virtually everyone (Guanyin, the Stove God); practices that were widespread (processions, pilgrimages); and the forms of temples and altars were much the same everywhere. Yet as soon as one looks closely at local ritual practice, whether domestic or communal, seasonal or liturgical, differences far outweigh similarities. And what else would one expect in a country where the population was measured in the hundreds of millions, where there was no established church, and where the organized religions that did exist were unsympathetic to the dogma-haunted sectarian mentalities that in the West produced creeds, catechisms, heresies, and excommunications?

PARTICULARS

The most important of the village rituals described below were still celebrated in southeastern Shanxi in the 1930s, as they had been for centuries. They were fabulous affairs involving hundreds of participants and thousands or even tens of thousands of spectators. People came from miles around to watch the processions that villages sent out with all the pomp they could muster to invite the gods of neighboring villages to their festivals. Some of the temples in which the offering rituals took place were massive structures with roofs of beautifully glazed tiles

---

12. Compare the practices of two neighboring Zhejiang villages described in two volumes by Xu Hongtu: *Zhejiang sheng Pan'an xian Shenze cun* and *Zhejiang sheng Pan'an xian Yangtou cun*.

13. See Wolf, ed., *Religion and Ritual in Chinese Society*, p. 20.

and walls painted the same dusty red as the imperial palaces, located in settings of considerable beauty away from villages and towns, from which they dominated the surrounding landscape like castles. Others were closer to inhabited places but still were imposing and well maintained because of the importance of their cults.

The villages of greatest interest to me, although I devote only half of this book to them, are located in the watershed of the Zhuozhang River and its main tributaries, whose central city is Changzhi. The waters of the Zhuozhang flow east, parallel to the Yellow River, through a gap in the Taihang Mountains and thence into the Grand Canal. The Taihangs are very rugged and form a significant barrier to communication.[14] The mountains to the west and north of Changzhi are also a challenge to travelers, and so the region is fairly self-contained. At its center is a fertile plain roughly forty by seventy kilometers, surrounded by ranges of hills that are heavily cultivated up to the point where the soil becomes too sparse to support anything besides grazing and forestry. Much of the soil is loess, and the deep water-carved gullies and ravines characteristic of the loess region are frequently seen.

The Changzhi region is heavily populated, its counties varying between 200 and 600 persons per square kilometer. But these statistics do not distinguish between cities and villages. Looking at the large-scale maps in the Shanxi Provincial Atlas of counties such as Tunliu and Pingshun is far more instructive: they are black with the names of villages.[15] Truly, this is village China. It is in villages such as these that the people we meet in this book lived, and in some cases still live: people like Xu Youyi, who preserved the last surviving copy of the liturgy of the Fan-drum ritual in Renzhuang village; Li Fubao of Lu village in Jincheng county, an Entertainer who accumulated over eighteen

---

14. But note that Shanxi dialect, or more precisely the Hanxin subgroup of the Jin dialect group, is spoken 75–100 km east of the southeast Shanxi border, which runs along the eastern base of the Taihang Range. From a geographical point of view this is hard to understand; is it a remnant of the forced Ming migrations from Shanxi to Hebei? See Wurm and Rong, eds., *Language Atlas of China*, map B7.

15. Oddly, areas in the heart of the plain, such as the eastern parts of Tunliu and Zhangzi counties and the western part of Lucheng, show much less dense concentrations of villages. Could this be a remnant of the "big fields" of the commune system?

exclusive ritual Territories in two decades; Yao Jitang and Zhang Yutang, who recopied the script of *Thrice Inviting Zhuge Liang* in the depth of the winter of 1925 in the village of Xinzhuang, hurrying to finish it before the New Year; Niu Zhenguo of East Big Pass village in Zhangzi county, who wrote down the *Handbook for Use Before the Gods of the Sai* in 1911; as well as the many others whose names have been lost forever.

For as long as there have been people who can be called Chinese, they have lived in southern Shanxi. Chinese culture was already very old in Shanxi when most of south China was still in the hands of indigenous peoples. Virtually every field in its river valleys has probably been cultivated for thousands of years. The Shang ritual center of Anyang, where the oracle bones were discovered, is just across the border in Hebei, and Houma, the site of a great Zhou bronze foundry, is in southwestern Shanxi. The maps in the Shanxi volume of the *Atlas of Chinese Cultural Relics* show southern Shanxi thickly covered with Shang, Western Zhou, and Eastern Zhou archeological sites.[16] Thus it is quite possible that some ritual performances in southern Shanxi, such as the killing of scapegoat figures to drive away evil influences, or the great fires at New Year (of which the lanterns now so closely associated with the holiday may be a domesticated substitute) go back a long, long time. Hou Yi, an ancient culture hero assumed by most sinologists to have been embalmed in literary legends as early as Han times, was the object of a flourishing cult in southeastern Shanxi as late as the 1930s. The festivals that are the subject of this book have histories counted in centuries, not millennia, but the long historical horizon of the region in which they emerged and flowered is not irrelevant, as we shall see.

No residents could avoid participating in their village's festival, and it is hard to imagine that anyone would have wanted to, since a village's festivals were at the heart of its inhabitants' sense of their place in the world, what made their village worthy of their neighbors' respect. In many places, important roles in the rituals and operas were passed from father to son, who presumably were among the most respected mem-

---

16. Guojia wenwuju, *Zhongguo wenwu ditu ji: Shanxi fence*, 1: 70–73.

bers of the community. But there was a place for non-elite villagers as well: they performed in shows of various sorts, gave demonstrations of martial prowess, and played in bands. Every village festival was different: there might be a distinctive display in the procession, or a unique opera during the offerings in the temple, or liturgies that were used nowhere else. And every one was taken very seriously.

Some of the largest festivals employed professional ritual masters and hereditary outcaste actor-musicians. These two types of specialists possessed ritual handbooks or opera scripts, which may have been in their families for generations. Their presence brought dignity and a certain consistency to the prayers, hymns, food offerings, operas, and the other activities that took place within the temples.[17] During the core rituals of the three days that most of these festivals lasted, the temple courtyard was packed with scores of participants, all wearing special costumes. Any remaining space must have been occupied by spectators. The temples were lavishly decorated: offering tables and all their paraphernalia were arranged in the offering hall; miniature thrones for the invited gods were set up in the main hall; special rooms set aside for the use of the gods were furnished with valuable furniture, paintings, and objets d'art; and in some of the temples intricately carved walls made of tiles fashioned from deep-fried dough extended across the entire width of the courtyard to set off the inner ritual space.

The gods feasted and watched operas, and so did the people. Those who could not squeeze into the temple courtyard to watch the gods' operas often gathered at temporary stages constructed near the temple where operas in popular regional styles were presented. Field or household work was put aside; the entire village was swept up in the excitement of the processions and feasts, buying and selling, gambling and drinking, and every other sort of enjoyable pastime. Authority, whether ecclesiastical or political, cast no shadow over the revelry. There were no Daoist priests or Buddhist monks, and no county officials, unless, as sometimes happened, the magistrate himself was the sponsor of the

---

17. The dominance of Daoist ritual specialists in southeastern China, with their fairly standardized ritual texts, may help explain why there was less variation in village rituals there.

festival, thus turning himself into an honorary commoner. These grand celebrations were the creations of the people, with no interference or direction from higher authority, and they knew it. The temple festivals were essential to their communal identity, sharpening differences that were already marked by dialect, costume, and cuisine.

A festival could not hope to be successful unless it was guided by villagers who were competent administrators. Planning for the next year's celebration began even before the current festival was over, with the selection of the sponsoring village (if the festival was sponsored by a village alliance). Under the supervision of a committee of villagers with executive authority, responsibility for everything from the stabling of horses and mules to the construction of temporary stages was assigned to specific individuals. Those who did not perform their tasks properly risked fines and even corporal punishment. Funds were collected from the community, generally on the basis of ability to pay, and a public accounting was made at the end of the festival.

In addition to temple festivals, the rural year was punctuated by seasonal festivals, the most important of which by far was New Year. At this time villages put on processions and other shows, some of them extremely elaborate. Fire, appropriate for the ending of winter, was used in many forms, ranging from lanterns to gigantic bonfires. There were usually exorcisms, and masked dramas and large-scale dances, performed on the ground, were common. These features have a strongly archaic feel to them. Since there was no approved model, either official or local, for New Year festivals, endless variations developed around certain basic practices, such as the display of lanterns. Seasonal festivals belonged to the people at large rather than village elites and local specialists. The carnival spirit was abroad, and formal rituals were much less in evidence, and for these reasons strong and even violent emotions sometimes surfaced.

Village festival life everywhere in prerevolutionary China, whether temple centered or seasonally based, was rich, complex, conservative, and extraordinarily diverse. Festivals and their associated rituals and other performances provided the symbolic and intellectual materials out of which ordinary people constructed their ideas about the human world and the realm of the Powers, presented in settings that guaranteed they would have maximum impact. These festivals took place throughout the year; in the more densely populated regions, a festival probably occurred within walking distance of any given village on average once every week or two. Without knowing a great deal about these aspects of rural life, it is quite impossible to understand Chinese history.

———

A brief word is in order about the sources I have used in writing. My attention was first drawn to southeastern Shanxi by the publication of a liturgical manuscript dated 1574 discovered in Nan Shê village, about seventeen kilometers north of Changzhi. Before long other liturgical manuscripts were located and (eventually) published. Such documents are extremely rare and are also very important because they are the only source of authentic information on the details of north Chinese village ritual practice. These texts form the core of the primary sources on which this book is based.

In addition, I obtained transcripts of oral histories of aging ritual specialists and musicians that had been prepared by local scholars and then edited for possible publication; copies of long and extremely detailed descriptions of one of the great *sai* prepared by an educated native of the place where it was celebrated; and published descriptions of various aspects of seasonal and liturgical rituals written by specialists but obviously based on extensive interviews with local people— although the sources of the information were not always specified, and the accounts appeared to have undergone extensive editing. During visits to southeastern Shanxi, I conducted interviews with villagers, including ritual specialists, that were recorded and later transcribed, and collected scarce publications and unpublished articles.

As I began to realize the degree to which I had underestimated the richness and vitality of village symbolic life, I simultaneously realized that hardly anyone with direct knowledge of it was still alive. A millennial change was under way; the old ways had vanished, and now even memories of them were disappearing. In addition to the intellectual program outlined above, I began to feel an obligation simply to preserve the knowledge of what some villagers had achieved and thus to restore to them something of the respect they deserved but which, because of our ignorance, they had never received.

My aim of describing as completely as possible the most important rituals of a few villages is what at least some anthropologists aspire to. But since almost none of the rituals are still performed, I have had to reconstruct them from texts and other evidence, which is what historians do. This has led me into the territories of both anthropologists and historians. Both are likely to be dissatisfied with the results, since my experience in the field was not extensive enough to allow me to write a solid ethnography, and the archival base is not rich enough to allow me to write a European-style local history.[18] But for all its limitations, I hope that this book, by showing the depth and complexity of Chinese village culture, will persuade its readers that they can never understand China if they ignore the country folk. If so, I will be content.

---

18. Cf., e.g., the sources available to Edward Muir for his *Civic Ritual in Renaissance Venice*.

PART I

Greeting the New Year
in Shanxi

The most important of the seasonal festivals was New Year. For the village as a whole, the New Year festivities centered on Yuanxiao, the day of the first full moon of the year. A nearly complete liturgy for the New Year ceremonies in the village of Renzhuang in southwestern Shanxi was discovered in 1987. Because of the interest aroused by the find, local scholars carried out extensive investigations of the village and its ritual life, and as a result Renzhuang's New Year rituals are exceptionally well documented. Another village New Year ritual that has been described in unusual detail was—and still is—celebrated in Guyi village in southwestern Hebei, which is located on an old road into southeastern Shanxi and like many other settlements in the area had close ties with that region. Its main New Year ritual was called "Capturing the Yellow Demon."[1] No liturgical material has yet been found in Guyi; the fine-grained descriptions come from fieldwork carried out in the village over a period of years by an assistant director of the Mass Arts Office in a nearby town who became fascinated by the performance, which had been completely unknown to him and his colleagues. To these two heavily documented rituals I added two more. These were the only other New Year festivals in Shanxi for which I could find detailed information derived from field research.

---

1. I use the past tense here and throughout this book when describing village rituals because using the present tense creates a misleading sense of continuity. I will note if any rituals are still being performed or have been performed recently.

The Nature of the Sources

It is exhilarating to move from the meager and formulaic descriptions of village festivals provided by local gazetteers to memoirs and reports based on fieldwork and filled with vivid detail about elaborate ceremonies and colorful customs unmentioned in the printed sources. But this wealth of detail and the authority we instinctively ascribe to eyewitness accounts should not lead us to see more in them than is actually there. For example, the many publications about Shanxi's temple festivals stimulated by the discovery of important manuscripts in the mid-1980s and later were written at least fifty years after the last natural performances, on the eve of the Japanese invasion of Shanxi in 1938. Much can be forgotten in fifty years, especially if they are as traumatic as the past fifty have been in China. Our informants in the 1980s and 1990s were separated from the last ritual performances in their villages by the Cultural Revolution, the Great Leap and its attendant great famine, one violent political campaign after another, land reform and collectivization, the fighting between Nationalist and Communist forces, and the war of resistance against the Japanese invaders.

The youngest informants to play a substantial role in the prewar festivals were in their seventies and eighties in the late 1980s. Even if we grant that they were much better able to remember small details of life fifty years earlier than we ourselves would be, surrounded as we have been since childhood by all the distractions of the mass media and modern life, still there is a limit to what one can expect from men and women of that age. And one must be especially careful with accounts based on interviews made by others. Hesitancies, contradictions, failures of memory, are almost never visible in the transcripts, much less in the printed reports. Finally, even if these informants had forgotten nothing, they knew only a few villages. There is a barely conscious tendency to expand from, say, the Fan-drum ritual of Renzhuang village in 1938 to "southern Shanxi village rituals in the late Qing" or even "North Chinese village rituals in late imperial times"—that is, to generalize from a few cases to an entire region, and from information collected at one point in time back through generations or even centuries. It is important to be sensitive to this tendency, not only because the temporal horizon of oral tradition is inherently limited—although there is no question that very old elements indeed can survive in it—but also and more especially because Chinese rural society everywhere underwent major periodic disruptions.

For example, the manuscript that has made possible the detailed reconstruction of the New Year rituals of Renzhuang village, one of the main subjects of Part I, is a copy made in 1909. In the preceding century, at least two events had a substantial impact on Renzhuang and on much of the rest of Shanxi: an attack by the Taipings in 1853 and the great famine of 1877–79.[2]

In 1852, horses intended for the Taiping armies, which probably were being herded south on a government road that skirted the village, damaged the crops on Renzhuang land. This resulted in a clash between villagers and the Taiping horse wranglers. Next year, as the Taipings under Li Kaifang and Lin Fengxiang advanced north along the same route, heading for Beijing, they took their revenge.[3] They burned the village to the ground, destroying "500 houses," most of the shops and small manufactories (including a dyeworks and a distillery), and the temples.[4] The genealogy of the dominant Xu lineage was lost at that time; presumably some of the part-scripts of the Fan-drum performances, to be discussed in detail in Chapter 1, were also destroyed then.[5]

A generation later the area was struck by one of the worst famines in Chinese history.

In 1877 there was no rain, and no crops were grown anywhere in Shansi, or four other provinces of North China—Chih-li, Shantung, Shensi and Honan. There was no rain in 1878 either, and again no crops. It was the same the fol-

---

2. Chen Gaoyong, *Zhongguo lidai tianzai*, lists only one year of serious drought in Shanxi in the nineteenth century (1810) before the drought of 1876 that set the stage for the great famine.

3. For the Taiping route of march in 1853, see *Zhongguo lishi ditu, xia*, p. 115.

4. Huang Zhusan and Wang Fucai, *Shanxi sheng Quwo xian Renzhuang cun Shangu shenpu diaocha baogao* (hereafter cited as Huang and Wang, "*Shangu shenpu*" *diaocha baogao*), p. 13. They quote a village ditty that says the first act of the "long-haired bandits" was to set fire to the temples.

5. Ibid., p. 20, says that one reason that twelve copies of the *Shangu shenpu* were made in 1909 was memory of the Taiping attack; Duan Shipu and Xu Cheng ("*Shangu shenpu chu tan*," pp. 94–95) point instead to memories of the great famine.

lowing year. . . . An estimated nine and a half million people died of starvation in the Great Famine. Nearly five and a half million of them, or more than one out of every three persons who lived in Shansi, died in that province alone.[6]

The sources seldom permit us to gauge the impact of the famine on a given village or even county, but there are some sobering statistics and a few suggestive anecdotes. The provincial population was 15,569,000 in 1879 and 10,744,000 in 1883.[7] The population of Quwo county (in which Renzhuang village is located) was 286,258 in 1840 and 35,813 in 1880.[8] (In 1988 the population was still only 191,000.)[9] The 1880 edition of the Quwo county history gives the population of Renzhuang as 118.[10]

To what extent did these calamities result in deformations or disruptions of local cultural traditions? This is one of the most difficult questions facing the historian of rural culture. We have many reasons to believe that villagers were intensely conservative, especially where ritual and religion were concerned. Yet when a culture is transmitted orally within small groups, the possibility of major breaks in the tradition must always be borne in mind. It would seem therefore that the richly detailed picture of village symbolic life offered by ethnographic reports can be safely extended back for only a few generations at most.

But this would be true only if the local culture was completely oral, which was emphatically not the case in southeastern Shanxi, or anywhere else in China. Most villagers were illiterate, but some could read and write, and there probably were always fairly well educated people

---

6. Brandt, *Massacre in Shansi*, pp. 20–21. This number is probably based on counts of the living, not the dead, and hence may be an overestimate. See Will, *Bureaucracy and Famine*, pp. 41–43, for information on the ease with which country folk migrated when they anticipated a crisis. There is no doubt, however, that the Guangxu famine was a catastrophe for many areas in north China. There is a large literature on the subject; a recent study with many useful references is Edgerton-Tarpley, "Family and Gender in Famine."

7. Liang Fangzhong, *Zhongguo lidai hukou*, p. 266.

8. Duan Shipu and Xu Cheng, "*Shangu shenpu* chu tan," p. 94, quoting the *Quwo xian zhi*. I have not been able to consult this work since the authors do not give bibliographic information or even *juan* or page numbers; therefore I cannot gauge the reliability of the figures.

9. Huang and Wang, "*Shangu shenpu*" *diaocha baogao*, p. 7.

10. Ibid., p. 14, quoting *Quwo xin zhi*, 13.12A.

living not too far away. Moreover, the written word was omnipresent in rural China, in temple murals, woodblock prints, shop signs, and children's clothing; in genealogies, land deeds, contracts, scriptures, broadside ballads, and a wide range of cheap books. Once we know that some villagers were literate, or that educated men, whether residents or not, played a regular part in village life, our assessment of the fragility of local culture necessarily changes.

And we should not overemphasize the fragility of even wholly oral culture. Sudden and substantial disruptions of local cultural traditions were probably very rare. If a third or even a half of the inhabitants of Renzhuang died or moved away in the famine of the 1870s, there still were two-thirds or a half who survived and who must have carried on the traditions they knew. (Specialist knowledge would have died if all the specialists died, but it could have been reconstituted with the help of surviving experts from areas nearby and by consulting the handbooks and other written material the specialists had used.) Furthermore, although local customs and beliefs inevitably change, this does not mean that they all change at the same rate. There are many hints—and sometimes more than hints—that some elements of Shanxi village culture were very old indeed, as we shall see.

A fair number of texts produced in late imperial times by people who lived in villages and small towns, or that directly influenced them, still exist and can be studied: scripts of local opera, especially truly local forms such as shadow opera; popular scriptures recited to villagers and sometimes read by them; almanacs; and so on. But they are almost never linked to a specific place. We justify using them by telling ourselves they are representative of what the people we are studying must have read or heard—an approach that raises many methodological issues.[11]

What is unusual about southern and especially southeastern Shanxi is that a number of liturgical texts and opera scripts have been discovered that can be linked with specific villages and temples there. These texts made possible the reconstruction of specific local festival traditions and enable us to say with a fair degree of certainty that some elements of the festival life of the 1930s existed in similar form far earlier than we

---

11. Genealogies, contracts, deeds, and the like are exceptions, but difficult to find.

could safely assume if we had just the memories of villagers interviewed in the past decade or so to go on. These documents obviously have the highest possible value; they provide fixed points of reference in what would otherwise be the endlessly shifting vistas of memory and oral lore, and they speak precisely where individual memory can be only approximate, at best. Most of the manuscripts come from the region of Changzhi, in southeastern Shanxi, but a notable one was discovered in the southwestern part of the province. It is the liturgy of the ritual celebrated at New Year in the village of Renzhuang.[12] The Yuanxiao festival, also known by its Daoist name, Upper Prime (Shang Yuan), was extremely important in all villages (unlike its trivialized modern form, the Lantern Festival). Since no liturgy for New Year rituals survives from southeastern Shanxi, this Part focuses on Renzhuang and three other villages for which we have good information, two in northeastern Shanxi and one in extreme southwestern Hebei not far from Changzhi. These New Year rituals provide a natural introduction to the communal rituals of rural Shanxi.

---

12. For an account of the origin and development of the Yuanxiao festival down to the Tang dynasty, see Wang Ch'iu-kuei, "Yuanxiao jie bukao."

I

Renzhuang Village

The Fan-Drum Roster of the Gods

GEOGRAPHICAL, RITUAL, AND SOCIAL CONTEXTS

Renzhuang is a small village (population 946 in 1988) about six kilometers south-southeast of Quwo town in southwestern Shanxi. It is situated on the edge of the fertile basin of the lower Fen River and its tributary, the Kuai; hills that rise just south of the village culminate in the 3,600-foot peak of Zijin Mountain. An ancient stone bridge spanning a deep ravine to the east of the village marks the route of the old government road that ran from Quwo south over Zijin Mountain to Jiang county. The village, enclosed by its wall, its many trees contrasting with the fields of ripe wheat around it, looked prosperous and peaceful when I visited in June 1992.[1]

Renzhuang lies in a region thick with important historical sites—Paleolithic, Neolithic, Shang, Zhou, Warring States, Qin-Han, and later. The age of the village itself is unknown. Of the many commemorative stelae that the village's temples must at one time have housed, only two, both dating to the Ming, are mentioned in a recent survey. One, dated

---

1. The basic sources on Renzhuang and the *Shangu shenpu*, both the manuscript and the ritual, are Huang and Wang, "*Shangu shenpu*" *diaocha baogao*; Li Yi, "*Shangu shenpu* zhushi," pp. 60–87; Duan Shipu and Xu Cheng, "*Shangu shenpu* chu tan"; and Zhang Zhizhong et al., "*Shangu nuo xi* luxiangpian wenben." The Huang and Wang book contains many useful illustrations, although the quality leaves something to be desired.

Map 2   Renzhuang and environs. 1 cm = 1.7 km (SOURCE: *Shanxi sheng ditu ji*).

1585, claims that both the village and the temple whose renovation it celebrates were founded in the Tang dynasty, and both suggest, we are told, that the village was populous and prosperous in late Ming times.[2] The other, commemorating the repair of the Lingfeng Chan Buddhist temple, records the names of over 210 donors.[3] This was probably a large proportion, though not all, of the male heads of household in the village and suggests that the total population was over 1,000.[4] As late as the mid-nineteenth century, the village had a government salt depot, a pawnshop, a dyeworks, a distillery, a tailor shop and/or cloth shop, a butcher shop, and a shop selling "mountain products," probably medicinal herbs.[5] This prosperity may have been due to the stationing of a

---

2. Huang and Wang, "*Shangu shenpu*" *diaocha baogao,* pp. 12, 13. They do not provide the texts of the inscriptions.

3. Ibid., p. 14. This stele is dated 1585 on p. 14 and 1606 in the caption to photograph no. 15, p. 184.

4. I assume an average of five persons per household.

5. Ibid., p. 13; Duan Shipu and Xu Cheng, "*Shangu shenpu* chu tan," p. 90.

garrison (*zhen*) there during the Qing, no doubt because of the post road from Quwo to Jiang county.[6] The nineteenth century brought some serious crises, but they were not enough to destroy the ritual life of the village. In 1909, when the manuscript of the *Fan-Drum Roster of the Gods* (*Shangu shenpu*) was last copied, there were apparently as many as seventeen temples and shrines in and around Renzhuang.[7] Their names and locations are known, but not one remains today. Most were destroyed in the Anti-Japanese War or the Cultural Revolution, but the last one—most likely the Lingfeng Chan Buddhist temple—was demolished and its carvings sold to an antique dealer by the village leadership in recent years, probably in the 1980s.[8]

Students of popular mentalities in modern China might wish to consider the implications for the collective psychology of the people of Renzhuang of the obliteration of all their temples in the space of a single generation, and ponder as well the total absence of any efforts to restore them. More relevant to the subject of this book is the ability of a village whose population may well have been as little as 500 in 1909 to support seventeen temples and shrines (plus an ancestral hall) despite a devastating famine just thirty years earlier. Nor was this rich provision of religious buildings unusual. The invaluable surveys by Willem Grootaers and his associates in the late 1940s of village temples in the regions around Xuanhua and Wanquan, frontier towns near the Great Wall northwest of Beijing, found an average of 4.2 and 6.5 temples per village, respectively. One large village near Wanquan had 32.[9] The gazetteer of Ding prefecture, in Hebei, records 25 temples in a village of 274

---

6. Ibid. Renzhuang is not listed as a *zhen* in the *Shanxi Provincial Gazetteer* (*Shanxi tongzhi*) (1990 rpt. of 1892 ed.), 26.2340. In my experience few southern Shanxi villages are walled, and large-scale prewar maps of the area also show very few walled villages; so Renzhuang's wall may have been connected with its *zhen* status. It should be noted, however, that when the great sinologist Berthold Laufer traveled from Taiyuan to Xi'an (in Shaanxi) in February 1909, he noted that "nearly all villages in Shanxi are surrounded by walls, like the towns" (Laufer, "Zur kulturhistorischen Stellung," p. 194).

7. The map in Huang and Wang, "*Shangu shenpu*" *diaocha baogao*, p. 135, lists nineteen temples, but two—numbers 1 and 3—were located inside the Patriarch Temple (number 2).

8. Interviews with Xu Cheng et al., Renzhuang, June 5, 1992.

9. Grootaers, "Rural Temples," p. 9; idem, "Temples and History," p. 217.

(above) Fig. 1   Rezhuang village looking north (photograph: David Johnson).

(right) Fig. 2   Plan of Renzhuang. (SOURCE: Huang and Wang, "*Shangu shenpu*" *diaocha baogao*). NOTE: not one of the temples survives.

Key to Fig. 2

1. Locust God Temple
2. Patriarch Temple
3. Cattle King Temple
4. Pusa Temple*
5. Lingfeng Temple (Chan Buddhist)
6. Grotto of the Clouds of the Law
7. Fire God Temple
8. Guan Di Temple
9. Guan Di Temple
10. Pusa Temple*
11. Fire God Temple
12. Guan Di Temple and Pusa Temple
13. Dragon King Temple
14. Tudi Temple (local earth god)
15. Eastern Peak Temple
16. Empress Earth Divine Mother Temple
17. Mountain God Temple
18. God of Literature Temple
19. Silkworm Goddess (lit. "Aunt") Temple

*Pusa is a generic term for deities; evidently the villagers had forgotten the god who originally received cult there.

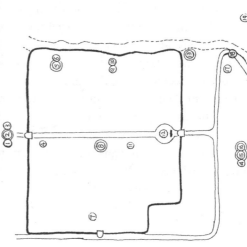

households and 20 in one of 96 households.[10] In the Ding County Experimental District in western Hebei, a unit of Ding prefecture, there was an average of seven temples per village in 1882, and this number was only slightly lower in 1914. But a militantly secularizing magistrate arrived in that year, and thereafter the number declined sharply.[11] Six of Sidney Gamble's "sample villages" in Hebei, surveyed in the early 1930s, had a total of 38 temples, with 15 in one village alone.[12] Thus, the density of temples and shrines in and around Renzhuang may have been above average for the region, but it was by no means extraordinary.

Of Renzhuang's seventeen temples and shrines, six are noted as "large" on the map in the report by Huang Zhusan and Wang Fucai that is one of my primary sources here. Moving from north to south, they are the Patriarch (Zushi) Temple, just outside the north gate of the village; the Lingfeng Temple, in the northeast corner of the village; the Guan Di Temple, in the center of the village; the Dragon King (Longwang) Temple, just outside the southeast corner of the walls; and the Eastern Peak (Dong yue) Temple and the Empress Earth (Houtu) Temple, located in a single compound on the slopes of Dragon Hill just south of the village.

The Patriarch Temple was dedicated to Pengzu, an ancient legendary figure said to have lived to the age of 800.[13] Cults to Pengzu are not common, but there was an important temple to him, said to have been constructed in the eighth century, on the north peak of Zijin Mountain, southwest of the village.[14] (The east and west peaks also had large temples, the former to Taishan, that is, the Eastern Peak, the latter to the

---

10. Kung-chuan Hsiao, *Rural China*, p. 276, presenting data derived from *Ding zhou zhi* (1850), *juan* 6–7.

11. Gamble, *Ting Hsien*, pp. 405–7.

12. Gamble, *North China Villages*, p. 119. Gamble had "no reports" on temples in another five sample villages, suggesting that his investigators may have ignored the smaller ones.

13. Yuan Ke, *Zhongguo shenhua chuanshuo cidian*, pp. 378–79.

14. Huang and Wang, "*Shangu shenpu*" *diaocha baogao*, p. 17, quoting an unspecified edition of *Jiang xian zhi*. See also Duan Shipu and Xu Cheng, "*Shangu shenpu* chu tan," p. 100, *n*1, which, however, cites no source. The east peak of Zijin Mountain has nothing whatsoever to do with the Eastern Peak, an alternative name for Taishan, the sacred mountain of the east.

Divine Mother, presumably Empress Earth.) In Qing times, the boundaries of three counties met at Zijin Mountain: Quwo, Jiang, and Wenxi, with jurisdiction over its north, east, and west peaks, respectively. These temples were the focus of festivals that must have resembled the great *sai* of southeastern Shanxi, although I have next to no information about them. All three festivals were sponsored by an alliance of seven *shê*.[15] The 1919 Wenxi county gazetteer says that villages "welcome" (*jie*) gods to give thanks for good harvests or timely rains. "Large villages form a *shê* by themselves, whereas smaller ones join together to form a *shê*. Five, six, sometimes even more than ten *shê* take it in turn to welcome the god(s)."[16] Renzhuang constituted a *shê* by itself, named the Star Fire *Shê* (Xing huo *shê*). It and six other *shê* managed the land belonging to the three temples, which was nearly 500 *mu* in the case of the Patriarch Temple, and organized the great annual festivals.[17]

At some point there was a dispute between Renzhuang and the other *shê* over the management of the temple land or the annual festival, and Renzhuang withdrew from the alliance and built its own Pengzu temple. (This tells us something about the resources available to the village for religious purposes in premodern times. Unfortunately the date of construction is not given in the reports.)[18] The Cattle King and Locust God also received cult there. The new temple had a stage over its main gate in typical Shanxi style.

The Dragon King Temple is not described, nor is any information given about the Chan temple, although, as mentioned above, it probably survived into the 1980s. The Guan Di Temple occupied a large space in the middle of the village. It had a main hall, an offering hall, side halls, and a stage, but the stage, contrary to usual practice, was not positioned on the central north-south axis of the temple complex. Instead, it was offset to the west due to the presence in the southeast

---

15. Huang and Wang, "*Shangu shenpu*" *diaocha baogao,* p. 17.

16. Quoted in Ding Shiliang and Zhao Fang, *Zhongguo difangzhi minsu ziliao huibian: Huabei juan,* p. 700.

17. Duan Shipu and Xu Cheng, "*Shangu shenpu* chu tan," p. 100, *n*1; Huang and Wang, "*Shangu shenpu*" *diaocha baogao,* p. 17.

18. Huang and Wang, "*Shangu shenpu*" *diaocha baogao,* pp. 17–18; Duan Shipu and Xu Cheng, "*Shangu shenpu* chu tan," p. 100, *n*1.

corner of the compound of the ancestral hall of the Xu lineage, which was dominant in the village. The large courtyard between the stage and the offering hall, which measured about thirty yards north to south and twenty yards east to west, was where the annual New Year ritual called the *Fan-Drum Roster of the Gods* was performed.

The main halls of both the Eastern Peak and Empress Earth temples were three bays wide. We are not told if they had stages. The cult of Empress Earth, the ancient earth goddess, had long been popular in southwestern Shanxi. The center of the cult was the great Empress Earth Temple (Houtu miao), now located at the village of Miaoqian (lit., "In front of the temple"), about ninety-five kilometers west of Quwo in Wanrong county, on the bluffs overlooking the Yellow River. This was one of the most sacred places in China. Emperors had personally come to make sacrifices there from the time of Han Wudi in the second century B.C.[19] The Renzhuang Empress Earth Temple was also known as the Niangniang Temple,[20] and the goddess was believed to be a sender of sons. Clay dolls were presented at the annual festival by people praying for a son, and some women would steal them to take home. The Empress Earth Temple was the most active of all the village temples.[21]

In addition to these six large temples there were eleven others, not counting the Xu ancestral hall. Four were Buddhist: three to Guanyin, plus a Grotto of the Clouds of the Law (Fa yun dong). There were also two to Huo Shen, the god of fire, two more to Guan Di (one sharing space with a temple to Guanyin), one to the local earth god (Tudi; in the same compound as the Empress Earth and Eastern Peak temples), one to the Mountain God (Shan shen), one to Wenchang, the god of literary arts, and one to the Silkworm Goddess (Cangu).[22]

There were festivals every year on the second day of the second lunar month at the Dragon King Temple, on the eighteenth of the third

---

19. See Zhao Kuifu, "Fenyin shangu nuo xi," pp. 213–15, for a list of imperial sacrifices at Shanxi's Houtu miao between Former Han and Song.

20. "Niangniang" usually means "grandmother" or "mother" in that part of Shanxi. See Ding Shiliang and Zhao Fang, *Zhongguo difangzhi minsu ziliao huibian: Huabei juan*, p. 699, quoting *Wenxi xian zhi* (1919); and Lu Chengwen, *Shanxi fengsu minqing*, p. 100.

21. Huang and Wang, "*Shangu shenpu*" *diaocha baogao*, p. 16.

22. Ibid., pp. 17–18, 135.

month at the Empress Earth Temple, and on the twenty-eighth of the third month at the Eastern Peak Temple. In addition, the great annual festival at the Patriarch Temple on Zijin Mountain began on the second of the third lunar month, and Renzhuang was one of the sponsoring *shê*, at least until the dispute.[23] People in Renzhuang believed that the rituals at the Patriarch Temple could not begin until their gong and drum troupe arrived. This custom was said to date to the founding of the temple in the Tang dynasty.[24] Whether or not this was actually the case, Renzhuang's percussion troupes certainly must have been famous, since they performed every year at the Dragon King Temple festival at Nanlinjiao village and the Nine Dragon Temple festival in Jingming village, somewhat larger settlements a couple of miles to the east.[25] They also performed at a New Year's folk culture exhibition in Linfen, thirty miles to the north, in 1954, and in recent years in exhibitions in Quwo.[26]

There were three gong and drum troupes in Renzhuang, one for each "section" (*jie*)—East, West, and South—of the village. Each troupe had sixteen members, who played two large drums, two small drums, two pairs of cymbals, eight regular gongs, and two small gongs. Fathers began to teach sons when they were eleven or twelve years old, and the boys would practice after supper and during breaks in field work by beating out the rhythms on their thighs.[27] A number of copies of the scores of the pieces in their repertoire were in circulation, and one still exists.[28] The troupes performed at temple festivals in neighboring villages. Only the best troupe was selected to represent the village at a given festival, and so there must have been a strong rivalry among the three sections.[29]

---

23. Duan Shipu and Xu Cheng, "*Shangu shenpu* chu tan," p. 100, *n*1; Huang and Wang, "*Shangu shenpu*" *diaocha baogao*, p. 17, quoting *Jiang xian zhi*, pt. III, sect. 2.

24. Duan Shipu and Xu Cheng, "*Shangu shenpu* chu tan," p. 100, *n*1.

25. Huang and Wang, "*Shangu shenpu*" *diaocha baogao*, p. 18. It is unfortunate that we are not given the dates of these festivals or of the other annual festivals in Renzhuang.

26. Duan Shipu and Xu Cheng, "*Shangu shenpu* chu tan," p. 100.

27. Huang and Wang, "*Shangu shenpu*" *diaocha baogao*, pp. 18, 95–96; interviews with Xu Cheng et al., Renzhuang, June 5, 1992.

28. The score is published in Huang and Wang, "*Shangu shenpu*" *diaocha baogao*, pp. 97–106.

29. Ibid., p. 18.

Renzhuang's festival culture was thus very rich. The village participated formally in at least five multivillage temple festivals, what were
called "great *sai*" in southeastern Shanxi, and there were probably six
major festivals in the village, one for each of its "large" temples. The
villagers also celebrated in grand style the great Yuanxiao festival on the
fourteenth to the sixteenth of the first lunar month. We usually know
almost nothing of what happened at such festivals, but Renzhuang is an
exception, because we have a copy of the script, or liturgy, of its New
Year ritual, which the villagers called *Fan-Drum Roster of the Gods* (*Shangu
shenpu*). As far as we know, this ritual was unique to Renzhuang, and
possibly very old. For three days there were invocations, dances, skits,
and other activities, all performed by villagers led by twelve men called
the "Godly Ones" (*shenjia*).[30] The Godly Ones inherited their positions,
and their families almost certainly constituted one of the village elites.
In the second decade of the twentieth century, each of these families
had a copy of the liturgy, and one of the copies, nearly complete,
somehow survived both the Japanese army and the Red Guards. The
text was discovered by representatives of the Quwo County Cultural
Affairs Office in 1985.[31] Its publication in the journal *Zhonghua xiqu* in
1988 created a sensation. A replica performance was organized and
videotaped in 1989. Considerable scholarly attention has been devoted
to the Fan-drum ritual, especially to tracing the origins of its various
elements.

Renzhuang's entire population was mobilized for the Fan-drum ritual, with virtually every household supplying at least one participant
and sometimes more, according to one estimate.[32] Preparations began
on the eighth day of the twelfth month, when a meeting was called by
the *xiangyue*—a village official appointed by the county magistrate who

---

30. This term could be applied to both individuals and families, and it is not always
clear which meaning is intended. Used of individuals, it meant something like "specialists on the gods," just as diviners were called *kan yu jia*, "specialists in investigating the
universe"; hence the translation here. When used of families, the term should be translated "godly families" or "divine families."

31. Huang and Wang, "*Shangu shenpu*" *diaocha baogao*, p. 23. On p. 3, 1987 is given as
the date of discovery, but the account on p. 23 is highly circumstantial.

32. Duan Shipu and Xu Cheng, "*Shangu shenpu* chu tan," p. 90.

served as liaison with the county government—to decide whether the Fan-drum ritual should be held at the upcoming New Year.[33] At the meeting were the head (*zuzhang*) of the Xu lineage, other respected members of the lineage, the leader of the gong and drum troupes (called the *Shê* Head [*shêshou*]), and the leader of the twelve Godly Ones, the hereditary performers who were the backbone of the ritual.

The roles of the Godly Ones were not interchangeable; the right to each descended in a particular family. Thus, not only the composition of the village ritual elite but also the relative rank of its member families was fixed: the position of Head of the Godly Ones (*shentou*) stayed in one family, and so also for the Second Godly One and the rest.[34] If a Godly One died without an heir, a successor was chosen at the meeting on the eighth of the twelfth month. The new Godly One was required to be a member of the Xu lineage, to reside in the village, to be familiar with the ritual, and to have the ability to perform creditably.[35]

Rehearsals began on the twenty-third day of the twelfth lunar month (the day the Stove God was believed to leave the kitchen on his annual journey to Heaven to report on the behavior of the family), under the general direction of the Head of the Godly Ones. Other important personnel were the *Shê* Head, who selected the players other than the Godly Ones who would have the honor of performing at the Fan-drum ritual and who supervised their rehearsals; the leader of the flower-drum troupe, who selected the young performers of the flower-drum dances and was in charge of their rehearsals; and the stage manager, who had overall responsibility for preparing the courtyard of the Guan Di Temple and making ready the ritual accessories.[36] Perhaps the most

---

33. Huang and Wang, *"Shangu shenpu" diaocha baogao*, p. 24, says that economic conditions could lead to a negative decision, but given the exorcistic function of the ritual and the central importance of New Year in the ritual year, I suspect that the Fan-drum ritual was almost always held. (I am aware that the more common meaning of *xiangyue* is "community compact.")

34. Ibid., p. 25. There is some ambiguity in Huang and Wang's account, however; they suggest that the *shentou* was the leader because he knew how everything was supposed to be done, which presumably would not have been the case with a young man who had just inherited the position.

35. Ibid.

36. Ibid., pp. 25–26.

important of these were baroque towers up to six feet tall made of hardened wheat-flour dough, which were placed around the Eight Trigram Altars (which marked out the ritual arena in the temple courtyard); these were made by the village women.[37] Despite the fact that dough sculpture was one of the great Shanxi folk arts, and despite the importance of the towers in the Fan-drum ritual—not to mention their beauty—none of the writers on the ritual explains how they were made or even describes them.[38]

The Godly Ones had by far the most important roles in the ritual. Each of them began learning his part from his father as soon as he could talk; it was considered part of his education.[39] They played the fan-shaped drums that gave their name to the ritual, took part in intricate dances at the Eight Trigram Altars, and performed various invocations and skits. For these last there were written scripts, evidently to ensure that no changes were introduced. Originally there had been only one complete copy, which was stored in the lineage hall. (This resembles the practice of the Entertainers of southeastern Shanxi, whom we will meet in Part III.) From that master copy, each *shenjia* family made a part-script with its own lines. But, as mentioned above, the disasters of the late nineteenth century led the village elders to have twelve complete copies made. Three members of the Xu lineage did the copying and proofreading in 1909.[40] When Japanese troops shelled and burned

---

37. Interviews with Xu Cheng et al., Renzhuang, June 5, 1992.

38. For pictures of the Renzhuang towers, see Fig. 4: Wen Xing and Xue Maixi, *Shanxi minsu*, p. 418; and Huang and Wang, "*Shangu shenpu*" *diaocha baogao*, pp. 191–94. For pictures showing the use of dough sculptures on other ritual occasions, which was common in Shanxi, see Wen and Xue, *Shanxi minsu*, pp. 58, 65, 118, 127; Li Yuming, *Shanxi minjian yishu*, pp. 34–38; and Bo Songnian and Duan Gaifang, *Zhongguo minjian meishu*, 4: 112–50.

39. Interviews with Xu Cheng et al., Renzhuang, June 5, 1992; Huang and Wang, "*Shangu shenpu*" *diaocha baogao*, p. 25.

40. Ibid., p. 20. Most unusually, Huang and Wang name the person who provided this information: Xu Cheng. On pp. 3–4, we are told that he was born in 1930. He joined the PLA when young and did not return for a long time. He retired to the village and is now the most influential resident. One son is the current village head, and another is the principal of the local high school. Xu Cheng was instrumental in arranging for the videotaping of the Fan-drum ritual (interviews with Xu Cheng et al., Renzhuang, June 5, 1992).

the village in July 1938, all but one of the scripts were destroyed, along with costumes, instruments, props, and other paraphernalia. One copy survived because the owner, Xu Yuyi, lived outside the village in a cave on Dragon Hill. This is the text that was discovered in 1985, in the possession of Xu Yuyi's son. It bears the date Xuantong 1 (1909) on the cover, along with the name of Renzhuang village. The manuscript is incomplete; the scripts of three skits are lacking. These have been reconstructed with the help of old villagers who memorized them when young.[41]

After the performers had been selected and rehearsals were well under way, the Eight Trigram Altars had to be prepared. These were temporary structures that were disassembled after the ritual was completed. Eight altars, made by stacking up ordinary household tables and chairs and then covering them with hangings, were set up facing inward, creating a circular space about forty feet in diameter within which most of the ritual action took place.[42] The altar on the north was about twelve feet high, the three at the other cardinal directions about ten feet high, and the rest about eight feet. Each was elaborately decorated.

The tables of the northern altar were mostly covered with blue cloth, with square red and black banners hanging in front, concealing the tables' legs. The lowest level was furnished like an altar with candlesticks, an incense burner, vases, and plates holding 55 buns shaped like peaches (but not colored).[43] Just behind these objects and also on the lowest level were three of the dough towers mentioned above, intricately carved and modeled and covered with hundreds of tiny colored flowers, insects, and animals, also made of hardened dough. Small paper-cut banners and other decorations made of paper hung from the towers. (Paper-cutting is another famous Shanxi women's folk art.) Two large square ritual vessels stood about head high in the middle level of the structure, flanking the towers. From the base of each, a yellow paper hung down on which was written in cinnabar, in the elaborate style of calligraphy used in charms,

---

41. Huang and Wang, "*Shangu shenpu*" *diaocha baogao*, pp. 20–22.

42. The sources for the following description of the Eight Trigram Altars are ibid., pp. 26–28; and photographs in the author's collection, unless otherwise noted.

43. The information on the buns comes from Huang and Wang, "*Shangu shenpu*" *diaocha baogao*, p. 28.

Fig. 3 The ritual arena for the *Fan-Drum Roster of the Gods*
(SOURCE: Wen Xing and Xue Maixi, *Shanxi minsu*).

Fig. 4 The main altar with dough tower
(photograph courtesy Yang Mengheng).

"Accept the command to behead demons." Above these, at the very top of the structure, was a container (called a *dou*—"peck measure") filled with five varieties of grain, in which paper "spirit tablets" of some of the hundreds of gods invited to the ceremony had been inserted, together with colorful paper-cut banners. The other seven altars were similar in style, though smaller. The general effect was rather splendid, for unlike permanent decorations inside temples, which cannot be seen clearly in the gloom and in any case are darkened by incense smoke and dust, these were fresh and bright and placed out in the open air.

A ninth altar, called the Table of the Kinfolk (*jia qin zhuo*), was placed to the northeast of the eight main altars. On it were the usual altar furnishings, plus a realistic pair of hands, palms together in a gesture of reverence, made of hardened dough. The offerings on this table were intended for distant Xu ancestors as well as orphan ghosts and wild demons.[44]

How closely did the Eight Trigram Altars prepared for the video-taping in 1989—from which all our visual documentation comes—resemble those that were constructed in the 1930s and earlier? Were the altar decorations perhaps less elaborate than in the past, or different in some other way? Our chief source, the report by Huang Zhusan and Wang Fucai, does not broach this troublesome question, nor do the other published studies. When I inquired of village leaders in 1992 how the recent performance compared to those before the war, everyone agreed that the old ritual was much bigger, and the performers more polished, but I did not press for details. Even if I had, what could I have learned? The oldest informant named in the preface to Huang and Wang's report was 31 years old in 1945, the date of the last real performance, the next oldest was 22, the next 20. When the ritual was reconstructed, every aspect of it not found in the *Shangu shenpu* manuscript or in the percussion score—the dances and costumes, the construction and decoration of the altars, the food offerings, and so on—depended on the memory of those men and other villagers their age who are not named, including the women. Since the percussion troupes continued to perform occasionally after 1949, memories con-

---

44. Huang and Wang, *"Shangu shenpu" diaocha baogao*, p. 29.

cerning them are no doubt fairly reliable. But what about the rest of the ritual?

The only possible answer is that we do not know how seriously the tradition was disrupted. We have the *Shangu shenpu* manuscript, which provides a foundation for a reconstruction, but there is much more to a ritual performance than the liturgy, more to an opera than the script. In the case of Renzhuang, we do not even know the relationship of men like Xu Cheng, the village leader, to the twelve prewar Godly Ones, and this is true of virtually all the others who are our main sources. (The exception is Xu Shiwang, the son of Xu Yuyi, who, since he possessed one of the scripts, was probably a Godly One.) What, then, are we to make of the information we do have? It would be as foolish to reject it uncritically as to accept it uncritically. We can, I think, feel confident that we know the general structure of the ritual, and we probably know all the main elements. But it would be a mistake to put too much faith in any detail, nor should we assume that the appearance of the altars or any other element of the reconstructed performance has anything more than a general resemblance to what was done in the 1930s—not to mention in the centuries before that. Nevertheless, given these constraints, we still know an immense amount about the New Year rituals of Renzhuang village.

FIRST DAY: The "Invitation to the Gods" and the Mamazi Exorcist

The Eight Trigram Altars were constructed and decorated on the twelfth and thirteenth of the first month. After breakfast on the fourteenth, a small procession composed of the gong and drum troupes, a man holding a large banner with the words "Solemnly carry out the *nuo* ritual; expel disease and drive out illness," the twelve Godly Ones, and the flower-drum troupe circled the Eight Trigram Altars three times and then marched through all the main streets of the village, working from north to south and east to west. This served as formal notification that the ritual was about to begin.[45] After completing its tour of the

---

45. Ibid., pp. 29–30.

village, the procession returned to the courtyard of the Guan Di Temple and circled the Eight Trigram Altars once in a counterclockwise direction. Then, after walking around each of the eight altars in the sequence north, west, south, east, northeast, northwest, southwest, southeast, the Godly Ones took their seats in chairs beside the altars, two each at the altars of the cardinal directions, one at each of the remaining four. The leader's place was in the chair on the west side of the southern altar, facing the main, northern, altar. The Godly Ones then began playing their fan-drums, and chanted the "Invitation to the Gods."[46] Since the name of the ritual as a whole derived from this invitation, it undoubtedly was an important part of it, and I translate it in full.[47]

Invitation to the Gods

First Godly One: This is the *jiyou*[48] year of the Xuantong reign [1909];

Second Godly One: At the Yuanxiao festival, we will burn masses of [sacrificial] money.

Third Godly One: The twelve Godly Ones invite the gods

Fourth Godly One: To protect the village and bring blessings and longevity to all.

Fifth Godly One: Virtuous men and devout women burn incense,

Sixth Godly One: Praying to the gods and immortals to preserve our tranquillity.

Seventh Godly One: Because our horses and donkeys increase year by year

Eighth Godly One: And our oxen and sheep fill their pens, we give thanks to Heaven.[49]

Ninth Godly One: The breezes are gentle, the rain timely, and every family joyful;

---

46. Huang and Wang, "*Shangu shenpu*" *diaocha baogao*, pp. 29–30.

47. I follow the text as given in ibid., pp. 32–39, supplemented by Li Yi, "*Shangu shenpu* zhushi," pp. 61–73; and the facsimile of the manuscript given in Huang and Wang, "*Shangu shenpu*" *diaocha baogao*. Note that in the manuscript, all the lines for each Godly One are in a single block. The editors broke up those blocks of speech and set the lines out sequentially. Not surprisingly, there is some disagreement between the two versions as to where the breaks between the speeches should come.

48. Reading 己 for 乙.

49. Note that Heaven rather than a popular deity is being thanked.

TENTH GODLY ONE: There is a bumper crop of all the grains, we celebrate a golden age.

ELEVENTH GODLY ONE: Sons and grandsons fill the houses, wealthy and distinguished;

TWELFTH GODLY ONE: Fathers are merciful, sons obedient, and tranquillity is attained.

FIRST GODLY ONE: The four words "scholar," "farmer," "craftsman," and "businessman"

SECOND GODLY ONE: Represent the whole population.

THIRD GODLY ONE: Those who read serve as officials;

FOURTH GODLY ONE: They should eliminate the people's grievances.

FIFTH GODLY ONE: Those who work at farming need to be diligent and thrifty;

SIXTH GODLY ONE: They arise at dawn and do not go to sleep until midnight.

SEVENTH GODLY ONE: Those who work at crafts are highly skilled;

EIGHTH GODLY ONE: There is nothing they do not know how to do.

NINTH GODLY ONE: Those who do business buy and sell;

TENTH GODLY ONE: Their wealth is in the millions.

ELEVENTH GODLY ONE: Now let all idle chatter cease

TWELFTH GODLY ONE: As we respectfully invite the thronging gods to come to our altar.

FIRST GODLY ONE:

> The incense is in the brazier, the candles on their stands;
> The flowers in the vases open wide their blooms.
> Cup after cup of wine is offered up;
> In plate after plate the fruit is arranged.

We invite the starry lord, Green Emperor of the first and second [heavenly] stems and of the eastern quarter and the element wood, to come and receive the incense smoke.

SECOND GODLY ONE:

> The Blessing of Heaven is the sun, moon, and stars;
> The Blessing of Earth is gold, silver, and the five grains;
> The Blessing of the State is loyal ministers and virtuous generals;
> The Blessing of the Family is filial sons and worthy grandsons.

The first blessing is gentle breezes and timely rains, the second blessing is the nation prosperous and the people at peace; the third blessing is a bumper crop of the five grains; the fourth blessing is old and young both at peace; the fifth blessing is two ears on each stalk of grain; the sixth blessing is two spikes on each stalk of wheat; the seventh blessing is nine seeds in each cotton boll; the eighth blessing is three ridges on each sesame seed; the ninth blessing is prosperous trade; the tenth blessing is the tranquillity of domestic animals. We invite the starry lord, Red Emperor of the third and fourth stems and of the southern quarter and the element fire, to come and receive the incense smoke.

THIRD GODLY ONE: We invite the starry lord, White Emperor of the fifth and sixth stems and of the western quarter and the element metal, to come and receive the incense smoke.

FOURTH GODLY ONE: We invite the starry lord, Black Emperor of the seventh and eighth stems and of the northern quarter and the element water, to come and receive the incense smoke.

FIFTH GODLY ONE: We invite the starry lord, Yellow Emperor of the ninth and tenth stems and of the central quarter and the element earth, to come and receive the incense smoke.

SIXTH GODLY ONE: We respectfully invite the Eastern Peak, Mount Tai, to come and receive the incense smoke.

SEVENTH GODLY ONE: We respectfully invite the Southern Peak, Mount Heng, to come and receive the incense smoke.

EIGHTH GODLY ONE: We respectfully invite the Western Peak, Mount Hua, to come and receive the incense smoke.

NINTH GODLY ONE: We respectfully invite the Northern Peak, Mount Héng to come and receive the incense smoke.

TENTH GODLY ONE: We respectfully invite the Central Peak, Mount Song, to come and receive the incense smoke.

ELEVENTH GODLY ONE: The five peaks of the five quarters are all invited.

TWELFTH GODLY ONE: Once again we invite all the gods.

FIRST GODLY ONE:

> One thread of incense smoke forms two lines of writing;
> Invitations to all the gods [are carried] on the incense smoke.
> If there are deities who have not come,
> Prepare more cards inviting them.

We respectfully invite

> His Honor the Grand Defender who was ugly when born,
> Who holds a steel whip ribbed like bamboo.[50]

---

50. Zhao Gongming.

> Other villages don't invite you;
> Come to Renzhuang village to receive the incense fire.

We respectfully invite His Honor the Grand Defender to come and receive the incense smoke.

We respectfully invite

> His Honor the Lord of the Stove, surnamed Zhang,
> Whose temple is erected at the corner of every stove.
> Say nothing of the rice and flour that were spilled,
> Speak only of our burning incense with clean hands.[51]

We respectfully invite His Honor the Lord of the Stove to come and receive the incense smoke.

SECOND GODLY ONE: We respectfully invite the green-faced Earth God (Tudi) of the east, the white-faced Earth God of the west, the red-faced Earth God of the south, the black-faced Earth God of the north, the yellow-faced Earth God of the center, the Earth God who announces events before the terrace of the Jade Emperor,[52] the Earth God who receives fire before the Fire-Star Grandmother, the Earth God who hastens birth before the Sons-and-Grandsons Grandmother, the Earth God who brings the rain before the Dragon King, the Earth God who makes medicines before the Medicine King, and the Earth God who rescues from suffering before Guanyin—we invite them all to come and receive the incense smoke.

We respectfully invite the Earth Gods of our capital, our province, our prefecture, our county, our village, and this courtyard; the Earth Gods of the regions in front of the mountain, behind the mountain, to the left of the mountain, to the right of the mountain, on top of the mountain, at the foot of the mountain, and halfway up the mountain; the Earth Gods of the mountain god, of the patroller of the mountain,[53] and of the thirty-six villages [*li*]—we invite all Earth Gods to come and receive the incense smoke.

THIRD GODLY ONE: We respectfully invite the city gods of our national capital, our provincial capital, our prefectural capital, our county capital, and our region, and the General of the Five Ways at the Crossroads—we invite you to come and receive the incense smoke.

---

51. This is an interesting reflection of the prohibitions and directives of the Stove God scriptures that circulated all over China. See Robert Chard, "Master of the Family: History and Development of the Chinese Cult to the Stove" (Ph.D. diss., University of California, Berkeley, 1991), chap. 10.

52. Reading 玉 for 王.

53. Reading 土地 for 大王.

FOURTH GODLY ONE: We respectfully invite the Earth God and Earth Mother, Elder Earth-Uncle and Younger Earth-Uncle, Earth Son and Earth Grandson, the Nine Walls of the Earth Prefecture, the Great God Most High, the Thousand-Pound Divine Demon, the Great Star That Controls the Years— we invite all the gods of the earth to come and receive the incense smoke.

FIFTH GODLY ONE: We respectfully invite the rain-giving Dragon Kings of the five lakes and the four seas, the nine rivers and the eight streams, the Dragon Kings of wells and springs, and the Dragon King of the Spring Where the Sword Was Drawn[54]—we invite all the Dragon Kings to come and receive the incense smoke. We respectfully invite the Heroic and Unyielding General, the Three Kings of the White Dragon, and the heir apparent of the Bright and Numinous King, to come and receive the incense smoke. We respectfully invite the Wind Earl and Rain Master, the Thunder Lord and Lightning Mother, the Dragon Son and Dragon Grandson, and all dragon spirits to come and receive the incense smoke.

SIXTH GODLY ONE: We respectfully invite the Ox King and Horse King, the Great King of the Water Trough, His Honor the God of the Sheepfold, the Fodder-Chopping Boy, and the Horse-Feeding Lord to come and receive the incense smoke.

SEVENTH GODLY ONE: We respectfully invite the Exalted Ancestor Marquis and King[?], the Dark Duke of Locusts, the God of Granaries, and the Earth God of Young Shoots to come and receive the incense smoke. We respectfully invite His Honor the Granary Official to come and receive the incense smoke.

EIGHTH GODLY ONE: We respectfully invite the ten kings of Hell, King Qinguang, King Chujiang, King Songdi, King Wuguan, King Yanluo, King Biancheng, King Taishan, King Dushi, King Pingdeng, and King Zhuanlun to come and receive the incense smoke. We respectfully invite the Demon on the Left and the Judge on the Right, Ox-Head and Horse-Face, the Three Bureaus and the Six Boards, and Grandmother Superintending the Offices to come and receive the incense smoke.

NINTH GODLY ONE: We respectfully invite the Divine Immortals of the Upper Eight Grottoes, the Divine Immortals of the Lower Eight Grottoes, the Divine Immortals of the Middle Eight Grottoes, the Divine Immortals of

---

54. This is just south of the village. A local legend says the spring appeared when Emperor Guangwu of the Han dynasty thrust his sword into the rock there and pulled it out (Li Yi, "*Shangu shenpu* zhushi," p. 66, *n*17).

the twenty-four Grottoes, all the Divine Immortals to come and receive the incense smoke.

TENTH GODLY ONE: We respectfully invite Aunt Cat, Aunt Vinegar, Aunt Hemp Twine,[55] Aunt Haosi,[56] Aunt Silkworm, all the Aunts to come and receive the incense smoke.

ELEVENTH GODLY ONE: The incense smoke twines upward, the divine doors open; our invitation arrives on the incense smoke.[57] Invited is Grandfather Five Plagues[58] who comes from the south holding his seven-star tablet with golden characters. In life he liked to ride big horses; now he mounts the clouds and rides the mist on his way to the assembly.[59] We respectfully invite the Eight Heavens of the eastern quarter,[60] the Eight Heavens of the western quarter, the Eight Heavens of the southern quarter, the Eight Heavens of the northern quarter, thirty-two Heavens in all, adding one for His Honor the Jade Emperor makes thirty-three, to all come and receive the incense smoke.

TWELFTH GODLY ONE: We respectfully invite the most humane, most holy Humane and Courageous Great Emperor, His Excellency the Holy Guan [Guan Yu], the loyally humane, loyally righteous Awesomely Martial Numinously Responding Holy Lords of the Peach Garden Liu [Bei] and Zhang [Fei], and their lordships Zhou Cang and Guan Ping[61] to come and receive the incense smoke.

FIRST GODLY ONE: We respectfully invite the gods of the year, month, day, and hour and their Honors of the Left Gate, the Right Door, and the Impluvium[62] to come and receive the incense smoke. We respectfully invite

---

55. This refers to Magu, immortal and bestower of long life (Zong Li and Liu Qun, *Zhongguo minjian zhu shen*, pp. 719–24).

56. Li Yi, "*Shangu shenpu* zhushi," p. 67, *n*36, says *Taiping guangji, juan* 6, has a story about an immortal from Taiyuan named Aunt Haosi (same characters: 郝司). Actually, it is in *juan* 60 and concerns a shrine (*si* 寺) to Aunt Hao.

57. Reading 到 for 道.

58. Ding Shiliang and Zhao Fang, *Zhongguo difangzhi minsu ziliao huibian: Huabei juan*, p. 699, quoting *Wenxi xian zhi*, says *yeye* 爺爺 means "grandfather" in the local dialect. Wenxi borders Quwo to the south.

59. The section from "Grandfather" to "assembly" is in verse in the original.

60. Reading 方 for 風 throughout, following Li Yi, "*Shangu shenpu* zhushi," p. 67, *n*39.

61. Guan Yu's squire and son, respectively.

62. Reading 雷 for 魁. The facsimile shows that the manuscript is very defective at this point, and it is not clear how the editors established the text here. The association

the Supreme Thearch of the Dark Heaven Lord Zhenwu to come and receive the incense smoke. We respectfully invite the Divine Marshals Deng, Xin, Gou,[63] Bi, Ma, Zhao, Wen, Liu, Jiao, and Yao,[64] the banner-carrying and sword-brandishing Peach Blossom Maiden and the Duke of Zhou,[65] and the Tortoise General and Snake General[66] to come and receive the incense smoke. We respectfully invite the Holy Mother Grandmother Empress Earth to come and receive the incense smoke.

SECOND GODLY ONE: We respectfully invite His Honor the dragon-quelling tiger-taming Medicine King and the famous physicians of ten dynasties to come and receive the incense smoke. We respectfully invite the Pill-Rolling Lord and the Herb-Picking Lord to come and receive the incense smoke. We respectfully invite Mars, the Southern Star Lord of Fiery Virtue, and Grandmother Fire Star to come and receive the incense smoke.

THIRD GODLY ONE: We respectfully invite the Greatly Perfected Most Holy First Master Confucius, the Thearch Lord Wenchang, and Kuixing Who Lifts the Dipper to come and receive the incense smoke. We respectfully invite the Four who receive sacrifice in association [with Confucius] and the Ten Philosophers [i.e., Confucius' disciples], and all the worthies of the Sage's Teaching, the former worthies of successive dynasties, and the Seventy-two Worthies to come and receive the incense smoke.

FOURTH GODLY ONE: We respectfully invite the Ancient Mother of Mount Li, the Ancient Mother of the Intercalary Month, the Twelve Ancient Mothers, all the Ancient Mothers to come and receive the incense smoke. We respectfully invite the All-Transforming Heaven-Honored Thunder God Respond-

---

of the Impluvium (*zhong liu* 中霤) with the Gate and the Door goes back to Han times at least (see Bodde, *Festivals in Ancient China*, p. 55). I believe that the text has 中魁 (*zhong kui*) instead of 中霤 (*zhong liu*) because of the influence of the names of two other spirits: Zhong Kui 鍾馗, the famous demon destroyer; and Kui Xing 魁星, the god of literature.

63. Reading 苟 for 勾.

64. Reading 姚 for 挑. Most of these names are found among the 24 gods of the Thunder Bureau as recorded in the cosmological novel *Feng shen yanyi* (*The Investiture of the Gods*) and elsewhere. The exceptions are Ma, Wen, and Jiao; see Zong Li and Liu Qun, *Zhongguo minjian zhu shen*, pp. 155–57. I have corrected the punctuation of the printed editions here.

65. The struggle between these two wizards was a popular subject for local opera.

66. Companions of Zhenwu.

ing to the Primal in the Nine Heavens to come and receive the incense smoke.[67]

FIFTH GODLY ONE: We respectfully invite the Heavenly Immortal Holy Mother, the Heavenly Mother of Eyesight, the Heavenly Mother of Sons and Grandsons, the Grandmothers Who Hasten Birth and Send Pregnancy, Who Strike Down Typhus,[68] Who Nurture and Raise the Young to come and receive the incense smoke. We respectfully invite the Elder Brothers and Elder Sisters to come and receive the incense smoke.

SIXTH GODLY ONE: We respectfully invite Guanyin Who Saves from the Suffering of the Eight Difficulties,[69] Sudhana,[70] the Dragon Maiden, Weituo the Guardian of the Dharma, the Eighteen Lohans, Manjusri, and Samantabhadra to come and receive the incense smoke. We respectfully invite the Mahasthama Bodhisattva, the Thousand-Armed Thousand-Eyed Bodhisattva, all the bodhisattvas to come and receive the incense smoke.

SEVENTH GODLY ONE: We respectfully invite Shakyamuni Buddha, Tathagata Buddha,[71] Amida Buddha, Maitreya Buddha, Dipamkara Buddha, all the myriad myriad Buddhas to come and receive the incense smoke. We respectfully invite the Zhunti Boddhisattva Who Welcomes in the West and Compassionately Ferries All to Salvation [i.e., Guanyin], the Immortal Ancient of the Southern Pole Star, Pengzu [whose original name was] Qian Jian, Wang Chan of Guigu, Lu Ban the Sagacious Master, the four great Heavenly Kings, and General Heng and General Ha[72] to come and receive the incense smoke.

EIGHTH GODLY ONE: We respectfully invite the Bodhisattva Ksitigarbha to come and receive the incense smoke. We respectfully invite the Lord of the Dark Altar to come and receive the incense smoke.

---

67. I have followed the emendation of Li Yi, "*Shangu shenpu* zhushi," p. 70, *n*16, reading 九天應元雷神普化天尊 for 九天應愿雷聲普化南無天尊. Li states that there is a god in *Feng shen yanyi* with the same title.

68. Reading 梧值 for the editors' 培植, which makes no sense. 梧 is the reading in the manuscript.

69. The editors' emendation is incorrect here. See Soothill, *A Dictionary of Chinese Buddhist Terms*, p. 41, for 八難.

70. Reading 財 for 才.

71. Following the glosses in Li Yi, "*Shangu shenpu* zhushi," p. 71, *nn*28–29.

72. These last are *Feng shen yanyi* characters; they are also the names conventionally given to the two guardians that flank the entrance of every Buddhist temple (Prip-Møller, *Chinese Buddhist Monasteries*, pp. 16–17).

NINTH GODLY ONE: We respectfully invite the Master of the Teachings of the Three Purities, the Heavenly Worthy of Primordial Beginning, Lord Lao of the Primordial Chaos, the Great Duke Jiang Shang [Jiang Ziya], the men of the Twelve Gates, Jinzha, Muzha, Leizhenzi, Nazha, and all the gods of *Feng shen bang* to come and receive the incense smoke.[73] We respectfully invite the Holy Mother of the Primordial Lord, Grandmother Queen Mother, the Immortal Maiden of the Nine Heavens, and Moon-Dwelling Chang E to come and receive the incense smoke.

TENTH GODLY ONE: We respectfully invite the four stars of the Eastern Dipper, the five stars of the Western Dipper, the six stars of the Southern Dipper, the seven stars of the Northern Dipper, and the twelve stars of the center to come and receive the incense smoke. We respectfully invite the Star Lords of the Nine Brightnesses,[74] the twenty-eight Lunar Lodges, the Herd Boy and the Weaving Girl, the Golden Crow and the Jade Rabbit, and the Moon and the Sun to come and receive the incense smoke.

ELEVENTH GODLY ONE: The Sovereign of Heaven whose clear vapors rise up to floating Heaven, the Sovereign of Earth whose heavy turbidity makes the cold Earth[?], the Sovereign of Man whose hands control men's fate, plus Yao, Shun, Yu, and Tang—we invite them all. We respectfully invite the Official of Heaven, the Official of Earth, and the Official of the Water Office, Yin Jiao and Yin Hong, Day Traveler and Night Traveler[75] to come and receive the incense smoke. We respectfully invite the Three Sovereigns and Five Emperors of antiquity, and Yao, Shun, Yu, and Tang to come and receive the incense smoke. We respectfully invite Grandmother Nüwa to come and receive the incense smoke. We respectfully invite His Honor the Jade Emperor of the Central Heaven to come and receive the incense smoke. We respectfully invite the True Lord of the Marvelous Way and His Honor Erlang to come and receive the incense smoke.

---

73. *Feng shen bang* is the title given to operatic versions of the novel *Feng shen yanyi*, of which there were many. We have already seen three examples in the liturgy of the influence of this novel. It is exceptionally interesting that an opera or novel was considered to give authentic information about the gods. The sharp distinction between sacred and secular texts, so natural to us, virtually disappears here.

74. All the divinities named up to this point in the paragraph are found in *Feng shen yanyi*, according to Li Yi, "*Shangu shenpu* zhushi," p. 72, *nn*52–57.

75. Following Li Yi's emendation in ibid., p. 73, *n*64. The deities in this sentence can also be found in *Feng shen yanyi*.

TWELFTH GODLY ONE: We respectfully invite the True Ministers of the Three Realms of Heaven and Earth, the Ten Directions, and the Myriad Potencies, and all the deities who move about in the Void to come and receive the incense smoke. We respectfully invite the God of Wealth, the God of Happiness, the God of Blessings, Emoluments, and High Office, the Two Harmonious Saints [Hanshan and Shide], the Immortal Officer of Profitable Trade, the Wealth-Summoning Lad, and the Gentleman Who Presents Treasures to come and receive the incense smoke.

We respectfully invite the present emperor, long life to him, to come and receive the incense smoke.

We request that the myriad gods who come to the altar arrange themselves according to status, rank, seniority, and precedence, each taking the proper place.

We respectfully invite the Great Gentleman Who Is to Be Avoided, the King of the Demons, the three generations of ancestors of every family, and all orphaned ghosts to come and receive the incense smoke.

When the chanting of this imposing list of deities finally came to an end, the twelve Godly Ones performed a dance to pay honor to the gods, and then three village elders presented incense, made obeisance, offered wine, and burned a memorial in front of each of the four main altars, accompanied by the gong and drum troupe, the flower-drum troupe, and a crowd of onlookers.

What are we to make of this inordinately long list of divine invitees? It is very different from the welcoming of the gods during the *sai* in southeastern Shanxi, examined in detail in Part III. In a *sai*, the birthday of a god was celebrated in his own temple, and the ceremony appears to have been modeled on birthday festivities for revered elders. In a *sai*, the guests were gods of similar status from neighboring villages; each god received a special invitation, and his or her spirit tablet was brought in procession to the host temple. The gods were greeted individually, given separate places in the temple, and entertained with a great feast and lavish theatricals.

In Renzhuang, by contrast, the occasion was the New Year festival, not the birthday of a god. The welcoming ceremony was simple, no special offerings of food were made, and there was no host god. At the end of the ritual, the paper symbols of the gods were simply taken down and burned (the process is not described in detail in Huang and Wang's report), along with all the other paraphernalia of the Eight

Trigram Altars.[76] The villagers themselves called the ritual as a whole the "Fan-Drum Roster of the Gods," and the immense list of deities (nearly 550 by my count) must have been regarded as the central feature of the verbal side of the ritual. Yet it is excessively long and tediously mechanical. The Earth Goddess had a special role in the ritual (as we shall see), yet her name is effectively buried in the middle of the roster. The entire ceremony was held in the courtyard of the Guan Di Temple, yet Guan Di is given no special emphasis. The village had long been closely linked with a major temple to Pengzu a few miles away, and Renzhuang had its own temple to him just outside the north gate—but Pengzu is also treated as just one deity among many. Moreover, the status of the deities in the list varies widely, from the Fodder-Chopping Boy to the Jade Emperor, from Aunt Cat to Maitreya Buddha, from orphan ghosts to Confucius. This heterogeneity diminishes the psychological weight of the roster as a whole. And the sheer number of deities named reduces the significance of any particular one.

The roster also has a distinctly literati or official flavor. A large proportion of the gods are the sort favored by the literary and political elites: faceless supernatural personifications of natural forces and the five cardinal directions, earth gods connected to abstract rather than actual places, city gods arranged in a neat hierarchy. One also gets a distinct sense of padding. In short, although I cannot claim familiarity with all the popular pantheons in north China, I believe that many of the gods in the list had no popular base at all; it does not seem to be a reflection of the lived, organic, on-the-ground religious universe of the people of Renzhuang. This is borne out when the roster is compared with the lists of cults in various locations in northern Shanxi and northern Hebei compiled by Grootaers.[77] The pantheons deployed in the great *sai* of southeastern Shanxi also had far fewer deities.[78]

In addition, the author of the roster drew on that great engine for the systematization of popular cults, the novel *The Investiture of the Gods (Feng*

---

76. Huang and Wang, "*Shangu shenpu*" *diaocha baogao*, p. 92. The exception was the spirit "tablet" of Empress Earth, which was dealt with separately; see below.

77. In addition to the articles cited in note 9 to this chapter, see also Grootaers, "Les temples villageois"; and idem, *Sanctuaries*.

78. See Johnson, "'Confucian' Elements in the Great Temple Festivals," pp. 136–41.

shen yanyi) and its operatic versions. Besides the explicit mention of "the gods of *Feng shen bang*," many other gods listed can be found in the novel. Of course, this does not mean that in all those cases the roster drew on the novel, or the operas.[79] But it is extremely interesting that the *shenpu* of *Shangu shenpu* and the *shen bang* of *Feng shen bang* have almost identical meanings. Clearly, the opera *Feng shen bang* and the novel *Feng shen yanyi* were powerful influences on Renzhuang's roster of the gods.

All this suggests that, unlike the pantheons (*pai shen bu*) of the great *sai*, the roster was not a more-or-less objective reflection of the cults in the immediate vicinity of Renzhuang. Rather, it was compiled by a man or men of moderate to good education, familiar with *The Investiture of the Gods* as well as a certain amount of orthodox cosmology, who wanted to create the most imposing possible list of deities, but who either had little sense of which gods mattered to the villagers or didn't care. Was the entire ritual a literati construct, then? To answer this question, we need to look at the rest of it.

Following the formal offerings and obeisances made by the three village elders, an exorcism called "Collecting Disasters" (*shou zai*) was carried out. In emotional impact, it contrasted sharply with the recitation of the roster. The exorcist was a spirit-medium or, rather, a man playing the part of a spirit-medium without actually being possessed. This collector of disasters was called Mamazi—an untranslatable term—and was one of the Godly Ones. The Mamazi was chosen prior to the organizing meeting on the eighth of the twelfth lunar month. He had to be young and vigorous and, moreover, to have been born in a "horse" year.[80] Here we see not an actual spirit-medium but a villager

---

79. Li Yi appears to assume this in his edition.

80. This section is based on Huang and Wang, "*Shangu shenpu*" *diaocha baogao*, pp. 41–43. Note that these restrictions on who could perform the role of Mamazi appear to conflict, at least potentially, with the hereditary principle of the Godly Ones. The chances of being born in a horse year are one in twelve, since there are twelve zodiacal animals. On average, then, only one of the twelve Godly Ones would have been a "horse"; surely that person would frequently have not been "young and vigorous." Moreover, what was done on the occasions when none of the Godly Ones was born in a horse year?

playing the scripted role of a spirit-medium. This theatricalization
of the divine, the blurring of the distinction between ritual and drama
and between divine and human, is one of the most important characteristics of Chinese popular religion. We will encounter it repeatedly in
this book.

The Collecting of Disasters began with the Godly Ones, minus the
Mamazi, dancing and drumming in a circle around him in front of
the main (north) altar. As the drumming grew more insistent and the
circle tightened, the Mamazi stripped to the waist, so that he was wearing only red pants.[81] The *Shê* Heads (leaders of the percussion troupes)
rubbed his torso with *bai jiu* (distilled spirits), and then someone struck
him in the middle of the forehead with the point of a knife "until
red showed."[82] (Presumably this means "until blood flowed," but no
blood can be seen on the Mamazi's face in the report's photographs.)
The Mamazi then put on a short red apron and wrapped a plain
yellow cloth around his head. He clenched a knife between his teeth
and held a "sounding knife" in his left hand and a long rope whip in his
right.[83]

It is possible that the knife clenched in the Mamazi's teeth simulated
a steel pin piercing both cheeks, a not uncommon feature of the costume of spirit-mediums. For example, in the *sai* at the Bixia Temple in
Jia village, Lucheng county, in southeastern Shanxi, the procession was
led by a figure called the Mabi. Frothing at the mouth, he collapsed in a
fit when the procession started off. Then about half an hour later he
suddenly jumped up, stripped to his undershorts, grabbed a seven-inch-
long steel pin previously placed on a stand, and stabbed it through both
cheeks. With the blood running onto his chest, he then took up a five-
foot-long steel spear with nine large rings on one end and dashed to the
head of the procession, frightening everyone along the way. It was said

----

81. For pictures, see Huang and Wang, "*Shangu shenpu*" *diaocha baogao*, pp. 199–203.
82. Ibid., p. 41.
83. Photographs show the "sounding knife" to have been more like a halberd. It
consisted of three short blades bound side by side on one end of a wooden handle
three to four feet in length. At the other end of the weapon were several large metal
disks, which looked much like oversized Chinese coins. When shaken or kicked, the
weapon clanged or jingled, hence the name.

that the Mabi got enough money for his performance to live on for half a year.[84]

After putting on his apron and head-cloth, the Mamazi brandished his Sounding Knife and, to the sound of the fan-drums, cracked his rope whip toward each of the altars. He then left the courtyard and went to the Xu lineage hall. This was built into the southeastern corner of the Guan Di Temple complex, with its entrance on the south. Just to the left of the entrance an altar called the Table of the Village Elders (*xiang lao zhuo*) had been set up, with candles, incense, a wine pot, and cups. Two lineage elders knelt at each end of the altar table; on the ground in front of the table was a crude grid of millet stalks, with seven bowls in the seven openings, which was called the Seven Star Straw (*qi xing cao*). Two pieces of new brick or tile were arranged in the form of the character 人 (man).

The Mamazi engaged in a dialogue with the elders, speaking in the voice of Empress Earth:

MAMAZI: Elders!

ELDERS: Here!

MAMAZI: I was in the heavens passing by when I saw the bright lanterns and candles of your village; what is the reason for the roaring of your gongs and drums?

ELDERS: Everywhere in our village disasters have arisen; we are making offerings [lit., "burning incense"] to expel disease.

MAMAZI: Have you been harmed or not?

ELDERS: We have been harmed.

MAMAZI: You have been harmed; does the harm remain?

---

84. Zhang Zhennan, "Zhongguo Shanxi," pp. 37–38. In Zhang's draft biography of Li Yuanxing (Draft biographies of *sai* specialists), p. 60, he uses the term *mapo*. For a description of mediums in Taiwan with steel needles through their cheeks (and elsewhere) striking themselves on the forehead (and back) with their exorcists' swords, see Schipper, *The Daoist Body*, pp. 46–47. Whoever created the Mamazi's routine in Renzhuang must have known how possessed mediums behaved. The figure itself, the demon killer with weapons in both hands, might conceivably be an echo of the ancient *fangxiang*. See the illustration from an Eastern Han tomb relief on p. 123 of Bodde, *Festivals in Ancient China*.

ELDERS: The harm remains; disperse the harm.

MAMAZI: It shall be so. Pour three cups of wine, make obeisance in gratitude for my favor, strike up the gongs and drums, and wait for me to collect your disasters.

ELDERS: We make obeisance for your favor.[85]

The Mamazi then cut off a rooster's head, sprinkled drops of blood in each of the seven bowls, chopped the Seven Star Straw to pieces, and smashed the 人-shaped tiles. After the three cups of wine were poured, he set off to visit every house in the village. Each family had put out an offering table with incense, wine, food offerings, and a bowl of water in which was floating a paper-cut pomegranate blossom. When the Mamazi arrived, the head of the family poured out three cups of wine and poured the water with the paper blossom on the ground. The Mamazi cracked his whip three times, and an assistant gave the family a charm on which "Accept the command to behead demons" was written in red and "Secure the family—increase good fortune" in black. In return the household head gave the Mamazi a bowl containing the five kinds of grain and other food.

During the two hours or so it took for the Mamazi to visit every household, the gong and drum troupe and the flower-drum troupe performed at the Eight Trigram Altars. The songs sung by the flower-drum troupe were not written down, but most people in the village knew the words since the same ones were always performed. They were even taught to children in some families. The sources do not indicate how many songs were in the original repertoire; only two titles are mentioned, and only one could be reconstructed. It is a narrative song in ten-character vernacular rhyming couplets.[86] In it a young woman is sent a book by her beloved and a letter asking for an embroidered bag. With the help of her maid, she gathers the materials needed and embroiders ten designs. Since embroidery subjects were almost always representational and could therefore transmit ideas and values to those who could not read, it is worth listing them.

---

85. Huang and Wang, "*Shangu shenpu*" *diaocha baogao*, pp. 42–43.
86. The text is given in ibid., pp. 45–47.

The first is herself, "a girl of sixteen," in a boat by the riverbank, and the tenth is famous views from the eighteen provinces.[87] All the rest are tableaux involving historical or mythological characters, probably taken from local opera or popular religious narratives: three feature heroes of the Three Kingdoms epic; three are from the Yang Family Generals cycle; one features Zhang Tianshi, the head of the Orthodox Unity sect of Daoism; and one the Queen Mother (of the West?) and Ninth Daughter Star. That a romantic heroine would embroider such subjects on a bag for her beloved is an interesting illustration of the way themes from popular opera and stories were diffused via objects of everyday use, including woodblock prints and papercuts in addition to clothing and accessories.[88] I believe this song reflects local mentalities much more accurately than the roster, not surprising perhaps when one considers that the Godly Ones did not monopolize it. It is significant that it was not included in the written liturgy.

When the Mamazi finished his visits to the village households, he and his entourage returned to the Eight Trigram Altars. The flower-drum troupe then wrapped up its performance, and the first day's activities came to a close.

---

87. This dates the text to the Qing.

88. Even with no more than the bare hints provided in the description of the embroidery subjects, it is possible to tentatively identify the source in the *bangzi* opera repertoire (one of the most popular local opera forms in Shanxi) of the second (*Yellow Crane Tower* [*Huang he lou*]), the third (*Changban Slope* [*Changban po*]), the fifth (*Yang Wulang Becomes a Monk* [*Wu lang chu jia*]), and the seventh (*Seven Star Temple* [*Qi xing miao*]). There are a number of *bangzi* operas featuring both Zhao Defang and Wang Qiang, but none that I can find appears to match the plot as described for the eighth scene. (It is found in the novel about the Yang family generals, *Yang jia jiang yanyi*, *hui* 42.) The sixth is too general to connect with any opera, although it obviously has to do with the saga of the Three Kingdoms. The fourth and ninth appear to refer to the iconography of popular religion rather than to opera (Heavenly Master Zhang wearing his Eight Trigrams robe; Mother Wang, who gave birth to the Ninth Daughter Star). The first and the tenth scenes are the only ones that can be construed as merely decorative—in this case, landscapes.

SECOND DAY:
Welcoming and Settling the Gods

On the following day, the night of the full moon and the main day of the festival, the ceremonies began with a formal welcome to the gods who had arrived the day before and an invitation to any gods who may have been overlooked. The first and second Godly Ones each recited half of a short verse ("Settling the Gods—First Part" ["Qian xia shen"]), the fifth invited any overlooked deities ("Adding Gods" ["Tian shen"]), and then the first and second each chanted a longer verse introducing a specific god ("Settling the Gods—Second Part" ["Hou xia shen"]). This pattern was repeated with the eleventh, twelfth, and sixth Godly Ones taking the place of the first, second, and fifth, respectively.[89] The language of these verses is a rather jingling seven-character colloquial; the first one begins as follows:

FIRST GODLY ONE:
> Great wealth is due to fate, small wealth to hard work;
> The hardworking are wealthy and honored, the lazy poor.
> Hard work gives birth to wealth, wealth is born from hard work;
> Sloth is born within wealth, and sloth receives poverty.

The point here is a distillation of gritty experience: if you work hard, you can do reasonably well, but you have to be lucky to get rich; hard work is the key to success, but success breeds laziness in the next generation, and laziness brings poverty. This is the first of many examples in this book of the countryman's sense of the instability of economic and social status in late imperial north China. The verse continues:

SECOND GODLY ONE:
> The Jade Emperor [ ][90] his pavilion and seats himself
>   in the imperial carriage;
> All the gods come together at the assembly altar.

---

89. This is the sequence as given in Huang and Wang, "*Shangu shenpu*" *diaocha baogao*; Li Yi's version, which follows the manuscript, is somewhat different.

90. 駕 must be an error, but I do not know how to emend it.

Drinking liquid jade and thick fragrant wine,
They will live forever and ever.[91]

After the fifth Godly One invites the overlooked gods who are hovering above, the first chants again:

On the fifteenth of the first month the brilliance of
    the spring is disturbed;
I sit erect in the Hall of Heaven.
From atop the southern gate of Heaven I look down;
My divine eye sees the Eight Trigram Altars.
Gathering clouds and collecting mists,
I descend to the Eight Trigram Altars.
· ·
I receive your incense smoke and accept your memorial,
I take into my sleeve your village's afflictions of sickness and fire
    and carry them back through the southern gate of Heaven.
If you want to know my name,
I am none other than the Holy Mother Grandmother Empress Earth—
    I rein in[?] and dismount.

In similar language, the second Godly One introduces the next deity, the goddess of fire, the Fire Star, who also promises, in identical terms, to take away the village's diseases and fires.

The eleventh, twelfth, and sixth Godly Ones now make their entrance. Their first three verses are rather inconsequential. The fourth and fifth are addressed to Erlang—here in the guise of a rain god—and Guan Di. Rather than ask them to take away the evils that afflict the village, however, the verses supply potted biographies of the two gods.

This completed the welcoming and settling of the gods. The lack of intensity seen in the roster of the gods is apparent here as well. Although three of the four deities singled out for special mention had temples in the village, including the two asked to prevent diseases and fires, the language of the liturgy is pedestrian, the tone in no way elevated. And in sharp contrast to the great *sai*, no offerings or even prayers were made to the assembled gods. They were provided only

---

91. Huang and Wang, "*Shangu shenpu*" *diaocha baogao,* p. 48.

simple entertainments until they were sent off, with scant ceremony, at the end of the festival.

With the guest gods in their places, the twelve Godly Ones began a series of six skits or playlets, of which the first three were performed on the fifteenth and the remaining three on the sixteenth. All the skits, which were short and written in simple colloquial, were performed in the space marked out by the Eight Trigram Altars, for the entertainment of both gods and people.

"The Winds Blow" ("Chui feng"), the first skit, consists of brief dialogues between the central wind and the southeast, northwest, northeast, and southwest winds.[92] Each represents a different craft: mason, blacksmith, carpenter, tailor, and brick and tile maker. The dialogue merely identifies them, mentions their tools and products, and ends with the wish that the water they use in their crafts (e.g., in tempering steel) "carry the water of the Long River." This is puzzling; presumably it expresses a hope for plentiful rain.

In the next skit, "Opening the Granaries" ("Da zang"), the characters are the five directions, with the center questioning the other four. Each is asked what storehouse it has opened and answers with what amounts to a riddle. For example, West says that it has opened the millet granary. When asked where millet grows, West answers, "On a pepper tree." Center says that the branches and leaves don't look right, and West retorts that pepper seeds look like millet seeds. The final part, in which Center has to respond to questions by the others, is slightly more complicated, but the whole skit appears to be nothing more than a mild sort of rural banter with no particular point.[93] The final performance of the day was a comic dialogue, reminiscent of *xiangsheng*, that was considerably longer than the previous pieces.[94] It was lighthearted and very colloquial, beginning with a duel of wits about an unpaid debt, moving on to riddles, and ending with a sort of tall-tale contest. This is all we

---

92. "The Winds Blow" and "Opening the Storehouses" are not found in the *Shangu shenpu* manuscript but were reconstructed from memory by one of the villagers (Huang and Wang, "*Shangu shenpu*" *diaocha baogao*, p. 22).

93. Text in ibid., pp. 60–62.

94. *Xiangsheng* are comic routines involving a rapid-fire back-and-forth between two performers.

are told of the ceremonies on the fifteenth, but it seems certain that there was the usual lantern-viewing, promenading, and other activities associated with the first full moon of the year.[95]

THIRD DAY:
The Fiery Mountain and the
Departure of the Gods

The first skit on the sixteenth, the third day of the festival, was called "Guessing Riddles" ("Cai mi"), and in it the twelve Godly Ones did just that. Occasionally a performer would deliberately miss an answer, and the audience would get involved. The riddles were followed by the only selection with any dramatic character at all, "Picking Mulberries" ("Cai sang").[96] It is set in the Spring and Autumn period and tells the tale of how an ugly woman bested the King of Qi in both martial arts and wisdom and ended by becoming his wife. The story is very old, appearing in *Lie nü zhuan* (first century B.C.), and is the subject of many operas.[97] It is (or was) a popular folktale in southern Shanxi and indeed throughout China. There is an Ugly Aunt's Tomb east of Nanji village (about three miles north of Renzhuang), and two natural features south of Renzhuang, Mulberry Grove and Silkworm Aunt's Grotto, may be connected with local versions of the folktale as well.[98] The presumed connection of the Ugly Aunt with the Quwo region probably made it particularly welcome as a holiday entertainment, and the text is mildly interesting, adding to the story of a humble woman who gets the best of a powerful man a strongly didactic message: do not judge by appearances. But like the previous four skits, this has no discernible cultic content.

---

95. See Ding Shiliang and Zhao Fang, *Zhongguo difangzhi minsu ziliao huibian: Huabei juan*, pp. 640–83 *passim*, for information on New Year customs in the region around Renzhuang.

96. This text is also a reconstruction, prepared by three villagers for the videotaping in 1989.

97. See Li Yi, "Quwo Shangu nuo xi," pp. 7–8; Huang and Wang, "*Shangu shenpu*" *diaocha baogao*, p. 127.

98. See Zhang Zhizhong et al., "*Shangu shenpu nuo xi* luxiangpian wenben," p. 22; Huang and Wang, "*Shangu shenpu*" *diaocha baogao*, p. 127.

The final skit, "Seating Empress Earth" ("Zuo Houtu"), is both simple and somewhat mysterious. The Earth Goddess—an important deity in the village and the divine focus of the festival, insofar as there was one—is celebrating her 1,000th birthday, but only four of her five sons have left their homes on the five sacred mountains to come to the celebration. Each of the four has charge of a season; the fifth, it turns out, is sulking because he does not have a season of his own. The Earth Goddess comes up with a solution: every brother is to donate eighteen days of his season to the absent one, so that each of the five will have seventy-two. This mollifies the fifth son, who joins the celebration, and all ends happily.[99]

At the conclusion of "Seating Empress Earth" the villagers brought fireworks and firecrackers into the altar area and placed them on the ground before the northern altar so the gods could see them. This was called "Welcoming the Fire" (*ying huo*). The percussion troupe played a special piece, the twelve Godly Ones made obeisance to all the gods, and then the villagers took the fireworks around the corner of the Guan Di Temple and placed them on a small table outside the east wall of the Xu lineage hall, at the foot of a temporary structure called Ao Mountain. This was about nine feet tall and five feet wide, made of bricks arranged against the wall to form a square lattice with diamond-shaped openings. In each opening was placed a small lamp, consisting of cottonseed oil in a cup with a wick. Formerly there was an Ao Mountain for each of the three "sections" of the village. Altars were constructed in front of each one, and the lamps lit on New Year's Eve and kept burning until the twentieth of the first month.[100]

Back at the Eight Trigram Altars, the Godly Ones again made obeisances to the gods, and then the senior Godly One took down the

---

99. The text is given in Huang and Wang, "*Shangu shenpu*" *diaocha baogao*, pp. 88–91.

100. There are references to large structures with lanterns called "Ao Mountains" as early as the Song dynasty. Zhou Mi (Southern Song), *Wu lin jiu shi*, p. 368, states that numerous "lantern mountains" were erected around the imperial palace for viewing on the night of the year's first full moon. Another title by the same author, which appears to be closely related, mentions that there were many thousands of lanterns in the "mountains" (see *Han yu da cidian*, 12:1402, *s.v.* 鼇山). The custom continued in the palace through the Ming and into the Qing. We will see other echoes of Song court practices in the New Year customs described below.

paper spirit tablet of Empress Earth and stuck it in an incense burner placed on a table to one side of the north altar. Then the Godly Ones took down all the other paper spirit tablets from atop their altars, placed them in the center of the ritual space along with the paper banners, flowers, and other altar decorations, and burned them. As the gods departed, the fan-drums were played, but there was no special prayer or benediction.

Then the twelve Godly Ones, led by the percussion troupe and followed by the flower-drum troupe, placed the table holding the spirit tablet of Empress Earth in front of the Ao Mountain. That evening, the percussion and flower-drum troupes performed at the Ao Mountain, and after all the villagers had arrived, the fan-drums played and the fireworks and firecrackers were set off. If snow fell at that time, it was considered an omen of a good harvest. The Godly Ones, after making a final obeisance to Empress Earth, carried the table with her spirit tablet on it, accompanied by the usual procession, out through the south gate of the village to the foot of Dragon Hill. There her paper tablet was burned, and she returned to her temple, part way up the hill. Everyone shouted "Has she come up or not?" and the villagers stationed at the temple called back "Not yet." The question was shouted out a number of times, and finally the people waiting at the temple replied "She's come up!" Then the banner was furled, the gongs and drums put aside, and everyone walked home silently in the cold and the dark, without looking back, for fear that evil spirits would follow them. This eerie procession brought the Fan-drum ritual to an end.

THE ROSTER OF THE GODS RITUAL
AND THE ENACTMENT OF
LINEAGE DOMINANCE

Above I asked whether, in view of the peculiarities of the roster of the gods, the ritual might have been a literati construct. The answer, now that we have looked at the entire program, is clearly "no," but there is no denying that it was far less intense than other communal rituals. As already mentioned, few of the gods named in the roster had active cults in the village, and one senses that the list was put together by someone guided more by the cosmological principles of the high literary tradition and *The Investiture of the Gods* or its cognate operas than by local beliefs. The "Settling the Gods" segment, on the second day, seems less distanced: four gods descend to the village, and three of them have temples there (Empress Earth, Guan Di, and the Fire Star, that is, the Fire God). The Godly Ones speak in the voices of the gods, with two promising to take away the afflictions of the villagers and two telling their own histories. But their speeches are short and routine, and the Godly Ones who spoke them wore their regular costumes, without makeup, whereas in other villages it was common for the gods to be impersonated by actors wearing elaborate costumes and masks.[101] This factor is especially important in explaining why "Settling the Gods" seems unlikely to have aroused strong emotions in the audience. Finally, the skits seem utterly trivial, light holiday entertainments hardly appropriate for a time when the gods are being asked to protect the village from disease and fire. They barely touch on the vast ocean of historical subjects so common in the operas presented elsewhere in Shanxi during important festivals, nor do they present the world of gods and demons with anything approaching solemnity or awe. In short, they have a somewhat perfunctory quality.

In passages such as the invitation to the various earth gods[102] and many others, a mechanistic, impersonal, and simplistic cosmology has taken the place of local cults. It is hard to believe that the author had much sympathy with, or knowledge of, what the inhabitants of Renzhuang actually believed about their gods. Such intellectual or ideological sympathies as appear are quite congruent with run-of-the-mill late imperial orthodoxy. However, the language is simply not elevated, graceful, and allusive enough for it to be the work of a highly educated man. The text is something that could have been written by a village school teacher, or perhaps a local ritual master who had received a fairly conventional education.

There were two exorcisms among Renzhuang's New Year rituals: that carried out by the Mamazi, and that accomplished by the sending off of Empress Earth at the end of the festival. Exorcisms are found in

---

101. See the sections below on Aoshi village and Guyi village.
102. See p. 43 above.

virtually all village New Year rituals and have an exceedingly long pedigree in China. In Han times (and no doubt long before then), the eve of the La, or New Year, was the time of the Great Exorcism (*da nuo*).[103] The worship of large numbers of gods, the use of fire, the procession of the exorcist past all the houses of the village and even into them in some cases, and the driving off or killing of malevolent demons—all these elements were present in the Great Exorcism of Han times as well as the New Year rituals of nineteenth- and twentieth-century Shanxi.[104] Yet in the Renzhuang exorcisms, once again one feels the absence of an expected heightening of the emotions, of the excitement or tension or even hysteria common in communal exorcisms elsewhere in China.[105] One senses this above all in the figure of the Mamazi. As noted above, the Mamazi only simulated the trance of a spirit-medium. He spoke scripted lines and did not mutilate himself. The second exorcism, the sending-off of Empress Earth, gives us the only evidence in the entire ritual that people felt the presence of the Powers: the moment when, after her spirit tablet was taken outside the village in the dark and burned, everyone crept back to the village in silence and trepidation lest evil spirits follow them home. But even this was a good deal tamer than analogous rituals elsewhere in Shanxi.

Educated men were certainly capable of orchestrating vivid, moving local rituals, as we shall see. Could the somewhat distanced, muted quality of the exorcisms in Renzhuang, and of the ritual as a whole, be due to a simple weakening of the tradition? Did the Fan-drum ritual have the same style before the Japanese war and the upheavals of the Mao era? Unfortunately it is impossible to answer this question,

---

103. *Nuo* is the term most commonly used by Chinese scholars today to refer to exorcistic ritual drama, and it is sometimes used by the villagers themselves. Note the words on the processional banner mentioned above (p. 39): "Solemnly carry out the *nuo* ritual." The term seems to be more common in central and south China. One example among several provided by the reports in the *Minsu quyi congshu* series is Yu Daxi and Liu Zhifan, *Jiangxi sheng Nanfeng xian*, which has a photograph on p. 165 of a Temple of the *Nuo* God/Gods (Nuo shen miao).

104. See Bodde, *Festivals in Ancient China*, pp. 55, 57, 77n4, 78, 81–82.

105. See the numerous examples given in Johnson, "Actions Speak Louder Than Words," pp. 9–24.

although we know (as mentioned above) that some villagers said the old ritual had been much larger and more skillfully presented than the 1989 performance on which most of our information is based. Nevertheless, and quite critically, we have a liturgical manuscript copied in 1909 from an exemplar whose origins may have been very old indeed, and much of our sense of the tone of the Fan-drum ritual comes from that. If there was a decline from some grander standard, it occurred in the nineteenth century or earlier.

The "skits" are a case in point. The scripts of three—"Guessing Riddles," the comic dialogue, and "Seating Empress Earth"—are in the 1909 manuscript; the other three—"The Winds Blow," "Opening the Granaries," and "Picking Mulberries"—were reconstituted from memory in the mid-1980s by old residents of the village. These reconstructions may be imperfect, but, unless the informants' memories were extremely defective, we have the core of the plot in each case. It is hard to believe they could ever have been substantial ritual dramas. "Picking Mulberries" is by far the most complex, but it is a didactic anecdote in dramatic form, no more. As for the three whose scripts survive, two are light entertainments. "Seating Empress Earth" touches on cosmological themes but is so slight that it is almost impossible to interpret. This opacity makes it somewhat mysterious but does not lend it symbolic weight. It features the most important deity in the entire festival, and yet the point of the skit appears to be nothing more than an explanation of the origin of the so-called *tu wang ri*, the first six days of every lunar month—something unlikely to have been of interest to ordinary villagers.

This does not mean that some or all of the skits might not be old, or descend from distant ancestors. Scholars of Shanxi ritual drama have done a good deal of work on this subject and, although frequently tempted to speculate beyond the evidence, have turned up some interesting facts.[106] Of these, one is worth recounting here. *Zhou yuexing tu*, a a *sai* liturgy found in southeastern Shanxi dated 1547, has in a list of

---

106. Huang and Wang, "*Shangu shenpu*" *diaocha baogao*, pp. 125–30; Li Yi, "Quwo Shangu nuo xi"; Zhao Kuifu, "Fenyin shangu nuo xi," pp. 207–9; and idem, "Bei Song nuo xi."

mimed skits one called "The Five Peaks Come to the Court of Empress Earth" ("Wu yue chao Houtu"). The text tells us nothing of the plot, but it does list the characters, more than a few of whom appear in "Seating Empress Earth." In addition, and what is most interesting, the story found its way to Japan, where it was turned into a popular folk drama.[107] To have become part of Japanese village culture, it must have arrived in the islands very early, and hence been well established in China at an early date also. All this raises the intriguing possibility that "Seating Empress Earth" is not a decayed remnant of some grand early ritual performance but part of a very old stratum of simple village dramas that spread from China throughout East Asia.

But this does not explain the "distanced" quality of the entire ritual program. Could it be due to the fact that the celebration of the first full moon of the year—Yuanxiao—was a seasonal ritual as opposed to a temple-based liturgical ritual? I do not think so; we shall shortly look at some examples of New Year's rituals that were very intense. What then was the reason? Certainly part of the cause was the fact that the ritual had ceased to be practiced and the version on which the reports are based was little more than an imitation of a genuine performance. Yet the reconstruction was based on an authentic liturgical manuscript that at the very least is direct evidence of nineteenth-century practice and probably preserves forms that are much older than that. Thus the most likely explanation is that the Fan-drum ritual was in all important respects a monopoly of the Xu lineage elite.[108]

Local histories reveal that Xus were already established in Quwo county in Northern Song and Yuan times. One of the Song dynasty Xus is said to have lived in Gaoxian commandery, which is modern Gaoxian, a few kilometers north-northwest of Quwo town.[109] The home villages of other early Xus are difficult to discover, since biographies

---

107. Huang and Wang, "*Shangu shenpu*" *diaocha baogao*, p. 129, quoting a paper given by Suwa Haruo at a 1991 conference in China. Unfortunately I have been unable to obtain a copy of Suwa's paper or determine if the conference papers were published.

108. A recent study that documents the revival of local religion in the interest of local elites is Chau, *Miraculous Response*.

109. See the references given in Huang and Wang, "*Shangu shenpu*" *diaocha baogao*, p. 15.

in large local histories such as the *Shanxi Provincial Gazetteer* (*Shanxi tong-zhi*) generally give only the subject's native county.[110] We know that the Xus were dominant in Renzhuang by 1585, since some 160 of the approximately 210 donors to the reconstruction of the Chan temple completed that year were surnamed Xu. In the 1930s, roughly 80 percent of Renzhuang's population still belonged to the lineage.[111] A conservative estimate of the reign of the Xus in Renzhuang village would therefore be four centuries—and it might well be longer. Once again we are reminded that we must be prepared to use a very long time horizon in thinking about Chinese rural culture. Chinese farming families have often demonstrated descents comparable in depth to those of the European nobility. We therefore should not be surprised by great antiquity in village institutions.

Some time during the very long period of Xu dominance in Renzhuang, its unique New Year ritual came to be entirely controlled by them. They owned all copies of the liturgy, their lineage head directed the performance, and only Xu lineage members could take the parts of the twelve Godly Ones and the Mamazi exorcist, by far the most important roles in the ritual. The Fan-drum ritual did not employ professional ritualists like the Masters of Ceremonial (*zhu li*) who directed the great *sai* of southeastern Shanxi. Nor did it use professional actors or musicians. Since all the key roles were inherited, ritual knowledge or literary ability were obviously secondary to pedigree as a qualification for holding them. Moreover, since being a Godly One must have brought great prestige, it seems probable that the most powerful families—as opposed to the most talented—vied to succeed to the occasional vacancies. Given such a situation, the general lack of complexity and depth in the liturgy, the exorcism, and the skits is easy to under-

---

110. The Xu genealogy would be the obvious source for information on the early history of the lineage, but it does not appear to exist. We know that one copy was destroyed by the Taipings (see above, p. 21), and I was told in 1992 that the genealogy was lost. But why would the *Shangu shenpu* script have been restored—and in twelve copies, at that—and not the genealogy? No doubt it was lost in more recent times; or perhaps the Xus, for whatever reason, prefer not to show it to outsiders. (Huang Zhusan apparently did not use a genealogy of the lineage in preparing the survey report.)

111. Huang and Wang, "*Shangu shenpu*" *diaocha baogao*, p. 14.

stand. If, for example, the Mamazi had been a spirit-medium who was actually possessed rather than a Godly One merely simulating possession, he would certainly have elicited a stronger response.

But granting that closing the ritual to outside influences and insulating it from change by making it a prerogative of the village elite served to make it less effective at mobilizing the emotions and expressing the fears and hopes of the people than comparable rituals elsewhere, there was a time when the Fan-drum ritual was new; yet it is hard to believe that it was even then an adequate expression of the villagers' religious universe. Of the three main parts of the ritual—the inviting, welcoming, and sending-off of the gods; the skits; and the Mamazi's exorcism— only the last, together with the sending-off of Empress Earth, seems likely to have summoned up intense emotions among the villagers, and neither is in the *Shangu shenpu* manuscript. The immensely long invitation, with its indiscriminate and chaotic pantheon, and the skits, of which even those that are something more than mere divertissements seem to convey nothing of any weight, cannot possibly be expressions of popular religiosity in the ordinary sense of the term. Why then is this text as it is?

The only evidence is the manuscript itself, and its form and content suggest that the author was a man of moderate to good education who had no particular allegiance to local cults and put little stock in local traditions—someone like a teacher in a lineage school, as I suggested above. But we would expect a liturgy composed by such a person to include some sort of didactic message, and there is almost none of this in the Fan-drum ritual. On the other hand, if a local ritualist wrote it, we would expect to see at least some evidence of genuine devotion to the gods, but that, too, is absent from the liturgy. If the purpose of the author, conscious or unconscious, was neither instruction nor devotion, what was it? I believe the intent was to create a means of enacting the social superiority of the lineage elite. The exorcistic elements may well belong to an older level of New Year ritual, as indeed may the drumming and dancing, which after all play an important role in the ritual as a whole. But the old elements were overshadowed by the new lineage ritual.

This account of why the Fan-drum ritual took the form it did is speculative, of course, but of its peculiar ritual style there can be no doubt. And that style gives much food for thought. Above all, it suggests that even a festival as universally celebrated as New Year can take on a virtually unique form in any given village. This *ritual autarky* is one of the leading characteristics of premodern Chinese communal religious life, although it is seldom found in such an extreme form and is never absolute.

———

Other village New Year rituals give a very different impression from the Fan-drum ritual, and yet share a number of motifs with it. The remaining chapters in this part look at three of these, two from northeastern Shanxi and one from a village in southwestern Hebei with easy access to the Changzhi basin of southeastern Shanxi, the home of the great *sai*.

Two Northeastern Villages

I. AOSHI: EXORCISM AND PROCESSION

The Setting and Preliminaries:
The Chicken-Feather Monkey

The village of Aoshi lies about fifty-five kilometers east-southeast of Datong in northeastern Shanxi, a few kilometers from where Mount Liuleng, part of the northernmost extension of the Hengshan Range, rises abruptly from the floodplain of the Sanggan River.[1] The report by

---

1. The main source for Aoshi's Yuanxiao ritual is Ren Guangwei, "Sai xi, naogu za xi chu tan." Ren did fieldwork of an unspecified sort in Aoshi in the 1950s and 1960s, and again in 1979, when he says, "conditions had changed greatly" (p. 195). Among other things, the traditional scripts, known as *zonggao*, had been destroyed in the Cultural Revolution, and few people could perform the local "*Sai* operas." Ren states that the tradition of this ritual was "unbroken" down to the Japanese invasion (p. 196), and the Shanxi volume of the *Encyclopedia of Chinese Drama* tells us that Aoshi even had an organized amateur troupe of *Sai* opera performers, known as the Hehe troupe, down to that point (*Zhongguo xiqu zhi: Shanxi juan*, p. 140). Ren gives no information on how the tradition fared after 1949, but it is safe to assume that the performance he saw in 1979 represented a revival of the tradition after an interruption of unknown duration and severity. The *Zhongguo xiqu zhi: Shanxi juan* notes a festival performance in Datong by an Aoshi troupe in 1960, which reminds one of the folk festival appearances of the Renzhuang percussionists. We can only guess at how much of the tradition had been lost by 1979. It is well to keep in mind when reading what follows that the "superstitious" exorcistic elements are likely to have been more vulnerable after 1949 than the entertaining ones.

Ren Guangwei that is the source of everything we know about Aoshi's New Year ritual tells us nothing about the village itself. The lack of information about its temples is particularly regrettable, since it makes it impossible to place the New Year rituals in the broader context of village cults and beliefs. Yet we can speculate with some confidence about the temples that are likely to have existed there before 1949, because Willem Grootaers surveyed the temples of this region in 1941–43, personally visiting 140 villages mostly east and southeast of Datong, including Aoshi.[2] He did not publish an inventory of the temples in each village as he did in later studies, but he found 401 temples in 134 villages (not counting four Muslim villages and two with no temples). In Grootaers's experience, even an average village in that region at that time was "sure to have" a Zhenwu temple, a Dragon King (Longwang) temple, a Guanyin temple, and a Five Ways (Wudao) temple, and quite possibly also a Guan Di temple or a monastery.[3] Aoshi must have been a large village in the 1940s and hence may well have had more temples than Grootaers' average.[4] How many were in existence when Ren visited is unknown, but certainly the Aoshi New Year ritual in its heyday was held in a place that was well supplied with temples and was also a good deal larger than Renzhuang.

There is a link between Aoshi and the region of southwestern Shanxi in which Renzhuang is located. Some of the important lineages of Aoshi trace their ancestry to migrants from the areas around Linfen and Yuncheng who moved as a group from "the big ash tree" (*da huaishu*) in Hongdong county between 1370 and 1375.[5] Some Aoshi residents

---

2. Grootaers, "Les temples villageois," p. 163.

3. Ibid., p. 209.

4. http://www.fallingrain.com/world/CH/a/A/o/ states that the approximate population in a seven-kilometer radius around Aoshi is 17,385. (The source and date of the data are not given.) The map in *Shanxi sheng ditu ji* shows approximately ten villages in that area, and satellite imagery (but not the atlas) shows them to be as large or larger than Aoshi. So its current population may be anywhere from 1,500 to 5,000.

5. Ren Guangwei, "Sai xi, naogu za xi chu tan," p. 196. The name refers to an actual tree, not a village. It was "to the left of the Guangji Temple north of the city [of Hongdong]" (Huang Youquan et al., *Hongdong da huaishu*, p. 2). The forced migration of tens of thousands of people from southwestern Shanxi in early Ming is a remarkable story

Map 3 Aoshi and environs. 1 cm = 1.7 km (SOURCE: *Shanxi sheng ditu ji*).

believe that those families brought *Sai* Operas from southwestern Shanxi with them, and that they were handed down generation after generation until the Japanese invasion.[6] They were performed to bring rain during droughts, to drive away disease, and to prevent fires, as well

---

that we will encounter again in Chapter 3. Hongdong's Guangji Temple served as an official collection and dispatch center for those about to be sent off to Hebei and elsewhere, and for centuries their descendants identified themselves by reference to the great tree outside the temple. There were even folk rhymes on the subject: "Wen wo shizu lai he chu? Shanxi Hongdong da huaishu" 問我始祖來何處? 山西洪洞大槐樹 (You ask from whence my forebears came? Hongdong Big Ash Tree's the name). I have no doubt that the lineage traditions recorded by Ren Guangwei in Aoshi are accurate. Philip Huang (*The Peasant Economy and Social Change in North China*, p. 114) encountered this tradition in the Mantetsu materials, and Prasenjit Duara engages with it in *Culture, Power, and the State*, pp. 7–9, but it deserves to be studied in detail. The Chinese book cited above is the best place to start. I am grateful to David Faure for this reference.

6. Ren Guangwei, "Sai xi, naogu za xi chu tan," p. 196. Huang Youquan et al., *Hongdong da huaishu*, p. 182, claims that Big Ash Tree migrants took Pu zhou *bangzi*, a popular Shanxi opera form, with them.

as to celebrate the New Year.[7] A note on the last surviving "combined script" (*zonggao*), that is, a script with all the parts, stated that it was a copy of a manuscript revised (not created) in the Ming Jiaqing period (1522–66).[8] (The *Zhou yuexing tu*, an important liturgical manuscript discovered recently in southeastern Shanxi, about which I shall have much to say in due course, is also a copy of an older text dating to the mid-sixteenth century.) According to Ren Guangwei, in northern Shanxi "most performers" (not otherwise specified) believed their *Sai* Opera (also called "Village *Sai*" [*xiang sai*] and "Operatic *Sai*" [*ju sai*]) originated in Northern Song. There was also a local tradition that the first script brought from southwestern Shanxi stated that *Sai* Opera had been handed down from the Song dynasty.[9] Although we have to withhold judgment for the moment on the claims to Song ancestry, there is little doubt of the connection between Aoshi and southwestern Shanxi, in particular with its ancient Gong and Drum *Za* Opera (*luogu za xi*).[10]

We have a fairly detailed description of the 1979 New Year festival in Aoshi, which I summarize below.[11] The man with overall authority was known as the *Shê* Head (*shêshou*), a term used in Renzhuang (where it was the title of the leader of the percussion troupe) and elsewhere.[12] The *Shê* Head summoned all the performers and other participants on the morning of the thirteenth of the first lunar month to inventory the costumes and props for the operas. Some time after this, a procession consisting of the King of Humanity (*ren zhong zhi wang*) and two goddesses (*niangniang*) accompanied by the usual attendants with banners and parasols formed up "in the space in front of the village stage" (presumably at one time the courtyard of an important village temple). The king wore a royal headdress and a yellow robe with jade pendants at the waist, and the goddesses were attired in phoenix headdresses and court

---

7. Ren Guangwei, "Sai xi, naogu za xi chu tan," p. 196.

8. Ibid. The manuscript was destroyed in the Cultural Revolution.

9. Ibid., p. 197.

10. Although Renzhuang is near the area where *Za* Opera was popular, the Fandrum ritual appears not to have been influenced by it, further evidence for my hypothesis about its character.

11. Ibid., pp. 197–200. Since Ren does not say how long he stayed in Aoshi, we do not know how much of the ritual he witnessed.

12. We are not told who this was or how he came to hold the position.

robes. As they left the assembly area, they were confronted by the curious figure of the Chicken-Feather Monkey, an exorcist/scapegoat. The Monkey, who was chosen by the entire village, had to be a strong and clever young man.[13] He wore a short yellow gown over colored trousers; his face makeup consisted of three white "tiles" outlined in black. In a burlesque of operatic generals, pheasant feathers were stuck in his head scarf, and he wore a triangular banner of command on his back. He held a bamboo staff about a yard long with a short crosspiece near the top. Over this framework a small jacket had been fitted, through the neck of which sprouted a duster made of chicken feathers. This was the Golden Chicken Staff.[14]

The Monkey, accompanied by a retinue, made obeisance to the king and the goddesses, who evidently then ordered him to make a tour of the village. He set off, pursued by a gang of villagers, some playing gongs, drums, cymbals, and the like. Everyone wanted him to visit their courtyard since that kept misfortune away for an entire year, but he also ran fast because it was important that he not be caught. According to a local tradition, in the old days if the Monkey were caught he could be killed. This is hard to understand, since if people thought he could protect their families from harm the last thing you would expect them to do is try to injure or kill him. We shall see other cases of scapegoats in what follows, but they all differ sharply from exorcists—the scapegoats victim-like, the exorcists priest-like—even though both helped rid the community of evil influences. I suspect that by the time Ren Guangwei visited Aoshi, the Chicken-Feather Monkey had taken on the roles of both exorcist and scapegoat, roles that earlier had been played by separate characters.[15]

---

13. Ren Guangwei, "Sai xi, naogu za xi chu tan," p. 198.

14. Ibid., pp. 197–98.

15. In the general account of *Sai* Opera in northeastern Shanxi given in *Zhongguo xiqu zhi: Shanxi juan*, a somewhat different procession is described. It took place on the first full day of the festival celebrating the birthday of a god. The entire troupe of actors, who often were hereditary Entertainers (*yuehu*), paraded in costume through all the streets and lanes of the village to drive away demons. They then paid homage to the god at his temple and performed *Teasing the Demons (Tiao gui)*, one of the most important pieces of the entire festival. This was probably related to or identical with the demon dance (*tiao gui*) in Aoshi's New Year celebration (see below), although the *Encyclopedia* account merely says

The Monkey's run took place on the afternoon of the thirteenth. When it was over, one or two *Sai* Operas were performed, bringing the day's activities to a close.

First Day: "Zhenwu Expels the Ten Evil Spirits"

On the morning of the fourteenth, the first day of the celebration proper, an important exorcistic drama was enacted on the ground in front of the village stage. (As we have seen, the Fan-drum skits were also performed on the ground. It is generally agreed that the earliest Chinese dramas were performed on the ground, later moving to open-air platforms, and finally to covered stages,[16] but whether the Aoshi *Sai* Operas and Renzhuang's Fan-drum ritual were survivals of that most ancient stratum of theater is impossible to say.) Aoshi's drama was called *Zhenwu Expels the Ten Evil Spirits* (*Zhenwu chu shi sui*), or *Arraying the Troupes* (*Bai dui*). This appears to have been a typical ritual drama, and I will translate it in full.[17]

The characters included Lord Zhenwu, Ding He (also known as Heavenly Master Zhang),[18] the Peach-Blossom Girl (also called "Third Master" [San lang]),[19] the Civil Judge, the Yang Judge, the Fiery Judge, Tan Fourth (a female attendant played by a village woman), the Tortoise and Snake Generals,[20] a troop of demons, and soldiers.[21] With the exception of Ding He, all the characters wore masks.

---

that seven masked actors portraying demons mounted the stage from the ground and capered about as they received the instructions of their chief, the City God.

16. Liao Ben, *Zhongguo gudai juchang shi*, chap. 1.

17. Ren copied a recording or transcript, not a script (Ren Guangwei, "Sai xi, naogu za xi chu tan," p. 210, *nn*1–2).

18. See ibid., p. 210, *n*1. Zhang Tianshi was the name by which every head of the Celestial Master school of Daoism was known, but in popular imagination the name no doubt simply connoted a great wizard.

19. Reading 挑 as 桃.

20. The tortoise and snake were iconographically inseparable from Zhenwu; see below.

21. Ren Guangwei, "Sai xi, naogu za xi chu tan," pp. 198–99.

Zhenwu Expels the Ten Evil Spirits

Enter Ding He, preceded by soldiers carrying Flying Tiger banners and accompanied by a fanfare on gongs, drums, shawms (suona), *and so on. He stands solemnly in the middle of the performance space.*

DING HE (*chants an "introduction"*):[22] Wei! On the fourteenth day of the first lunar month of _____ year, _____ village presents a festival (*shê huo*)![23]

Gongs and drums play.

DING HE (*sings*):

> Gongs and drums resound together just as I arrive;
> May every family enjoy peace and happiness and
> never suffer illness.
> I reverently offer the god three cups of wine
> And place some sticks of incense in the bronze burner.

He offers wine and incense. A Great Melody (daqu) *is played, followed by a* quban.[24]

> My staff beats the wind into gusts,
> The wind scatters the dust raised by the horses.
> Do not covet improper debts;
> Remember there are merciful people.

(*Speaks*) I have two demon servants—when I call them, they come; but if they don't, they don't.

(*Chants*) Suddenly I hear the sound of gongs and drums; at the third drumroll the demon servants come.[25]

The drums beat three times; the demon servants enter; the soldiers make a road-blocking formation; the demon servants do a demon dance (tiao gui). *The three Judges enter and dance a judgment dance with the demons. The dancing ends.*

(*Speaks*) I have a Pathfinder (*xianxing*)—when I call her, she comes; but if she doesn't, she doesn't.

Drumming starts. The Pathfinder (xianfeng; *also called the Peach-Blossom Girl*) *enters.*

PATHFINDER (*sings*):

> Almond eyes, peach cheeks, willow-leaf eyebrows—
> I carry on my shoulder a banner with the
> word "command."

---

22. See *Hanyu da cidian*, definition 2 *s.v. kou hao* 口號.
23. Blanks were left for the date and the name of the village.
24. I have not been able to determine the meaning of this term.
25. Reading 響 for 上.

The [ ] Earl[26] has vowed to fight the world;
I mount my horse to spread the news.

The Pathfinder mounts a horse and gallops once around the grounds. Tan Fourth, facing east, makes a threefold welcome. Lord Zhenwu, leading the Tortoise and Snake Generals, blocks the demon servants' exit. Lord Zhenwu, grasping his treasure sword, announces the commands of the Law. He points in the four directions and establishes their places. He mounts a high table; all the demons prostrate themselves; all the people fall on their knees.

DING HE (*chants*):

> On Mount Wudang he practiced acting in accord
>   with the self-so (*zizai*),
> And cut off the love between husband and wife.
> Trampling on the Tortoise and Snake Generals,
> Lord Zhenwu subjugates the Ten Evil Spirits.

Performers and audience give three shouts. Everyone sings the "Song of Subjugating the Demons," drums and shawms send off the god, and the performance ends.[27]

The Zhenwu cult was important in northeastern Shanxi and northwestern Hebei, and no doubt elsewhere in North China as well.[28] Grootaers says that virtually every village of average size or greater in the survey area that included Aoshi had a Zhenwu temple,[29] so it is virtually certain that Aoshi also had one, probably as late as the 1930s. Grootaers also did extensive fieldwork on the Zhenwu cult and its hagiography in the region around Datong, fifty-five kilometers to the west of Aoshi, and in Wanquan and Xuanhua counties in northwestern Hebei.[30] Since Aoshi is roughly midway between those two areas, the hagiography of the cult in Aoshi probably resembled that reported by Grootaers for the other places. In popular belief, Zhenwu was the ruler of water, as befitted his northern location (water is the element associated with the north),

---

26. The text is imperfect here.

27. Ren Guangwei, "Sai xi, naogu za xi chu tan," pp. 199–200. The Ten Evil Spirits must be the "troops of demons" included in the *dramatis personae*.

28. Grootaers, "Les temples villageois," pp. 195–98; idem, "Temples and History," pp. 248–53; idem, "Rural Temples," pp. 57–60.

29. Grootaers, "Les temples villageois," p. 195.

30. See "Hagiography of the Chinese God Chen-wu," reprinted in Grootaers, *Sanctuaries*.

and an adversary of evil spirits.[31] This explains why it was he who expelled the "Ten Evil Spirits" in Aoshi's New Year ritual, and why the same ritual drama was performed at times of drought and pestilence.

According to Grootaers, in temples in the Xuanhua region the image of Zhenwu was always accompanied by those of the Peach-Blossom Girl and the Duke of Zhou. He was depicted with a sword in his right hand and with a tortoise and snake at his feet.[32] The snake and tortoise are sometimes interpreted not as vanquished demons but as celestial lieutenants, as in the Aoshi play.[33] Popular prints usually show him holding the seven-star "treasure sword" given him by the Jade Emperor, with the tortoise and snake either at his feet or literally underfoot.[34] (In the earliest written version of his life and deeds, he crushes a demonic snake and dragon [not tortoise] under his feet.)[35] In the murals recorded by Grootaers, he is commonly shown becoming an immortal (often by removing his viscera) after leaving his parents and practicing austerities on Mount Wudang for many years. It is also said that he battled evil spirits, taught the Law in the palace, and brought rain.[36]

The Aoshi drama clearly drew on a tradition similar to the versions of the hagiography recounted by Grootaers. Zhenwu is accompanied by the Peach-Blossom Girl (the Pathfinder), subdues demons with his treasure sword, and is said to have practiced self-cultivation on Mount Wudang, to have trampled on the tortoise and snake, and to have abandoned his family (his wife, not his parents as in the versions given by Grootaers).[37] However, his announcing of the commands of the Law and fixing of the four directions, mentioned in the script, are not found in any of the versions discussed by Grootaers or in the novel *Journey to the*

---

31. Maspero, "The Mythology of Modern China," pp. 339–40; Goodrich, *Peking Paper Gods*, pp. 234–35.

32. Grootaers, "Rural Temples," p. 58.

33. Maspero, "The Mythology of Modern China," p. 340.

34. Ibid., fig. 62 (p. 341) is the classic image. For cruder versions, see Goodrich, *Peking Paper Gods*, p. 416; and Wang Shucun, *Paper Joss*, pl. 61. This is one of the best-known images of a Chinese folk deity.

35. Grootaers, "Hagiography of the Chinese God Chen-wu," p. 146, citing *San jiao yuanliu da quan*.

36. Ibid., pp. 163–81 *passim*.

37. In none of the versions reported by Grootaers does Zhenwu marry.

North (*Bei you ji*), which is the most complete version of the story.[38] It appears that Aoshi has added a few touches of its own. Perhaps the local Zhenwu temple had murals showing these acts. But even if there were no murals, Zhenwu's story would have been well known to the villagers, and the action of this opera would have been instantly recognizable. It was as if the statue of the god had come to life and stepped down from the throne in his temple to demonstrate to the villagers his concern for their welfare.

The length of the script is deceptive. Contrary to what one might expect from the translation given above, the performance, even in 1979, lasted two hours and was said to have been skillfully done.[39] The pre-war version was almost certainly longer, and its exorcistic and devotional content more pronounced, since these are precisely the areas of popular drama most severely repressed since 1949. In addition, most of the performers were masked, and nothing heightens the impact of ritual drama more than masks. Finally, it is critically important to note that at the climax of the performance the entire audience joined in, first falling on their knees and then giving three great shouts with the actors and singing the "Song of Subjugating the Demons." There can be little doubt that *Expelling the Ten Evil Spirits* had a substantial emotional impact on the residents of Aoshi. There was nothing comparable in the Fan-drum ritual of Renzhuang.

Later in the day on the fourteenth, the village head and a number of other people climbed a nearby mountain[40] to get "holy water." They

---

38. One of the murals seen by Grootaers has Zhenwu teaching the Law in the palace ("Hagiography of the Chinese God Chen-wu," pp. 176 and 177; in the latter passage I take "heavenly general" to be Zhenwu). Note that "preaching the Law" appears in the title of two other mural panels (pp. 168, 171), but the preacher is not Zhenwu. At one point in the novel Zhenwu exhorts his father, the king (Grootaers' summary, p. 154, 28b), but this does not seem equivalent to preaching the Law. It is an interesting question which Law it was whose commands Zhenwu "announced" in the Aoshi opera. Daoist elements seem to predominate in the versions Grootaers collected, but there were Buddhist elements as well (pp. 155, 178–79). For a study and translation of the novel, see Seaman, *Journey to the North*.

39. Ren Guangwei, "Sai xi, naogu za xi chu tan," p. 200.

40. The report says "Mount Wutai," but this must be an error, since Wutai is over 140 km away.

brought this back in a Buddhist alms bowl and presented it at the Guanyin temple, to be used on the following day (see below). In the evening there were more *Sai* Operas.[41]

Second and Third Days:
The Great Procession; "Demons Snatch
the Meat"; "Lord Guan Beheads Chi You"

On the morning of the fifteenth a group of ten or more men, wearing masks, costumed as warriors, and mounted on horses or donkeys[42] galloped through the four streets of the village, accompanied by drums and wind music. The function of this is obscure, although its name— "Increasing Good Fortune" (*tian cai*)—supplies a hint.[43] In the afternoon there were *Sai* Operas, and in the evening there was a procession. It was led by a person called the Lantern Official together with Buddhist monks and Daoist priests and featured stilt-walkers, the Old Man Carrying the Old Woman on His Back, the Big-Headed Monk Fighting Liu Cui, lion dancers, bucking donkeys, and other festival staples. The procession paraded through all the streets of the village; families lit bonfires as it passed their gates, believing that would expel demonic influences and bring good luck. Then the monks performed a *jiao*, sprinkling in the four directions the "holy water" brought from the mountain the previous day. The monks also sang "Buddhist melodies" (*fo qu*).[44]

There were *Sai* Operas during the day on the sixteenth, and at dusk there was another exorcistic skit, of a type common in southern Shanxi and, no doubt, elsewhere. The skit was entitled *The Demons Snatch the Meat* (*Gui gua rou*) or, more formally, *Presenting [Offering] Tables* (*Shang zhuozi*). Twelve offering tables were set up on the ground to one side of the stage; each held five bowls containing pieces of meat. (We are not told whether the meat was raw or cooked.) These offerings to "the hundred spirits" were contributed by everyone in the village. After they

---

41. Ren Guangwei, "Sai xi, naogu za xi chu tan," p. 200.
42. Ren says oxen took part as well, but that seems unlikely.
43. Ren Guangwei, "Sai xi, naogu za xi chu tan," pp. 200–201.
44. Ibid., p. 201.

were set out, people hid in places from which they could watch the tables without being seen. Two men costumed as demons and wearing masks then began a dance (*tiao gui*) on the stage. When they finished, they sneaked off the stage, hurried to the tables, and began stuffing the offerings into their hats as fast as they could. At that point the people came swarming out from their hiding places and snatched the meat back from the "demons," watching one another to make sure that no one took too much. People believed that eating this meat brought good luck and protected against disease. The "demons" could well have been handled roughly at this point. Some time after this a Daoist priest, beating a small gong, walked to the front of the stage and sang the song "Requiting the Pleasures of Spring" ("Bao chun xi").[45] This prayer for the protection of the villagers during the coming year brought Aoshi's New Year rituals to an end.

Even from Ren Guangwei's somewhat sketchy description, it is clear that the two most important parts of this ritual were the exorcisms and the operas. (There appear to have been few invocations, hymns, or prayers.) As we have seen, there were four exorcistic or good-luck-bringing performances: the Chicken-Feather Monkey, *Zhenwu Expels the Ten Evil Spirits*, the gallop through the village called "Increasing Good Fortune," and *The Demons Snatch the Meat*. What of the *Sai* Operas, which were performed on the afternoon or evening of the thirteenth, the night of the fourteenth, the afternoon of the fifteenth, and the morning or afternoon (or both) of the sixteenth? There were two types: history plays and dramatized hagiographies and exorcisms. I describe the latter first and, for simplicity's sake, refer to them as "ritual operas," although in fact they were not fully developed operas.

As we have seen, there was a village oral tradition that their last Combined Script was a revision made in the Ming Jiaqing period. Moreover, Ren Guangwei has made a fairly persuasive case that Aoshi's *Sai* Operas were brought from southwestern Shanxi in the 1570s. Unfortunately, we are given little information about the repertoire. We do know that the ritual operas were *Lord Guan Beheads Chi You* (*Guan gong zhan Chi You*), *Beheading Han Ba* (*Zhan Han Ba*), and *Beheading Zhao*

45. Ren Guangwei, "Sai xi, naogu za xi chu tan," p. 201.

Wanniu (*Zhan Zhao Wanniu*). According to the general article on north-eastern *Sai* Opera in the *Encyclopedia of Chinese Opera*, *Beheading Han Ba* took place on the second day of a three-day festival, the most important day. The performance began with a character called Zhao Wanniu committing certain unspecified unfilial acts. (This is reminiscent of the Yellow Demon of Guyi; see Chapter 3.) At noon the actor playing this role became Han Ba. His costume included a fresh sheep's stomach worn over his head.[46] At the end of his performance (which is not described), Han Ba was driven off the stage by four guardian gods and ran straight into the audience, who surrounded him, shouting loudly and throwing stones and clods of dirt. He escaped by splattering them with sheep's blood he was carrying in a bowl and ran madly through the streets pursued by the gods and villagers. All the shopkeepers had their best things on display on tables lining the streets, and Han Ba could take what he wanted. He was chased back to the stage, where he threw to the crowd the things he had grabbed during his run. He was then captured and beheaded.[47]

Ren Guangwei's brief description of the opera as it was performed at New Year's in Aoshi accords well with this account: after Han Ba jumped off the stage, the audience together with the other actors chased him down to the riverbank where they caught him, tied him up, and dragged him back to the stage for execution. So too when the actor playing Zhao Wanniu was about to be captured (in Aoshi two actors must have taken these parts), he reacted in a now-familiar manner by jumping off the stage into the audience and then running out into the main street, where he snatched up food from stands set up along the street until he was finally captured and taken back to the stage to be executed.[48]

---

46. In the *Beheading Han Ba* of Wusai county in northwestern Shanxi, a pig's stomach with holes cut in it for eyes and mouth was used (Wang Zhijun, "Tan sai xi," pp. 100–101).

47. *Zhongguo xiqu zhi: Shanxi juan*, p. 141.

48. Ibid., pp. 203–4. Here again we see large-scale participation by the villagers, in sharp contrast to Renzhuang. The differences between Aoshi's *Han Ba* and that described in the *Zhongguo xiqu zhi: Shanxi juan* are examples of the theme-and-variation form typical of all folk literature.

Lord Guan Beheads Chi You is by common consent one of the most ancient of all Shanxi operas, although scripts are rare. In southwest Shanxi it was said to be the ancestor of *Za* Opera, and in northern Shanxi it was believed to be the ancestor of *Sai* Opera.[49] The ritual opera was based on a well-known legend. In the reign of Song Zhenzong, a drought caused by the ancient drought demon Chi You is destroying the salt ponds of Xie prefecture, an imperial saltworks. The Jade Emperor commands Lord Guan (Guan Di, the divinized Guan Yu), in his role as earth god (Tudi) of Xie, to save the people. Guan Yu sends rain and kills Chi You after a great battle. Chi You was undoubtedly executed in the Aoshi drama, in view of the title and the climax of Aoshi's *Beheading Han Ba*.

Leaping from the stage, snatching up goods set out by shopkeepers, and "beheadings" can be found in ritual operas throughout Shanxi. It is tempting to see these performances as simulations of what were once, at some time in the distant—or perhaps not so distant—past, actual ritual killings. Along with the masks and elaborate dances, they may well represent a stratum in the ritual that was very old indeed.

The history operas may have preserved old performance traditions, too.[50] Although not as ancient as I imagine the beheading skits to have been, they may well have contained features of early Chinese drama. Masks were used until late Qing times; the *Shê* Head took many minor parts, moved the scenery, and in general oversaw the stage;[51] there was little distinction between song and speech;[52] the style of the narrative resembled prosimetric literature;[53] there was a strong emphasis on dances, called "formations" (*zhen*);[54] and only percussion instruments

---

49. Ren Guangwei, "Sai xi, naogu za xi chu tan," p. 206.

50. These are discussed in more detail in Part II.

51. This is similar to the *dabao zhe* of *Za* Opera, whom we will meet in Part II, and the *Shê* Head of Guyi, introduced in the next chapter.

52. Ren Guangwei, "Sai xi, naogu za xi chu tan," p. 202.

53. Ibid., p. 205. Southwestern Shanxi *Za* Opera (also known as Gong and Drum [*luogu*] *Za* Opera) is described in almost identical terms in Yang Mengheng and Xie Yu-hui, "Shanxi sheng Linyi xian," pp. 144–45.

54. Ren Guangwei, "Sai xi, naogu za xi chu tan," p. 204. The scripts are said to have included diagrams of many "formations." The *Shangu shenpu* script has a similar diagram

were used.[55] It is possible that Aoshi's *Sai* Operas, both ritual and historical, and others like them elsewhere in Shanxi, such as the *Za* Operas of southwestern Shanxi (as well as the Mask Operas of Guyi, in southwestern Hebei), represent an early type of dramatic performance that survived into late imperial times and was strongly influenced by solo storytelling or ballad singing.[56]

Aoshi's New Year ritual had some features in common with the Fandrum ritual of Renzhuang. It appears to have been almost entirely a creation of the villagers themselves (or, more properly, their ancestors). Although Buddhist monks and Daoist priests (or perhaps only one of each) took minor parts,[57] in form and content the rituals were neither Buddhist nor Daoist but exorcistic. Interestingly, however, in neither Renzhuang nor Aoshi were the exorcist figures actual ritual specialists or possessed spirit-mediums, nor were they portraying demon-subduing gods such as Zhong Kui. The Renzhuang exorcist was a simulated spirit-medium, and in Aoshi the Golden Chicken Monkey was as much scapegoat as exorcist and was hardly a figure to inspire awe and fear.

Overall, however, Aoshi's New Year ritual must have been a far more intense experience than Renzhuang's. It had masked exorcistic drama (*Zhenwu Expels the Ten Evil Spirits*) and staged beheadings that were also clearly exorcistic, one of which at least (*Lord Guan Beheads Chi You*) was extremely ancient. Masked actors portrayed deities with local cults, and ordinary villagers joined in the action at moments of heightened emotion, such as the climaxes of *Zhenwu Expels the Ten Evil Spirits* and *Beheading Han Ba*. Nor is there any sign that a lineage elite monopolized the right to perform, and indeed Aoshi was not a lineage village. (The existence of an established amateur *sai* troupe before the war and

---

of a "formation" on its front cover (Huang and Wang, "*Shangu shenpu*" *diaocha baogao*, p. 146).

55. Ren Guangwei, "Sai xi, naogu za xi chu tan," pp. 202–3.

56. It is of course possible that the *Sai* Operas represent an extremely unsophisticated attempt to imitate "real" opera, that they represent a regression, rather than a survival. But that interpretation strikes me as the less plausible of the two, given the inherent conservatism of ritual opera.

57. There was a Buddhist ceremony on the evening of the fifteenth, which must have been overwhelmed by the activities of the Lantern Festival, and a Daoist priest pronounced something like a benediction at the end of the whole festival.

the selection of the Golden Chicken Monkey by the villagers also suggest that roles were not dominated by specific families.) Aoshi, like most villages, had gradually developed a ritual repertoire that met its residents' needs. Its New Year ritual was above all an occasion during which the villagers themselves, with little or no outside help, drove dangerous influences away and tried to ensure that the coming year would be fortunate. The means they employed were their own versions of rituals widely diffused in Shanxi and no doubt elsewhere. How they reached the particular form they took in Aoshi is impossible to say, but we know it was not a recent development, since the tradition went back to the sixteenth century, if not earlier. We also know that it was not imposed by officials, or "landlords," or clerical elites.

II. Sand Hill: Novel and Labyrinth

The Story Troupes and
the Shui hu zhuan

About twenty-five kilometers southwest of Aoshi, across Yellow Sheep Peak and the other outliers of the Hengshan Range that march along the southern side of the Sanggan valley, is a village of about 2,000 people with the unpromising name of Sand Hill (Shagetuo). It lies at an elevation of 1,300 meters, about fifteen kilometers northeast of the capital of Hunyuan county. The New Year ritual at Sand Hill is reminiscent in some ways of Renzhuang's, and it is worth describing, even though the only extant report provides little detail.[58] It was called *Shua gushi* (Playing [or playing at] stories).[59] It had this name because the main performers were costumed as characters from the episode in

---

58. Wang Fucai, "Hunyuan minjian shehuo," unpublished 1991 conference paper in the author's collection. This report appears to be based on a single visit to the village together with research in the archives of the county cultural affairs office. It is manifestly incomplete (for example, the sending-off of the spirits of the ancestors is described, but not their welcoming), and also is unclear on certain crucial matters, as will become apparent.

59. Although the ritual was extremely durable and evidently is still alive, I use the past tense here to avoid giving the impression that it has not changed.

Map 4 Sand Hill and environs. 1 cm = 1.7 km (SOURCE: *Shanxi sheng ditu ji*).

chapter 72 of the great novel *Shui hu zhuan* (translated variously as *All Men Are Brothers*, *Water Margin*, and *Outlaws of the Marsh*), in which a number of the heroes create an uproar in the Song capital, Kaifeng, during the New Year festival.[60] *Shua gushi* is said to have been widespread in Hunyuan county. It must have been very deeply embedded indeed in local culture, because people in Hunyuan continued to perform it through most of the Cultural Revolution, when such customs were being ferociously suppressed elsewhere. They managed this by having the county cultural affairs office label it a folk dance and changing the characters from the heroes of *Shui hu zhuan* to heroes of socialist reconstruction: workers, peasants, and soldiers, or characters from Jiang Qing's model operas.[61]

---

60. Actually, of the fourteen characters named in the report, only four appear in chapter 72. Five others who do figure in that chapter were not portrayed in the performances. The author does not mention this major discrepancy.

61. Wang Fucai, "Hunyuan minjian shehuo," p. 1.

There were no operas in Sand Hill's New Year festival, and almost no ritual or liturgical activity (if we can believe the report, which is completely silent on anything having to do with local temples and cults). Instead, processions and dances by *Shui hu* characters appear to have been the main kind of performance. Preparations began on the twelfth day of the first lunar month with the collection of coal for the Great Fire(s) (*wang huo*), which were an important part of the New Year celebrations in many places in Shanxi.[62] The coal was trimmed into "fist-sized" bricks and used to construct a hollow tower resembling a miniature pagoda. Firewood was placed inside, and, when lit, the fire blazed out spectacularly through gaps left between the coal bricks.[63]

The thirteenth was devoted to making lanterns and to rehearsals by the musicians and the "story troupes."[64] In the old days, money to buy food for the performers was raised by a levy on the owners of oxen, and other villages evidently cooked the meals. During "the period of the communes," work points were levied and additional funds were raised by sending New Year's "cards" (*tie*), on which were written auspicious phrases, to village cadres, "responsibility households," "specialist households," and families with members working outside the village, just as before the revolution they were sent to shopowners and other well-to-do families.[65]

A story troupe was made up of nine pairs of performers. Each of the eighteen performers was costumed as a *Shui hu* character, but in procession they just performed various turns: one pair wore big-headed masks and dueled with cudgels, another wore headdresses made of paper flowers and played gongs, yet another played waist-drums and danced with

---

62. Wen Xing and Xue Maixi, *Shanxi minsu*, pp. 81B–82A; pictures on pp. 109, 110. Coal is extremely common in Shanxi.

63. Wang's account ("Hunyuan minjian shehuo," p. 5) is confusing and incomplete; I have supplemented it with educated guesses based on the material in Wen Xing and Xue Maixi, *Shanxi minsu*.

64. Wang Fucai, "Hunyuan minjian shehuo," p. 5. Wang says that the story troupes rehearsed on the fourteenth (p. 6), but this must be a mistake, since he makes it clear that they performed on the morning, afternoon, and evening of that day. See below.

65. Ibid., pp. 5–6. The socioeconomic hierarchy obviously survived the revolution in Sand Hill.

swinging, winding steps, and so on.[66] This is puzzling, since they appear at no time to have acted out scenes from *Shui hu* or even to have tried to impersonate the characters. Did the people enjoy imagining that the figures from the novel had somehow decided to come to their festival and entertain them by playing gongs and dancing? Or had the performance decayed to the point where all but the names of the characters had been forgotten? Whatever the explanation, it is clear that popular fiction (and drama) still had a powerful grip on the popular imagination.

On each of the three days of the festival, these troupes (there were several of them, organized by age) "trod the streets" (*cai jie*) three times in the morning and four times in the afternoon. Their winding routes were called "garlic braids."[67] The rest of the daylight hours were spent performing dances, called *taolu*, in an open space not further identified (at one time, no doubt, the courtyard of a large temple). Originally there were ten of these dances; recently only two have been performed. (One of the eight no longer performed was called "Gold Coin Eyes," which irresistibly brings to mind the bear-skin headdresses with four golden eyes worn by shamans during the Great Exorcism at the Han court.)[68] I think it is reasonable to assume that Sand Hill's dances were similar to the "battle formations" put on during the New Year performances at Aoshi and the choreographed movements of the Godly Ones in Renzhuang's Fan-drum ritual.[69]

Walking the "Nine Bends of the Yellow River" and Dispatching the Disease Gods

In the evening of each of the three days, the story troupes, with lanterns on their heads, joined by people performing Dragon Lanterns, Boats on Dry Land, and similar festival fare, danced around the Great

---

66. Ibid., pp. 2–5.

67. Ibid., p. 7. Wang adds that on the sixteenth old performers who could no longer restrain themselves would sometimes rush into the performance area and join the show, although he doesn't make clear what was being performed (p. 6).

68. See Bodde, *Festivals in Ancient China*, p. 81.

69. For diagrams, see Wang Fucai, "Hunyuan minjian shehuo," pp. 15–16; and Huang and Wang, "*Shangu shenpu*" *diaocha baogao*, pp. 140–43.

Fire and then walked through a giant maze of lanterns called the Diagram (or Formation, or Lanterns) of the Nine Bends of the Yellow River (*Jiu qu Huang he tu/zhen/deng*). In Sand Hill, as elsewhere in northern Shanxi, this was an array of nineteen rows of nineteen small "lotus-flower" lanterns on five-foot tall stakes, about six and a half feet apart. This yielded 361 lanterns, but the central one was replaced by a stout pole twenty to thirty feet high with a large red lantern on top, which was called the *lao gan*. Cords strung between the lantern stakes formed an intricate pattern of pathways. According to David Holm, the Nine Bend arrays in northern Shaanxi traced out nine *yinyang* symbols or "diagrams of the Great Ultimate," each representing a cosmic region, centered on the supreme ruler.[70] It is easy to imagine that in other cases the path also traced out esoteric symbols or even giant characters.[71] Men were specially assigned to keep the lotus-flower lamps filled with oil, as well as to prevent their theft, since they were coveted as potent charms for the conception of sons. After the story troupes and other acts wound their way through the Nine Bends, the rest of the villagers followed. Once people entered, they had to follow the path through the entire array. In some places, it was believed that stroking the *lao gan* kept one healthy for the entire year.[72] The stream of people moving through the huge array of lanterns under the icy full moon was an impressive sight.[73]

The Nine Bends were sometimes called a "formation" (*zhen*), a term we have already encountered in Aoshi. Formations, which were dance-

---

70. Holm, *Art and Ideology*, p. 196. The Nine Bends array described by Holm differs in some details from Sand Hill's.

71. Wen Xing and Xue Maixi, *Shanxi minsu*, p. 81A. The impulse to assume a relationship between the number of lanterns and the number of days in the year should be resisted, since the traditional Chinese lunar year had 353–55 days (some months had 29 days and others 30). The number must have had some larger significance but I have not been able to discover what it was.

72. Wang Fucai, "Hunyuan minjian shehuo," pp. 9–10; Wen Xing and Xue Maixi, *Shanxi minsu*, p. 81.

73. I have a videotape that shows hundreds of people walking a Nine Bends array in Hebei, the lantern field stretching away into the darkness. There is a diagram of Sand Hill's Nine Bends on p. 17 of Wang's paper, and colored photographs of an unidentified Nine Bends on p. 489 of Wen Xing and Xue Maixi, *Shanxi minsu*. My account uses the latter to supplement Wang's report.

like, not opera-like, and took place on the ground not the stage, were an important part of many Shanxi festivals, a topic well worth pursuing given their military-cosmological nature. But the Nine Bends Formation has a special interest because it is another example of a link between Sand Hill's New Year rituals and a popular novel. The story of the creation of the magical Nine Bends Formation to trap the allies of the Zhou takes up chapters 47–50 of the great late Ming cosmological novel, *The Investiture of the Gods*.[74] Since there were operas based on this episode in many of the local opera genres of north China, it clearly was a popular theme.[75] Moreover, a lantern maze constructed by villagers between the eleventh and sixteenth of the first lunar month called the Nine Bends of the Yellow River is mentioned in the *Di jing jing wu lue* of Liu Tong (*jinshi* 1634).[76] Thus Sand Hill's Nine Bends may have been rooted in a stratum of popular cosmological symbolism older than the novel.

The most important exorcism of the Sand Hill festival took place on the evening of the sixteenth. First the villagers "sent off" the spirits of their ancestors. (We are not told how or when they were invited.) Carrying lanterns, they went to the ancestral tombs, where they burned incense and made offerings. No gongs or drums were allowed, and the Great Fire and the lanterns of the Nine Bends could not be lit until this ceremony had been completed. This was followed by "Sending Off Diseases" (*song wen*). An "eminent man" from the county town was invited to act as the Official in Charge of Sacrifices (*zhu ji guan*). He was costumed as a civil official and rode in a palanquin accompanied by four Masters of Ceremony (*li sheng*). *Li sheng* were employed all over China to lead non-Buddhist, non-Daoist family and communal rituals.[77] The Official in Charge of Sacrifices may have belonged to the elite of the county's *li sheng*, somewhat like the Masters of Ceremonial (*zhu li*) in southeastern Shanxi, or he may have simply been an admired local

---

74. As we have seen, this novel was also a major influence on Renzhuang's New Year performance.

75. Yang Mengheng et al., eds., *Zhongguo bangzi xi jumu da cidian*, p. 11; and Tao Junqi, *Jingju jumu chutan*, p. 8.

76 . Beijing guji chuangshe ed. (2000), chap. 2, p. 66.

77. For an introduction to this important group of specialists, see Yonghua Liu, "The World of Ritual."

scholar. If the latter, we see a possible link between village ritual and orthodox Confucian ritual, a subject I shall address in the Conclusion of
Part III. Another, quite different figure, called the One-Beam Official
(*yi gen chuan de guan*), accompanied the *li sheng*. He sat at one end of a
long beam supported in the middle by a short crosspiece held by two
men. People pushed down on the free end of the long beam see-saw
fashion causing the Official to bounce up and down. He bantered with
the spectators and set off firecrackers in front of various shops. But
people in the crowd also threw firecrackers at him and battered him,
and by the time the procession reached the place northwest of the village where the diseases were to be "dispatched," his clothes were in tat-
ters, his shoes and stockings torn off, and his face so smudged he was
unrecognizable. Once again, as with the Chicken-Feather Monkey, we
have a victim of ritual abuse who was also the village protector.

All the performers and residents followed the two Officials to the
place where diseases were dispatched. The Official in Charge of Sacrifices read a prayer, incense was lit and firecrackers set off, and a memorial was burned. Then a big fire was lit, and the disease gods sent off—
presumably by being thrown into the flames. The people returned to the
village in silence, forbidden to look back until they had walked a hundred
paces, lest the disease gods follow them home.[78] (The poor One-Beam
Official limped along behind, walking barefoot on the frozen ground,
hoping to retrieve his shoes and stockings back in the village.) This was
the end of the ritual, at least as described in Wang's report.[79]

Sand Hill's New Year rituals were strikingly different from both
Renzhuang's and Aoshi's—the use of characters from the novel *Shui hu
zhuan* in the street performances, the teaming up of a ritual expert and a
scapegoat in the exorcism, and above all the spectacular Nine Bends of
the Yellow River Formation and the Great Fire: all these had no counterparts in the other villages. Of course, there were similarities—all had
elaborate processions and dances, were centrally concerned with exor-

---

78. Wang Fucai, "Hunyuan minjian shehuo," pp. 10–11. See Chapter 1 for a similar
custom in Renzhuang.

79. Wang Fucai (ibid., pp. 7–8) notes that another village was sometimes invited to
take part in the festivities and describes the tensions that arose when the guest troupe
entered the host village.

cism, and used fires or lanterns in some way—but the most important features were not shared. Even the general *tone* of the ritual was quite different in each case: Renzhuang's rather distanced, with no strong heightening of the emotional ambience; Aoshi's bringing Zhenwu and other gods to life in masked ritual operas and exorcisms; Sand Hill's touching on the deepest levels with its Great Fire and labyrinth of lanterns—light against darkness, fire against demons. It is true that Sand Hill's Nine Bends and Great Fire had counterparts in other north China villages, but this does not significantly lessen the general impression of village ritual autarky. And the final example of a New Year ritual to be presented here, which is almost as well documented as the Fan-drum ritual of Renzhuang, also was unique.

3

Guyi Village

Killing the Yellow Demon

Guyi village is in the eastern foothills of the Taihang Range in southern Hebei, in the same dialect area as the southeastern Shanxi region that was home to the great *sai*.[1] In late imperial times the village was near the important road that connected southern Hebei with southeastern Shanxi.[2] This is probably the reason it was quite prosperous "in the old days," when it had dealers in carts and horses, restaurants, and many shops. In addition, men from Guyi traded in Shanxi, as well as Liaoning, Zhejiang, and Inner Mongolia. It was an administrative village (*li*), with authority over twenty-three neighboring villages, and hence must have been fairly populous. (The current population now is over 2,700—a good deal larger than Renzhuang, substantially smaller than Aoshi, and about the same size as Sand Hill.)[3]

---

1. The most important sources for Guyi's New Year rituals are three works by Du Xuede: *Yan Zhao*, which despite its title is almost entirely devoted to Guyi; "Hebei sheng," which is heavily dependent on the book; and "Guyi." These studies complement one another to a certain extent; where they disagree I have followed the book, which has much more detail. I have also been able to consult videotapes of Guyi's New Year rituals, including *Catching the Yellow Demon*, kindly supplied to me by Wang Ch'iu-kuei and Sarah Jessup.

2. The road probably followed the line of the modern railway between Handan and Changzhi, the only rail crossing of the Taihang Range south of Shijiazhuang. See map in Du Xuede, *Yan Zhao*, p. 150; and, e.g., *Zhonghua renmin gongheguo fensheng ditu ji, Hanyu pinyin ban* (1983), map 5.

3. Du Xuede, *Yan Zhao*, p. 7.

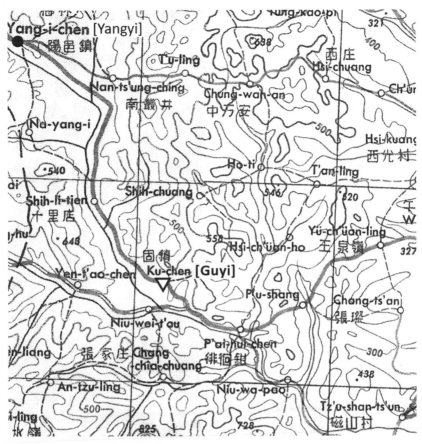

Map 5   Guyi and environs. The village is labelled "Ku-chen" on the map. 1 cm = 1.7 km
(SOURCE: U. S. Army Map Service series L531, 1:250,000. Compiled 1945 from
China Central Land Survey 1:50,000, aerial photography 1944–45, and
Chinese Road Maps and Intelligence Reports, 1943–45).

RITUAL GEOGRAPHY, FOUNDING LEGEND, TYPES OF PERFORMANCE

Guyi was divided into four neighborhoods: Big West Shê (Da xi shê), Southern Wang Ward (Nan Wang hu), Eastern Wang Ward (Dong Wang hu), and Liu Village Ward (Liu zhuang hu), each of which may originally have belonged to a single lineage but now is occupied by several surnames. Roles in the New Year ritual were passed down in families from generation to generation, as in Renzhuang, and the most important roles were monopolized by Big West Shê lineages. The leading Big West Shê lineages, the Dings, the Lis, and the Mas, had come to Guyi from Hongdong in southern Shanxi some time during the Ming;[4] here again we encounter members of that remarkable diaspora. Formerly each lineage had its own ancestral hall, which probably helped define the territory of the wards. (At least one of them, that of the Lis, is still standing.)[5] There were also temples to Buddhas, Guanyin, Guan Di, the River God, the three goddesses of Taishan, the Jade Emperor, the Dragon King(s), the Fire God, the Earth God (Tudi), Laozi, the God of the Five Ways, Lü Dongbin, and the Three Teachings, as well as an important one known simply as the Hall of the Immortal(s). Remarkably, most of these were still standing in 1998.[6]

Local people called Guyi's New Year festival *Catching the Yellow Demon* (*Zhuo huang gui*), after its central ritual drama. It was a huge production with operas, processions, prayers, and other performances involving hundreds of villagers.[7] Its purpose is succinctly described in a self-referential verse that, as we shall see, is characteristic of the *Yellow Demon* liturgy:

> At the New Year festival we delight in the New Year,
> Wearing costumes civil and military, we drive calamity and
>   disease away.
> Raising shields and gripping lances, we perform the Nuo ritual;
> The five grains will flourish, we will celebrate great peace.[8]

The age of the ritual is unknown, but there is an interesting local tradition about its origin. At some unspecified time in the past, a native of Guyi named Ding Duan was "cutting opium" in Yu county, which is about 145 km west of Beijing and over 240 km north of Guyi. He fell ill

---

4. Du Xuede, *Yan Zhao*, p. 8.
5. Ibid., p. 149.
6. Ibid., pp. 9–10.
7. According to Du Xuede, "Hebei sheng," p. 154, over 600 people were directly involved in the 1995 performance. Even though *Catching the Yellow Demon* is still performed, I use the past tense in this account. See Chapter 2, *n*59.
8. The text in Du Xuede, "Guyi," p. 167, is superior to that in idem, *Yan Zhao*, p. 78.

in late autumn and by the twelfth month still had not recovered. One night, when he had fallen into a sort of waking dream, a huge figure appeared before him. He was dressed like a general, and his eyebrows were white as snow. He said he was a Guyi man, and when Ding, not recognizing him, asked where he lived, he replied "Guyi's Little South village." He gave Ding two packets of medicine and said that if he took them he would recover in a few days. Ding asked how he could thank him, and the visitor said "Bring me a pair of scrolls (*duilian*) when you return." Ding asked where to get them, to which the visitor replied, "You'll get them on the way," and left. Ding was about to rush out to continue questioning the man when he woke up. As he lay on the *kang* (heated sleeping platform), he recalled the statue of Third Master White Eyebrows in the Goddess Temple in Little South village on the outskirts of Guyi and realized that it was the Third Master himself who had visited him.

Ding's illness immediately began to improve, but when the New Year season came, his employer warned him that he was still too weak to travel, and so he stayed in Yu county. Now it so happened that Little Wutai Mountain, not far away, had a famous New Year festival, and Ding decided to go. (That a particular New Year festival could be famous tells us that some were better than others, and hence that there was variety.) When he got to the main gate of the temple, he paused to rest—he was still convalescing—and looked back down the way he had come. He saw performers and shows, including *Catching the Yellow Demon* and *Cen Peng and Ma Wu Contend to Be Top Graduate*, lining each side of the road, like a pair of scrolls. Ding realized that it was the festival itself his dream visitor wanted him to bring home. (Note that the festival is thought of as a coherent program, since it can be taken somewhere. That there were local committees to organize and finance them shows the same thing.) He found out everything he could about the performances, especially *Yellow Demon* and *Cen Peng*. When the weather warmed up a bit and he had fully recovered, he went home to Guyi. He told his kinfolk about the god's request, and they agreed to adopt the new style festival. It was too big for them to do alone, however, and they recruited the Li and Ma lineages, who also lived in Big West Shê. But when word got out, the rest of the villagers insisted that they be included. Big West Shê agreed, with the proviso that the others take only the less important roles, and so the festival began.[9]

No date is given in the story, but Du Xuede says that Ding Duan brought *Catching the Yellow Demon* to Guyi in mid-Ming.[10] This does not fit with the opium theme, since the drug was not widely cultivated in north China before the early eighteenth century.[11] However, the Dings are said to have emigrated from Hongdong some time during the Ming. There is abundant evidence of forced transfers of people from Shanxi via Hongdong to southern Hebei in Ming times; half the villages in Handan county, which is near Guyi, are said to have been founded by Hongdong people.[12] It is not impossible therefore that a man named Ding brought *Catching the Yellow Demon* to Guyi in the Ming, not from northern Hebei but from Shanxi.

Shanxi references in various performances during the festival make this seem more likely. There also had been ritual operas featuring yellow demons in southeastern Shanxi for a long time. Two important old liturgical handbooks, the *Zhou yuexing tu* (1547) and the *Tang yuexing tu* (1818 in part), both list among their ritual operas ("skits" might be a better word) one called *Beating the Yellow Consumption Demon* (*Bianda huanglao gui*).[13] Pieces with this title were in fact performed in southeastern Shanxi in late imperial and early Republican times. In them the part of the Yellow Consumption Demon was played by a hereditary Entertainer (*yuehu*), who wore only a pair of shorts and whose body was smeared with yellow, much like Guyi's Yellow Demon, as we shall see. The demon entered the stage pursued by a judge (*panguan*), and soon jumped off the stage and ran through the streets, with judge and musicians in pursuit. During his run, the demon grabbed as much as he

---

9. Du Xuede, *Yan Zhao*, pp. 26–28. This lineage-based exclusivity reminds one of Renzhuang; there was no trace of it in Aoshi and Sand Hill.

10. Ibid., p. 3.

11. Spence, *The Search for Modern China*, pp. 88–89. There may, of course, have been local exceptions to Spence's dating.

12. Huang Youquan et al., *Hongdong da huaishu*, pp. 114–16.

13. Or perhaps Hepatitis-Consumption Demon. See Han Sheng et al., eds., "*Yingshen saishe lijie* . . . zhu shi," p. 95; and Li Tiansheng, "*Tang yuexing tu* jiao zhu," p. 31. (There are other editions of these key texts, but discussion of them is deferred to Part III.)

could from the stalls, throwing it into a bag carried by a helper. (Shop-keepers considered it good luck if he took some of their wares.) Eventually the demon ran back to the stage, where his pursuers finally caught him. He was strung up to a roof beam and beaten by the judge. (All this is highly reminiscent of the pursuit and punishment of Han Ba and Zhao Wanniu in Aoshi.) As the demon screamed and groaned, a man came on stage with an incense tray. The material on the tray, when lit, filled the stage with thick smoke. When the smoke cleared away, the demon had disappeared. Sometimes men who played the role of the Yellow Demon put a hollowed-out yellow melon filled with a mixture of sand and red-colored water on their heads and then smashed it at the climax of the performance. This must have had a spectacularly shocking effect.[14] Although, as we shall see, this scenario differs in many respects from Guyi's *Catching the Yellow Demon*, the two certainly are related, and a Ding ancestor could well have brought a version from Shanxi to Guyi as early as the Ming dynasty.

Catching the Yellow Demon and much of the rest of Guyi's traditional New Year performances were revived in 1987 after a lapse of "over fifty years" and were put on again in 1990, 1991, 1992, 1995, 1997, and 1998.[15] Du Xuede first learned of Guyi's New Year performances from photographs in an informal exhibition. No one in Handan, where he was assistant director of the Mass Arts Office, could tell him anything about the festival (Guyi is all of fifty-five kilometers from Handan), so he mounted his own expedition in March 1990.[16] He appears to have

---

14. The material on Yellow Demon performances in the nineteenth and twentieth centuries is from Yuan Shuangxi, "Shangdang nuo xi ji qi liubian," unpublished paper in the author's collection, 1990, pp. 7–8. (The detail about the sand and water mixture is taken from Yuan's description of a similar performance called *Beheading Han Ba* [ibid., p. 8].) See also Han Sheng et al., eds., *Shangdang nuo wenhua*, pp. 350–51.

15. The statement about a hiatus of over fifty years is part of a reported conversation with village leaders (Du Xuede, *Yan Zhao*, p. 60). But a performance in 1964 is mentioned on p. 12 along with those from the 1990s.

16. Du's account of his "discovery" of the ritual and his abortive attempts to attend it before 1992 shows that the gulf between city-based functionaries and the life of the countryside did not end with the advent of a new political system in the twentieth century (ibid., pp. 162–66).

observed the ritual in 1992 and 1995, and possibly also in 1997.[17] According to Du, the driving force behind the revival of *Catching the Yellow Demon* was Ding Deyu, a Guyi resident and the retired principal of an elementary school in the town of Zhitao zhen, about five km northwest of Guyi. He was assisted by other Guyi natives: Ding Shiquan, a retired cadre; Li Qilai (b. 1914), who had served as Staff-holder, or master of ceremonies, in the 1930s, was a member of one of the twenty-five elite *Shê* Head families (see below), and had a large collection of liturgical manuscripts and opera scripts;[18] and Li Zhengnian (b. 1917), who had served as a scout (*tanma*) in the prewar performances.[19] The work of restoration was formidable: the masks were in such poor condition they could not be used,[20] and although the scripts of a number of Mask Tableaux and *Sai* Operas had been preserved, along with liturgical materials, the performances themselves—music, costumes, and everything else not found in scripts—had to be reconstructed. Even though Ding Deyu had the help of two men who had had important roles in the prewar performances, inevitably the restored ritual was incomplete.[21] But *Catching the Yellow Demon*, complete or not, was still a remarkable show. Qu Liuyi, the former head of the Chinese *Nuo* Drama Research Association, wrote that none of the many ritual drama performances he had observed since 1985 impressed him as much as Guyi's.[22]

Each of Guyi's four wards had specific responsibilities in the staging of the ritual. Twenty-five families from Big West Shê, who were called the *Shê* Head households (*shêshou hu*), were in charge.[23] They were divided into five groups (*zu*) of five families each, and the right, or duty,

---

17. Du Xuede, *Yan Zhao*, pp. 58–62.

18. He was illiterate, but knew almost all the Staff-holder's lines (ibid., p. 61).

19. Ibid., pp. 58–59, 61–62.

20. Ibid., p. 13.

21. See ibid., pp. 56–58, for a list of acts that have not yet been reconstituted; in addition there must be gaps and changes in the restored version that are impossible to identify.

22. Ibid., p. 131.

23. As we have seen, the term *Shê* Head was used in Renzhuang to refer to the leaders of the gong and drum troupes and also in Aoshi, where it was the title of the man with overall authority. This is a reminder of the importance of the *shê* as a geographic unit, discussed in the Introduction.

of organizing the ritual passed from group to group in a regular rotation.[24] *Shê* Head household status stayed in a given family until it was no longer willing or able to shoulder the administrative, ritual, and financial responsibilities the role entailed. If that happened, a replacement family was selected, always from within Big West Shê.[25] Big West Shê also supplied all the performers in the Mask Tableaux (literally, "face operas" [*lian xi*]), *Sai* Operas, and *Catching the Yellow Demon*, as well as the Staff-holder, whose role is described below.[26]

The other three wards contributed over 300 performers and at least thirty-three acts. For the most part they were typical New Year fare—boats on dry land, stilt-walkers, dragon dancers, lion dancers, *yangge* singers, and so on. A few are worth mentioning, although they had no special ritual significance. For example, all three wards had acts that featured what seems to have been a mock official. In the Liu Village Ward it was called "The Nobody Official Riding a Lofty Palanquin" (*Mo guan zuo qiao jiao*).[27] A child, presumably dressed in official costume, rode on a two-wheeled cart bearing the following sign: "This small official is from No Family village (*Mojia zhuang*) of Qin county in Shanxi, and my given name is No Ability (*Moneng*). I am traveling to Changzhi [in Shanxi] to take up my post. I cross the Qingzhang River astride a river horse."[28] The Eastern and Southern Wang wards both put on an act called the "Rank Seven Sesame Official" (*qi pin zhima guan*), which must also have featured some sort of carnivalesque anti-official.

The Lius also had an act called "Refugees Pushing a Cart," which portrayed two old people and a child fleeing to Shanxi from the earthquake-ravaged town of Wu'an, not far from Guyi. This must have

---

24. Du Xuede, *Yan Zhao*, p. 11.

25. Du Xuede, "Guyi," p. 164.

26. Du Xuede, *Yan Zhao*, pp. 15–17; idem, "Guyi," pp. 147–50. This is reminiscent of the Godly Ones in Renzhuang, except that more than one lineage was involved.

27. The humor here turns on the word *mo*, which can be a family name and a place-name, but also means "not," "un-," and so on.

28. Du Xuede, *Yan Zhao*, p. 18. The Shanxi setting is notable. The reference to Changzhi is further evidence that communication between Guyi and southeast Shanxi was relatively easy. The Qingzhang River crosses from Shanxi to Hebei at virtually the same place as the Guyi–Changzhi road. There seems never to have been a Qin county in Shanxi. I do not know the implications of riding a river horse (*he ma*).

struck an oddly discordant note amid all the prayers for good crops and protection from natural disasters.[29] The Southern Wangs had something resembling a *Sai* Opera, titled "Interrogating Ma Long" ("Shen Ma Long"). It was called a "bamboo horse opera"; evidently all the characters were fitted with costumes that made it appear they were mounted.[30] Most interesting of all, though, is the fact that each of the three ritually subordinate wards fielded a large martial arts troupe; Eastern Wang's is said to have had 100 men. It is almost as if the ritual dominance of Big West were being deliberately counterbalanced by the martial might of the other three wards. Perhaps the acts that mocked officials represented a similar challenge.[31]

As we have seen, the status of *Shê* Head Household was hereditary; so too were all tasks connected with the festival. This included not only roles in the operas, as in Renzhuang's *Shangu shenpu*, but also membership in the groups that made willow clubs (which were used in large numbers), built temporary stages, made artificial smoke, and cared for the horses and donkeys. The duties of a man who had no son were inherited by his nephew or son-in-law. Those who had such responsibilities were expected to return to Guyi at New Year's even if they were living elsewhere.[32]

Although gods were invited, welcomed, and sent off, and prayers and invocations recited, the most important elements in Guyi's New Year celebration were the theatrical performances and processions. Villagers distinguished two types of drama: *Sai* Opera and *Dui* Opera. (Both these terms were also used in southeastern Shanxi, although they referred to somewhat different sorts of performance.) *Sai* Operas in Guyi resembled mainstream local opera in certain respects: they had historical subjects and were performed on stage with actors wearing face makeup, not masks, and used ordinary dialogue rather than narration by the

---

29. Du Xuede, *Yan Zhao*, pp. 17–18. Once again, the orientation is toward Shanxi. These casual mentions of Shanxi provide additional evidence to support the suggestion that Guyi's New Year performances came to southern Hebei with the *Da huaishu* diaspora.

30. Ibid., p. 34.

31. For a complete list of the three wards' acts, see ibid., pp. 17–19.

32. Du Xuede, *Yan Zhao*, p. 12.

Staff-holder.[33] However, only percussion instruments were used, and the actors moved very little when speaking or singing.[34] As I have said, roles in *Sai* Operas and in almost all the other theatrical performances were reserved for members of Big West Shê.[35] Seventeen scripts (*duben*) of eleven *Sai* Operas are extant, only three of which were performed when Du was present.[36] They must have been rather unimportant compared to *Catching the Yellow Demon*. The oldest of the *duben* is dated 1834; two are dated 1875; and one 1876, the eve of the great famine in Hebei.[37]

The villagers lumped rather different kinds of performance under the label *Dui* Opera, the second of the two types. To avoid confusion I divide what they called *Dui* Opera into two subtypes: stories narrated by the Staff-holder and mimed by masked actors, which I call Mask Tableaux (avoiding Du's confusing "Mask Operas," since they were not operas); and all the rest, which had little in common besides the use of face makeup instead of masks. These I call *Dui* rather than *Dui* Operas, since even the longest of them barely rises to the level of real opera. Seven Mask Tableaux and five *Dui* are extant. The five *Dui* included the two that, if one can judge by the origin legends, were very closely associated with the New Year ritual in the villager's minds: *Catching the Yellow Demon* and *Cen Peng and Ma Wu Contend to Be Top Graduate*.[38] *Catching the Yellow Demon* was particularly important and is discussed at length below.

---

33. Ibid., pp. 39–41. For the Staff-holder, see below.

34. Du Xuede, "Guyi," p. 159. This resembles a number of Shanxi ritual opera genres, such as the Gong and Drum *Za* Opera of the southwest and Aoshi's *Sai* Opera.

35. Du Xuede, *Yan Zhao*, pp. 17, 40.

36. For the eleven titles, see idem, pp. 40–41. Only three titles of *Sai* Operas are mentioned in the detailed account of the ritual, pp. 42–55. Du evidently was not allowed to study the scripts, which are still owned by the family of Li Qilai, the former Staff-holder who preserved them through the Cultural Revolution (p. 41), since he has nothing to say about the content of the remaining eight. The term "*duben*" was also used in southeastern Shanxi to refer to the scripts of certain ritual operas (Han Sheng et al., eds., *Shangdang nuo wenhua*, p. 134).

37. Du Xuede, *Yan Zhao*, pp. 40–41; Bohr, *Famine in China and the Missionary*, pp. 13–16.

38. The other three are *Interrogating Ma Long*, a military opera, the only opera not performed by the men of Big West Shê; *The Big-Headed Monk Sports with Liu Cui* (*Da tou heshang xi Liu Cui*), a comedy; and *Ten Drumbeats* (*Shi bang gu*), a farce. Du gives no

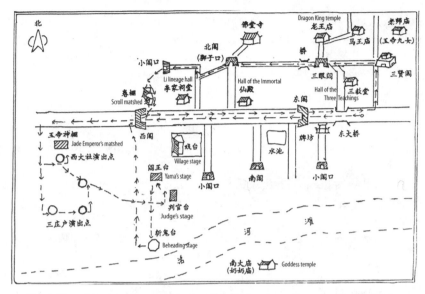

Fig. 5 Plan of Guyi showing the main sites of the Yellow Demon ritual, including the route of the procession and the stages (SOURCE: Du Xuede, "Hebei sheng").

Most of the Mask Tableaux were performed on the village stage, but some were presented on the ground in front of the Jade Emperor's Matshed (*Yuhuang peng*), a temporary shrine built just outside the village.[39] They were always narrated by the Staff-holder—the actors themselves were silent. The narratives appear to have been strongly influenced by storytelling. For example, in *Stealing a Horse*, a change of scene is signaled by the phrase "We'll speak no more of that, but turn instead to . . . (*zhe hua mo ti, zhi yin* . . .)," and the dynasty during which the action takes place is not called the Three Kingdoms, but rather "the *Historical Romance of the Three Kingdoms*."[40] Similar locutions can be found in *Levying Demon Soldiers*.[41]

Narrator-director figures like the Staff-holder were important in many other ritual drama genres in Shanxi: the *Shê* Head in Aoshi's *Sai* Opera,

---

information as to when the last two were performed. Both were very short; see Du Xuede, *Yan Zhao*, pp. 32–33.

39. Ibid., pp. 29, 43–44.

40. Ibid., p. 72.

41. "We'll speak no more of that" (*zhe qie bu jiang*) (ibid., pp. 70, 71).

the Announcer in the Gong and Drum *Za* Opera of southwestern Shanxi, and the Leader (*qianhang*) in southeastern Shanxi's *Dui* Opera. Although in these genres the main characters spoke their own lines, the dialogue often had a strong narrative quality. In Gong and Drum *Za* Opera, for example, the lines spoken by the main characters at times appear to have been taken over from prosimetric storytelling narratives with little or no change, and in the *Sai* Operas of Aoshi, whose scripts have clearly retained characteristics of prosimetric narrative, the main characters sometimes stand and declaim for four or five minutes at a time.

Dui were presented at a number of venues: the village stage, the Jade Emperor's Matshed, and three temporary stages used only for *Catching the Yellow Demon*: Yama's Stage, the Judge's Stage, and the Demon-Beheading Stage. The village stage was just south of Front Street. It was oriented east and west, had row seating made of plastered brick, and was not connected with a temple, which strongly suggests that it was built after 1949. If it was, it is almost certain that a major temple, with its stage, formerly occupied that site. The Jade Emperor's Matshed was constructed of poles covered by canvas on a site west of Guyi's west gate. It faced south and had an altar inside, like a rudimentary temple. On the morning of the fifteenth, a villager costumed as the Jade Emperor took a seat in it, probably behind the altar in the place a statue of the god would occupy in a temple. (This is the first of many examples in Guyi's New Year of the gods "coming to life" but also being reduced to roles played by actors.) Theatricals presented here were performed on the ground. By contrast, performances at the three temporary stages took place on raised platforms of boards. Yama's and the Judge's stages had cloth sides and a backdrop; the Demon-Beheading Stage was open on all sides, although blue cloth concealed the space beneath it. Yama's Stage faced south; the Judge's Stage, located just southeast of Yama's Stage, faced west. Directly opposite Yama's Stage, fifty yards away, was the Demon-Beheading Stage, also known as the South Stage. It faced north and was constructed so that the floor boards could be moved apart, allowing the Yellow Demon to drop beneath the stage at the climax of the performance.[42]

---

42. Ibid., pp. 44–45.

The figure known as the Staff-holder was the most important per-
former in the ritual.[43] This role was another Big West Shê monopoly
and, like all the others, was passed down in a single family.[44] The Staff-
holder wore white face makeup and no beard and was costumed in a
red court robe and a black Song-style hat. He introduced almost all the
operas and skits and narrated the otherwise-silent Mask Tableaux. He
also recited invocations and prayers throughout the three days of the
festival. His symbol of office was a staff about two feet long and "as
thick as a hen's egg," whose upper part was split vertically into thirty
strips bound together with red thread. This he used to direct the action
on stage, introduce the characters, and so on.[45] Du states that the Staff-
holder and the staff itself are "living fossils" of Song dynasty stage
practice. Remarkably, a twelfth-century stone engraving from Gaoping
county (now municipality) in southeastern Shanxi, a region where *sai*
were commonly performed, shows a troupe leader holding a similar
staff.[46] The Staff-holder and his staff are very reminiscent of the Leader
(*qianhang*) of the actors and musicians of the great *sai* of southeastern
Shanxi, whom we will encounter in Part III, and so it is striking that the
Staff-holder refers to himself as "Leader" in the script of *Introducing the
Eight Immortals*: "Today is the proper *sai*—we will present the *Dui*
Opera about the Eight Immortals. Each has his own name—listen
while the Leader tells you who they are."[47] This is yet another hint that
Guyi's ritual repertoire was influenced by the communal ritual culture
of southeastern Shanxi.

---

43. In *Yan Zhao*, Du always renders this character's title 長(掌)竹 (*zhang [zhang] zhu*),
presumably a reflection of a disagreement among his informants as to the correct character. (One pronunciation of 長 is identical to the pronunciation of 掌 [*zhǎng*].) But in
"Hebei sheng," he uses only 掌竹, which makes much better sense. My translation reflects this usage.

44. Du Xuede, *Yan Zhao*, p. 17; idem, "Guyi," p. 155.

45. Du Xuede, *Yan Zhao*, p. 19, with photograph on p. 153; idem, "Guyi," p. 155. Du
Xuede, "Hebei sheng," p. 165, says there were twenty-eight strips.

46. Du Xuede, *Yan Zhao*, p. 6; idem, "Hebei sheng," p. 154. For illustrations of the
Song engraving and a modern counterpart, see Han Sheng et al., eds., *Shangdang nuo
wenhua*, pls. 13–14, 46–47. Han and his collaborators have a detailed article on the engraving: "Cong Song Jin yuewu dui xi."

47. Du Xuede, *Yan Zhao*, p. 80. The term *fenjie*, here translated as "tell who they
are," is also a storyteller's locution used in fiction.

PRELIMINARIES AND THE
SHÊ PROCESSIONS

Preparations for Guyi's New Year festival began early in the tenth lunar month, when the twenty-five *Shê* Heads met to decide whether it would be staged during the coming New Year season. (Presumably each *Shê* Head household sent one representative.) If they decided to proceed, all the performers from Big West Shê were invited to a dinner of rice and vegetables hosted by the *Shê* Heads. On the following evening, the performers from the other three wards were invited to a similar meal. After this formal beginning, all the performers began practicing, at first by themselves, and then, after the start of the twelfth month, in ensembles. During these practices, the *Shê* Head households were responsible for supplying fuel, water, and other necessities for the Big West Shê performers, as were the heads of the other wards for their performers.[48]

On the first day of the twelfth month, the mask of Third Master White Eyebrows, which had previously been carefully cleaned, was taken by a procession of all the performers, led by the *Shê* Heads, from the Goddess Temple south of the village to a place called the Scroll Matshed (*juan peng*), which was set up temporarily in the outer part of the Guanyin Temple near the west gate. There it was placed on a square block of stone that had "Ten Thousand Years to the Emperor, a Thousand Autumns to the Heir-Apparent" engraved on the front, and "The Breezes Gentle, the Rains Timely" and "The Realm Prosperous, the People Serene" on the sides.[49]

Around the tenth of the first month, construction of the other temporary stages and matsheds along with the preparation of all the other things used in the performances, such as the willow clubs and the stabling for thirty-five pairs of horses and donkeys, was begun.[50] The Hall of the Immortal was decorated, and banners were hung across Front Street.[51] On the morning of the twelfth, all the performers gathered

---

48. Ibid., p. 42; Du Xuede, "Guyi," p. 165.
49. Du Xuede, *Yan Zhao*, pp. 14–15.
50. Ibid., p. 44; Du Xuede, "Guyi," p. 165.
51. Du Xuede, *Yan Zhao*, pp. 44–45.

before the mask of Third Master White Eyebrows in the Scroll Mat-shed for a purification ritual. They were told to abstain from sex until the end of the festival, and the *Shê* Heads reviewed the preparations and gave a formal invitation card to each participant.[52] Two days later, on the morning of the fourteenth, a group from Big West Shê including one *Shê* Head, the Staff-holder, a "sacrificer" (*duan xiangzhi gongpin zhe*), a gong and drum troupe, and masked actors representing the City God and his seal-bearer together with the Military Judge, the God of the Five Ways, the Earth God, and the Small Green-Faced Demon went in procession from the Li lineage hall to the site of the former Dragon King temple, in the northeastern part of the village. There the *Shê* Head offered incense and sacrificial money before a tablet of the Dragon King and recited an invitation to him.[53] This invitation was used on at least four other occasions during the ritual with only slight modifications.

> Face like black lacquer, like the bottom of a wok,
> A hero uglier than any human,
> In charge of the pens and cages [of the Nether World],
> He is enfeoffed as the Venerable Way-Opening Demon.
>
> Restraining this world's villains and rewarding the good,
> He comes to check the records when you die;
> In charge of rebirth into the Six Kinds of Existence,
> He is enfeoffed as the Demon Judge of the Old City.
>
> At his temple where the streets meet,
> The evil demons of the five directions gather.
> He beheaded the *Sang* God in the Golden Hall,
> And is enfeoffed as the venerable Golden God of
>   the Five Ways.
>
> The pearls of the Literary Duke Han [Yu] are densely strung,[54]
> The yellow thread is tightly tied around his waist.
> Because he was impartial and just,
> He was enfeoffed as the Earth God of this village.

---

52. Du Xuede, *Yan Zhao*, p. 45; idem, "Guyi," p. 165.
53. Du Xuede, *Yan Zhao*, pp. 45–46.
54. 密系; the translation is tentative.

Their ancestral tombs were in Tangyin county,[55]
When they played gongs and drums, it was not to the point of
    arousing martial passions.[56]
Because they were honest and impartial,
They were enfeoffed as the four Grand Defenders (*tai wei*).

There are four gods who do not part from the sun,
Transforming like Heaven,[57] moving like the wind.
They control the year's four seasons,
The four *Zhi* Gods of the year, month, day, and hour.

In this world he brings order to the realm,
After you die, you appear before him.
Because he was honest and impartial,
He was enfeoffed as our county's City God.

Yesterday the *Zhi* Gods descended from the remotest heaven;
The hooves of their horses scattered the clouds of the
    four directions.
Before them came the Little Demon, leading the way;
Then came the Military Judge, following along behind.
Earth God, Five Ways, the four *Zhi* Gods,[58]
And the City God of the county town all came to invite
    the god [the Dragon King].

As auspicious clouds float in the clear sky
We offer fresh tea and fruit to the god.
Playing a melody of unearthly beauty,
We invite the honored god to ascend to his temple.[59]

This text is for the most part an introduction to the gods who issue
the invitation to the Dragon King, there in the flesh, so to speak, played
by villagers wearing masks and costumes. Thus, although it originally

---

55. In Henan, about 100 km south-southeast of Guyi.

56. Du Xuede's proposed emendation (*Yan Zhao*, p. 20, *n*4) is excessively complicated; it seems better to simply drop the 道, since there is an extra syllable in the line in
any case.

57. The text reads 化如天邊; 天邊 is used a few lines later in a context where it
must mean something like "Heaven."

58. Reading 四 for 司.

59. Du Xuede, *Yan Zhao*, pp. 19–20, 46–47.

took place in a temple and had a ritual purpose, this segment is more akin to a Mask Tableau than to a prayer or invocation. When the text speaks of a god, it is referring to one of the masked and costumed villagers gathered at the Dragon King's temple, not to a divine being— or rather, to both at once. As with the Mamazi exorcist in Xinzhuang, this theatricalization of the divine effectively erases the distinction between deity and actor. (These deities, who appear over and over during the ritual, are for the most part divine officers concerned with the administration of the Other World, not gods with distinctive personalities or histories. This is the type of deity favored by the educated elite. Han Yu's recruitment as the local Earth God also points to literati involvement.)[60]

After the Staff-holder recited the invitation, more spirit money was burned, and the *Shê* Head, the Staff-holder, and the villagers portraying the gods made obeisance to the Dragon King. Then his spirit tablet was taken to the Hall of the Immortal, where it was placed beside a spirit tablet representing all the gods.[61] (In earlier times, there were over sixty spirit tablets on the altar, representing all the gods who had come to the festival.)[62]

While the representatives of Big West Shê were inviting the Dragon King, a troupe made up of performers from the other three wards went to the Goddess Temple south of the village—the place where the mask of Third Master White Eyebrows had been stored—to invite the wooden statues of the three Third Masters, which were also kept there: Third Master White Eyebrows (Bai Mei San Lang), Third Master White Face (Bai Mian San Lang), and Third Master Red Peak (Chi Feng San Lang). After receiving incense and obeisance, the statues were brought to the Scroll Matshed, where the mask of Third Master White Eyebrows had been brought two days earlier. The statues were placed on

----

60. Han's native place was far away from Guyi, just inside the Great Wall near the sea at Changli 昌黎. He seems not to have had a connection with Guyi.

61. Du Xuede, *Yan Zhao*, p. 46.

62. This is reminiscent of the practice at the great *sai*, as we shall see, and also at Renzhuang's New Year ceremony. Du implies (ibid., p. 15) that a single collective tablet is now used because the Hall of the Immortal has been replaced in whole or in part by a workshop, and hence there is less altar space.

each end of an altar on which the tablets of the Gods of the Five Grains, the Dragon Kings of the Five Directions, All the Gods, the Gods of Wind, Rain, Thunder, and Lightning, and the Gods Participating in the New Year Ceremonies had already been placed.[63]

Later in the day there was a gigantic procession of all the performers in what amounted to a dress rehearsal. This was called "Brightening the Brains" (*liang naozi*). The scale of the New Year activities at Guyi is apparent from the roster of participants. For Big West Shê, the procession consisted of a banner reading "Big West Shê of Guyi," with the name of the village written 顧義, said to be an older form;[64] a large frame drum, a hall drum, two large cymbals, two hall gongs, and two "clearing the way" gongs; one greeting banner, four hexagonal lanterns, six flying tiger banners, two six-foot-tall signs reading "Directorate of Education," two reading "Tribute Student," one reading "Court Gentleman for Promoted Service," and one reading "Gentleman for Good Service";[65] two parasols, one yellow and one blue, each seven feet tall, and a giant fan, eight feet tall; a pair of "clearing the way" signs, each with a five-foot handle and a tall green placard reading "Third Master—Spiritual Penetration," a pair of five-foot-long red-painted cudgels, a pair of "golden melons" (a type of mace), a pair of battle axes, a pair of "heaven-facing stools," a pair of halberds, a pair of long-handled knives, and a pair of "dragon heads" (presumably another type of weapon); plus all the actors in the *Dui*, the Mask Tableaux, and the *Sai* Operas in full costume, together with the Staff-holder and the two Scouts, one dressed all in white, the other in black, both mounted on horses.

Then came the Liu Village Ward delegation. It was led by a banner with the word "Liu" on it and comprised a thirty-man martial arts troupe plus five men performing the Boat on Dry Land, stilt-walkers costumed as characters from *Journey to the West*, two men playing Galloping

---

63. Ibid., p. 46.
64. Ibid., p. 7.
65. The title Gentleman for Good Service (*xiu zhi lang*) ceased to be used after the Ming, according to Hucker's *Dictionary of Official Titles in Imperial China*, no. 2611. Is its use here a Ming survival?

Donkeys, twenty schoolchildren singing *yangge*, twenty others perform-ing The Tyrant's Whip, five lion dancers, a Galloping Pig, a Pigsy Car-rying His Daughter-in-Law on His Back, a decorated cart, a Refugees Pushing a Cart, a Pepper-Tree Spirit, and (as mentioned above) a No-body Official Riding a Lofty Palanquin.

They were followed by a 100-man martial arts group from the East-ern Wang Ward with a banner saying "United-in-Obedience Troupe of Guyi." That ward also provided a Flower Cart, a Galloping Donkey, characters from *Journey to the West*, a Sesame Official troupe, thirty schoolchildren performing songs and dances, a large team of dragon dancers, and four men playing martial music.

The Southern Wang Ward contingent brought up the rear of the procession. They were led by a banner with the words "Middle South-ern Region" and had a martial arts troupe of thirty, a percussion troupe of six, four lion dancers and their musicians, the performers in the bamboo horse skit, a Donkey Galloping to Mother's House, a Sesame Official, twenty schoolchildren performing The Tyrant's Whip, thirty schoolchildren singing *yangge*,[66] four singers of *sanjuban*,[67] and two men performing "Selling Ointment."[68]

This enormous procession set off from the west end of Front Street and headed east through the village. As it passed the Hall of the Im-mortal, all the riders dismounted, and the Staff-holder recited again the invitation used at the Dragon King's temple, although this time it was probably directed at all the gods. The procession went out through the east gate, returned via Rear Street, and dispersed. It was, as I have said, a dress rehearsal, an opportunity for the *Shê* Heads to make sure that all the costumes were in order and the performers well prepared. With this, the preliminaries were complete, and the ritual proper ready to begin.[69]

---

66. It is possible to sense a connection between the large contingent of school-children and the fact that the prime mover in the revival of the festival was once the principal of a nearby primary school.

67. I have not been able to identify this.

68. This description of the procession is based on the statement that every per-former took part (Du Xuede, *Yan Zhao*, p. 46, plus the full roster given on pp. 15–19).

69. Ibid., pp. 46–47.

FIRST DAY:
Killing the Yellow Demon and
Other Performances

Very early on the morning of the fifteenth, the Big Demon, the Junior Demon, the Scouts, and twenty villagers armed with willow clubs assembled at the ancestral hall of the Li lineage, where they put on their costumes and walked past a bonfire in the courtyard. Thus purified, they went to the Hall of the Immortal and then to the Jade Emperor's Matshed, where they invited the Jade Emperor and all the other gods to the festival. After they returned to the Li lineage hall, an elaborate process combining the exorcism of demons and the welcoming of gods began. The two Scouts rode out about a kilometer from the village in each of the cardinal directions and returned, then rode out half a kilometer and returned, and finally rode out just to the village boundary. This was to welcome the gods. At the same time, the Big Demon, the Junior Demon, and the twenty men armed with willow clubs drove away evil influences. The gang went out about half a kilometer from the village in each direction, making four sorties in all, and then went through all the village streets. After this, the Demons and the Scouts returned to the Hall of the Immortal, made obeisance to the spirit tablets, and announced that the gods had been welcomed, evil influences driven away, and all preparations completed. By that time it was around 6:30 A.M.[70]

At 7:00 A.M., all the performers of non-operatic acts assembled at the Hall of the Three Teachings, outside the East Gate. There they lined both sides of the street leading from the Hall to Front Street. The Big Demon and the Junior Demon, accompanied by the Hopping Demon, who moved by jumping back and forth, brought the Yellow Demon out of the Hall and along the path formed by the two lines of performers.[71] The faces of the first two were painted with a swirling pattern of black and white lines, and they wore wigs of long unkempt

---

70. Ibid., pp. 47–48.

71. We are not told when the Yellow Demon was put in the Hall of the Three Teachings.

gray hair and yellow costumes painted with stylized black tiger stripes. (See Fig. 7.) The Hopping Demon wore a broad-brimmed hat and a blue robe covered with embroidery, his makeup was black sand on a white base, and he carried a sign of command. The Yellow Demon was an utterly depraved creature who had killed his parents and committed other monstrous crimes. His face and body were smeared with a yellowish substance and he wore yellow-orange shorts and a short-sleeved yellow shirt. He was pulled along by a chain looped about his neck and stage knives pierced his arms and legs. His hair was in disarray, his face wore an expression at once corrupt and moronic, and his whole body trembled.[72]

The idea was that the Yellow Demon had been captured—presumably during the early morning sweep by the Big Demon, the Junior Demon, and the twenty villagers—and was now being taken to the divine judge for sentencing. As the two chief demons dragged him along, he was tormented by the Hopping Demon. A way was cleared through the press of people by the two mounted Scouts, who earlier had gone out to welcome the gods. The whole assembly progressed slowly along Front Street toward the west gate, where the opera performers were waiting. The augmented procession then headed for the Jade Emperor's Matshed, where the Yellow Demon seems to have been left for the time being. Meanwhile, the actors got ready to perform the *Dui* called *Cen Peng and Ma Wu Contend to Be Top Graduate*.[73]

Cen Peng, a brief farce, was performed on the ground in front of the Jade Emperor's Matshed. The characters wore conventional Chinese opera makeup and costumes[74] and recited their own lines. The action is set in the reign of Wang Mang (A.D. 9–23), at the first military examination to have been held in eight years. Cen and Ma are the only two candidates found worthy, and they match each other feat for feat until Ma finally loses on what seems a technicality, accuses Cen of bribery, and

---

72. *Zhonghua xiqu* 18 (1996.5), fourth color photograph; Du Xuede, *Yan Zhao*, pp. 48–49; idem, "Guyi," pp. 152, 149.

73. The Demons were invited to stop at houses where evil influences were felt to be at large, since their presence could put demons to flight or at the very least bring good luck (Du Xuede, *Yan Zhao*, p. 49; idem, "Guyi," p. 153).

74. *Zhonghua xiju* 18 (1996.5), eighth color photograph.

goes off in a huff.[75] The work is simply light entertainment with no detectable lesson to teach, not unlike several of the skits in Renzhuang's
Shangu shenpu.

Before the performance began, the Staff-holder issued an invitation
to the Jade Emperor identical to the one issued earlier to the Dragon
King (see above, pp. 106–7). The Staff-holder then told the Little
Green-Faced Demon to place an incense tray on the altar and bow to
the Jade Emperor. The *Shê* Heads placed lighted incense on it, and a
memorial called "Inviting the Superior Sage" was burned. The Green-
Faced Demon then mimed mounting a horse, "opening the way," in-
specting the area, and rejoining the other gods.

This was the first of the *Dui*, and it was followed by two Mask Tableaux, just as simple, called *The Four Zhi* and *The Four [Grand] Defenders.*[76] In each, the masked actors entered and acted out bowing to the
Jade Emperor, mounting their horses, making an inspection, and returning. The Staff-holder introduced each of these skits, but we are not
given his lines.[77] Here again we see the gods brought to life by village
actors, the theatricalization of the divine. And recall that the Jade Emperor, before whom these brief skits were performed, was also a villager in costume.

The masks worn in these and other Mask Tableaux were kept in the
village storehouse and taken down, cleaned, and offered incense on
the twelfth of the first month by the *Shê* Heads.[78] Because they were
unusually large and had strong—not to say grotesque—features, they
create a striking impression even in snapshots; in real life they must
have been awesome, even frightening. (See Fig. 6.) This is particularly
true of Duke Guan and the Thirteenth Prince in *Levying Demon Soldiers,*
whose masks were disturbingly bizarre.[79] With only a very few exceptions, the masks represented gods, including the City God, Guan Di,

---

75. Du Xuede, *Yan Zhao*, pp. 82–86.

76. The word *diao* 刁, when it appears in Mask Tableaux titles, means "wear the costume of" or "to be costumed as," and I have not attempted to translate it. It does not
appear to be used in this sense in the titles of standard operas.

77. Du Xuede, *Yan Zhao*, pp. 39, 49–50.

78. Ibid., p. 23.

79. See the photograph in Du Xuede, *Yan Zhao*, p. 152.

Third Master White Eyebrows, the Star of Longevity, the "military" god of wealth Zhao Gongming and his tiger, the regular God of Wealth, the Stove Lord, the Judge, the Four *Zhi*, the Four Grand Defenders, the Earth God, the God of the Five Ways, the Ox King, the Horse Ancestor, the Small Green-Faced Demon, and Tan shen.[80] There are no strictly local gods in this group, with the sole exception of Third Master White Eyebrows. Nor are they Buddhist, Daoist, or sectarian. On the contrary, all are familiar mainstream popular deities. It is as if the barbaric nature of the central act left no psychic space for anything but the most domesticated gods to be portrayed in the other performances.

After the preliminary Mask Tableaux ended, the other three wards presented some of their acts, such as lion dancing and stilt walking, in the arenas just south of the Jade Emperor's Matshed.[81] During those performances, all the Big West Shê performers, including the three demon guards of the Yellow Demon, accompanied by their gongs, drums, banners, and signs, went in procession to the Li lineage hall. Yama, ruler of the Underworld, and his Judge, who were waiting there, were then escorted by the whole crew to the stages constructed for them to the east of the Jade Emperor's Matshed, due south of the west gate, Yama enjoying the dignity of a yellow parasol, the Judge of a blue one. They took their seats behind their respective altar tables—again the sense of gods come to life—while the performers went back to the Jade Emperor's Matshed to get the Yellow Demon. After the minor entertainments ended, all the performers again formed two lines, as they had earlier when the Yellow Demon was taken from the Hall of the Three Teachings, and the three Demons, supported by eighty club-wielding villagers, harried the Yellow Demon amid the roaring of the packed crowd from the Jade Emperor's Matshed to the Judge's Stage. When they arrived, the Judge unrolled the scroll on which his judgment was written and displayed it to the crowd. The Yellow Demon was then

---

80. Du Xuede, *Yan Zhao*, pp. 22–23. I have been unable to find information on Tan shen (lit., "the *Tan* god"). Other gods that almost certainly were represented by actors wearing masks, including Guanyin, are mentioned on p. 54.

81. The statement in ibid., p. 50, that these were performed at the same time as the *Dui* cannot be correct; in any case it is contradicted in the next paragraph.

Fig. 6 Performers in Guyi's *Dui* Opera (SOURCE: Du Xuede, *Yan Zhao*).

Fig. 7 Yellow Demon with his guards, the Big Demon and Little Demon
(SOURCE: Du Xuedu, "Guyi").

dragged to Yama's Stage, a few yards away. The Staff-holder read the judgment and said, "Shackle him and take him to the Southern Stage; pull out his guts and skin him!"[82]

After this hair-raising command, the Staff-holder sang a most revealing verse from Yama's Stage:

> I exhort all of you not to deceive your parents and forget who
>   gave you life.
> If you are obstinate and unfilial, the Lord of the Ten Courts of Hell
>   [Yama] will find it hard to forgive you.
> He will command the two Demons to tie you up and take you
>   to the Southern Stage, where you will be gutted and flayed!
> In the end good and evil each have their recompense; how can
>   you be human and not honor your father and mother!
> If you want to know the name of this *Dui* Opera, it is "The Lord
>   of the Ten Courts Pulls Out Guts."[83]

The use of ritual opera to reinforce community values could not be more obvious. However, it is extremely significant that the Staff-holder explicitly refers to the Yellow Demon's judgment and execution as an opera. Indeed, the Staff-holder's very presence on the stage, commenting on the action, aligned this performance with the other Mask Tableaux and *Dui* in the minds of the audience. They were being reminded, in effect, that what they were watching was "only a play." This was taken to another level when the audience members were told that if they were unfilial, they would be "taken to the Southern Stage"—not Hell—and executed. Were they to imagine that divine judgment was meted out on a temporary stage outside their own village? This seems a contradiction in terms; but then, so does the alternative: that their punishment for being unfilial would be no more than a play. Once again, the boundaries between religion and drama collapse—this time creating deep ambiguities.[84]

---

82. Du Xuede, "Guyi," pp. 153–54; idem, *Yan Zhao*, p. 50. That the Staff-holder read the judgment is clear from the video.

83. Du Xuede, *Yan Zhao*, p. 21.

84. The ambiguities may seem more severe to us than to the intended audience, but they must have been there even for the villagers. Very few Chinese rituals or operas, especially those presented to rural audiences, called attention to their own theatricality.

This ambiguity may have had a purpose. Scapegoat figures are too common in the New Year rituals we have looked at to ignore the possibility that at one time communal exorcisms included human sacrifice. If Guyi's "Yellow Demon" ritual did indeed have such grisly origins, the theatrical version powerfully illustrates a point I have made elsewhere: that by late imperial times ritual had been partly displaced by opera as the bedrock of Chinese symbolic culture. If there had at one time been an annual ritual in Guyi that involved the sadistic murder of a scapegoat, it had been replaced by a theatrical representation of such a killing. Thus the theatricalization of Chinese culture naturally led also to its humanization.

After the Staff-holder's verse, the Yellow Demon was dragged off to the Southern Stage, followed by the entire population of the village in a frenzy of excitement. The Yellow Demon and his guards mounted the open platform, which was surrounded by the villagers with their clubs, the masked gods, the martial arts troupes, all the other performers of the four wards, and the entire population of the village. Suddenly the Big Demon and the Junior Demon began striking the Yellow Demon with their weapons, chicken guts soaked in red fluid were pulled from a bag concealed in the Yellow Demon's shorts and flourished in the air, and thick smoke boiled up, obscuring the scene. While the stage was hidden in smoke, the floorboards were pulled apart, and the Yellow Demon dropped into the curtained space beneath it. When the smoke cleared, he was gone.[85]

The performers, followed by the villagers, then returned to the village for an elaborate victory celebration. Six altars called "incense and paper [i.e., spirit money] tables" had been set up at the Scroll Matshed in the Guanyin Temple, the Hall of the Immortal, and elsewhere. At each altar, the *Shê* Heads burned a memorial announcing the punishment of the Yellow Demon, and the Staff-holder sang a verse, such as the following:

> The divine carriage has left Heaven and descended to
>   this mortal world.
> We respectfully welcome all the gods to our village,

---

85. Du Xuede, "Guyi," p. 154; idem, *Yan Zhao*, pp. 50–51. In these descriptions I am also drawing on the video of the ritual supplied to me by Wang Ch'iu-kuei.

> We make offerings of incense on bended knee to
>   Heaven and Earth.
> We offer wine to the Dragon God in celebration
>   of the rich harvest [to come].[86]

It was then around 2:00 P.M., and everyone dispersed for a few hours of rest.[87]

Later in the afternoon a Mask Tableau and a *Sai* Opera were presented on the village stage, and in the evening another pair was performed at the same location. The *Sai* Operas were familiar titles in the standard northern local opera repertoire, *Changban Slope* (*Changban po*) and *Tiger Pen Pass* (*Hulao guan*), and are of little interest. But the two Mask Tableaux are far from familiar and are extremely interesting.

The one presented in the afternoon has the title *"Stealing a Horse"—Fifteen Man Troupe* in the manuscript.[88] The Staff-holder enters and, after adjusting his hat and striking a pose, recites the following verse:[89]

> The blossoms of the pear tree fill the courtyard,
> The battle flags hang limp, the pennons furled.
> If you would know great peace with no killing,
> Men of great peace celebrating years of great peace,
> Then seldom raise the hurtful sword,
> And constantly whet the blade of self-control.
> When the world relies on Heavenly Principle (*tian li*),
> Disasters naturally vanish.[90]

Next a fisherman and a woodcutter, conventional figures of detachment from the world, meet, talk, and part, with the fisherman advising

---

86. Du Xuede, "Guyi," p. 156.

87. Ibid., pp. 154, 156; Du Xuede, *Yan Zhao*, p. 51.

88. We have both the script and a description of the action: Du Xuede, *Yan Zhao*, pp. 72–74, 36–37, respectively.

89. Three other Mask Tableaux, two of which—*Levying Demon Soldiers* and *Introducing the Eight Immortals*—were of considerable ritual importance, begin in almost identical fashion.

90. Du Xuede, *Yan Zhao*, p. 72; also p. 36. The appeal to the central Neo-Confucian concept of Heavenly Principle suggests the involvement of educated men at some stage in the composition of this liturgy, as surely as does Han Yu's appearance as the Earth God.

his friend not to concern himself with petty affairs. Then the Staff-holder motions the main characters, Guan Di and Tan shen, onto the stage. Guan Di sits on a chair placed on a table at the rear of the stage; thus the actor playing this part is elevated well above the stage, strengthening the resemblance to a statue of a god in a temple. Tan shen makes an inspection, bows, and offers incense to the god. At this point a *Shê* Head enters with a memorial, which is read and burned:[91]

FIFTEENTH, [AFTER]NOON, TEXT ON "STEALING A HORSE," TO BE BURNED BEFORE THE TABLET OF THE SUPERIOR SAGE GUAN[92]

Today, the *Shê* Heads _____, of _____ village, Wu'an county,[93] Zhangde prefecture, Henan [province] of the Great Qing, leading the men of their *shê* in respectfully offering gifts of incense, spirit money, and many delicacies as sacrifices before the seat of the august sage, say:

> A myriad sages gather like clouds,
> Ritual distinguishes the noble and base.
> The common people are ignorant,
> Knowing nothing of the causes [of things].
> We gaze up at the venerable god,
> Every one in his proper place.
> Above, below, left, right,
> There we take our places!
> Reverently preparing the offerings,
> Worshipfully presenting them at the jade steps,
> With a myriad wishes for the descent of blessings.
> Awaiting the moisture [of your beneficence] amid
>   the dust [of the world],
> We humbly ask that you partake of the offerings.

The Shê Heads _____ make obeisance.[94]

---

91. Du's account does not say it was read.

92. The title suggests that there was a spirit tablet. There was none at the village stage, but there *were* tablets at the Hall of the Immortal. Were these Mask Tableaux performed there before the war?

93. Wu'an was the county with jurisdiction over Guyi.

94. Du Xuede, *Yan Zhao*, pp. 64–65. The condescending reference to the "common people" once again hints at literati involvement in the development of the script.

Then the performance shifts from the liturgical to the dramatic again, as the Staff-holder briefly narrates the high points of Guan Yu's life. He asks in what dynasty the events took place, and answers "*The Historical Romance of the Three Kingdoms*."[95] When the Staff-holder reaches the story of Yan Zhao's attempt to avenge his father's death at the hands of Guan Yu, the narration becomes more detailed, and Guan Di, the god, descends from his elevated seat to take on the role of the historical Guan Yu contending with Yan Zhao.[96] The two characters mime combat as the Staff-holder continues his narration. When Yan is at last vanquished, the Staff-holder launches into an encomium (*zan*) of Guan Di listing his triumphs and giving his noble title.[97]

There is nothing about stealing a horse in what we have read so far, nor are fifteen performers required. The answer to the conundrum this poses is suggested by the lines that follow the end of the action:

The dragon-and-phoenix carriage descends from Heaven; wine, fruit, and fragrant tea are all prepared. We offer a piece of melodious music, "Guan Di Steals a Horse in the Thick Pine Wood." (Fifteen members of the troupe in all: the Four *Zhi*, the Four [Grand] Defenders, Zhou Cang, Guan Ping, Yan Zhao [who takes a robe and carries a belt], Zhao, Lu, and Wang, supplemented by Tan shen.)[98]

Evidently in the original version, some sort of performance that featured Guan Yu stealing a horse was presented immediately after this prologue. What is striking is that there is no such incident in the novel or in the better-known operas based on it. It probably derived from a local operatic or storytelling tradition, like the scene with Yan Zhao.[99]

---

95. Du Xuede, *Yan Zhao*, p. 72. The functional meaning of the term *yanyi* is something like "historical novel." One could not ask for a better illustration of the fusing of history and fiction in popular consciousness.

96. Yan Zhao and this scene are not in the current versions of *The Romance of the Three Kingdoms*. The text is probably drawing here on a local dramatic tradition.

97. For the script, see Du Xuede, *Yan Zhao*, pp. 72–74.

98. This translation is very tentative. Tan shen is considered supplementary presumably because Guan Yu is counted among the fifteen, even though he is not listed. I am indebted to Stephen West for helping me understand the probable function of this passage.

99. This conclusion is based on a search of Shen Bojun et al., *San Guo yanyi cidian*.

Du's reports give no hint of what *Stealing a Horse* was like, but I suspect that it was something like a static tableau showing a well-known scene from a local opera of that title. If this is true, it suggests deep local sources, offsetting the hints of literati influence mentioned above.

Catching the Yellow Demon proceeds without words except for Yama's execution order and the moral pronounced by the Staff-holder. There is no ambiguity on the level of the primary action—an evil creature is killed and morality is both served and taught. *Stealing a Horse*, by contrast, is an offering, not an exorcism, and its point would have been incomprehensible without the Staff-holder's narration. It seems to have nothing of the cathartic quality of *Catching the Yellow Demon*; instead, it is a combination of prayer and exhortation that suddenly takes on dramatic form, something found in many other local community rituals. The focus is on Guan Di, one of the chief gods of the village,[100] and the bulk of the Staff-holder's lines are a rehearsal of his great deeds. This is at once hagiography and (operatic) history—Guan Yu's exploits were familiar to everyone from popular opera and stories, yet in this setting they were also the actions of the village god. At the outset the deity is seated on a raised throne, like his statue in the village temple, and the *Shê* Head makes offerings to him (or at least speaks as if offerings are to be made), just as would be done during rituals in his temple.[101] But then Guan Di descends from his throne and assumes the persona of the theatrical Guan Yu, to do battle with Yan Zhao.

Hence this Mask Tableau is both a ritual and a masked drama; there is a complete fusion of ritual and opera. The actions recounted by the narrator are not miracles, or supernatural transformations, or epiphanies, but simply the exploits of a great warrior who is firmly embedded (as far as the audience was concerned) in history. So there is a fusion also of history and cult, with the inevitable consequence that the

---

100. Du Xuede, *Yan Zhao*, p. 10, tells us that the Guan Di Temple at one time owned 45 *mou* of land, which was lent for short terms to farmers who had lost their land.

101. Our sources do not describe the actual presentation of offerings, even though they are explicitly mentioned in the memorial of sacrifice. It is difficult to decide whether this is further evidence of theatricality, or whether the ceremony has lost something here in its restored form.

actions of the historical Guan Yu and the orthodox values they exemplify take on divine authority. This is precisely analogous to the great Mulian operas of south China, although on a much smaller scale.[102]

The manuscript of the "memorial" recited by the *Shê* Head has blanks for not only the name of the officiant but also the name of the village. This means that the liturgical manuscripts in the possession of the former Staff-holder Li Qilai were not intended for use exclusively in Guyi, but in other villages in Wu'an county as well. This probably was also true of the opera scripts. And yet the role of Staff-holder was hereditary in Guyi and not filled by an outside expert as in the multivillage *sai* of southeastern Shanxi. Did Guyi's Staff-holder perform in the smaller villages that fell under its jurisdiction as an administrative village? Perhaps we have here an example of how the ritual forms of a single village could begin to spread through a wider area. Or possibly someone in Guyi obtained a collection of ritual texts and used one of them in constructing the village New Year rituals. Obviously village ritual autarky was not absolute.

On the evening of the fifteenth, another fascinating Mask Tableau was performed. It is entitled *"Levying Demon Soldiers"—Thirteen Man* [*Troupe*]. It is similar in form to *Stealing a Horse*, and presents similar puzzles (along with some uniquely its own). Its prologue is identical to that of *Stealing a Horse*, with an opening poem in praise of peace and Heavenly Principle and an appearance by a fisherman and a woodcutter. Third Master White Eyebrows probably enters and seats himself on a raised chair after this segment. Following this, Tan shen arrives, makes his inspection, and reports. Then a memorial is burned. (As with "Stealing a Horse," we have the text.)[103] Two offerings are presented to the Third Master: a long-handled demon-terrifying mace made of gold, silver, and jade, and a *Dui* called *Levying Demon Soldiers*. As in *Stealing a Horse*, the narrator states that the action of the opera takes place in a period named after a novel: "the time of *The Historical Romance of the*

---

102. See Johnson, "Actions Speak Louder Than Words"; and idem, "Mu-lien in *Pao-chüan.*"

103. Du Xuede, *Yan Zhao*, p. 66. It has a fill-in-the-blanks date with the Guangxu reign-name.

Spring and Autumn Warring States" [sic],[104] and then continues with a biography of the Third Master. Thus historical fiction is equated with history in both of these ritual playlets. But Third Master White Eyebrows is a historical figure in only the most tenuous sense, unlike Guan Yu in *Stealing a Horse*, and what the Staff-holder presents here is essentially the hagiography of the most important god of the village, or at least of the New Year festival.[105] The god's biography is calmly equated with historical fiction; evidently the distinction was not considered important. This parallels the fusion of (real) cult and (imaginary) opera, a theme we have been following throughout this section.

According to the script, "the Lord" (*lao ye*), as he is called throughout the text, is the thirteenth son of King Zhuang of Qin. He has fled the kingdom of Jin (modern Shanxi) after killing a villain there—once again a connection with Shanxi—and is being pursued by Jin soldiers when he comes to Zhendian village in Tangshan county, Xunde prefecture.[106] Hearing the clamor of gongs and drums, he asks what the occasion is. The *Oumen*[107] replies: "The village is making offerings (*sai*) to Heaven and Earth and sacrificing to the Dragon God." The prince says, "It is a virtuous act." He then tells the story of his flight from Jin and asks to be hidden from his pursuers. The *Oumen* suggests a ruse: let the prince put on a mask and costume and hide among the *sai* performers. Thus the real Third Master is in his temple; a villager playing the role of Third Master is on stage, receiving offerings in a posture like that of the god in his temple; and this character watches a re-enactment of an episode in the life of the man who would become the Third Master in

---

104. No such novel exists.

105. It is interesting to note that in "Guyi," Du Xuede, when recounting the legend of the god's origins, attributes it to "old village performers," evidently not realizing that they were simply telling him what was in their opera. Other local "oral" traditions may also have had their source in opera or fiction.

106. Xunde was abolished in the Republic. Tangshan county was probably abolished sometime in the early Republic also; *Zhongguo diming da cidian* 中國地名大辭典 (1931) lists it, but atlases of the mid-twentieth century and later, such as *Zhonghua minguo dituji* 中華民國地圖集 (1961), do not. It is almost certainly the modern Yaocheng 堯城, about eighty km north-northeast of Wu'an county in southwest Hebei. (Du [*Yan Zhao*, p. 24] mistakenly identifies it with Longyao 隆堯 county, not far from Yaocheng.)

107. I have not been able to discover what this term means.

which he puts on a mask and costume during a village ritual much like the one in which the whole performance is embedded.

When the Jin soldiers arrive, they too ask about the music and are given the same answer. They too say the ritual is a virtuous thing, adding that "it can only lead to peace,[108] it will not cause disorder." After they leave, the *Oumen* gives the prince a horse and he makes his escape. When he reaches Magpie Goose Mountain (Que'e shan), south of Guyi, he falls ill and sores erupt all over his body, but the God of Medicine appears and gives him two pills, one red and one white, which cure him. Afterward, his eyebrows turn white and are so long they hang down below his chin.[109] This section of the script ends by stating that he "was transformed" (became a god) on Magpie Goose Mountain.

The focus then shifts to an emperor with the unlikely name of Third Younger Brother Zhengzong (*san di Zhengzong*), who visits an unnamed temple at an unspecified time to pray for a son. When he passes Magpie Goose Mountain, the Third Master creates a violent windstorm, from the midst of which the tinkling of his horse's bells can be clearly heard. The emperor asks what god is there and hears a voice say "I was a general of the Warring States period; I have come to protect Your Majesty." The emperor returns to the palace and orders a search for such a god among the seventy-two "offices" (*si*) of the temple (of the Eastern Peak?).[110] When no such god can be found, the emperor creates a new "office" and enfeoffs the god as chief inspector of the Bureau of the Throat (*Yanhou si du xun'an*). At this point, the narrator gives a brief reprise of Third Master White Eyebrows' career, and the play ends with these lines: "He likes to ride a white horse and wear red robes; he manifests his awesome spiritual power at Magpie Goose Mountain. Holding a mace with which to scatter the incense smoke, Third Master White Eyebrows Levies Demon Soldiers."[111]

---

108. Literally, "the dispersing of troops."

109. Earlier in his book, Du (*Yan Zhao*, p. 24) gives a local legend about the prince's illness: it was the villagers who provided the medicine, and after he recovered he did much good for them. His cult began when the grateful villagers made a statue of him and placed it in the Goddess Temple on Magpie Goose Mountain.

110. See ibid., p. 71, *n*2.

111. The entire text of the opera may be found in ibid., pp. 70–72.

The first section of this script recounts the origin legend of an important local deity, Third Master White Eyebrows, and the second provides an account of his admission into the orthodox pantheon and an explanation of his official title, "Chief Inspector of the Bureau of the Throat." The patron deity of the hereditary caste of ritual Entertainers (*yuehu*) of southeastern Shanxi was the Throat God (Yanhou shen).[112] There were temples to Yanhou in the county towns of Gaoping, Lingchuan, Changzhi, and Xinxian.[113] A Yanhou temple still exists in the village of East Chenzhanggou in northwestern Lingchuan county, which is in extreme southeastern Shanxi, about 100 km from Guyi. This was one of the most important temples of the Shanxi Entertainers, who conducted elaborate rituals there every year on the eighth day of the twelfth lunar month.[114] Unfortunately, all the stelae were destroyed in the Cultural Revolution,[115] and much of the history of the temple has been irrevocably lost, but some surviving wooden inscription boards provide precious information.[116] One gives two titles or attributes of the god: "Chief Supervisor of Instruction of the Thirty-third Heaven; Throat God of the Seventy-two [ ]."[117] Another says: "The Song emperor Zhenzong enfeoffed him as Throat [ ]."[118] Another fragment says "In recompense for his goodness in healing Zhenzong's throat." And finally: "Snowy brilliance shines from white eyebrows; the divine

---

112. *Zhongguo xiqu zhi: Shanxi juan*, p. 143.

113. Xiang Yang, *Shanxi yuehu yanjiu*, p. 153. For a report on the remains of the Yanhou temple in Gaoping city, see Han Sheng et al., eds., *Shangdang nuo wenhua*, pp. 639–41; a stele from it is reproduced on p. 60.

114. *Zhongguo xiqu zhi: Shanxi juan*, p. 143. For a report on this temple, see Yuan Shuangxi and Li Shoutian, "Fang Lingchuan xian." (The character 犬 in the article's title is an unfortunate typo for 丈.) There is a photograph of the temple and objects from it in Han Sheng et al., eds., *Shangdang nuo wenhua*, pp. 62–63.

115. Yuan Shuangxi and Li Shoutian, "Fang Lingchuan xian," p. 545.

116. Ibid., p. 546.

117. Yuan and Li (ibid.) have 罡 here, which I suspect is a mistake; note that in the text the emperor has the god searched for among the seventy-two "offices" 司.

118. In the space left blank here, Yuan and Li have *ci* 祠, which makes no sense. I suspect it should be *si* 司, because one of the local names for the god was Yanhou si 司 (Du Xuede, *Yan Zhao*, p. 72, n2), and as we have seen, he is said in the script to have been enfeoffed as *Yanhou si du xun'an*. There must be an error in the original inscription or, more likely, in the transcription.

radiance is dazzling." The god of this Yanhou temple had white eyebrows and was made head of the Throat Bureau by Emperor Zhenzong of the Song dynasty. There can be little doubt that Guyi's Third Master White Eyebrows was the same as the patron deity of the Entertainer families of Shanxi. The Zhengzong of this text is an obvious homophonic error for Zhenzong; "Third Younger Brother" must reflect the fact that Zhenzong was the third son of Song Taizong.

There was a Shanxi tradition that the Throat God was a man of the kingdom of Chu in Warring States times who after a defeat "fled into an Entertainer troupe."[119] This tradition is echoed in a recent report from Xiangyuan county in southeastern Shanxi, which is quite easily reached from Guyi. It cites local informants who said that all temple musicians and amateur instrumental troupes (of the sort that played at festivals and other ritual occasions) worshipped a god called Third Master, or Yanhou, or Chuanggeda.[120] He also lived during the Warring States period, but in the kingdom of Han, and was honored there for having invented a way of communicating on the battlefield by using flutes.[121] Third Master White Eyebrows, who on first acquaintance seems likely to be a deity of very limited range, perhaps unique to Guyi, turns out to be closely related to the patron saint of ritual musicians in Shanxi and probably southern Hebei as well, especially venerated by the hereditary Entertainer families. And the cult was supported by ordinary people too, since there is a large shrine to Yanhou in the great Jade Emperor Temple of Fucheng village, not far from the city of Jincheng in southeastern Shanxi.[122]

Levying Demon Soldiers was more than just an account of the origins and official recognition of a local god. In the script, both the fugitive who would become Third Master White Eyebrows and the Jin soldiers praise the social value of a village ritual that closely resembles Guyi's;

---

119. *Zhongguo xiqu zhi: Shanxi juan*, p. 143.

120. Strangely enough, two of the characters in the description of the ailment afflicting Third Master in *Levying Demon Soldiers*—瘡疥—are very similar to two in this name: 瘡疣. Did his disease in one version become one of his names in another?

121. Xiang Yang, *Shanxi yuehu yanjiu*, p. 148, quoting *Xiangyuan minjian yinyue* (1989, not formally published).

122. I saw the shrine on a visit in 1993.

the Third Master-to-be even puts on a mask and costume and joins the other performers. Thus were Guyi's New Year rituals legitimated, and a hint left in the air that a masked participant in the procession of gods might actually be a god. And note that the mask of the Third Master was treated by the villagers as a sacred object: it was stored in the Goddess Temple and taken in procession to the Scroll Matshed, where it was placed on an altar-like stone block before which a ritual of purification was performed. The mask of the Third Master must have shared in the supernatural potency of his statue; this made it all the easier to see the figure on stage as something closely akin to the god himself.

After the summary of Third Master's life and honors, the script ends with the words "He likes to ride a white horse and wear red robes; he manifests his spiritual power at Magpie Goose Mountain. Holding a mace with which to scatter the incense smoke, Third Master White Eyebrows Levies Demon Soldiers," the final phrase referring to the title of the tableau, which evidently was displayed immediately thereafter.[123] So, in the midst of a ritual that involved making offerings to and burning a memorial before a villager playing the role of Third Master White Eyebrows, the audience is told that a tableau featuring the Third Master is about to begin. The villager costumed as Third Master presumably left his stage throne at this point and joined the troupe of "demon soldiers." The offering to the real Third Master (if the term makes any sense at this point) thus consisted in part of an opera in which he was the leading character.

This is all rather dizzying to us, with our rigid categories of sacred and secular, reality and representation. Did it create tension in the minds of its intended audience? I doubt it. I think they felt that the carved representation of the god in his temple and the operatic representation of the god on stage were closely related: both had divine potency, both were proper objects of sacrifice. By the same token, the gods parading through their streets were something more than their neighbors wearing masks and costumes. After all, the real Third Master had at one time taken part, incognito, in precisely the sort of ritual performance they were watching at that minute.

---

123. The thirteen-man troupe of the title would have performed this.

For the audience in Guyi the distinction between ritual and theater, between deity and masked actor, became untenable, and perhaps unthinkable. This must have had two results: the awesomeness of the divine was diminished; yet any seemingly ordinary person might be a god, and any everyday event be supernatural. In addition, at certain points we see that the performances were simultaneously proceeding on two levels: naïve representation and self-conscious awareness of the act of representation. All this in the New Year celebrations of an obscure village in a remote corner of Hebei after generations of social and economic decline.

SECOND AND THIRD DAYS:
The Eight Immortals Appear;
Rituals of Closure

At 8 A.M. on the morning of the sixteenth, two *Shê* Heads, the Staffholder, percussionists, and a martial arts troupe, plus performers wearing the masks and robes of the City God, the Military Judge, the God of the Five Ways, the Earth God, and the Little Green-Faced Demon left the village and proceeded south to the foot of South Mountain to sacrifice to the Locust King and then north of the village to sacrifice to the Dragon King in charge of hail. Two men carried trays with incense and sacrificial money, and a third carried on a shoulder pole buckets filled with water in which wheat flour and millet had been sprinkled. As the water-bearer passed, all the villagers came out to offer incense, sacrificial money, and grain. On both journeys, when the entourage reached the site of the sacrifice, dirt was heaped up into a small mound, incense sticks put in it, and colored paper banners stuck in the ground around it. Then the Staff-holder recited a prayer, once again highly self-referential, once again conflating the theatrical and the divine:

> Yesterday the *Zhi* Gods descended from the remotest heaven;
> The hooves of their horses scattered the clouds of the
>   four directions.
> First came the Little Demon, leading the way;
> Then came the Military Judge, following along behind.

Earth God, Five Ways, the four *Zhi* Gods,[124]
The City God of this county—all sacrifice to the
    Locust King.
As auspicious clouds float in the clear sky,
We offer fresh tea and fruit to the god.
Playing a melody of unearthly beauty,
We invite the honored god to ascend to his temple.

Then the percussionists played, a blunderbuss and mortars were set off, the water scattered about, and the *Shê* Heads burned sacrificial money, read a prayer for blessings, and led the company in making obeisance to the god. The sacrifice to the Hail Dragon was similar, except that a white rooster was sacrificed.[125]

Starting around 9 A.M. there were many performances in the streets by the three non-elite wards, and at 3 P.M. the final pair of entertainments was presented. The *Sai* Opera was *Attacking Jing Zhou* (*Tao Jing zhou*), yet another Three Kingdoms story; the Mask Tableau was called *Introducing the Eight Immortals* (*Kai ba xian*).[126] As in the other Mask Tableaux, a memorial was burned by one of the *Shê* Heads near the beginning of the performance.[127] The tableau opens with the Star of Long Life—the presiding deity—seated on his throne. The Staff-holder recites the same auspicious prologue that prefaced *Stealing a Horse* and *Levying Demon Soldiers* and then says "Today we have the *Dui* Opera about the Eight Immortals, in which the Old Man Star descends to earth." After mentioning the Star's daily compounding of potions and pills of immortality and briefly reviewing the creation of the universe by Nüwa, the Staff-holder relates that the Eight Immortals, Laozi, and the Queen Mothers of the East and West are coming to pay their respects to the Star, presumably on his birthday. Then the Old Man Star is described—with many of the legendary attributes of Laozi as well as those of the Star of Longevity—and the Eight are introduced: "Today is the proper *sai*, broad and bright; we will present the *Dui* Opera about

---

124. Reading 四 for 司.

125. Du Xuede, *Yan Zhao*, pp. 51–52.

126. *Kai* as a stage term meaning "self-introduction" is found in Song and Jin dynasty *Za* Opera and *yuanben* (Qi Senhua et al., *Zhongguo qu xue da cidian*, p. 821).

127. Du Xuede, "Guyi," p. 161.

the Eight Immortals. Each has his own name—listen while the Leader (*qianhang*) [128] tells you who they are." After brief introductions, the Staff-holder enumerates all the blessings the *sai* will bring and concludes with a flurry of auspicious pronouncements ending "The Emperor is enlightened, the people content, the five grains luxuriant, and the granaries full."[129]

The Immortals then make their appearance, one by one, led by Lan Caihe. (They wear makeup; only the Old Man Star wears a mask.) Lan introduces himself[130] and then greets Han Zhongli, the next Immortal. They perform a brief dance, Lan goes to his place, and Han introduces himself. Then Lan comes out again to greet the next immortal, who introduces himself, and so it goes until all are onstage, half lined up on the right, half on the left, with the Star of Longevity on his throne at the center rear of the stage.[131] At the very end, a Willow Tree spirit comes on stage, introduces himself, then goes to the rear. The Staff-holder then brings the performance to a close.[132]

This Mask Tableau differs in several ways from *Stealing a Horse* and *Levying Demon Soldiers*. Only one character is masked, and other characters besides the Staff-holder speak lines. More important, the Old Man Star is not a deity like Guan Di or Third Master White Eyebrows; rather, he is an auspicious emblem like the Eight Immortals. Representations of him, with his enormously elongated head, protruding forehead, and short body, were familiar to everyone, just as representations of the Eight Immortals were. If the other Mask Tableaux brought the gods in local temples to life, this one brought popular woodblock prints to life. In fact, although this is not made explicit in the script, the entire performance can be seen as a dramatization of the print in which the

---

128. See above, p. 104, for the significance of the term "Leader."

129. Du Xuede, *Yan Zhao*, pp. 80–81.

130. Du states this explicitly (ibid., p. 81, *n*2), although in Mask Tableaux normally only the Staff-holder speaks.

131. There are in fact nine immortals in the script, not eight, and there is some deviation from the standard roster.

132. Du Xuede, *Yan Zhao*, pp. 79–82, 37–38. The script has no concluding lines for the Staff-holder, but the description on p. 38 states that he has them, and this seems likely.

Eight Immortals gather for the birthday of the Star of Longevity (*Ba xian qing shou*).[133]

This was the last New Year drama performed for the general population of Guyi. In the evening, the Southern Wang and Liu Village wards performed songs and dances at the village stage,[134] and no doubt there was lantern viewing on this and the other evenings as well, although this is not mentioned in the sources.

The seventeenth was devoted to rituals of closure. In the morning the villagers split into two groups: one returned the tablet of the Dragon King to the site of the Dragon King Temple northeast of the village, and the other took the statues of the three Third Masters[135] back to the Goddess Temple south of the village. At each place the Staff-holder intoned verses virtually identical to those used to welcome the gods on the fourteenth (the word "invite" was simply changed to "send off" throughout), a memorial was burned, incense offered, and obeisances made, after which everyone returned to the village. This was followed by a ceremony in which responsibility for the festival was formally transferred to the five *Shê* Heads who were to manage it the following year. The accounts and any surplus funds were handed over at that time.[136] A large troupe of performers in gods' masks visited the house of each of the new leaders, where the Yellow Tiger rolled around on the sleeping platform to expel evil influences and Guanyin put a cloth doll on it, symbolizing male babies. Such were the supernatural benefits that offset the very real costs of this particular kind of village leadership.

A Mask Tableau called *"Passing the Kitchen"—Troupe of Eighteen—* named for the route followed by the gods who were to take up

---

133. A print of this scene from Xinjiang county is reproduced in Bo Songnian and Duan Gaifang, *Zhongguo minjian meishu*, 4: 157. One from Hongdong county is reproduced in Zhongguo meishu xuehui, Shanxi fenhui et al., *Jinnan muban nianhua ziliao*, p. 70. Both counties are in southern Shanxi. For an impressive Qing dynasty print of the same subject, in which one can almost see the tableau staged in Guyi, see Wang Shucun, ed., *Zhongguo meishu quanji*, 21: 13.

134. Du Xuede, *Yan Zhao*, p. 53.

135. See above, p. 108.

136. Ibid.

residence in the family shrines of the new leaders—was performed for the same select group.[137] It began with a veritable roll call of the gods, most of whom are already familiar from the other Mask Tableaux: the Door Gods, the Earth God, the Stove Lord, the Horse Ancestor, the Ox King, Guan Di, Erlang, Marshal Zhao (the "military god of wealth"), the God of Wealth, and Guanyin.

> As all the gods ascend to the family shrines, they go past
>   the kitchen;[138]
> As we change the *Shê* Heads, all of them ascend to their
>   family shrines and secure their households.
> Fresh tea and good wine are arranged on the table,
> Incense and [spirit] money, treasures, and horses are
>   burned in the street outside.
> All the families of the *Shê* Heads jointly offer up prayers,
> All the gods and sages draw near.
> At the Yuanxiao Festival, we delight in the New Year,
> Wearing costumes civil and military, we drive calamity
>   and disease away.
> Raising shields and gripping lances, we perform the
>   Nuo ritual;
> The five grains will flourish, we will celebrate great peace.
> These two candles [on the offering table] illumine the world,
> These three incense sticks perfume Heaven's Terrace.
> All the *Shê* Heads make obeisance in the street
> As they welcome the divine carriage that preserves them
>   from harm.[139]

This Mask Tableau, like *Introducing the Eight Immortals*, uses only the most familiar deities, and, also like that script, it is self-referential: its subject is the very ritual of which it is a part.

---

137. Du does not mention this in his section on Mask Tableaux (ibid., pp. 36–39), nor does he list it as a *Dui* (pp. 29–30)—and all Mask Tableaux were *Dui*. Yet its title and form are very similar to Mask Tableaux such as *Levying Demon Soldiers*, and I treat it as one.

138. Reading 升 for 聖.

139. Du Xuede, *Yan Zhao*, p. 78; ibid., "Guyi," pp. 166–67. The latter has a more complete version of the text.

As the festival began with a great communal meal for the participants, so too it ended with one, at noon on the seventeenth. They ate
the same types of food they had been served at the inaugural banquet,
plus the food offerings that had been made during the ritual. This was
the last formal act of Guyi's New Year celebration.

———

From start to finish—from the driving away of evil spirits by the Scouts
and their twenty club-wielding escorts early on the fifteenth to the return of the tablet of the Dragon King and the statues of the three Third
Masters to the Goddess Temple on the seventeenth—the entire village,
not just a select group of hereditary performers, was heavily involved in
Guyi's New Year festivities. The number of performers and the variety
of acts were remarkable for a single village, and the grand processions
in which all the performers took part must have been spectacular. But
the emotional high points were surely the Mask Tableaux involving
Guan Di and Third Master White Eyebrows, both important deities in
the village, who were portrayed by villagers wearing frightening masks
of unusual size, and, above all, the capture, trial, and execution of the
Yellow Demon.

Of course the *Sai* Operas had their own significance. Like all historical operas in premodern China, they brought to life elements of the
national or regional story and, in so doing, inculcated values and ideas
at two levels. By providing memorable scenes featuring courageous
(and treacherous) generals, loyal (and corrupt) officials, and virtuous
(and evil) rulers, they gave ordinary people models of good behavior
and bad. By focusing on political and military affairs, they simply took
the institutions of the traditional state for granted, and their audiences
naturally did the same. So the *Sai* Operas were important in their
own way, but there were few of them. They carried no special ritual
or religious weight and were unlikely to have stirred the deeper emotions of the villagers. They were virtually submerged by the other
performances.

The response to the Mask Tableaux must have been quite different.
Gods and immortals appeared in them, and not in standard stage
makeup but wearing large masks that made their heads look dispropor-
tionately big. Even modern replicas in poorly reproduced photographs

can look very alarming.[140] And the villagers almost certainly believed that the masks had supernatural powers; this is clear in the case of the Third Master's mask. Moreover, those who wore the masks were silent—no human voices emerged from the masks to demystify them. Those mysterious and unsettling figures also strode through the streets of the village and observed the disemboweling of the Yellow Demon. Deities that the villagers had seen in temples since they were children came to life and walked among them, appeared on stage while their lives and deeds were recounted with pomp and circumstance, and even took roles in some performances.

Even more powerful as symbolic theater, as the tangible representation of central values and beliefs and unquestionably the emotional climax of the New Year ritual in Guyi, was the capture and barbaric execution of the Yellow Demon. It is notable that here, and only here, the meaning of the staged action was made completely explicit, in the verses spoken by the Staff-holder after Yama sent the Yellow Demon to be gutted and flayed. And what was the message? Respect and obey your parents. The Yellow Demon was a loathsome creature who committed many terrible crimes in addition to the murder of his parents, but the message preached before his punishment was simply "Don't be unfilial." In *Catching the Yellow Demon* the most effective techniques available for the inculcation of values were mobilized in the service not of enlightenment, world renunciation, universal compassion, or transcendence, but of conventional domestic morality.

Surely there is something odd here: filial piety had been preached for millennia in story, verse, and picture without the need for such a barbarous and shocking display. The means seem not only disproportionate to the end but almost antithetical to it. Bloody sacrifice, above all human sacrifice, had been opposed by the Chinese educated elite, clerical and lay, for centuries. Yet we have encountered scapegoat figures in three of the four New Year rituals looked at here: the Chicken-Feather Monkey in Aoshi, the Single-Beam Official in Sand Hill, and the Yellow Demon in Guyi. Even Renzhuang's Fan-drum ritual, clearly the most diluted and secularized of the four, had the Mamazi exorcist. The real

---

140. See Du Xuede, *Yan Zhao*, p. 152.

or simulated abuse and perhaps even killing of human scapegoats, including officials, may well have been fairly widespread at one time. But scapegoats were the living embodiment of everything the community feared and hated, not just lack of filial piety, and we are told specifically that the Yellow Demon had committed other crimes besides parricide. Thus there is a double puzzle: the disemboweling of the Yellow Demon seems an excessively violent way of promoting filial piety, and in any case the Yellow Demon was guilty of many crimes in addition to lack of filial piety. Why then did the Staff-holder explain the meaning of the opera as he did?

I suspect that it was to help bring under control the violent emotions stirred by the simulated ritual murder. I have already mentioned that the execution was explicitly labeled an opera by the Staff-holder. In addition, the Yellow Demon undergoes a legal process just as does a human being who has committed a crime. The world of superstition, demons, and savagery is being hedged around by the forces of rational morality, of legal process, of hierarchy. But it is only hedged around, not eliminated. The horrific spectacle remains, filling a need that the guardians of public morality may have been able to blunt but not eradicate.

Catching the Yellow Demon was not typical of the overall tone of Guyi's New Year celebration. The first impression one gets is that the ritual was concerned above all with the inculcation of conventional village values, which were not wholly shared by officials and the highly educated. Foremost among these was submission to parents and reverence for the gods, and those were things only the most narrow-minded local magistrates would have found fault with. Nevertheless, a visiting local official would not have felt entirely comfortable at Guyi's New Year celebration, quite apart from the barbaric spectacle of the Yellow Demon: the gods of the village's temples had come to life and were moving through the streets, alien and disturbing. Martial arts troupes, perhaps better called local defense squads, were making shows of force. Dozens of men armed with clubs were marching through the streets of the village and out into the surrounding area. And no representatives or symbols of the state were in evidence, except on stage, nor were there any Buddhist or Daoist clergy.

With so many disturbing elements present, it is not surprising that the prologue to the Mask Operas warned against resorting to armed violence and invoked Heavenly Principle, one of the central ideas of the state-approved Neo-Confucian orthodoxy, or that *Levying Demon Soldiers* included lines assuring the audience more than once that the ritual was a virtuous act. Such insistent protestations of innocence suggest that the creators of the ritual had their doubts. So our first impression appears to be incomplete. The New Year rituals did uphold conventional village morality, but they did other things as well.

Most of the deities who made an appearance in the performances and processions were mainstream gods such as the God of Wealth, the Star of Longevity, the Stove God, and the Ox King, and in particular gods involved in the administration of divine justice: the City God, the Judge, the God of the Five Ways, the Earth God. But their masks, grotesque and disturbing, suggest they were something quite different from conventional heavenly bureaucrats. Moreover, not all the gods were mainstream. The most important, Third Master White Eyebrows, although he was related to a god who received cult in a fairly wide region in southwestern Hebei and southeastern Shanxi, had been made fully Guyi's own. Certainly he was not a mainstream deity. Then there was the Yellow Demon and his captors, emissaries from a darker and more primitive world.

This combination of orthodox and heterodox elements is extremely disconcerting—to us. But it is highly unlikely that it bothered the residents of Guyi. They were in complete control of the ritual and presumably were seeing exactly what they wanted to see. For them, this is how the gods looked when they attended the New Year festival. Our discomfiture by the use of a representation of human sacrifice to teach filial piety, or by having the gods portrayed by villagers wearing grotesque masks, or by the juxtaposition of images of violence with images of order strongly suggests that we simply do not understand the symbolic world in which the people of Guyi lived. This is one of the most important lessons I have drawn from reflecting on this material.

There are other striking features of Guyi's New Year rituals. One is the large role played (in every sense) by the gods. They were not immobile statues before whom rituals and operas were performed; rather, they paraded through the streets and performed on stages. Unlike statues of gods in temples, which almost always looked human, these looked like figures from a nightmare. It was the eruption of an alien pantheon into the village streets. Yet—and this is another notable point—they were not purely gods; the masks certainly helped project some sense of the numinous, but at the same time the men wearing them must have gotten their steps wrong from time to time, or perhaps bumped into one another. Everyone knew who the men behind the masks were as well as the deities the masks represented. Thus the distinction between the divine and the human blurred and virtually disappeared. Third Master White Eyebrows was both a god and a villager; rituals were operas and vice versa; stages were temples. The dualisms so familiar to us of sacred and profane, solemn and entertaining, temple and street, seem not to have been relevant. Instead there was a single unified symbolic realm for which we have no good name.

The masks were crucial; the aura of the sacred they preserved would have dissipated if the actors had appeared only in makeup. But masks must also have reinforced the sense that the rituals were theater. It was not unusual for large assemblies of gods to be present at important community rituals in China, whether in the visualizations of Daoist priests, or in spirit tablets, or in the form of statues. But those gods were immobile and silent. They could move only if they were carried and speak only if they possessed someone—but possession was usually unscripted, spontaneous, and therefore uncontrolled. Guyi's gods moved and gestured and (sometimes) spoke, but in ways that they themselves, in their words and actions, acknowledged to be scripted performances. Opera had largely displaced ritual, but without banishing the numinous.

Conclusion

This part began with a description of the New Year ritual in Renzhuang village, about 240 km southwest of Guyi. This is a considerable distance, over rugged terrain. Moreover, as is clear from a dialect map, southwestern Shanxi, where Renzhuang is located, is culturally somewhat distinct from southeastern Shanxi and southwestern Hebei. The differences between the two regions should not be exaggerated. In early Ming and after, many migrants from southwestern Shanxi settled in the villages of southwestern Hebei, including Guyi, and presumably brought much of their culture with them. Yet the differences between Renzhuang's *Fan-Drum Roster of the Gods* and Guyi's *Catching the Yellow Demon* are extraordinary.

The Fan-drum ritual was controlled, remote, even perfunctory. The only signs that fearsome supernatural forces might be involved were the simulated spirit-medium, the Mamazi, and the dispatch of Empress Earth's spirit-tablet at the very end of the ritual. There was no opera worthy of the name, no masks or even face makeup, no real exorcisms. In Guyi, by contrast, there was an abundance of masked tableaux featuring a wide variety of deities, including one that provided a hagiography of the chief god of the ritual. And there was, above all, the symbolic ritual murder of the loathsome Yellow Demon.

The contrast is not merely between Guyi and Renzhuang. The execution of the Yellow Demon and the performance of masked ritual tableaux with narration, the parts of Guyi's New Year performances with probably the greatest impact on audiences, had no real analogues in any of the three Shanxi New Year rituals we have looked at. Similarly, Guyi appears to have had nothing like the elaborate dances performed on the ground that we noted in Renzhuang, Aoshi (the "battle formations"), and Sand Hill (the *taolu*). Nor did it have any rituals to expel diseases (as opposed to malign influences in general), although they were central to the New Year ceremonies in the three Shanxi locations.

Does this point to different Shanxi and Hebei traditions? No; after all, the three Shanxi celebrations of New Year were very different from one another. Are we dealing with regional or subregional traditions, then? Renzhuang, Guyi, and Aoshi certainly are in different regions— but Aoshi and Sand Hill are only about twenty-five kilometers apart. What we see is not regional differentiation—although that existed—but *village ritual autarky*. This simple notion is the key to understanding the symbolic culture of the common people in premodern China and has profound implications for our understanding of Chinese society.

The four festivals were not completely different; they shared a number of elements. All had some sort of exorcistic ritual, though these ranged from the mild (the Chicken-Feather Monkey) to the horrifying (the Yellow Demon); all had elaborate processions; and all had skits or dances performed on the ground. Perhaps these were elements of a very old stratum of New Year ritual—there certainly seem to be echoes of the Great Exorcisms performed on the eve of the New Year at the Han court, as well as of Sui and Tang practices in court and country[1]— and if so, that would be interesting and important. It is clear, however, that, old though they may have been, they did not amount to much in the context of the rituals as a whole. Of greatest interest to us is what was unique to each village, because just those elements appear to have been the most spectacular or dramatic and hence probably had the greatest impact. These unique elements were, for Renzhuang, the dough towers on the Eight Trigram Altars and the recitation of the "Roster of the Gods"; for Aoshi the Mask Tableau *Zhenwu Expels the Ten Evil Spirits*; for Sand Hill the Yellow River Lanterns (although this was found in other places); and for Guyi *Catching the Yellow Demon*.

---

1. Bodde, *Festivals in Ancient China,* pp. 81–85; Wang Ch'iu-kuei, "Yuanxiao jie bu-kao," pp. 10–33.

This exuberant ritual creativity is significant and has a number of implications. First, it suggests that at least some villages were both willing and able to devote considerable resources to their communal religious life. These four New Year rituals were costly undertakings, and they were only a small part of village ritual life. The total expenditure on seasonal and liturgical rituals in any given year must have been enormous. (This is even more obvious in the great *sai* of southeastern Shanxi, dealt with in Part III.) This speaks eloquently of the importance to ordinary farmers and townspeople of communal religious activities, and it should be borne in mind by anyone studying premodern rural China.

Village ritual autarky is another facet of "the insularity of the villages of the North China plain" noted by Philip Huang in his study of North China villages.[2] He argues that "even in the 1930s, all but the most highly commercialized villages of the North China plain were still relatively insular communities"—socially, economically, and politically.[3] Although the extreme isolation that he portrays for some villages (such as Shajing) is unlikely to have been matched in villages wealthy enough to support the sorts of ritual we have been looking at, and although the Shanxi *sai* provide powerful examples of routine joint sponsorship of temple festivals by village alliances as well as plentiful evidence of attendance at village festivals by friends, relatives, and others from neighboring villages, nevertheless Huang's portrait of village social, economic, and political insularity dovetails perfectly with the ritual insularity obvious in the evidence presented here. Villages that could afford to do so seem to have developed unique forms of seasonal rituals with no reference to outside ritual or ideological authority, whether popular or elite. These rituals were probably virtually unknown to and unaffected by the county magistrates and education officials, nor do Daoist or Buddhist clerics appear to have had any discernible influence on them.

The great variation in New Year rituals was not just due to the ritual autarky of insular villages, however. Because New Year is a seasonal

2. Philip Huang, *The Peasant Economy and Social Change in North China*, chap. 13 and *passim*.

3. Ibid., pp. 219, 224. His data are concentrated in northern Hebei and northwestern Shandong.

festival, not a god's birthday, none of these rituals was centered in a temple (although the wholesale destruction of village temples in the past fifty years may create a misleading impression on this score). More important, in not one of the rituals were offerings of food to the gods of much importance. Incense was offered everywhere, of course, and wine in Renzhuang and Guyi. In Guyi, tea was also offered, and sacrificial money burned.[4] But the only things resembling food offerings were, at Renzhuang, plates of fruit and the fifty-five peaches made of dough on the main altar, although the peaches seem to have been decorations rather than offerings (nothing in the liturgy refers to their being offered to the gods); unspecified offerings to the ancestors in Sand Hill; a white rooster for the Hail God in Guyi; and—the only case involving substantial amounts of food—the meat offerings at Aoshi. These were set out on twelve tables, each holding five bowls, and are said to have been offerings to the "hundred gods." But there appears to have been no formal liturgical recognition of this offering, no point at which the meat was given to any deity. Instead, the meat offerings turned into a parody of sacrifice when two masked demons tried to steal them and were prevented by the villagers—who then took the meat home instead of re-dedicating it to the gods. (Food offerings in the great *sai* were sometimes disrupted in a similar way, as we shall see, but those episodes never subverted the offerings as a whole, which were central to the ritual.)

Since it was the New Year festival and not the birthday of a particular god, it is not surprising that food sacrifice was of little importance. But this had important implications. The absence of formal sacrifice meant less need for a liturgical structure in which the sacrifices were embedded, and hence less need for ritual professionals. This in turn meant that potent forces for the creation of ritual norms—the ritualists and their proprietary liturgies, whether Buddhist, Daoist, governmental, or local—were not present (although the *Shê* Heads of Guyi may have been an incipient version of such specialists). This is another way of saying that New Year belonged more to the realm of custom than of cult.

---

4. In Sand Hill there was an Official in Charge of Sacrifices, but no sacrifices are described.

But there was more to rituals than sacrifice. At least one other activity was also significant: exorcism. Just as in some village ceremonies, such as the New Year rituals, sacrifice played only a minor role while in others, such as the *sai*, it was central, so also some rituals had few exorcistic elements or none, while in others exorcism was extremely important. This allows us to create a typology of Chinese village rituals and bring order to their seemingly limitless variety: there were rituals in which both sacrifice and exorcism were central—for example, the great *sai* of southeastern Shanxi, examined in Part III; those where sacrifice was unimportant but exorcism important—for example, many of the New Year rituals studied in this part; those where sacrifice was important but exorcism unimportant—for example, lesser temple rituals such as the birthday of the Earth God of Lituo, Sichuan, observed by D. C. Graham in 1930,[5] and perhaps most of the village temple rituals of southwestern Shanxi at which *Za* Opera was performed; and those where neither sacrifice nor exorcism was particularly important—for example, certain seasonal festivals such as the Full Moon Festival.[6] My research in north China suggests that for non-Buddhist, non-Daoist rituals, as the importance of food sacrifice increased, so did the role of ritual professionals, and with it a tendency to develop forms shared by more than one village; by contrast, the greater the importance of exorcism, the less such ritual experts were involved and the greater the tendency toward ritual autarky.[7] But all village rituals, no matter what their type, were characterized by the immense creativity of the popular religious imagination, unconstrained by orthodoxy either doctrinal or liturgical and independent of the practice of Buddhist and Daoist clerical elites.

---

5. Graham, *Folk Religion in Southwest China*, p. 154.

6. This typology is designed for rituals in which the ritualists were neither priests nor monks; therefore I exclude rituals that were purely Daoist or Buddhist.

7. Exorcism was important in the New Year rituals, but spirit-possession was not; the closest approach is the simulated spirit-medium of Renzhuang, the Mamazi.

PART II

Shanxi Village Ritual Opera, an Overview

HISTORY

The New Year rituals examined in Part I did not take place in temples, did not provide offerings of food to the gods, and did not employ professional ritualists, although exorcistic elements were common in all of them. A second type of annual village ceremony is the main concern of this book: rituals in honor of the birthday of a local god. These were the very heart of the symbolic culture of the countryside, the bedrock of mainstream Chinese popular religion. They usually featured elaborate food offerings, were often led by specially trained ritual specialists, focused more on the temple than the street or field (although their theatricals could escape the temple stage and spill into the streets), and featured full-scale operas mounted on temple stages as opposed to skits, pantomimes, and processions. Above all, they were focused on specific gods and their temples and their central activity was sacrifice. These liturgically dense, highly choreographed communal celebrations were very different from the ancient annual customs of the New Year, grounded in magic and exorcism.

Temple-based liturgical rituals as they were celebrated in late imperial north China were more highly evolved than seasonal rituals and could not have existed without the models provided by the Buddhist, Daoist, or "Confucian"—i.e., state—ritual regimes, even though they might not have been directly influenced by any of them. Because they were dedicated to specific deities, their ritual programs were relatively focused and complex; they were concerned more with sacrifice than with exorcism, although exorcism almost always played a part. The largest ones were the richest, deepest, most consequential expressions of Chinese village culture ever created, and Part III focuses on some spectacular examples from southeastern Shanxi, called *sai*, that by a happy chance are well documented—perhaps as well documented as any premodern Chinese rural temple rituals can be.

Operas performed on stages as offerings were virtually mandatory in temple rituals; indeed, a large stage was an integral part of many temples in southern Shanxi. Only extreme poverty prevented a village from staging operas on the birthday of a god, and prosperous villages and village alliances sponsored extravagant programs of them.[1] Ritual and opera thus formed an integrated, seamless performance complex. This kind of village opera—which should not be confused with the well-known "local" or "regional" opera genres (*difang xi*)—was truly *of* the people: the jealously guarded scripts were regarded as part of a village's patrimony and were often performed by the villagers themselves.

We have striking evidence of the importance of village opera from a scholar who was a native of southwestern Shanxi and knew from personal experience what it had been like before 1949:

Every village, large and small, had nonprofessional performances of its own operas. The farmers called this "family opera" (*jia xi*). Virtually every village had this. After liberation[2] a single county (*xian*) could have had over 200 nonprofessional opera troupes. . . . I remember that in my home town, Yishi, and its suburbs, there were over eighteen stages, and it was only an ordinary small town. Larger villages usually had five or more stages, and the smallest ones had at least two.[3]

---

1. Poor villages would hire puppet troupes if they could not afford proper opera. Only the most impoverished places would have had no opera at all—and they may not have had a temple in which to stage them.

2. Du must mean "before" or "at the time of," since one of the first things the Communist government did after 1949 was to take complete control of the performing arts. Amateur village troupes had no place in the new dispensation.

3. Du Lifang, "Lun Longyan za xi," p. 353.

For Shanxi as a whole, the Cultural Relics Bureau estimated that there were nearly 10,000 stages before the Cultural Revolution,[4] and this was after the havoc of the New Life movement, the warlord period, the anti-Japanese war, and the Civil War. In the high Qing, the numbers must have been considerably greater. For opera to have achieved such prominence in rural Shanxi, where, like everywhere else in village China, few people had much extra money to spend, it had to have filled an important need, and it had to have developed over a long period of time.

How long? This is a matter of central importance to any assessment of the significance of village temple rituals. If the operas were old and were performed only on temple stages during rituals, then the ritual programs were also old. The older they were, the more embedded they must have been in local culture and the greater their influence on it. Specific operas were not unchanging, nor would every script have had the same proportion of older and newer elements; so we cannot expect to date them precisely. However, we can try to get a general sense of their age.

The only ritual operas from any part of Shanxi that have survived in significant numbers are the *Za* Operas of southwestern Shanxi, which were collected in villages there between the 1950s and 1980s.[5] Specialists refer to these as Gong and Drum *Za* Operas (*luogu za xi*) or Cymbal and Drum *Za* Operas (*naogu za xi*), but local people generally called them just *Za* Operas, often with the name of a village or temple as a prefix.[6] The operas presented at the great *sai* in southeastern Shanxi—called *Dui* Operas, *Sai* Operas, or—confusingly—*Za* Operas—differed from Gong and Drum *Za* Operas in that they were the monopoly of a hereditary caste of actors and musicians known as *yuehu*, or Entertainers, whereas the southwestern *Za* Operas were performed by the villagers

---

4. Wang Fucai, "Shanxi zhongnan," p. 25. See also the remarkable map of extant Shanxi opera stages in Guojia Wenwuju, *Zhongguo wenwu ditu ji: Shanxi fence*, 1: 84–85.

5. I have copies of forty-three *Za* Opera manuscripts, most of which have never been published, and have made a close study of a number of them. My comments on the genre in what follows is based on this research.

6. A word of warning to the unwary: "*Za* Opera" (*za xi* or *za ju*) is a term that has many meanings; it by no means refers to a single, clearly defined genre.

themselves. Although there were substantial differences in the content of *Dui* Operas and Gong and Drum *Za* Operas, there is persuasive evidence that their formal features were similar. This strongly suggests a common origin and a single tradition distinct from regional opera forms such as Shanxi *bangzi* that became dominant in the Qing.

A number of scholars of Shanxi village opera, including the authors of the two earliest reports on southwestern *Za* Opera, thought that because the farmers refused to change the scripts, they probably were very old. In 1958 Wang Xiaju wrote:

[The villagers] have for a long time performed only the repertoire with which they are familiar; so it probably has had very little contact with other genres and has preserved its original character. . . . They say this genre [*Za* Opera] is very old, but even they do not know how old. . . . They have no desire to elevate or develop it, saying that these operas are offerings to the gods and cannot be lightly changed, and that if they were changed, they couldn't be used as offerings. So they have been passed on from generation to generation in their original form.[7]

In a 1959 article Du Lifang even suggested that the farmer-actors did not understand their own lines.

If one asks the farmers to read [their scripts], they cannot understand them. Even if they are read to them, they do not necessarily understand. Although they perform them every year, they merely know their parts by rote. They are unable to understand the content, the meaning of the sentences. . . . [As a result,] the farmers have sacralized [the scripts], regarding them as sacred things used to worship the gods. Thus if they cannot understand something, they memorize it, and even if they feel something does not make sense, they dare not add or change a line.[8]

In conditions such as these, change would come slowly. However, Du and Wang were writing when the tradition was almost moribund, and in earlier times the villagers may have better understood their own operas and have been more willing to alter them. This is strongly suggested by the fact that the surviving *Za* Opera scripts from a single vil-

---

7. Wang Xiaju, "Jianjie," p. 118A.
8. Du Lifang, "Lun Longyan za xi," pp. 346–47.

lage are not all of the same age; obviously, new items must have entered the repertoire from time to time. Moreover, some scripts were edited by educated men.[9] Nevertheless much about *Za* Opera, and other village ritual opera genres, is far from the mainstream of Chinese opera, and possibly archaic. Just how far back can we trace this tradition of operas without role-types or song-suites, with no string and few wind instruments, performed by village amateurs?

The farmers who passed these operas on from generation to generation believed they were old, and students of Chinese culture ignore such traditions at their peril. In this connection it is worth mentioning a fascinating comment in a report by one of the first historians of Shanxi drama, Mo Yiping. In 1948 he heard a famous actor distinguish between "New *Za* Opera"—Yuan dynasty *zaju*, which dates to the late thirteenth and early fourteenth centuries—and "Old *Za* Opera," that is, Gong and Drum *Za* Opera.[10] And I have already noted that people in Aoshi, in northeastern Shanxi, believed their *Sai* Operas had been brought by their forebears from southwestern Shanxi in the late fourteenth century, when they must have already been old.[11] However, the only reliable way to establish the age of village opera in Shanxi is to study village stages. At least thirteen extant stages dating to Song, Jin, and Yuan times have been identified in Shanxi, the most in any province.[12] The existence of over twenty others that are no longer extant can be confirmed by stone inscriptions. Many of these are found in the middle of the *Za* Opera region in southwestern Shanxi, and there is no reason to believe that they are any less old on average than those elsewhere in the province (see table).

All thirty-eight of these Shanxi stages (with the exception of the one in the Yongle gong, which was an imperially sponsored Daoist

---

9. See the colophons referenced in note 84 below.

10. Mo Yiping, *Puju shihun*, pp. 18–19. In what follows, the Chinese term for *Za* Opera from the Yuan dynasty will always be written "*zaju*." All other kinds of *Za* Opera will be written "*za ju*."

11. See Chapter 2, pp. 70–71.

12. There are only ten in the accompanying table because I have excluded three that cannot be dated at least to a reign-period.

Stages in Shanxi: Song, Jin, and Yuan Dynasties
*(Extant stages are in boldface; the dates shown
are those of construction or repair)*

Date	Location
1005–7	Houtu Temple, Qiaoshang village, Wanrong county 萬榮縣橋上村后土廟
1080	Guansheng Temple, Qin county seat 沁縣城關聖廟
1100	Jiutian Shengmu Temple, Donghe village, Pingshun county 平順縣東河村九天聖母廟
1137	Houtu Temple, Miaoqian village, Wanrong county 萬榮縣廟前村后土廟
1157	**Dongyue Tianqi Temple, Zhidi village, Jincheng municipality** 晉城市治底村東岳天齊廟
1190–96	Han Hou Temple, unknown location in Lingshi county 靈石縣韓侯廟
1199	**Dongyue Temple, Tuncheng village, Yangcheng county** 陽城縣屯城村東岳廟
1202	Bailong Shrine, Mt. Yan, Yangcheng county 陽城縣崦山白龍祠
1203	Dongyue Temple, East Gate village, Ruicheng county seat 芮城縣城東關村東岳廟*
1208	The "great temple," Dou village, Yangcheng county 陽城縣豆村大廟
1218	Shengmu Shrine, East Kang village, Linfen municipality 臨汾市東亢村聖母祠
1271	Jiwang Temple, Taizhao village, Wanrong county 萬榮縣太趙村稷王廟
1283	**Niuwang Temple, Wei village, Linfen municipality** 臨汾市魏村牛王廟
1287	Anle Temple, Southern Dujian village, Hongdong county 洪洞縣南渡澗村安樂廟
1293	Dongyue Temple, Qingjian village, Hejin county 河津縣清澗村東岳廟
1294	City God Temple, Fencheng town, Xiangfen county 襄汾縣汾城鎮城隍廟
1294	**Yongle Palace, Ruicheng county** 芮城縣永樂宮

Early Stages in Shanxi, *cont.*

Date	Location
ca. 1297– 1307	Taishan Temple, Xiedian town, Wanrong county 萬榮縣解店鎮泰山廟 (stele dates from Ming)
1301	Fengbo Yushi Temple, Mt. Gu, Wanrong county 萬榮縣孤山風伯雨師廟
1312	Gaomei Temple, Lianbo village, Hejin county 河津縣連伯村高禖廟
1312	Lingkuang Temple, Shangzhang village, Hongdong county 洪洞縣上張村靈貺廟
ca. 1314– 20	Hedong Gong Temple, Le village, Wenshui county 文水縣樂村河東公廟
1318	**Houtu Shengmu Temple, Hudun (?) village, Hejin county** 河津縣滹淹村后土聖母廟†
1318	Daiyue Temple, Ruicheng county seat 芮城縣城岱岳廟
1320	Unnamed temple, Ganjian village, Hejin county 河津縣干澗村無名廟
1322	**Sanlang Temple, Dong village, Yongji county** 永濟縣董村三郎廟
1324	**Qiaoze Temple, Wuchi village, Yicheng county** 翼城縣武池村喬澤廟
1328	Guandi Temple, East Lü village, Ruicheng county 芮城縣東呂村關帝廟
1341	Hulu Temple, Xinjiang county seat 新絳縣城葫蘆廟
ca. 1341– 68	**Sisheng Palace, Caogong village, Yicheng county** 翼城縣曹公村四聖宮
1342	Niuwang Temple, Jing village, Hongdong county 洪洞縣景村牛王廟
1344	Longwang Temple, Hailong Pond, Qinshui county 沁水縣海龍池龍王寺
1345	**Dongyue Temple, East Yang village, Linfen county** 臨汾縣東羊村東岳廟
1347	**Shengmu Temple of Mt. Dian Monastery, Zhangjiahe village, Shilou county** 石樓縣張家河村殿山寺聖母廟
1354	Dongyue Temple, West Jing village, Wanrong county 萬榮縣西景村東岳廟

Early Stages in Shanxi, *cont.*

Date	Location
1362	Yudi Temple, Qinshui county seat 沁水縣城玉帝廟
1364	Unnamed temple, North Gaoyu village, Xiangfen county 襄汾縣北膏腴村無名廟

*According to *Zhongguo xiqu zhi: Shanxi juan*, p. 562, the temple was in the "eastern corner" of Ruicheng town; Liao Ben (*Zhongguo gudai juchang shi*, p. 17) says "Eastern Gate"; neither indicates it was in a village. But there was an "East Gate" village just east of Ruicheng, which I think is the more likely location. The temple no longer exists.

†The village name as found in Yang and Cao, *San Jin xiqu*, p. 975, is preferable to that given in Liao Ben's list. The reading of the second character is unclear.

SOURCES: Based primarily on Liao Ben, *Zhongguo gudai juchang shi* (together with the very similar list in Liao Ben, *Song Yuan xiqu wenwu*, pp. 130–34), supplemented by the list in *Zhongguo xiqu zhi: Shanxi juan*, pp. 562–64. I have used only entries in these lists that are based on epigraphic evidence. (Unfortunately, the dates of the inscriptions were seldom noted by the authors.) No entries based solely on local monographs or other literary evidence were used. Some of the steles are no longer extant. Since some inscriptions commemorate the repair or reconstruction of a temple or stage, a number of stages are actually older than the date assigned to them. I have excluded from the list an extant stage said to be of Yuan dynasty provenance: Sanguan Temple, Sanluli village, Yuncheng Municipality 運城市三路里村三官廟. For additional information on early stages in Shanxi, see Huang Zhusan et al., "Cong Bei Song," pp. 32, 34; Mo Yiping, *Puju shihun*, p. 16; and *Zhongguo xiqu zhi: Shanxi juan*, p. 9.

monastery) were in temples, temples moreover of the mainstream popular religion, whose deities ranged from the humble Cattle King to the august, imperially supported Empress Earth. Buddhist and Daoist monasteries played no part (except for the Yongle gong). Twenty-eight of the thirty-eight were in villages or other rural places. Furthermore, the county seats in which the rest were found were quite small in the Song-Yuan period.[13] So these early Shanxi stages were profoundly *rural*.

---

13. If we use the census figures of A.D. 1102—and the population in Jin and especially Yuan was likely to have been lower—for the three prefectures (*jun*) in which most of the stages were found—Jin, Jiang, and Hezhong—we get an average population of about 21,000 per prefecture. If 10 percent of a prefecture's population lived in its administrative seat, which seems a reasonable guess for north China in this period, then a typical prefectural town at that time and place would have been home to around 2,000 people—a village by modern standards.

Some other material offers evidence on early opera in southern Shanxi. In 1978–79 a large number of magnificent tombs, probably dating from the late twelfth century, were discovered in Jishan county in southwestern Shanxi.[14] These underground burial chambers are made of fine-textured gray brick decorated with high-relief carvings of spectacular quality. A number include depictions of roofed stages with actors placed directly opposite seated figures representing the two occupants of the tomb, a husband and wife. This clearly echoes the placement of temple stages, which typically faced the statues of the gods in the main sanctuary. Just as the gods were the primary audience for operas performed in temples, so the deceased couple was the audience for this performance in the afterlife.[15] The ultimate model of the stages in the Jishan tomb carvings, which are very substantial structures, must have been temple stages. Opera clearly had penetrated deeply into the culture of the local elite in southwestern Shanxi by the second half of the twelfth century.[16]

One final piece of physical evidence must be mentioned because of its exceptional quality, although it may depict a performance at something like one of the great *sai* celebrations (to be discussed in Part III) rather than village opera of the sort I have been discussing. I say this because the temple is not located in a village, but near a large spring, and hence the rituals there were probably sponsored not by a single village but by those that were party to the agreement that fixed the distribution of the spring's water; and the *sai* of southeastern Shanxi were also sponsored by village alliances. The evidence is a mural in the Hall of the Brilliant and Responsive King (Mingying wang dian), known locally as the Water God

---

14. For the basic archaeological reports, see *Wenwu* 1983.1: 45–72.

15. Although the actors are in costume, they do not appear to wear makeup (personal visit, August 1997; Liao Ben, *Song Yuan xiqu wenwu*, color pls. 20–27, pp. 177–185; *Zhongguo dabaike quanshu: xiqu, quyi*, pls. 2–6). This is also true of the famous set of five figurines found in an early thirteenth-century tomb near Houma, in southwestern Shanxi (*Zhongguo xiqu zhi: Shanxi juan*, color pls., unnumbered p. 4). Jishan and Houma are on the northern edge of the Za Opera region. The absence of makeup in these representations of actors is interesting because one of the characteristics of southwestern Za Opera as it was performed in the first part of the twentieth century was that the actors often wore no makeup.

16. I say "local elite" because the tombs were obviously very costly.

Temple (Shuishen miao), about fourteen kilometers east of Hongdong in southwestern Shanxi. It is dated 1324 and shows a troupe of actors on a stage, as if taking a bow. According to a banner painted across the upper part of the mural, the troupe had come from "Yao's capital," that is Pingyang, the modern city of Linfen, about thirty kilometers south of Hongdong. So this is a professional troupe, not farmers giving a holiday performance. The high quality of the opera mural and the other murals in the Hall of the Brilliant and Responsive King strongly suggests that the temple enjoyed the patronage of the local elite.[17]

The evidence just presented is important for this study because it demonstrates that when opera first appeared in the Shanxi countryside—which must have been very near the time when opera first appeared in China—it was already intimately connected with ritual life, and continued to be so.[18] In the Song, Jin, and Yuan dynasties, village opera was ritual opera, and ritual opera was village opera. Moreover, once opera was introduced, it appears to have spread from village to village with great speed.[19] In a world where ritual played a central role, this new kind of symbolic performance was immediately welcomed. What happened after that?

Historians of Chinese opera have concentrated on tracing the origins of the major genres, such as Yuan *zaju*, Ming *chuanqi* and *kunqu*, and

---

17. A recent publication with much information on this temple, its rain rituals, and its pictorial program is Jing, *The Water God's Temple.*

18. I am aware of the abundant evidence attesting the presence of professional performers, dramatic and otherwise, in the Northern Song court and capital. (See, among many studies, Idema and West, *Chinese Theater, 1100–1450*, pp. 14–56, 95–102.) The familiarity of the accounts in well-known texts such as *Dongjing menghua lu* and the nearly universal habit of treating metropolitan literati culture as if it were the only thing that mattered or, at least, that it can adequately represent Chinese culture as a whole have created the impression that Song opera was an essentially urban phenomenon. In the present state of our knowledge, it is impossible to argue that Chinese opera *originated* in the villages of southern Shanxi, but there is no doubt that it spread widely among them in the course of the eleventh century.

19. This is proven by the fact that the three earliest stages for which we have epigraphic evidence were in widely separated locations in the southern part of the province: Wanrong county, on the western border of southern Shanxi (1005–7), Pingshun county, on the eastern border (1100), and Qin county, well north of them in central Shanxi (1080).

important regional forms like Peking Opera that arose in the Qing. Few have paid much attention to the evolution of village opera, because it is of inferior literary merit and is extremely difficult to study due to the lack of evidence. But it has not been completely ignored and two interesting hypotheses concerning Shanxi village opera have been proposed by the theater historians Liao Ben and Yang Mengheng. Liao Ben believes that "[southeastern Shanxi] *Dui* Opera, [southwestern Shanxi] Gong and Drum *Za* Opera, and [northern Shanxi] *Sai* Opera all arose from popular prosimetric narrative genres; they were the product of popular Shanxi prosimetric forms from the Song and Yuan dynasties combined with ritual performances."[20] Yang Mengheng, a specialist on the history of opera in Shanxi, has a more fully developed theory:

In Shanxi for century after century operas were performed constantly, during both prayers for good harvests and temple rituals, and although we cannot be certain just what types of opera were performed on every occasion, we can assert that in general, on the basis of sources known to us at present, before the middle of the Qing dynasty old *Sai* Opera had the leading role in temple rituals.[21]

Yang defines "old *Sai* Opera" as Gong and Drum *Za* Opera of southwestern Shanxi, *Dui* Opera of southeastern Shanxi, and *Sai* Opera of northern Shanxi—all of which were village ritual opera genres. He believes that "the old *Sai* Opera system was formed by the transformation of the old opera of Song and Jin in the villages of Shanxi. This system not only took over the legacy of the old opera of Song and Jin, it also gave impetus [much later] to the rise of Shanxi regional opera," including the important *bangzi*, or Clapper Opera.[22] (His "old opera of Song and Jin" probably refers to Song and Jin *zaju* and *yuanben*.)[23]

According to Yang, although the "old *Sai* Opera" of Shanxi emerged from the same sources as Yuan *zaju*, it had very little humor and was heavily influenced by Song dynasty history storytellers and by written fiction. It continued to be used in village temple rituals century after

---

20. Liao Ben, "Jin dongnan," p. 156.
21. Yang Mengheng, "Gu ju zheguang," p. 23.
22. Yang Mengheng, "Song Jin," p. 59.
23. Yang Mengheng, "Gu ju zheguang," p. 25.

century, changing very slowly, with only village writers contributing to the repertoire. Later on, around the mid-seventeenth century, southern opera began to infiltrate Shanxi. However, its influence was felt most strongly in professional performances sponsored by elites in cities and wealthy temples and did not displace the "old *Sai* Opera," which continued to be performed in its various forms on Shanxi village stages into the twentieth century, although its popularity declined.[24] Other scholars also seem to believe that Chinese opera developed along two tracks, one reasonably well documented and with a distinct urban and elite bias, the other profoundly rural, presented in temples on ritual occasions and often acted by amateurs, although they do not develop the idea.[25] Do we have concrete evidence for this hypothesis?

Yuan *zaju,* the first Chinese operas to be praised by later critics for their literary merit and the source of all major operatic genres, arranged tunes into suites and used role-types,[26] but Shanxi's "old *Sai* Opera" used neither song-suites nor role-types. This alone strongly suggests that it diverged from the main tradition at a very early point. In addition, investigators in the 1950s found signs of extreme conservatism in southern Shanxi opera. We have already seen that scholars who did field research on the Gong and Drum *Za* Operas of southwestern Shanxi stressed the reluctance of the villagers to change their scripts because of their ritual function and claimed that they sometimes learned them by rote. We have also noted that as late as the 1950s, the inhabitants of Aoshi in northeastern Shanxi believed that their ancestors had brought *their* ritual operas from southwestern Shanxi in the 1370s.[27] Supporting these views is some impressive textual evidence.

In late imperial times and down to the 1930s, the ritual programs of the largest temple festivals in Zhangzi and Lucheng counties, and probably many other counties in southeastern Shanxi as well, were directed by ritualists known locally as Masters of Ceremonial (*zhu li*).

---

24. Yang Mengheng, "Gu ju zheguang," pp. 23–24. Evidence of rural patronage of opera is presented below.

25. See, e.g., *Zhongguo xiqu zhi: Shanxi juan*, p. 83; Liao Ben, "Jin dongnan," p. 156; and Dou Kai and Yuan Hongxuan, "Shilun Shanxi luogu za xi," p. 74B.

26. Nienhauser, *Indiana Companion*, pp. 14–15.

27. See above, pp. 70–71.

(They also served as diviners—*Yinyang* Masters [*yinyang xiansheng*]—and geomancers—Experts on Examining the Earth [*kanyu jia*].)[28] These men used handbooks with outlines of rituals, texts of prayers and invocations, lists of ritual dishes for the food offerings, and so on. Sixteen such texts have been discovered in southeastern Shanxi in recent years.[29] The oldest one of any substance is dated "thirteenth day of the first month of the second year of the Wanli reign-period"—that is, February 4, 1574.[30] It was found in a village in Lucheng county, in southeastern Shanxi. The text is known by various names (there is no proper title page); in this study I refer to it as the *Zhou yuexing tu*.[31] In 1989, four years after the *Zhou yuexing tu* came to light, another liturgical handbook, titled *Tang yuexing tu*, was discovered in a village in Zhangzi county, which is just west of Lucheng. This manuscript is in two distinct parts. The second contains the date Jiaqing 23 (1818), and the first part may be substantially older than that.[32] These texts contain the titles of hundreds of operas.

In the *Zhou yuexing tu* of 1574, three opera genres are named: *zhengdui*, also known as *Dui* Opera, *yuanben*, and *Za* Opera. No one knows what the *Dui* and *Za* Operas of the late sixteenth century were like, but it seems virtually certain that they had no connection with the southern opera genres of that epoch, since they were designed specifically for performance during the grand temple rituals to which the *Zhou yuexing*

---

28. The Masters of Ceremonial are discussed in detail in Part III, Chapter 2.

29. Some of the major references on this topic are Liao Ben, "Jin dongnan"; idem, *Song Yuan xiqu wenwu*, pp. 358–70; Han Sheng, "Dui xi," pp. 282–309; Yang Mengheng, "Song Jin"; Huang Zhusan, "Wo guo xiqu"; and Li Tiansheng, "*Tang yuexing tu* sanlun."

30. The cover, on which the date is found, is not original. Indeed, Li Tiansheng, one of the few scholars who has firsthand knowledge of the original manuscript, says that the cover shown in an early photocopy is different from the cover it has now, but that that also was not the original. See "*Tang yuexing tu* sanlun," pp. 49B–50A. However, no one to my knowledge has questioned the authenticity of the date. The earliest of all the manuscripts, a list of ritual dishes, is dated 1522.

31. For a general introduction to the *Zhou yuexing tu*, including the punctuated and annotated text, see the articles in *Zhonghua xiqu* 3 (1987).

32. For a general introduction to the *Tang yuexing tu*, including the punctuated and annotated text, see *Zhonghua xiqu* 13 (1998) and *Xiyu* 1990, special issue. Detailed discussion of the dating of these and other Shanxi liturgical manuscripts is presented in the Introduction to Part III.

tu was a guide. In short, this ritual handbook provides solid evidence that there was a second, virtually invisible, village-based track in the history of Chinese opera, and that it dated at least to the early sixteenth century. Closer to the period of our fieldwork evidence, the 1818 *Tang yuexing tu* also gives the titles of many *Za* Operas and hence provides further evidence of the "village track."

Both ritual handbooks also list titles of a type of opera called *yuanben*.[33] In contrast to *Dui* and *Za* Opera, we know a good deal about the history of *yuanben*, and it may tell us something about the history of the others.

During *sai*, *yuanben* were performed at night behind the locked gates of the temple, and women and children were not allowed in the audience. This rule was enforced by a special watchman.[34] Villagers I spoke with in Xiaozhang village, near Zhangzi, in October 1993 still remembered their off-color character. Zhang Quanlong recalled that Entertainer families performed ribald skits including *Nao wu geng* (*Making a Commotion All Night Long*) at the great *sai* at the Sanzong Temple on Longquan Mountain (the subject of Part III, Chapter 2). As soon as he mentioned them, all the onlookers laughed; they knew what the performances had been like even though no one had seen one for sixty years.[35] No scripts of *yuanben* survived, but some old performers remembered two of them, *Nao wu geng* and *Tudi tang* (*The Temple of the Earth God*). Yuan Shuangxi and Li Shoutian wanted to record them, but the old men, worried that someone would hear them reciting indecent dialogue, refused to cooperate until Yuan and Li rented a room in a local hotel, where the recording session could take place behind closed doors.[36]

---

33. For Shanxi *yuanben*, see *Zhongguo xiqu zhi: Shanxi juan*, p. 143; Yuan Shuangxi and Li Shoutian, "Shangdang," p. 467; Han Shuwei, "Yuanben," unpublished paper in the author's collection.

34. Yuan Shuangxi and Li Shoutian, "Shangdang," p. 467. See also Zhang Zhennan, "Yueju yu sai," p. 243; *Zhongguo xiqu zhi: Shanxi juan*, p. 143; and Han Shuwei, "Yuanben," p. 6, quoting a member of an Entertainer family.

35. Interview at Xiaozhang village, 10/15/93. The reconstructed script of *Nao wu geng* can be found in Han Sheng et al., eds., *Shangdang nuo wenhua*, pp. 304–11.

36. Yuan Shuangxi and Li Shoutian, "Shangdang," p. 467; Han Shuwei, "Yuanben," pp. 1–2. The editorial work was done in 1985.

The legends villagers told about the origin of the *yuanben* further confirm their character. For example, one tradition had it that the gods gathered at the temple for the festivities naturally wanted to have a good time but worried that the wife of Jiang Ziya, Madame Ma, who was notoriously prudish, would spoil their fun. They therefore had *yuanben* performed, knowing that the vulgar language would offend her and drive her away.[37]

During the Jin and Yuan dynasties, *yuanben* were "farce skits" with five role-types: two clowns (*fumo* and *fujing*), an official (*zhuanggu*), a functionary or gentleman (*moni*), and the play leader (*yinxi*).[38] Later, but still in the Yuan dynasty, another type of *yuanben* appeared: a short slapstick farce with two main actors, the butt (*fumo*) and knave (*fujing*).[39] Remarkably enough, the two reconstructed *yuanben* from southeastern Shanxi, *Tudi tang* and *Nao wu geng*, resemble the two types of Jin and Yuan *yuanben*. *Nao wu geng* is a short knave-and-butt farce, and *Tudi tang* has five characters, of whom two are clowns, one a lower degree–holder, one a nontitled member of the local elite, and the fifth a student of the degree holder. The first four of these have close analogues in the five-role-type *yuanben*. It is hard to see this as mere coincidence.

Even though some early seventeenth-century scholars believed that old-style *yuanben*—the kind performed in Jin and Yuan—had virtually disappeared,[40] we know that it did survive, because short bawdy farces called *yuanben* are attested in the 1574 ritual handbook—one is even labeled a *fumo* (written 附末 rather than 副末) *yuanben*—and were still being performed as part of southeastern Shanxi temple rituals as late as the 1930s. Because the old genre was performed only during village temple festivals, it was invisible to the educated men who wrote about

---

37. Zhang Zhennan, "Yueju yu sai," p. 245. For similar legends, see Yuan Shuangxi and Li Shoutian, "Shangdang," p. 467. The combination of ritual drama with farcical interludes is not uncommon in world drama: *Nō* operas had their *kyōgen*, Greek tragedies their comedies and satyr plays.

38. Idema and West, *Chinese Theater, 1100–1450*, p. 85. There are a number of Song and Jin visual representations of the five role-types. See Liao Ben, *Song Yuan xiqu wenwu*, black-and-white pls. 2 and 3, color pl. 29, and the line drawing on p. 187, among others.

39. Nienhauser, *Indiana Companion*, pp. 958–59.

40. See Hu Yinglin (1551–1602), *Zhuang yue ji tan*, quoted in Hu Ji, "Jin Yuan yuanben," pp. 89–90; and Shen Defu (1578–1642), *Gu qu za yan*, p. 2b.

opera, since they knew little about village ritual life. But it became an integral part of the standard ritual program for the great temple festivals, or *sai*, and was passed on from generation to generation in the villages of southeastern Shanxi.

A further point: an important characteristic that Ming and even Jin dynasty *yuanben* shared with the *yuanben* of early twentieth-century Shanxi is the relative unimportance of music. In *Tudi tang* there is no singing at all, and *Nao wu geng* has only one short sung passage. Li Kaixian (1502–68), an educated man who wrote six *yuanben*, said: "In Southern Lyrics (*nanci* [i.e., *chuanqi*]), there is much music and few words; in Northern Lyrics (*beici* [i.e., Yuan-style *zaju*]), words and music are balanced; and in *yuanben*, there are many words and little music."[41] Xu Chong (b. 1518) wrote: "That which has speech and song is called *zaju*, that which uses stringed instruments is called "suites" (*tao*), and performing opera scripts by hopping about and not singing is called *yuanben*."[42] Han Shuwei quotes a number of other passages from Ming sources that speak of "doing" (*zuo*) rather than "singing" (*chang*) *yuanben*, further supporting the impression that they were mostly stage business and dialogue.[43] Earlier evidence about *yuanben* performance is scarce, but a well-known Jin dynasty description of an urban theater, probably dating from the early thirteenth century and depicting what is almost certainly a *yuanben* performance, makes no mention of singing. A villager is recounting what he saw in a theater on a visit to town. (A *yuanben* is specifically said to be on the program for which he buys a ticket.)

> One [actor] dressed up as Squire Zhang,
> The other changed to Brother Two,
> Walking, walking, they said as they walked that they were
>   on the way to town.
> Seeing a young girl standing under a shade,
> The old man bent his mind and schemed to get her to wife.
> Brother Two he went off to speak for both sides,
> What she wanted was beans and grains, wheat and rice,

---

41. Preface to *Xi ye qun you ci*, quoted in Hu Ji, "Jin Yuan yuanben," pp. 88–89.
42. *Nuan shu you bi*, quoted in Han Shuwei, "Yuanben," p. 6.
43. Ibid., pp. 6–7.

She never asked for floss or fine silk, satin or cotton.
Making the Squire twist forward, daring not twist back,
Causing him to raise his left foot, daring not raise
    the right.
Back and forth, up and down, all because of *that one*
    [Brother Two]!
Now the Squire's heart is fuming and burning,
And he strikes with his flesh bat,[44] breaking it in half.
And I say this will give rise to depositions and claims,
    and I have to laugh again.[45]

Since at this point the narrator has to leave, we do not know how the performance ended, but the general impression is clear enough: knave and butt, horseplay on stage, and speech rather than song—"hopping about and not singing" indeed.

All in all, it is not out of the question that the *yuanben* performed at the *sai* in southeastern Shanxi as late as the 1930s belonged to a type of village ritual opera already well established in the late sixteenth century that quite possibly was descended from a dramatic genre that originated in the twelfth century, and thus was older than Yuan *zaju*.[46] It apparently disappeared from the written record in late Ming but continued to be performed in the villages of southern Shanxi for ritual purposes—it was an invisible tradition. It is not unreasonable to suggest, especially in view of the other evidence adduced, that the other ritual opera genres that appeared with *yuanben* in the 1574 handbook had a similar history. The "old *Sai* Opera" may have been very old indeed.

---

44. This recalls the cudgels held by some of the figures in Jin dynasty tomb carvings.

45. "A Country Bumpkin Knows Naught of the Theater," in Idema and West, *Chinese Theater, 1100–1450*, p. 189. Wade-Giles romanization changed to pinyin, one other minor change.

46. Note that *Tudi tang* is one of the eight *yuanben* titles in the 1574 *Zhou yuexing tu*. Two more of the eight have clear analogues among the titles of *yuanben* given in the mid-fourteenth-century *Zhuogeng lu*: *Pima zhuang* (*Zhou yuexing tu*) and *Si ruo pima zhuang* (*Zhuogeng lu*), *Shuang she zhi* (*Zhou yuexing tu*) and *Shuang she zhi cuan* (*Zhuogeng lu*). *Zhou yuexing tu* text in *Zhonghua xiqu* 3 (1987), pp. 73 and 90; 99 and 103; and 100; *Zhuogeng lu* (Siku quanshu Wenyuange intranet ed.), 25.14a, 25.15a.

PERFORMANCE

What were these village ritual operas like in performance? The best available description of southeastern Shanxi *Dui* Opera is found in Zhang Zhennan's immensely detailed account of the great *sai* held annually on the sixth day of the sixth lunar month at the Sanzong Temple in the Big West Gate quarter of Zhangzi town. Zhang, a native of Zhangzi, witnessed the local temple festivals in his youth and carried out extensive fieldwork on the *sai* after retirement.

The music for *Yue* Opera was extremely simple; there were only percussion instruments, no strings.[47] There also were no parts for shawm (*suona*). Onstage there was an Incense Gong [or Gongs] and a *Shê* Drum. {The former was about a foot in diameter.}[48] The latter had heads about twenty-one inches in diameter. They also used small gongs, and large and small cymbals. As for repertoire, they mostly performed martial operas with historical themes. Their manner of performance resembled that of grand opera (i.e., Shanxi *bangzi* [Zhang's note]), but the skills of the actors were far inferior. Their techniques of singing, gesturing, declaiming, and fighting {obviously were rather crude}. The melodies had tones but no harmony, and no subtlety whatsoever. It was like a combination of recitation and singing.[49] The rhythm did not vary, despite changes in the dramatic situation. After a line was sung, the gongs and drums would play twice, and after every four lines they would all wildly dash off a passage. The style of speaking was also very free; sometimes there were long passages of speech with no music at all.[50]

---

47. He calls the genre "*Yue* Opera" because it was performed by Entertainer families—*yuehu*—but there is no question that he is referring to what other writers call *Dui* Opera. The terms *Sai* Opera and *Za* Opera are also sometimes used to name the main dramas performed at *sai*.

48. Unless otherwise noted, all material in braces is supplied from p. 9B of another version of Zhang Zhennan's article, entitled "Yueju he sai."

49. In the surviving script fragments, the rhymed sections are marked "says" not "sings."

50. Zhang Zhennan, "Yueju yu sai," pp. 246–47. As to the last point, an old man who had been a Master of Ceremonial in his younger days stated in a 1990 interview that in the village of Nan Shê the part of Xiang Yu in the opera *Da hui gai* was so long—it had a total of 1,800 lines—that two actors had to share it (Li Tiansheng, interview with Cao Zhan'ao, *Zhonghua xiqu* 13 [1998], p. 124). Incidentally, this opera, under

Li Yuanxing, a native of Nan Shê, a village about thirty-five kilometers northeast of Zhangzi town, in his youth played the drum at his village's *sai*. Nan Shê's single-village festival was modeled on a multi-village *sai*. Since it had Entertainers to train the performers, its operas may well have resembled the regular *Dui* Operas. He writes that the form of Nan Shê's *Dui* Operas was "very primitive. The singing had only two pitches, high and low, and the only accompaniment was five gongs and a big drum about thirty inches in diameter." The big drum was from the village drum tower, and the gongs were the ones used by the night watchmen. Thus the instruments used in Nan Shê's ritual operas were also used to mark out the rhythms of daily life.[51]

Yang Mengheng, whose general account of the history of Shanxi ritual opera we have already reviewed, has also done extensive fieldwork on village drama in southern Shanxi and writes that although elements in Nan Shê's *Dui* Opera derived from Shangdang *bangzi*, or Clapper Opera, there were also older elements: the second line in the rhymed sections repeated the—presumably tonal—contours of the first, and there was very little melodic character. When recited, the verse sounded like chanting (the *yinsongqiang* style). The only accompaniment was percussion. According to Yang, the style of singing and drum accompaniment in southeastern *Dui* Opera was similar to that in southwestern Gong and Drum *Za* Opera, and seven- and ten-character lines were typical in both.[52] In a later article he writes:

The form of *Dui* Opera as seen in the scripts that have been discovered . . . is the same as that of the Gong and Drum *Za* Opera of southwestern Shanxi. The sung sections are for the most part in the seven- or ten-character declamatory rhyme form (*zanyun*), interspersed with prose for the spoken parts. In performance they sing in the *yinsongqiang* style. No stringed instruments are used in accompaniment, only gongs and drums to beat the time.[53]

---

the title *Shi mian mai fu*, was also in the southwestern Shanxi Gong and Drum *Za* Opera repertoire.

51. Li Yuanxing, "Zhui shu Nan Shê 'Tiao gui,'" p. 463. In my 1993 interview with him, Mr. Li mentioned several other percussion instruments.

52. Yang Mengheng, "Lucheng Nan Shê," pp. 19B–21B.

53. Yang Mengheng and Zhang Zhennan, "Shangdang gu sai," p. 92.

Finally there is this comment by Li Tiansheng, another expert on the ritual opera of southeastern Shanxi:

The [prosody of] the *Za* [i.e., *Dui*] Operas that were performed at the big temple festivals [in southeastern Shanxi], as we know from documents that we can now study and from [local] investigations . . . was similar to that of the *banchang cihua* of the Jin and Song [a prosimetric genre], using the lyric declamatory prosimetric form (*shizan jiangchang*). . . . This kind of *Za* [i.e., *Dui*] Opera is commonly called Gong and Drum *Za* Opera in the southwest, and *Sai* Opera in northern Shanxi.[54]

A good deal of information is also available about the performance style of southwestern *Za* Opera. To begin with, the repertoire consisted almost entirely of "history" plays—martial (*wu*), not civil (*wen*), to use the traditional Chinese categories—and much of the action involved combat between warriors, during which the actors frequently used real weapons and struck heavy blows, weapon against weapon. The fighting was tightly choreographed; if a number of warriors were on stage, their movements were called formations (*zhen*). Each had its own name,[55] as did the specific moves in the duels. They were probably martial arts moves performed in an exaggerated style.[56] In some villages, the actors' armor was made of dried clay on a paper or fabric base. These costumes were heavy and clumsy, and this, according to some scholars, was one of the reasons the actors' gestures were slow and exaggerated.[57] The actors wore face makeup, not masks, but they did not use the makeup patterns traditionally associated with their characters in mainstream opera.[58] Wang Xiaju thought the face makeup resembled that of the door gods on the gates of villagers' houses and suggested

54. Li Tiansheng and Tian Sulan, "Saishe jili," p. 229.

55. Du Lifang, "Lun Longyan za xi," pp. 347–48; Wang Xiaju, "Jianjie," p. 119B; Yang Mengheng, "Luogu za xi," p. 23B; Ren Guangwei, "Sai xi, naogu za xi chu tan," p. 209. Both Du and Wang state that stage weapons were used.

56. Wang Liang, "Luogu za xi," p. 210.

57. Ibid., p. 211; Wang Xiaju, "Jianjie," p. 119A; Dou Kai, "Luogu za xi," p. 234.

58. Du Lifang, "Lun Longyan za xi," pp. 349–50. A color painting of a *Za* Opera performance in Wangwu village (about twenty-eight kilometers west of Linyi) made in the 1950s is reproduced in *Xiqu yanjiu* 6 (1958.2), together with colored illustrations of the face makeup of six characters.

that the clay armor was modeled on the armor of the guardian gods of temples, who traditionally were represented as fierce warriors, one standing on each side of the main gate.[59] If so, this is impressive evidence of the intimate connection between ritual opera and village life, like the use of the drum tower's drum and the night watchman's gong to accompany opera singing.

One performer wore neither makeup nor costume and had few if any lines to speak, yet was essential to the action and is considered by all scholars to have been one of the defining features of southwestern *Za* Opera. This was the Announcer (*dabao de, dabao zhe*). Among other things, he took all the small parts, such as servants, soldiers, offstage voices, and the like, which had only the simplest of lines. (Aside from the Announcer, there were virtually no minor roles in *Za* Opera.)[60] At times he helped arrange the stage furnishings and props. In one amusing case, he even played a tree, around which a duel between Cao Cao and Ma Jiao was fought.[61] According to Wang Liang, he also made offerings and obeisances to the gods, pronounced a prayer, and at the start of the program led the whole troupe onto the stage. He also came on stage before every opera and summarized the plot and then used his triangular yellow banner to invite the actors to join him.[62] This is confirmed by Ren Guangwei, who did fieldwork in southwestern Shanxi in the early 1950s. He reports that the Announcer was played by the *Shê* Head, who paced about the stage with an "apricot-colored" banner, announced the name of the opera, and then took a seat at the left of the stage, getting up to help out as needed.[63] Du Lifang reports that, in the southwestern *Za* Opera he was familiar with, opera teachers and other knowledgeable men took the part of the Announcer.[64] His costume—an official's hat, a long robe, and a short jacket—indicated he was a person of high status.

---

59. Wang Xiaju, "Jianjie," p. 119A.

60. Dou Kai, "Luogu za xi," p. 233.

61. *Terrace of the Bronze Bird* (*Tong que tai*), *Shanxi difang xiqu huibian* edition, pp. 400–401.

62. Wang Liang, "Luogu za xi," p. 210.

63. Ren Guangwei, "Saixi, naogu za xi chu tan," p. 208.

64. Du Lifang, "Lun Longyan za xi," p. 344.

We have encountered this narrator-director figure in the ritual opera of other villages: in Aoshi the *Shê* Head (*sheshou*) and in Guyi the Staff-holder (*zhangzhu*) carried out these functions. And there is an analogous figure in the great *Sai* Operas of southeastern Shanxi: the Director (*qianhang*). The Announcer and his analogues had a dual role, part liturgist and part director. This parallels the dual nature of village ritual opera, part ritual and part entertainment. I agree with the scholars who think the Announcer must be a survival from an unsophisticated and probably early form of opera.[65] His functions suggest origins in a time when the division of labor on stage was in its infancy, a time when it was not yet considered important to maintain the theatrical illusion consistently throughout an opera and the technical means of handling small but crucial actions such as informing a general that the enemy was attacking had not yet been developed. Note that one of the role-types in Song dynasty *za ju* and Jin *yuanben* was the "Director" (*yinxi*), who was something like a stage manager who also played the minor roles.[66]

In *Za* Opera scripts, the only Shanxi ritual opera scripts of which more than fragments survive, characters are identified by name and not role-type. This is contrary to the custom in the scripts of most other Chinese opera genres from Yuan times on[67] and is yet more evidence that *Za* Opera may be a very old form little influenced by later changes in Chinese drama. This impression is further reinforced by the extreme simplicity of its music, whether in the arias or the accompaniment. As the name indicates, the accompaniment of Gong and Drum *Za* Opera consisted almost entirely of percussion instruments: drums of various sizes, and gongs or cymbals.[68] *Suona* were used in some villages, but

---

65. E.g., Du Lifang, "Lun Longyan za xi," p. 345.

66. See Qi Senhua et al., *Zhongguo quxue da cidian*, p. 47B; and Dolby, *A History of Chinese Drama*, p. 26. Remarkably enough, the same term was used instead of "Announcer" in the *Za* Operas of Longyan monastery (about seven kilometers northeast of modern Linyi town), the last place where *Za* Operas were performed. See Du Lifang, "Lun Longyan za xi," pp. 341–54.

67. Chung-wen Shih, *The Golden Age of Chinese Drama: Yuan Tsa-chü* (Princeton: Princeton University Press, 1976), p. 50; Yang Mengheng and Xie Yuhui, "Shanxi sheng Linyi xian," pp. 144–45; Dou Kai, "Luogu za xi," p. 233.

68. Wang Xiaju, "Jianjie," p. 118B. His testimony is important, since he witnessed actual performances.

only at entrances and exits, and not to accompany singing.[69] No string instruments were used at all.

Furthermore, the drums and gongs were used in the simplest possible manner. In verse passages, they came in at the end of every line or couplet, and each section concluded with a long passage of drumming and gong-playing.[70] Prose passages were sometimes punctuated with a cymbal clash after every phrase. The actors seemed to some observers to move to the beat of drums and cymbals like marionettes.[71] The singing and other vocal work seems to have been equally crude. Song-forms, the hallmark of mainstream opera from Yuan times on, were almost never used, and if they were, the performers may not have known their names.[72] Vocal technique was not subtle: according to some observers the performers simply sang as loudly as they could, with no modulation or variation.[73] In other cases, listeners were reminded of spirit-mediums reciting spells or monks chanting scriptures, or of the recitation of poems on historical subjects (*shishi*).[74] Some observers said that the performers made little distinction between speech, the chanting of verse, and singing.[75] One author calls this declaiming the apotheosis of the local dialect.[76] Verse was almost invariably in lines of uniform length, usually seven characters, sometimes ten.[77] The verse passages were chanted in the style used by storytellers.[78] In a few operas some speeches are immensely long, more like narrative than drama, and some scripts are divided into *hui* "chapters" rather than acts. These are

---

69. Ibid.; Du Lifang, "Lun Longyan za xi," p. 344; Ren Guangwei, "Saixi, naogu za xi chutan," p. 209.

70. Wang Xiaju, "Jianjie," p. 118B; Dou Kai, "Luogu za xi," p. 234.

71. Yang Mengheng and Xie Yuhui, "Shanxi sheng Linyi xian," p. 150.

72. Ibid., p. 147; Dou Kai, "Luogu za xi," p. 234; Du Lifang, "Lun Longyan za xi," p. 347.

73. Du Lifang, "Lun Longyan za xi," pp. 345, 348; Dou Kai, "Luogu za xi," p. 234.

74. Dou Kai, "Luogu za xi," p. 235; Wang Xiaju, "Jianjie," p. 120B.

75. Wang Xiaju, "Jianjie," p. 120B; Du Lifang, "Lun Longyan za xi," p. 349.

76. Wang Liang, "Luogu za xi," p. 211.

77. This statement is based on a survey of over twenty *Za* Opera scripts.

78. Yang Mengheng and Xie Yuhui, "Shanxi sheng Linyi xian," pp. 146–47; *Zhongguo xiqu quyi cidian*, p. 671, s.v. 詩贊.

additional reasons why some scholars think that *Za* Opera descended
from storytelling or was influenced by it.[79]

The stress on declamatory narrative rather than mimetic action, the
use of percussion at the ends of lines, and exclusive reliance on chanting and speech rather than song were also characteristic of the *Dui*
Opera of the southeast, as we have seen, and the *Sai* Opera of Aoshi.[80]
In fact, almost all Shanxi village ritual opera is described in these terms.
This is opera at its least sophisticated; it suggests that all the genres are
very old, and are related.

THE ABSENT GODS

Operas performed as part of the ritual program at Shanxi village temple
festivals belonged to a rural dramatic tradition little influenced by developments in mainstream local opera. With few exceptions, it was unknown to outsiders, including theater scholars, until the 1950s. Many
villages seem to have had their own scripts, which were considered a
legacy from earlier generations and, in some cases, were never shown to
outsiders. There must have been an intense emotional bond between
the villagers and their operas; this is explicit in the few surviving colophons and implicit in the fact that the operas were performed by villagers rather than professional actors. In many villages, the right to perform a particular role in the temple ritual operas passed from father to
son, and performing in an opera was probably a marker of local elite
status. This must have woven the operas even more tightly into the social fabric of the village and made them that much more resistant to
change. In addition, they were regarded as offerings to the gods, and
the villagers were therefore reluctant to modify them. It is not surprising that they appear to preserve an archaic performance style.

This highly conservative form was the vehicle for a wide range of
stories. We know from surviving scripts and the titles of lost scripts

---

79. Yang Mengheng and Xie Yuhui, "Shanxi sheng Linyi xian," p. 144; Yang
Mengheng, "Luogu za xi," pt. 2, p. 31; Du Lifang, "Lun Longyan za xi," p. 345; Dou Kai,
"Luogu za xi," p. 242.

80. Yang Mengheng and Xie Yuhui, "Shanxi sheng Linyi xian," pp. 144–45; Ren
Guangwei, "Saixi, naogu za xi chutan," pp. 202–5.

that it was unusual for a village to have an opera with a unique plot. It was more common for a village opera to give its own version of plot lines that circulated widely in novels, *chantefables*, and storytelling. Since already in the oldest *sai* liturgy (dated 1574) we see titles that refer to popular stories, this had been the case for a long time. Evidently if village playwrights used the accepted forms, they were free to use plots from a wide range of sources. It seems that just as with ritual, the important thing was to do opera the right way. Thus the Director, who was in charge of the operas in the great *sai*, was a close analogue of the Master of Ceremonial, who led the rituals. (We meet both in the following chapters.)

But there were limits. The operas performed on temple stages were never love or crime stories or farces. (The *yuanben* were a special case and treated as such.) The characters were figures from history (or more accurately, historical fiction or legend, but this was history to ordinary people), almost invariably warriors who spent a substantial part of the opera fighting one another, and not always for admirable motives. This raises an interesting question: What made such operas seem suitable as offerings to the gods? Why was dueling with swords or lances considered an appropriate accompaniment to prayers and invocations?

It is possible that we underestimate the importance of the military side of temple festivals. Recall the central role played by operaticized military formations (*zhen*) in the New Year's processions in Aoshi and Sand Hill, in northern Shanxi, discussed in Part I, Chapter 2. And in Renzhuang, most of the villagers performed military formations instead of Fan-drum Operas during the New Year rituals. The temple festivals of Heyang, just across the Yellow River from the *Za* Opera area of Shanxi, were accompanied by *Tiao* Opera, which closely resembled Shanxi's *Za* Opera and other village ritual opera forms. There was a tradition in Heyang that *Tiao* Opera had been staged in Yuan times to provide cover for boxing and staff-fighting practice, and that it had other military associations as well.[81] There could well have been a link between stage fighting and popular martial arts traditions. Village festivals, which reaffirmed village identity, may have been occasions for a

---

81. See Shi Yaozeng, "Heyang"; and Holm, "The Death of *Tiaoxi*."

display of military strength as well as ritual reverence. Staged demonstrations of martial arts, semimagical formations of troops, and explications of the moral foundations of the use of force—all these things could conceivably have been directly connected with village self-defense in the villagers' eyes. People knew they needed to protect their village against human as well as supernatural threats.

But this answer only leads to a more difficult question: Why were there so few religious or cultic operas? It is striking enough that, from the very beginning of opera in Shanxi, stages were constructed in temples. Even more striking, scarcely any religious plays seem to have been performed on them.[82] (Most of the many operas listed in the 1574 *sai* liturgy were on well-known historical subjects.) Deities almost never were protagonists in local opera, although Buddha, the Jade Emperor, and other very grand gods often put in token appearances. Guan Yu, who had temples all over China, appears in many plays, but as a historical person, not the god Guandi. And deities who had never been historical figures, such as (to take examples from southeastern Shanxi cults) Shen Nong, the God of the Eastern Peak, the Cattle God, the Two Immortal Ladies, the God of the Five Ways, and so on, virtually never became characters in operas.[83] The local gods of southern Shanxi (and probably most regions in north China) were never offered plays about themselves. Not for lack of materials—the story of a local god's life and miracles was frequently depicted in murals in the village temple and made the subject of narrative songs. The literate had access to scrip-

---

82. *Lord Guan Beheads Chi You* is the only title of an opera with supernatural protagonists we know, and, revealingly, no version has survived, even though it is claimed to be the source from which all Shanxi opera flows.

83. This is how it appears to me now, but I have not done a special study of hagiographic operas, and my conclusion is necessarily provisional. There were operas that had Buddhist or Daoist divinities as characters—the Mulian cycle, the Xiangshan cycle, the Enfeoffment of the Gods cycle, Daoist conversion operas—but although these were famous, they were not numerous. There may have been more in the marionette theater repertoire—see, e.g., Ye Mingshen, *Fujian Shouning.* Puppet theater played an important part in many rituals in southern China; whether this led to the writing of hagiographic operas in that region is a question awaiting further research. But in any case there seem to have been very few operas of any kind in Shanxi that featured deities from non-Buddhist, non-Daoist rural cults.

tures written in easy-to-read prose and verse. Hagiography was abundant in the countryside; why, then, was so little of it turned into drama? Why did villagers don masks of gods and parade through the streets but not dress up as gods and perform in operas about them?

At least some village rituals had scripts and thus had been written by literate men. The identity of the original authors will never be known, but the colophons of several scripts performed in the village of Xinzhuang in southwestern Shanxi show that by late Qing or early Republican times educated men resident in the village took an active part in the revision of its scripts. There is no reason to think that this was not the case in other villages in Ming, Yuan, or even Song and Jin times.[84] It would have been more natural for such men to write operas about historical figures than about gods. A man who had had even the beginnings of a classical education would have absorbed the cultural bias of the educated elite toward history and against "superstition." Every educated man read history and remembered what he read. It was a rare official or local leader who would defend a decision by reference to the scripture of a popular sect or local cult, but few would have hesitated to argue from historical precedent; after all, two of the five Classics were histories.

But what about the audiences? Would they not have enjoyed operas about their local gods, who were after all the reason for the festival? Could government prohibitions have discouraged them? It does not seem so. The monumental sourcebook on censorship in the Yuan, Ming, and Qing dynasties, *Yuan Ming Qing sandai jinhui xiaoshuo xiqu shiliao*, shows that officials were concerned because operas brought men and women together "at night" and the scripts were allegedly immoral, but except for occasional fulminations against Mulian operas and unspecified "Buddhist operas" they do not appear to have objected to op-

---

84. Two men, Yao Jitang and Zhang Yutang, recopied the script of *Thrice Inviting Zhuge Liang* in the depth of the winter of 1925. For the colophons they and others added to the text, see Yang Mengheng and Xie Linyi, "Shanxi sheng Linyi xian," pp. 137–41. Yang republished this article in two parts as "Luogu za xi kaolue"; the colophons, in versions that vary slightly from those published in the first article, can be found in the first part, pp. 19–20.

eras about gods.[85] This fits with the official policy of benign neglect toward local cults in general. Most officials worried about local religion only when it turned toward rebellion or when people spent too much money building temples and staging festivals. So village taste in ritual opera was not due to pressure from the state.

In medieval Japan there was a type of rural drama called *sangaku* or *sarugaku*.[86] Gotō Hajime, a leading historian of Japanese theater, found that in the Kamakura period (late twelfth–early fourteenth century) *sangaku* were performed at "popular religious services and festivals held primarily at minor shrines and temples in all parts of [Japan]." Eventually, "to the usual entertainment and honoring of the gods at shrines or temples, [the performers] added theatrical enactments of the myths celebrated in divine services," possibly to improve their "outcast" status. The actors wore masks representing local gods and spirits, and came to consider themselves Shintō priests. The two founders of Nō drama, Kan'ami and Zeami, emerged directly from this tradition.[87] There are strong similarities to Shanxi rural ritual opera here: the *sangaku* were performed to entertain the gods during rituals at local temples, and the tradition was deeply local; and as in southeastern Shanxi, the actors were a debased status group. But in Japan the form continued to develop: the performances became "the enactment of the myths celebrated in [the temple rituals]," with masked actors impersonating the deities. And this led directly to Nō, one of the most sublime forms of religious drama in world literature.

Nothing like this took place in the development of ritual drama in Shanxi. The rituals of the great temple festivals were not encounters with the Sacred; they vaguely resemble a combination of court ceremony and ancestral sacrifice in their emotional registers. The only time the gods appeared—something like real gods, with their irreducible otherness— was in certain processions, where villagers wearing large masks paraded

---

85. Wang Liqi, *Yuan Ming Qing*.

86. Donald Keene (*Seeds in the Heart*, p. 1043, *n*8) suggests that these are merely different pronunciations of the same Chinese loanword. *Sangaku* originated in Heian times, when it had a different form; the details are not relevant here.

87. See Ortolani, "Shamanism in the Origins of the Nô Theatre," pp. 172–73, summarizing Gotō's work.

through the streets or took part in simple skits or tableaux. And indeed, the masks were at times grotesque and unsettling. But, to my knowledge, such figures never appeared in operas on temple stages. It was on the ground or in temporary matsheds, not on the stage in the temple, that the village gods "came to life." And there they stayed.

The fundamental concern of Shanxi temple festivals was not worship or prayer or transcendence or salvation, but rather sacrifice, the making of offerings. Sacrifice involved people acting, not catharsis or inspiration. In that world ritual—prescribed acts properly performed— and opera—serious (or amusing) stories performed in the proper manner by the proper people—were at the heart of the symbolic culture of the educated and uneducated alike. The language and gestures of operas and rituals were meaningful for those who watched them, but as performed in village temples both were fundamentally offerings to the gods. And just as the rituals did not evoke awe or lead people to confront the deep questions of human existence, the operas performed on temple stages did not inspire pity and terror or aspire to transcendence.

This helps us understand why something like Nō did not emerge out of Shanxi village ritual opera. But we are left with the question why nothing like *sarugaku* appeared, or, to change hemispheres, medieval English mystery plays. The mystery plays were simple vernacular performances of important moments from the Bible, sometimes staged on wagons drawn through the streets of small towns.[88] It is not hard to imagine similar performances in rural Shanxi temples dramatizing the hagiographies of local gods. But none was written.

The great temple festivals called *sai*, celebrated for hundreds of years in southeastern Shanxi, which are the basis of my understanding of local ritual culture there, were imagined as something like birthday parties for important deities. The god being honored invited to the party deities of approximately equal rank from temples in nearby villages. It is possible that people thought about their local god, at least during the *sai*, as something like a revered elder; far more powerful than any person, of course, and needing to be treated most respectfully, but still likely to enjoy a lav-

---

88. There is an enormous literature on this subject. See, e.g., Rosemary Woolf, *The English Mystery Plays* (Berkeley: University of California Press, 1972).

ish party. In such a situation, presenting a dramatization of the god's life before his apotheosis would have risked irreverence (since gods often had rather colorful lives as humans), and a dramatization of his miracles risked failing to do them justice. And since the gods' taste was rather like the villagers', as can be seen from the food offerings, perhaps it seemed natural to provide them with the sort of operas that the villagers enjoyed.

I have made a basic distinction between festival performances that took place on the ground, such as processions and the simple skits that accompanied them (although the skits were sometimes performed on temporary stages), and the longer and more complex ritual operas, which were performed on permanent stages—spectacle and sacrifice. Processions and other performances on the ground seem to have been part of the traditional stock of local customs; they had many archaic features—bonfires, scapegoats, "formations"—and seldom had scripts. It was on the ground, not on stage, that the gods "came to life" and could be seen, often wearing masks, walking in processions, or sometimes engaging in simple actions on temporary stages in tableaux whose lines were spoken by a narrator-director. And on those occasions there was no risk of offending the gods, since the villagers were the audience; the gods were elsewhere.

Southern Shanxi and the rest of north China was saturated with temples, and large-scale sacrifices to the gods who occupied those temples took place constantly throughout the year. Both spectacle and sacrifice were there, but no sense of the sacred, no great central Story to be dramatized. There was no catharsis, no epiphanies. The tragic, the profound, the sacred—these never appear in the ritual operas I have knowledge of. The historical and contingent, not the eternal and immutable, supplied the stuff of dramatic action. The gods were not far removed from this world; they entered it with ease and behaved much as ordinary men and women did. And so they were diminished. True, they wielded considerable power, but so did the county magistrate or the wealthy landowner.

———

The most spectacular expression of the central role of ritual and drama in the religious culture of Shanxi was the *sai*. Those festivals are particularly worth studying because of their unique importance to the people of the villages that sponsored them. Some of them are also unusually well documented: we know a great deal about the ritual masters who supervised them, the actors and musicians who accompanied the rituals and staged the operas, and even the chefs who prepared the elaborate food offerings. The temples where the *sai* were performed were large and imposing, often built on splendid sites away from villages, out in the countryside. It is to these great temple festivals that we now turn.

PART III

The Great Temple Festivals of Southeastern Shanxi

INTRODUCTION

The village New Year celebrations we examined in Part I were tightly tied to the arrival of spring, that is, they were seasonal. The other major form of village ritual, the liturgical, focused on temples and celebrated the birthdays of gods. Even the simplest of these, sponsored by a single village, could be quite elaborate, but in southeastern Shanxi they were dwarfed by a special type of ritual, called by local people *sai*, *sai hui*, or *yingshen*.[1] Like single-village rituals, they focused on a local god, and their core ceremonies took place before temple altars. But unlike them, they were sponsored by village alliances, which were building blocks of the rural ritual-social-political-military order in southern Shanxi and perhaps many other regions; their operas were performed by members of a hereditary caste of Entertainers, who were both despised and ritually indispensable; they featured enormous food offerings prepared by

---

1. *Sai* as a term for offerings to the gods dates at least to Han times. I do not know how this meaning is connected with the modern meaning of the word: "compete" or "competition." It is commonly said that the link is competition between villages to put on the most spectacular festivals, but this is folk etymology at its worst. The better explanation, consistent with so much else in the *sai*, is that the term, like *nuo*, simply preserves its archaic meaning.

It may be more accurate to translate *sai hui* as "festival" rather than "ritual." But to avoid confusion, I use "ritual" to translate or refer to *sai* or expressions containing the word, and when I use "*sai*" I am referring to the ritual parts of the entire complex.

specially trained chefs; and they were overseen by professional liturgists known as Masters of Ceremonial, an elite group drawn from the ranks of local diviners and geomancers. They were last performed in Shanxi as authentic village traditions in the late 1930s, on the eve of the Japanese invasion of the province.

Starting in the mid-1980s, over a dozen manuscripts containing prayers, invocations, instructions, and outlines of the ritual programs for entire *sai* were discovered in a few southeastern Shanxi villages. These discoveries stimulated further research, including field investigations of particular *sai* and interviews with surviving participants. Although virtually all the scripts of the operas that were an integral part of the *sai* have been lost, most of them during the Cultural Revolution, a few part-scripts belonging to specific Entertainer households survived. From these we can gain a slight sense of what a handful of *sai* operas were like.

Sai were always centered on a specific temple, some of them monumental structures on grand sites far out in the countryside. To the best of my knowledge, none was in the heart of a village, although exact locations are often difficult to determine. (Some *sai*—including one of the three discussed in this part—were celebrated in temples in towns. In those cases, the wards of the city jointly sponsored the festivals, thus becoming the functional equivalent of a village alliance.) I cannot say whether there were grand temple festivals sponsored by village alliances elsewhere in north China—although I suspect there were. But whether the *sai* evolved thanks to a set of circumstances unique to southeastern Shanxi or existed in other regions, they are still of the greatest importance. Even more than the New Year rituals analyzed in Part I, the *sai* force us to revise a good deal of conventional wisdom about Chinese village life and rural culture. My goal therefore is quite simple: to show in detail the extraordinarily rich symbolic world that farmers, shopkeepers, craftsmen, and the like, quite without guidance from ecclesiastical or political authorities, created for themselves in the villages of southeastern Shanxi. If there had been no officials, no monks, and no Daoist priests, little if anything in the *sai* would have been different. This is not to say that these rituals and operas had no connection to the world of state ritual and orthodox doctrine, or to novels and other productions of the educated elite, because they did. But although the ideas, values, and cultural forms of the economic and cultural elites frequently left a mark, the *sai* always transcended them.

The *sai* were not as autarkic as the Yuanxiao rituals discussed in Part I. *Sai* of different places had many elements in common because the rituals were led by a relatively small number of specialists who relied on liturgical manuals, and because the operas were staged by professionals who had a monopoly on *sai* performances in their family territories. Nevertheless, each *sai* did look different from every other—as an experienced Master of Ceremonial told an interviewer in 1989, "Of ten *sai*, nine are different."[2] But the Shanxi *sai* are extremely unlike the *jiao* of southeastern China, which have received so much attention over the past several decades. I shall return to this point.

In each of the three chapters that follows, I describe in detail a multivillage *sai*. Each *sai* is paired with one of the three basic elements of festival life in China, opera, ritual, and feasting. Thus in Chapter 1, on the Temple of the Divine Mother of the Ninth Heaven, I include substantial material on the hereditary Entertainer families (*yuehu*). Chapter 2, on the Hou Yi Temple of Mt. Longquan, discusses those indispensable ritual specialists, the Masters of Ceremonial (*zhu li*). And finally, Chapter 3, on the Hou Yi Temple of Big West Gate, provides information on the great food offerings and the ritual chefs who prepared them.

Before proceeding, it is important to discuss the primary sources I have drawn on in my study of the *sai*, partly because they are both exceptionally rich and scarcely known, but also because some of them raise basic questions. In early 1983 the Ministry of Culture and other high-level organs of the Chinese government proposed the compilation of a *National Encyclopedia of Drama and the Performing Arts* (*Zhongguo xiqu zhi*). After consideration by other administrative bodies, the project was incorporated into the sixth and seventh five-year plans.[3] At about the same time, nine other encyclopedic compilations, on subjects such as dance, folk songs, and instrumental music, were also approved.[4] Editorial committees were set up in the provinces, municipalities, and

2. "Shi sai jiu bu tong" (Li Tiansheng, "*Tang yuexing tu* jiao zhu," p. 121).

3. *Zhongguo xiqu zhi: Shanxi juan*, "Xu yan" by Zhang Geng.

4. The entire series was called *The Ten Great Collections on Culture* (*Shi da wenyi jicheng*).

counties, and local drama specialists began searching for new material.[5] In 1985 two scholars, Li Shoutian and Yuan Shuangxi, who were probably then based in Changzhi city, one of the most important municipalities in southeastern Shanxi, uncovered fragments of *Dui* Operas and *yuanben*, which were performed during *sai*, and of prayers and invocations recited by the Director (*qianhang*) of the Entertainers during temple rituals. These findings roused the interest of provincial authorities, who decided to make audio and video recordings of rituals and operas reconstructed from the Li-Yuan material. During the filming, one of the specialists involved learned that a man named Cao Zhanbiao of Nan Shê village, Lucheng county, was in possession of an old ritual text.

The Cao family had for generations been *yinyang* masters, local specialists who knew how to calculate the proper time for funerals, find propitious grave sites, carry out vernacular rituals such as "Thanking the Earth" (*xie tu*) (which was needed when ground was broken for a new house or a grave), and so on. As a result, they were persecuted severely after 1949, especially during the Cultural Revolution, and Zhanbiao was extremely reluctant to have anything more to do with local cadres. But eventually he was persuaded that no harm would come to him, and he showed the researchers a remarkable document. On its title page was the date "Wanli second year, first month, thirteenth day" (February 4, 1574) and the title *Transmitted Records of Rituals for Welcoming the Gods and Sacrificing at the Shê, with Forty Melodies in [Twenty-eight] Keys (Yingshen sai shê li jie chuan bu sishi qu [ershiba] gongdiao)*. On the first page it called itself *The Diagram of the Musical Asterisms of the Zhou Dynasty (Zhou yuexing tu)*, a more authentic title, which I shall use (in transliteration) hereafter.[6] In the photographic reproduction of the text, the cover appears to be in a different hand from the main body of the text, and,

---

5. Much of what they collected was not published, and other material appeared only in limited-circulation sources such as Shanxi's *Xiju ziliao*. The location of the original reports and documents is something of a mystery. When I inquired of specialists in Shanxi in the mid-1990s, they all claimed not to know what had happened to them.

6. The text is not a "diagram" (*tu*), and any meaning of "musical asterisms" (*yuexing*) that can intelligibly be applied to the text escapes me, despite the glosses in the two published editions: Han Sheng et al., eds., "*Yingshen saishe lijie . . .* zhu shi," p. 56, *n*; and Liao Ben, *Song Yuan xiqu wenwu*, p. 371, *n*.

since the three columns of text on it are intended to be read modern fashion from left to right, it almost certainly is a fairly recent concoction. On this dubious cover the alleged Ming dynasty copyist's name is given as Cao Guozai. The same name (actually, the personal name) has been crudely added to the first line of the main text.[7] Both the date and the link with a distant ancestor of Cao Zhanbiao should therefore be regarded with considerable skepticism.

This find caused a sensation since elements in the manuscript, including opera titles and musical references, appeared to local drama

---

7. The cover and first page of the manuscript are reproduced in *Zhonghua xiqu* 3 (1987.4), pp. 2–3. The second of the two characters is illegible, but clearly intended to be 宰. But the printed text in *Zhonghua xiqu* 3, the first printed edition, transcribes the copyist's name on the cover as 曹國宪 but states in a note that the Cao brothers say that the name should be 國宰. That edition also reads the crude addition to the first line of the text as 國宰賽記 and adds that the 宰 was changed from 宪 (Han Sheng et al., eds., "*Yingshen saishe lijie . . . zhu shi*," p. 56, *n*3, p. 57, *n*3). Yang Mengheng ("Shanxi saishe yuehu," p. 244) says that the name on the cover is 曹國憲, with no further comment (宪 is the simplified form of 憲). Liao Ben, in *Song Yuan xiqu wenwu*, pp. 371, 372, *n*4, gives the name on the cover as 曹國宰, and that added to the first line of the main text as 國宰 also, but comments that the 宰 has been changed to 宪 there. Apart from demonstrating the folly of transcribing older texts with simplified characters, all this strongly suggests that the editors of the printed text in *Zhonghua xiqu* 3, and possibly Yang Mengheng as well, saw a cover that was different from the manuscript reproduced in that issue, perhaps the original photocopy. Li Tiansheng, who knew many of the principals personally and conducted many interviews in the area, claims that Cao Zhanbiao, on the pretext that the old cover page was damaged, tore it off and substituted the one that is on the manuscript now and presumably was used in the reproduction in *Zhonghua xiqu* 3.

Cao Zhanbiao claimed that he was a descendant in the twenty-second generation of Cao Zhenxing, who held the official position of *yinyang* master (*yinyang xue guan*), as did his son, grandson, and great-grandson. There is an inscription for a bridge at Nan Shê's Yuhuang Temple dated 1637 that has the entry "The Yinyang [Master] Cao Guozai." Zhanbiao claimed that he was the twentieth-generation descendant of Guozai, who thus would have been a grandson of Zhenxing. (See Liao Ben, *Song Yuan xiqu wenwu*, p. 356.) Having Guozai as a direct ancestor would in itself have been an advantage to Zhanbiao, for it would have given him a formidable pedigree and had the added benefit of strengthening his claim to ownership of the manuscript. This would have been a strong motive for changing the name 國憲 (or 宪) on the cover to 國宰. Note that Li Tiansheng says that the manuscript was originally the property of the Niu family of Jia village, whom we will meet in a moment. (See Li's open letter, "You 'Shanxi saishe zhuan ji,'" p. 186.)

historians to suggest strongly that it preserved a very old tradition. This encouraged local scholars to continue the hunt for manuscripts that had survived the bibliographic holocaust of the Cultural Revolution. In 1989 Zhang Zhennan, an elderly retired playwright with a deep interest in folk opera, heard that a *yinyang* master named Niu Xixian, who lived in East Daguan Village, about thirteen kilometers northeast of Zhangzi town, had managed to preserve an important ritual handbook that had belonged to his father and other forebears, who had also been *yinyang* masters and had officiated at *sai*. Zhang bicycled to East Daguan and persuaded Niu Xixian to show him the manuscript. This was the text now known as *The Diagram of the Musical Asterisms of the Tang Dynasty* (*Tang yuexing tu*). It was immediately obvious to Zhang that the manuscript was of great importance, and he asked Niu for permission, which Niu granted, to show it to the scholars working on the Shanxi volume of the drama encyclopedia. Not long thereafter, Niu gave thirteen more manuscripts either to Zhang or to Li Tiansheng, another local scholar and assistant director of the Changzhi Drama Research Unit. One of these was dated 1522.[8] The texts are mostly collections of prayers, hymns, memorials, and exhortations for use during a *sai*, but some are virtually templates for a full *sai* performance.[9]

Another important ritual manuscript was collected from Cao Zhanbiao in 1989 and published in 1991. It was "found among tattered old volumes on house and tomb geomancy" when he and his son were "cleaning out an old trunk." It has been given different titles in each of

---

8. Conflicting stories are told about the discovery of these manuscripts. Zhang Zhennan is said to have been given them by Niu Xixian in the biographies of himself and Niu Xixian; see Yang Mengheng, "Zhang Zhennan," p. 255; and Zhang Zhennan and Yang Mengheng, "Niu Xixian," p. 285. Zhang Zhennan himself, in his earliest account of the discovery of the *Tang yuexing tu* (Zhang Zhennan, "Ji Lucheng *Lijie chuan bu*," pp. 145–47) does not mention the thirteen additional manuscripts, although it is possible that the article was written before he learned of them. By contrast, Li Tiansheng says that Niu Xiaowu, Xixian's brother, gave the bulk of the manuscripts to *him*. I have not been able to reconcile these conflicting accounts.

9. Most of the thirteen additional manuscripts from the Niu brothers remained unpublished and virtually inaccessible until they were edited by Yang Mengheng and published, along with the *Tang yuexing tu*, in a single volume in 2000: *Shangdang gu sai xiejuan shisi zhong jian zhu* (hereafter cited as *Fourteen Manuscripts*). Fortunately I had photocopies of the originals.

its two editions, since the original cover is missing. One can be rendered as *Model Texts for Offerings and Melodies for the Presentation of Cups During the Welcoming of the Gods and Sacrificing at the* Shê.[10]

In addition to the sixteen manuscripts listed above, a wide variety of other material has been recovered, including scripts for the roles of individual characters in a number of *Dui* Operas. Most of these can be found in the collection edited by Han Sheng.

The liturgical manuscripts provide an unusual and possibly unique window on village ritual life in north China in late imperial times. But their value would be greatly reduced if we knew nothing about the settings in which they were performed: the villages, the cults, the temples, the processions and dances, the costumes, the music, the offerings, and so on—in short, the total experience of the *sai*. Fortunately we can reconstruct a great deal of that experience, but only by relying heavily on the memories of men of advanced age, an issue that needs to be carefully discussed.

Although I visited many sites in the *sai* area and took part in a number of interviews with villagers who had personal knowledge of the processions and sacrifices that took place during the festivals, most of the descriptions of the *sai* used here were written by local authors who either remembered them or had talked with older villagers who had observed them or participated in them. In addition, I have used a number of biographies of Entertainers and Masters of Ceremonial compiled on the basis of interviews with the subjects or with members of their families. Some of this material is highly detailed, but it is retrospective; it does not describe current practices. It is based on interviews and reminiscences, not long-term residence in the research sites (although some researchers are intimately familiar with the relevant villages). Nor is it derived from archival research, since there are no archives. In short, the various accounts are neither anthropological nor historical sources as traditionally defined. Rather, they are something like hometown or home-region ethnography. This is their strength, and I have used them

---

10. Published as Han Sheng et al., eds., "*Yingshen saishe jisi . . .* zhushi." The comment about the manuscript's discovery is found on p. 1. A version with less complete annotations was published in Han Sheng et al., eds., *Shangdang nuo wenhua*, pp. 500–536.

with gratitude. We are very fortunate that they exist; many of the inter-
viewees have already passed away, and soon there will be no one who
personally experienced those great rituals. But, as with all accounts
based on memories, reliability is an issue. Hence a certain amount of
caution is in order.

A NOTE ON *SHÊ*

At various points in this book, we have encountered the micro-
geographic unit known as the *shê*. In the areas familiar to me, a *shê* could
be identical to a natural village, or several small villages could combine
to form a *shê*, or a single large village could be divided into several *shê*.
Each *shê* focused on a particular temple, or perhaps a lineage segment.
David Holm refers to the *shê* as "that elusive form of organization . . .
that until recently formed the bedrock of rural social structure in North
China."[11] People identified with their *shê* and wanted its celebrations to
be the best, and this gave rise to intense, sometimes violent, rivalries
between *shê*. For example, the men carrying a deity's palanquin during
the festival celebrating the Dragon King's birthday in Xinli village, near
Heyang in eastern Shaanxi (just across the Yellow River from the Gong
and Drum *Za* Opera region of southwestern Shanxi), needed to be
careful not to cross from their *shê* into the neighboring one.[12] Another
example of *shê* particularism in the same district involves a certain
Wang Shunkui, a member of the East *Shê* of Xingjia village, who one
day early in the Republican era took a shortcut across the grounds

---

11. Holm, "The Death of *Tiaoxi*," pp. 868–69. There is further important information on *shê* in Holm, *Art and Ideology*, pp. 157–58; and Hsiao, *Rural China*, p. 58 (quoting a
statement by Zhang Zhidong). See also Dean, "Transformations of the *Shê*"; and Johnson, "Report on 堯山聖母廟與神社," *passim*. William Rowe somewhat underestimates
the importance of *shê* in *Saving the World*, p. 381. The *shê*, in southern Shanxi and east-
central Shaanxi at least, remind one of the *contrade* of Siena, Italy, the seventeen wards
of the city that probably date to the thirteenth century. In Siena, "each individual belongs first to his *contrada* and then to Siena. In the strictest sense, one is born into a *contrada*" (Dundes and Falassi, *La Terra in Piazza*, p. 12). It is the *contrade* that sponsor riders
in the ancient horse race known as the *palio*, which is run twice every summer and is
Siena's most important communal event.

12. Shi Yaozeng, "Heyang," p. 223.

where the West *Shê* performed a local form of ritual opera called *tiao xi*. For this blasphemous trespass, a gang of West *Shê* men attacked him and threw lime in his eyes.[13]

Additional evidence concerning the importance of *shê* comes from a passage in the 1919 Wenxi local gazetteer that provides invaluable information on temple festivals in southwestern Shanxi before the great upheavals of the middle decades of the century.

When the wheat harvest is over and the granaries are full, the larger villages put on operas to give thanks. In times of drought, when prayers have brought sweet moisture, they also often present operas to give thanks for the rain.[14] Small villages sometimes invite blind storytelling masters. Each village has a god that it welcomes. Large villages form a *shê* by themselves; smaller ones join together to make a *shê*. Also there are cases where five, six, ten or more *shê* join together and take turns welcoming a specific god. . . . For each *shê* whose turn it is, when the appointed time comes, they put on a lively festival with gongs and drums, and Flower Carts and Drum Carts pulled by oxen. There are also opera floats (*tai ge*) and stilt-walkers that act out stories, each striving to be the most unusual. . . . They must go through the village in which the temple is located and all the other villages in the *shê* [if it is a multivillage *shê*]. At the temple, the *shê* that is "sending off" the god has operas ready for presentation. When [the procession] arrives, the gongs and drums play several pieces, and then they arrange the banners, pick up their stilts, and go to the traveling palace that the members of the *shê* have built, where operas are performed for three days to pacify the gods.[15] . . . Every village [in the *shê*] has at least one "moon platter period" for which they build a colorful shed of excellent workmanship in which are arranged offerings of [food from] land and water, and during which they perform operas for three days.[16]

This passage, which reflects conditions at the end of the Qing and appears to be based on firsthand knowledge, shows clearly that *shê* played

---

13. Ibid., pp. 225–26.

14. The author points out later that Clapper Opera (*bangzi xi*) was the most common type of opera at temple festivals, but that "other forms are also sometimes seen."

15. This must refer to a temporary stage, and if so, it is extremely interesting that it is called a "palace" (宫), because that term can also mean "temple."

16. Ding Shiliang and Zhao Fang, *Zhongguo difangzhi . . . Huabei juan*, p. 700, quoting *Wenxi xian zhi* (1919), section on "Customs Connected with Beliefs" (*Xinyang fengsu*). (Other sources give a 1918 date for this local gazetteer.)

a role in the organization of temple festivals in southwestern Shanxi very similar to that in the Heyang district.[17]

Finally, we have the valuable eyewitness account by Fr. Willem Grootaers of *shê* in the region around Xuanhua, in Hebei about sixty kilometers northeast of the extreme northeastern corner of Shanxi. In fieldwork carried out in 1948, Grootaers and his assistants visited over 100 villages in the area to carry out a survey of rural temples and their cults.[18] The *shê* had administrative committees that met in temples or even had offices there; Grootaers believed that all important villages probably had such committees. In one village he was able to examine the account books of the *shê*, which were kept in the Dragon King temple, and discovered that "the list of expenses for several years showed conclusively that no important thing was done in the village except through [the *shê*]." The members of the *shê* committee were "the real masters of the village." According to Grootaers, in the Xuanhua region the *shê* committee took care "of everything pertaining to village government, waterways and irrigation, crops, charity works, legal suits, schools, temple feasts [i.e., festivals] and temple revenue." He suggests that the authority of the *shê* was particularly important in Xuanhua because of the need for a strong hand in administering the irrigation agreements There is little doubt that the *shê* encountered in southern Shanxi were similar to those known to Grootaers.

The ritual-sponsoring districts known as *shê* were a basic component of the social and political organization of rural north China; we will encounter them frequently in the following chapters. Better understanding of this social formation should be a high priority for future research.

---

17. Very similar also was the *shê*'s role in the great annual festival of the Lady of Miraculous Response of Mount Yao, in Pucheng county, west-central Shaanxi, about 60 km southwest of Heyang and 160 km west-southwest of Wenxi. See Qin Jianming and Marianne Bujard, *Yao shan shengmu miao*, chap. 2.

18. See Grootaers, "Rural Temples," pp. 39–41, esp. p. 40.

The Temple of the Divine Mother of the Ninth Heaven

□

The Entertainers (*Yuehu*)

The Temple and Its Founding

The Temple of the Divine Mother of the Ninth Heaven (Jiutian sheng-mu miao) was the site of one of the most famous *sai* in southeastern Shanxi. The temple is located on a hill just west of the very small village of Donghe in western Pingshun county, near the borders of Huguan and Lucheng counties. Donghe and the other villages in the Divine Mother alliance are in a valley separated from the eastern edge of the Changzhi plain by a substantial spur of the Taihang range.[1] The goddess, whom

---

1. Cao Zupeng and Cao Xinguang, "Pingshun xian Dongyugou," p. 1. On the 1:200,000 map of Pingshun County in the *Shanxi Provincial Atlas* (*Shanxi sheng ditu ji* [1995]) and the 1:100,000 map of Changzhi Municipality (Shanxi Provincial Carto-graphic Bureau, 1987) the village neighboring the Divine Mother temple is called He-dong 河東, and a village about six kilometers to the southeast is called Donghe 東河. However, on the 1:50,000 Chinese Army map of Pingshun (sheet 529, surveyed 1924, printed 1942), these names are reversed, with the village near the temple called Donghe. Scholars discussing the temple and its Song dynasty stele, including Yang Taikang and Cao Zhanmei in their *San Jin xiqu wenwu kao* (p. 353) and Cao Zupeng, who is a native of North Shê (Bei Shê) village, just a few miles away, and is assistant director of the local antiquities museum (interview), also call it Donghe. It would appear that either the village's name has been changed or the more recent maps are in error. An additional mystery is that Dongyugou village, identified as the site of the temple by our best lo-cal informant, Wang Jiaju, does not appear on any map I have seen. I suspect that

locals called simply "Grandma" or "Old Lady" (Lao nainai), was unquestionably a rain-bringer, as we shall see shortly. Unique in my experience of southeastern Shanxi temple festivals, the annual *sai* was held not on the goddess's birthday, always determined by the lunar calendar, but on a date in the solar calendar: the fifth *wu* day after the Beginning of Spring (*lichun*), thus in the third or fourth week in March. If the year had been a good one, a second *sai* would be held on the fifth *wu* day after the Beginning of Autumn (approximately the third or fourth week of September).[2] The *sai* was sponsored by an alliance of five *shê* comprising eight villages, with each *shê* taking responsibility in turn.[3] The temple is imposing, especially if approached by the long flight of steps leading to the single entrance in its massive south façade,[4] but its interior dimensions are surprisingly compact. I found the distance between the stage (located over the main gate in the southern Shanxi style) and the main hall to be about sixty feet, and the courtyard at its widest ninety-six feet. A roofed Offering Pavilion at least forty feet long nearly fills the space between stage and main hall, leaving courtyards on each side of it.[5] Over thirty stone stelae are preserved in the temple, many under the roof of the Offering Pavilion, reinforcing the impression that the temple was spared the worst ravages of the Red Guards.[6]

Dongyugou village somehow became Donghe village, because Wang Jiaju stated in our interview that the Divine Mother Temple was on the western edge of Dongyugou village (p. 54 of interview transcripts).

2. Yang Mengheng, "Pingshun xian Dongyugou," p. 323. The Beginning of Spring was February 4 or 5 and the Beginning of Autumn was August 8 or 9; the fifth *wu* day would come 41–49 days later.

3. The five *shê* were East Shê, Lower Shê, South Shê, North Shê, and West Shê, which comprised, respectively, Dongyugou village; Lower Shê and Changjia villages; South Shê and Dingliu villages; North Shê village; and West Shê and Hedong (*sic*) villages. (Interview with Mr. Wang Jiaju carried out in his home in North Shê village in October 1993. Interview transcripts, p. 57.) All these villages can be found on the 1 : 200,000 map of Pingshun in the official atlas of Shanxi, *Shanxi sheng ditu ji*, with the exception of Dongyugou, whose name, as I noted, has probably been changed. (Dingliu is in Lucheng county.) See Map 6.

4. For photographs of the stage, see Yang Taikang and Cao Zhanmei, *San Jin xiqu*, fig. 281; and Yang Mengheng, "Pingshun xian Dongyugou," p. 241. See also Fig. 8.

5. Some photographs of the interior can be found in Yang Mengheng, "Pingshun xian Dongyugou," pp. 338–41. For a detailed plan, see Fig. 9.

6. Feng Junjie, *Shanxi xiqu*, p. 34.

Map 6 Temple of the Divine Mother of the Ninth Heaven and environs. Villages that participated in the *sai* are highlighted. 1 cm = 1.7 km (SOURCE: *Shanxi sheng ditu ji*).

The oldest of the inscriptions is dated Song Yuanfu 3.12.15 (January 16, 1101).[7] It commemorates the renovation and enlargement of the temple and provides important information on its history and the cult of the Divine Mother. The temple "is located in the eastern part of Three Pond *li*; the elders refer to [it as] the 'Immortal's Village of the Divine Mother' (*shengmu zhi xianxiang*)." This suggests that it was sited in what was at that time the countryside, away from village sounds and smells; this would be consistent with what we know of other temples

---

7. This is probably the date of the official dedication of the stele, even though it had not been finished. (Such anticipatory ceremonies are not unknown even today.) Four other dates appear on the stele, in the following order: the first month of the Jianzhong jingguo era (February 1101); Yuanfu 3.12.23 (January 24, 1101; completion of the carving, probably of the front); Chongning 2.5.5 (June 11, 1103; setting up the stone); and Jianzhong jingguo 1.1.15 (February 14, 1101). The two dates in February 1101, which are the penultimate lines in the front and back of the stele, may refer to the carving of additional text, especially donors' names. The text, punctuated, can be found in ibid., pp. 28–32; and in Yang Mengheng, "Pingshun xian Dongyugou," pp. 334–37. Both transcriptions have errors.

where *sai* were celebrated. Donors are listed on the reverse, and their villages are named. Three of the twenty-odd villages—North Shê, West Shê, and Lower Shê—are among the eight villages that supported the *sai* in the 1930s; so their involvement with the Divine Mother temple went back at least eight centuries. But there is little sign of the village alliances that were the foundation of the great *sai* in late imperial times.[8] The inscription states clearly that one part of the project was the construction of a stage (*wu lou*). The word *lou* strongly suggests that this was a covered structure, not an open platform. Therefore this is one of the earliest known records of a stage in China.[9] Even today the Divine Mother temple is rather isolated; at the beginning of the twelfth century, it must have been quite remote. And yet at that time enough people were watching operas during temple rituals that there was a felt need for a new-style stage. This reinforces the point made in Part II about the virtually simultaneous rise of opera in countryside and city in Song times.

The text of the inscription reflects two rather different ways of thinking about the goddess. In one, her temple is set in a landscape rich in associations with Daoist worthies and described with Daoist imagery and allusions. But woven in with this literati Daoist material are a few references to popular lore about her powers as a rain goddess. "This is the place where Duke Wei . . . spent the night,[10] and having received the great favor of a banquet from the Divine Mother, rode auspicious clouds . . . into the heavens, where he raised thunder and rain to drench the Central Kingdom."[11] This is an allusion to a legend recorded in the ninth-century compilation *Xu xuan guai lu* concerning the early Tang

---

8. The only hint comes near the start of the text on the back of the stele, where it states that "all the *shê* in the eastern part of the jurisdiction of Three Ponds [*li*], at the base of Mt. Zhongnan and in Chen Family village" worked on the project (Feng Junjie, *Shanxi xiqu*, p. 30).

9. The present stage was built in the Qing. See Liao Ben, *Song Yuan xiqu wenwu*, p. 130.

10. There is a problem with the text at the ellipsis. The four transcriptions of the inscription available to me—Yang Mengheng, "Pingshun xian Dongyugou," p. 334; Feng Junjie, *Shanxi xiqu*, p. 28; Yang Taikang and Cao Zhanmei, *San Jin xiqu*, p. 356; and Shanxi shifan daxue xiqu wenwu yanjiusuo, *Song Jin Yuan*, p. 134—each give a different version of the characters between 雲 and 遇.

11. Yang Mengheng, "Pingshun xian Dongyugou," p. 334.

Fig. 8 General view of the Divine Mother Temple. The boxy structure on the right is a stage built in the 1950s (SOURCE: Yang and Gao, *San Jin*).

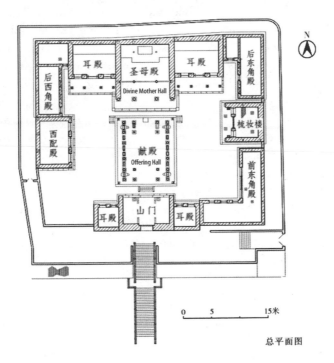

Fig. 9 Plan of the Divine Mother Temple
(SOURCE: *Zhongguo wenwu ditu ji: Shanxi fence*).

general and high official Li Jing, to whom many temples were dedicated in southeastern Shanxi.[12]

According to the legend, when Jing was still unknown, he lived in a mountain village and spent his time hunting. One day while out hunting, he lost his way and sought lodging for the night in a grand mansion over which a dignified lady presided. After some hesitation because her sons were away, she allowed him to stay. In the middle of the night, he heard an urgent knocking at the gate: a heavenly tally ordering rain for the area 700 *li* around the mountain had arrived. The lady then revealed to Jing that she and her sons were dragons. Since her sons were not at home, there was no one to carry out the order, and she asked if he would attempt it. She explained that he merely had to let his horse go where it wanted and, whenever it neighed, to put a drop of water from a magic flask on his mane. Jing agreed, and at once his horse leaped into the sky, his hooves thundering, and with every drop from the magic flask the lightning stabbed and the clouds parted. Then he saw the village where he had been staying. He had never been able to repay the villagers' kindness, and he knew they were suffering from drought; so he generously shook out twenty drops for them. Alas, when he returned he discovered that the twenty drops had generated twenty feet of rain and the village had been swept away.[13] The inscription text later says that "the Divine Mother receives heavenly tallies to stimulate the rain, attends the Jade Emperor at court, and hastens the thunder."[14] And there are constant (and highly esoteric) allusions in the text to lightning, thunder, and rain. An inscription of 1261 provides further evidence: "The Divine Mother of the Ninth Heaven is the daughter of the Darkly Efficacious King (Xuanmiao wang) in Heaven and is the Prime Ruler of the Great Unity (Taiyi yuanjun) on Earth. She commands the thunder and raises the lightning, she scolds the wind and upbraids the clouds."[15]

---

12. Feng Junjie, *Shanxi xiqu*, p. 33.

13. *Taiping guangji*, 418.10a–12a, quoting *Xu xuan guai lu*, cited in Feng Junjie, *Shanxi xiqu*, p. 33.

14. Feng Junjie, *Shanxi xiqu*, p. 29.

15. Yang Mengheng, "Pingshun xian Dongyugou," p. 321.

In the Song dynasty, at least, this rain-controlling mother of dragon kings was provided with a thick Daoist veneer. To judge from a quick survey of the other surviving inscriptions, it is doubtful that the Daoist aspect remained as strong in later dynasties, but to demonstrate this in detail here would take us too far afield.

ORGANIZATION OF THE *SAI* AND FIRST DAY

So much for the setting, the temple, and the goddess; what of the great ritual, the *sai*?[16] As mentioned earlier, it was sponsored by eight villages organized in five *shê*. All but one of the eight can be identified on the 1:200,000 map of Pingshun in the official atlas of Shanxi; they define a compact area about three kilometers by four kilometers, a good deal smaller than the areas covered by other village alliances we shall encounter.[17] Cao Zupeng, a native of North Shê, one of the participating villages, said that villagers' contributions to *sai* expenses were based on their landholdings. The money was collected after each *sai* and lent out at interest during the following year.[18] Neither Cao nor any of our other sources says much about the men who ran the *sai*. However, we know the names of the Masters of Ceremonial who presided at the last

---

16. The main sources for the following section are a long interview with Wang Jiaju (Interview transcripts, pp. 57–63); a shorter interview with Cao Zupeng, assistant director of the Pingshun County Antiquities Museum, at the home of the director of the county Cultural Affairs Office in Pingshun town, Oct. 18, 1993 (Interview transcripts, pp. 51–53); and Yang Mengheng, "Pingshun xian Dongyugou," pp. 315–46. Yang's article is the most important source. Yang took part in the 1993 interview with Mr. Wang, but information credited to him comes from his article unless otherwise noted. Yang says virtually nothing about the sources he used in researching his article, but internal evidence suggests interviews not only with Mr. Wang but also with other residents of villages near the temple. The information is so detailed that it must have come from participants and witnesses.

17. The grouping of "five *shê* and eight villages" is mentioned explicitly in a poem from the Qing Xianfeng era (1851–61) quoted in Cao Zupeng and Cao Xinguang, "Pingshun xian Dongyugou," p. 7; and in an inscription of 1875 quoted in Feng Junjie, *Taihang shenmiao*, p. 491. Hence, it had been customary for at least a century when the *sai* was celebrated in 1938.

18. Interview with Cao Zupeng, Oct. 18, 1993 (Interview transcripts, p. 52).

Divine Mother *sai* in 1938: Qin Laike and his brother Qin Xianke, who lived in Huangchi village, about four kilometers north of the temple.[19]

The activities of the *sai* stretched across six days: two preparatory days, three days for the *sai* proper, and one day to bring it to a proper conclusion. On the morning of the first day, the *Shê* Heads, who were the leaders of the sponsoring village and of the other villages in the alliance, surveyed the preparations. All the participants, including the actors in full costume, the banners and parasols, the musicians with their instruments, the floats, the palanquins, and the massive Four-Scene Carts (*si jing che*) gathered at a place called East Quarter and were inspected by the *Shê* Heads. While this was going on, twenty-four Spirit Mansions (*shen lou*)—elaborate palanquins—were arranged in two rows, one on either side of the main gate of the Divine Mother Temple. (They must have extended down the grand stairway.) These were made to look like multistory buildings, complete with architectural details like flying rafters and hanging cornices.

All the participants then paraded from East Quarter to the temple: at the head of the procession was the Director (*qianhang*) of the Entertainers, Wang Fuyun, carrying his Director's Staff (*xi zhu*). He led the troupe of Entertainers (*yuehu*), who wore red gowns with green borders and hats decorated with pheasant feathers. Then came the Masters of Ceremonial, Qin Laike and Qin Xianke, leading the *Shê* Heads, each of whom held a dragon-head staff and a copper censer wreathed in incense smoke. They were followed by four Incense Masters (*si xiang*), carrying bundles of "string incense" wrapped in white cloth, and four Candle Masters (*si zhu*), each with a red silk lantern. Then came ten or more Incense Elders (*xiang lao*), whose duty it was to accompany the *Shê* Heads with incense during the rituals, and a group of Water Officials (*shui guan*), youths of around fifteen who were responsible for serving tea and wine to the gods. Twenty-four Pavilioners (*tingshi*) and twenty-four Attendants (*weishi*) holding their "sounding staffs," long rods with rings at one end that jingled when they were shaken, brought

---

19. Yang Mengheng, "Shanxi saishe yuehu," p. 261. In my interview with Wang Jiaju, he stated that the Master of Ceremonial in 1938 was surnamed Qin and was from Huangchi village, confirming (or perhaps simply repeating) Yang's information.

up the rear. These men were in the service of the gods who would be present at the ceremony: the Divine Mother and her twenty-three guests.

All the members of the procession entered the temple courtyard and stood waiting quietly. The Master of Ceremonial said "Present the incense!" and the Incense Masters, Candle Masters, and Water Officials presented incense. Accompanied by music, they performed four obeisances, and the *Shê* Heads and Incense Elders kowtowed. Then the Master of Ceremonial wrote the name of each of the twenty-four gods on a slip of red paper, rolled each slip into a ball, and put it in a bamboo tube of the sort used to hold divination sticks. The Master of Ceremonial called out "Pavilioners, offer incense!" Each Pavilioner walked into the main hall, offered incense, bowed, took out one of the paper balls, and gave it to the Master of Ceremonial. He opened it up and read the name. The Pavilioner then went to the spirit tablets of the twenty-four gods, which were probably placed all together in the main hall, picked up the one for his god, and stood waiting reverently with his Attendant close behind him.[20]

After all the Pavilioners had been assigned a god, they formed into two lines and, holding the spirit tablets, filed out of the temple and put the tablets in the appropriate palanquins. At the Master of Ceremonial's order, each palanquin was lifted up by the two men assigned to it, firecrackers were set off, the musicians began to play, and all the ritual personnel, including the Pavilioners and their Attendants, the *Shê* Heads, and the Gods' Horses (one for each palanquin) and their grooms went back to East Quarter. This was the moment when formal invitations to the festival were extended to the twenty-three gods who were to be the guests of the Divine Mother. The Master of Ceremonial led the *Shê* Heads and Incense Elders to the Earth God Temple of East Quarter; there they offered incense and wine and then prostrated themselves while the Master of Ceremonial chanted the "Writ of Invitation." It said in part:

---

20. This random assignment of responsibility for the gods strongly suggests that there was no established hierarchy among the participating *shê*.

All you divinities, it is well that you draw near. We honor you with respectful libations of clear wine and announce that the Divine Mother of the Ninth Heaven has requested the Earth God of this place to inform her guests and the General of the Five Ways to open a divine road. In the Heavenly Palace and the Earthly Bureau, let the gods be informed that she has selected this day, the such-and-such day, for music and offerings to be presented in the temple of the Divine Mother of the Ninth Heaven, and that the offerings will continue for three days. As your carriages draw near, they will be welcomed respectfully.[21]

Then the participants dispersed, leaving the ritual paraphernalia in East Quarter overnight, under guard.

That night there was a ritual at the Temple of King Yu (Yuwang miao) in North Shê, the village in charge that year, to welcome the Star of Long Life. This ritual was presumably a privilege of the sponsoring village. (The Temple of King Yu was itself fairly large, but when I visited in 1993 there was no sign of religious activity there; the Offering Pavilion had been demolished, the main hall was used for storage, and the side chapels had been converted to private use.) An offering table was set up in the Offering Pavilion and the spirit tablet of the Great Emperor of the Southern Polestar and Long Life was placed on it. Led by the village's *Shê* Head, the Incense Elders and others offered wine and incense, and the Master of Ceremonial chanted the "Writ for Inviting [the Star of] Long Life":

[On behalf of] the starry lord of the Southern Pole, "whose virtue is as that of Heaven and Earth, whose benevolence is as fine as the Sun's and the Moon's," let the *Shê* Head so-and-so, holding incense, and the Incense Elders of the associated villages bow their heads and earnestly invite "the honored God to come to this service and accept our offerings."[22]

Then the Master of Ceremonial called out, "Receive the Star of Long Life!" and he and the Director led the *Shê* Head, the Incense Elders, and the musicians, playing their instruments, out of the Offering Pavil-

---

21. Yang Mengheng, "Pingshun xian Dongyugou," p. 325, places these words in quotation marks, but gives no indication of the source.

22. Ibid., p. 326. Here Yang has placed quotation marks within the quotation but does not say why.

ion and through the temple gate. They arranged themselves in front of the Nine-Dragon Wall, the Master of Ceremonial announced, "The carriage of the Star of Long Life has arrived!" and the Director continued with the courteous invitation: "Star of Long Life, if you please." Then the whole company, led by the musicians, filed back into the Temple of King Yu, went through the East and West arcades, and took their places in the Offering Pavilion. The Master of Ceremonial said, "Let the Star of Long Life take his seat!" and the Director said, "The Monkey will present fruit." A young Entertainer, made up and costumed to look like a monkey, came on stage turning somersaults and capered about with a large "peach of immortality" made of paper. He eventually lay down on his side on a red blanket in a posture of presenting the peach, and the Master of Ceremonial sifted wheat flour over and around him. He then hopped nimbly up, leaving behind an image of "Monkey Presenting a Peach." (This bit of stage business turns up frequently in other *sai*.)

Then a brief ritual opera called *The Eight Immortals Welcome the Star of Long Life* was presented. The actors representing the Eight Immortals came on stage carrying representations of clouds, evidently painted on flat pieces of wood. They danced so their movements imitated floating clouds, the formations changing constantly, and sang auspicious songs. In the end they used the "clouds" to spell out the phrase "A great man of the first rank" (*yipin daren*). A large golden *shou* (long life) character was placed in the middle. Then they performed two more operas, selected by the *Shê* Head of North Shê. This concluded the first of the two preliminary days.

A FAMILY OF HEREDITARY ENTERTAINERS (*YUEHU*)

The Director of the Entertainers at the Divine Mother Temple *sai* in 1938 was Wang Fuyun, and remarkably enough we know a great deal about his family.[23] (I discuss the caste of Entertainers at some length below.) Wang Fuyun of West Shê village belonged to an Entertainer

---

23. The information on the Wang family in this paragraph is taken from Yang Mengheng, "Shanxi saishe yuehu," pp. 260–63; and Li Tiansheng, "Xishe cun."

Headman (*yuehu ketou*) family, whose senior member had authority over ordinary Entertainer families. This authority probably derived from forebears who at one time had the duty of providing entertainment at the county yamen.[24] Elite *ketou* status seems to have stayed in particular families. Lucheng county was said to have had eight *ketou* families; Wang Fuyun was a member of one of them.[25] At the 1938 *sai,* Fuyun's father, Genwang, was the *ketou,* coordinating the work of all the Entertainers, including those brought in from other counties. In addition, Fuyun's elder brother Xiyun probably was a member of the troupe of actors, and his younger brother Laiyun probably played *suona.* When young, Fuyun had studied with his father and older brother; later he studied at the school run by Li Ertu of Raven village in Huguan county. Students of an Entertainer master were virtually indentured to him and underwent many hardships.[26]

Fuyun became skilled at using the *suona* to imitate the singing of famous non-Entertainer actors. He is said to have known a great number of opera melodies and to have been an excellent reciter of stories from novels. His colleagues called him "Catchall" for the wide variety of things he knew. By 1938 he was ready to replace his father as Headman, since he had proven he was able to direct both musicians and actors and work successfully with a Master of Ceremonial. But then the Japanese army occupied southeastern Shanxi. All *sai* were suppressed, and the prohibition remained in force when the Communists came to power. Fuyun turned to farming but was also a member of the West Shê ritual music troupe, which played locally for weddings and funerals. In addition he organized a number of troupes of young musicians and taught music to his relatives, some of whom later had significant

---

24. Yang Mengheng, "Shanxi saishe yuehu," p. 256; Xiang Yang, *Shanxi yuehu yanjiu,* pp. 94–96. The Entertainer Headmen are discussed in detail below.

25. Yang Mengheng, "Shanxi saishe yuehu," pp. 257, 260. The eight are mentioned frequently. Since West Shê was under the jurisdiction of Pingshun county from 1528 to 1764, thereafter reverting to the jurisdiction of a much-enlarged Lucheng county (see below), it seems likely that the "Eight Entertainer Headmen Families of Lucheng" is a grouping that dates from after 1764.

26. See the contract in Qiao Jian et al., *Yuehu,* p. 99. There is a chart showing Li's many students and *their* students on p. 101.

careers as regional opera performers. In 1985 he donated a number of *Dui* Opera part-scripts when he heard that the compilers of the Shanxi volume of the *Encyclopedia of Chinese Opera* were searching for original source materials. These scripts form a significant portion of the pitifully small remnant of southeastern Shanxi ritual opera texts that survived the depredations of the Red Guards and party censors. He also reconstructed from memory the script of the short opera *The Temple of the Earth God* (*Tudi tang*) in the final three weeks before his death and, despite ill-health, did much to assist the scholars trying to recover the operas performed at the great *sai*.[27]

The Wangs of West Shê originally lived in a village called Wang Bend (Wangqu), eighteen kilometers north-northeast of West Shê as the crow flies (much farther than that by road). According to family tradition, at some unknown time in the past, the village of West Shê called in three *yinyang* masters to see if they could determine the cause of the village's poverty. The three masters declared that a nearby mountain was a sleeping dragon, which, if awakened, could make the village prosperous. To wake the dragon, they recommended bringing in musicians to play music all day long. (Anyone who has heard rural Chinese festival music will understand why they made this suggestion!) So an invitation went out to the Wang family, and they moved to West Shê. (It is not clear if this origin legend is meant to apply to all six lines of the West Shê Wangs, or just the line of Fuyun, which is by far the best known.) The family still has tombs near Wang Bend, and for a long time they continued to have exclusive rights to perform ritual music in that area—that is, it was their Territory (*polu* or *yifan*).[28] (I discuss the Territories in detail in the section on the Entertainer caste, below.)

There is no record of when the Wangs came to West Shê to awaken the dragon. In 1995, 320 Wangs in six descent lines were living there.[29] Fuyun's line traces its ancestry to a man named Wang Jiancheng and has in its possession a promissory note dated 1775 (Qianlong 40) in

---

27. See his biography by Li Shoutian and Yang Mengheng, "Wang Fuyun," pp. 260–63.

28. Li Tiansheng, "Xishe cun," p. 100.

29. Ibid., p. 99.

which Jiancheng borrows 5,000 "big coins" from Guo Fuming,[30] an Entertainer who lived in Miaozhuang village, about five kilometers south of West Shê on a main road.[31] This suggests that Jiancheng had already moved to West Shê, since West Shê is much closer to Miaozhuang than Wang Bend is. In the genealogy of the descendants of Wang Jiancheng, Wang Fuyun appears as a descendent of Jiancheng in the sixth generation.[32] He was born in 1914.[33] In another line of descent from Jiancheng, a man in the fifth generation was born in 1896.[34] Jiancheng is therefore likely to have been born between 1730 (assuming an average of thirty years per generation) and 1750 (since he would probably have had to be at least twenty-five for anyone to have been willing to loan him 5,000 "big coins").

According to official sources, Pingshun county was created in 1528 out of parts of Licheng, Huguan, and Lucheng counties, eliminated in 1764 by being completely absorbed into Lucheng, and then restored in 1911, abolished, and restored for good in 1913.[35] Surprisingly enough, a contract of 1839 between one of Jiancheng's sons and two of his grandsons, seventy-five years after Pingshun county had officially ceased to exist, refers to service at the Pingshun yamen as a present obligation of the family; another contract, between two of Jiancheng's sons, dated 1827, mentions service at the "civil and military yamens of the old county seat of Pingshun."[36] This means that some time before 1764 Jiancheng or a forebear began serving at the Pingshun yamen. (They might have still been living in Wang Bend or already have moved to West Shê.) That Jiancheng's descendants were still serving in the Pingshun "yamens" in 1827 and 1839 shows that the county continued to exist in the eyes of its residents long after it had been formally abolished by the central government. Could it have been a grand imposture that

---

30. Li Tiansheng, "Xishe cun," p. 113.
31. Assuming it is the present Miaozhuang zhen.
32. Li Tiansheng, "Xishe cun," p. 119.
33. Yang Mengheng, "Shanxi saishe yuehu," p. 260.
34. Hanchen; Li Tiansheng, "Xishe cun," p. 103.
35. Zhang Jizhong, *Shanxi lishi zhengqu dili*, pp. 221, 227; Yang Mengheng, "Shanxi saishe yuehu," p. 260.
36. Li Tiansheng, "Xishe cun," p. 114, contracts nos. 3 and 2.

somehow benefited the local elite, or was it simply a matter of intense local conservatism?[37]

Imposture or not, it had ended by 1890, since a contract of that year contains a list of villages, several of which presumably were once in Pingshun county because that is where they are located now, all said to belong to Lucheng.[38] And also in 1890 the Wangs had a contractual arrangement to take part in the Officials' *Sai* (*guan sai*) at the Lucheng City-God Temple (it was called an Officials' *Sai* because it was sponsored by the county magistrate) as well as in the great fourth-month *sai* at Jia village, also in Lucheng county.

Wang Fuyun, the Director of the *sai* at the Divine Mother Temple in 1938, was thus a member of a widely ramified line of hereditary Entertainers who had been performing ritual music and opera in southeastern Shanxi since the mid-eighteenth century, and quite probably longer. His family had belonged to an elite of eight hereditary or semi-hereditary Entertainer Headman families in Lucheng county for a long time. They had exclusive rights to perform at weddings, funerals, and *sai* in dozens of villages in Lucheng and Pingshun counties, and also were said to have taken part in *sai* in Huguan, Zhangzi, and Tunliu counties.[39] The story of Wang Fuyun and his family, with their two-hundred-year tradition as ritual performers, reminds us forcibly just how rich and deep the cultural and historical context of the *sai* actually was. If we had enough information, every element of the great festivals would look equally complex: the Masters of Ceremonial (some of whom we meet in the next section), the music, the rituals, the temples and their decorations, the village alliances, the villages themselves. These temple festivals, celebrated in the remote countryside and supported by mere farmers, had evolved over the centuries into something deep and rich. They should be studied with this in mind.

---

37. The 1839 contract is especially convincing. When Li Tiansheng (ibid., p. 100) says that the family continued to owe service to the *Lucheng* yamen after they moved to West Shê, I believe he has silently corrected his sources.

38. Ibid., p. 116, contract no. 6.

39. Li Tiansheng, "Xishe cun," p. 109.

THE FOUR-SCENE CARTS
INVITE THE GODS

The second of the two preliminary days of the Divine Mother *sai* was what made it one of the most famous festivals in all of southern Shanxi, for on that day the great Four-Scene Carts made their run. In the morning the Entertainers, Incense Elders, and all the others who had participated on the first day went to the open area at East Quarter, where the Spirit Mansions and the Four-Scene Carts had been left the evening before. They were joined by a large number of floats and small "acts," complete with musicians, from nearby villages.[40] These formed up in a horseshoe-shaped arc, with the twenty-four Spirit Mansions and the four Four-Scene Carts facing one another across the open end of the horseshoe.[41] At this point actors wearing the masks of the Earth God and the General of the Five Ways, together with a troupe of actors portraying gods, also wearing masks, entered the space marked out by the Mansions, Carts, floats, and acts, and performed a Mask Opera, which presumably was essentially a dance, like the formations (*zhen*) at a number of New Year rituals (see Part I).

Each of the five *shê* had its own Four-Scene Cart; at every *sai* four were brought out (the sponsoring *shê* was exempt). The Carts were spectacular structures nearly forty-five feet tall, each pulled by a team of six black oxen.[42] According to the description of Cao Zupeng, who very likely saw an actual Cart, plus my own copy of a photograph of it, the tower consisted of five parts: a square red base about six feet high on a large two-wheeled cart; on that a roof-like structure about five feet in height; then a pavilion over fourteen feet high with a gallery around it and crowned by an elaborate roof; and finally a ten-foot pole piercing

---

40. It is not clear whether these came only from the eight villages that sponsored the *sai* or from other villages as well.

41. The detail about the Mansions and Carts facing one another comes from the interview with Wang Jiaju of North Shê. Yang Mengheng's description in "Pingshun xian Dongyugou" (p. 327) is much more complete than Mr. Wang's, but I still have had to supplement it here and there.

42. There is a drawing in ibid., p. 344, but better is the small color photograph of a restored or replica Cart in Wen Xing and Xue Maixi, *Shanxi minsu*, p. 483. See Fig. 10.

Fig. 10 Reconstructed Four-Scene Cart, some time in the 1980s
(SOURCE: photograph David Johnson of photograph in the collection of Wang Jiaju).

three colored globes, finished with a five-foot-long pheasant feather. Every square inch of the surface was covered with colored silk, gold foil, glass, and scenes and motifs of the four seasons, one per side.[43] After the Mask Opera, these magnificent juggernauts began to move around the open space at East Quarter, gradually picking up speed.

At the same time, a grand repayment of vows made to the Divine Mother on behalf of children during the preceding year was taking place. Each child who had been helped or protected by the goddess sat on a mule holding a placard on which was written his or her eight natal characters. The mule was followed by the child's father holding a willow staff and was led by another man. A third man held a parasol decorated with the beautifully embroidered collars the child had worn, jewelry (if he or she had any), and other decorative objects.[44] All the

43. Last details from Yang Mengheng, "Pingshun xian Dongyugou," p. 325; Cao Zupeng, "Si jing che jianjie," p. 1; and Zhang Zhennan, "Pingshun xian de pao che hui," pp. 36–37.

44. For Shanxi children's collars, see Bo Songnian and Duan Gaifang, *Zhongguo minjian meishu*, vol. 4, pls. 38 and 39; and Li Yuming, *Shanxi minjian yishu*, pp. 23, 25.

children—and there could be over a hundred of them[45]—rode in procession to the Temple of the Divine Mother and made offerings. This was called "repaying [the goddess's] nourishment" (*bao shi*). After they were finished, they returned to East Quarter, which the Four-Scene Carts were still circling.

At this point a gigantic procession formed up and set off for the village of Nanchui, the supposed birthplace of the Divine Mother. (Her statue was said to have been carved from the wood of a willow tree that grew there.)[46] The highlight of the procession must have been the Four-Scene Carts, each pulled by six oxen (which had been rested and fed special food for a month in advance) and accompanied by teams of men straining against the guylines that held it upright, but there were also the twenty-four Spirit Mansions, the twenty-four Spirit Horses for the invited deities to ride should they tire of their palanquins, and the hundred-odd children on their mules, with their little retinues of father, parasol holder, and mule wrangler.[47] In addition, the villages supplied troupes of musicians, silver umbrellas, floats, banners, and placards in which each attempted to outdo the others.[48]

What I am calling floats included beautifully costumed women who appeared to be standing on tall poles[49] and almost certainly also included a type of float in which young people or children, dressed as

----

45. Wang Jiaju said "over 200" in his interview (Interview transcripts, p. 59).

46. I have not been able to locate this village on any map, but we are told it was near South Shê, which is virtually contiguous with Donghe on the 1:50,000 Chinese Army map of the area, for which the survey was done in 1924. Because of the difficulty of moving the Carts, it could not have been very far from the Temple of the Divine Mother and was probably at more or less the same elevation.

47. For special treatment of the oxen, see Wang Jiaju interview, p. 60; for the instability of the Carts and the use of guylines, there are two very similar accounts: the biography of Li Yuanxing (draft biographies of *sai* specialists, p. 59); and Zhang Zhennan, "Pingshun xian de pao che hui," p. 36. Since Zhang wrote Li's biography, that text should be considered the primary source.

48. Some details here from Cao Zupeng, "Si jing che jianjie," p. 1. It is unclear which villages participated in this way. I suspect it was every village from which one of the twenty-three guest gods came, although I have no idea how many villages that would have been, since there could easily have been more than one substantial temple per village.

49. *Kang zhuang*; for a photo, see Wen Xing and Xue Maixi, *Shanxi minsu*, p. 482.

figures from well-known scenes in famous operas, were carried along seemingly suspended in midair. (Actually they were secured to iron rods hidden by their costumes.)[50] The sources describe one float in some detail. It featured a fierce lion with a precious vase on his back. Set in the vase was a large gold *shou* character and tied to that was the "Pennon of the Sacred Command" (*sheng zhi fan*), which quite possibly was the Sacred Edict (*sheng yu*) of the Kangxi emperor.[51] Protecting the Sacred Command was a yellow silk parasol, which was crowned with a tuft of multicolored chicken feathers.[52]

This huge procession, with altogether over thirty types of "story" and over 200 individual units,[53] was watched by thousands of people, some of whom came fifty *li* to see it.[54] It first went, as far as I can tell, to Nanchui village, where the local god (not identified) entered the spirit tablet in his spirit mansion, that is, his palanquin.[55] At this point, the teams of oxen were changed for fresh ones, and new men took over carrying the palanquins.[56] The procession then went to the Temple of the Jade Emperor in South Shê to welcome the Jade Emperor to the *sai*. (He was believed to be the Divine Mother's uncle.) His spirit mansion, with the spirit tablet inside, was carried into the temple, while the other palanquins waited outside the main gate in two rows, with the Divine Mother at the head of one and the Nanchui god at the head of the other. All the ritual personnel went into the temple in order; music was played and offerings made. The Master of Ceremonial invited the Jade Emperor to take leave of his hall; at the same time his palanquin

---

50. Ibid., pp. 482–83. We will meet this sort of float again in the Big West Gate *sai*. An exceptionally attractive woodblock print depicting this type of float deserves to be mentioned here, even though it comes from Sichuan. See Gao Wen et al., eds., *Mianzhu nianhua*, pls. 126, 130.

51. Alternatively, it may have referred to an order or orders of the Divine Mother (*shengmu*).

52. Wang's description of this in his interview (p. 59) differs somewhat from Yang's, which I have followed.

53. Cao Zupeng and Cao Xinguang, "Pingshun xian Dongyugou," p. 6.

54. Li Yuanxing biography, draft biographies of *sai* specialists, p. 60. For the number of spectators—"like a city"—see Yang Mengheng, "Pingshun xian Dongyugou," p. 327.

55. No source says this explicitly, but nothing else makes sense.

56. Wang Jiaju interview, p. 60.

was lowered to the ground and his Pavilioner raised the curtain to let him enter it. The Master of Ceremonial then ordered the palanquin to be lifted up, and all the participants left the temple and rejoined the procession. The palanquins of the Jade Emperor and the Nanchui god shared the honor of leading it.

When their palanquins came to a narrow place in the road, each crew politely requested the other to go first, but this little show of mutual deference always ended with the Nanchui god giving way. The procession then visited a number of other villages (how many is unknown, although certainly the eight villages of the alliance were among them). Two squads of young men riding horses, called Mounted Scouts (*tanma*), rushed back and forth along the route ahead of the procession to clear any obstacles and to give notice of its arrival.[57] We are told that the procession did not stop, but that the appropriate palanquin was simply made available to the local god as it passed. I suspect that what in fact happened was that the procession stopped briefly, the local god or gods were welcomed by lowering his or her palanquin and holding the curtain aside, and then the procession moved on. However it was done, the procession gradually picked up the spirits of all the gods who had been invited to the festival.[58]

Eventually the procession arrived at the Temple of the Divine Mother. The Pavilioner responsible for the Divine Mother took her spirit tablet from her palanquin and, accompanied by his Attendant and flanked by actors wearing masks of the Earth God and the General of the Five Ways, entered the temple. Behind them came the *Shê* Heads, the Incense Elders, and the Director and his musicians. They made a circuit of the courtyard, ending at the main gate. The Divine Mother had now assumed her role as hostess.

The Master of Ceremonial chanted a greeting: "We go out and greet all the gods, who have drawn near the mortal world. We respectfully invite you honored gods, fatigued by your journey, to alight from your

---

57. Li Yuanxing says two horses, not two squads (Li Yuanxing biography, draft biographies of *sai* specialists, p. 59).

58. As noted above, this was not a birthday party, as was virtually always the case elsewhere, but a celebration linked to a solar date in the spring. Nevertheless, in all respects it resembled the birthday celebrations of conventional *sai*.

royal carriages." The Director cried out in a loud voice: "Honored gods, kindly alight from your royal carriages!" Then, to the thunder of drums and the roar of firecrackers, the Pavilioners took the spirit tablets of the gods from the palanquins and the Master of Ceremonial, standing in the main hall, invited them into the temple in the order given in the Diagram for Arranging the Gods (*pai shen bu*). First came the Jade Emperor. The Master of Ceremonial called out, "The Supreme Lord of the Golden Palace of the Heavens, the Jade Emperor, is invited to enter the hall and take his place!" [59] The Director, standing closer to the gate, repeated the invitation. At this, the Jade Emperor's Pavilioner and his Attendant entered the temple, went to the main hall, and placed the Jade Emperor's tablet on the appropriate table. The rest of the gods followed one by one, with the Divine Mother bringing up the rear. As the Pavilioners, Attendants, *Shê* Heads, and Incense Elders stood in ranks, the Master of Ceremonial led them in offering incense, presenting offerings, and making obeisances. The Master of Ceremonial then read the "Writ of Commands" ("Ting ming wen"), which announced the Jade Emperor's regulations for the *sai* and outlined the duties of all the participants.[60] After further offerings and obeisances, all the ritual personnel left the hall, and the formal activities of the second preparatory day came to an end. (While these solemn ceremonies were proceeding inside the temple, where space was limited, the many village troupes and bands performed informally outside the temple before what must have been large crowds.)

Cup Offerings and the Jian Zhai God

The next three days were the most important part of the Divine Mother *sai*: the focus shifted from outside to inside the temple, from movement to stability, from spectacle to sacrifice, from processions to ritual and opera. But because the documentation is less rich than for the first two days, I will just summarize here how the Cup Offerings fit

---

59. Yang Mengheng, "Pingshun xian Dongyugou," p. 328.
60. An example of one of these important texts is discussed in the next section.

into the overall ritual program and defer a detailed description of the core ritual, the offering of "Cups," to the next chapter.[61]

First thing in the morning of the third day, the first day of the *sai* proper, the Master of Ceremonial called the roll of the Pavilioners, and then they, their Attendants, the *Shê* Heads, the Incense Elders, and the rest processed around the temple courtyard, through the two entrances in the Flowery Offering (*hua ji*) and into the main hall.[62] The Water Officials, Incense Masters, and Candle Masters took up the Spirit Platters and wine cups from a niche and gave a platter and cup to each Pavilioner. They went back to the courtyard, made a circuit, and re-entered the main hall, where each cup was filled. Then at the Master of Ceremonial's command, the Water Officials took the cups, lifted them up, and emptied them on the ground. This was done three times altogether.[63]

Then the formal food offerings, called Cups (*zhan*)—a term used in imperial banqueting in the Song dynasty—began. There were seven on the first day, twelve on the second, and eight on the third. Each Cup involved the carrying of dishes prepared in the ritual kitchen to the Offering Hall or the tables in front of the gods' spirit tablets. After the third Cup on the first day of the *sai*, there was an important ritual called "The Dance of Jian Zhai."[64] An Entertainer played the part of Jian

---

61. The account of the Longquan *sai* may also be more reliable. Yang Mengheng may have fleshed out his account of the Divine Mother *sai* with material from the single-village *sai* at Nan Shê village, in Lucheng county. See note 63 below.

62. The Flowery Offering was a screen made of intricately carved tiles of hard, deep-fried dough that in the Divine Mother Temple was about nine feet high and twenty-five feet wide. It was extravagantly decorated, by all accounts a masterpiece of folk art. Since eyewitness descriptions of the *hua ji* at the Big West Gate *sai* outside Zhangzi town are more detailed than those of the Divine Mother's, I defer my discussion to that chapter.

63. Yang Mengheng, "Pingshun xian Dongyugou," pp. 329–30. This account is similar to a passage in Yang's earlier report on the single-village *sai* at Nan Shê (Yang Mengheng, "Lucheng Nan Shê," p. 10A). It is difficult to know whether the two *sai* shared this particular action, or whether Yang is embellishing his description of the Divine Mother *sai* by borrowing a detail from the Nan Shê *sai*.

64. The Chinese term given is *tiáo Jian Zhai* 調監齋 (to regulate Jian Zhai)—although *tiào* 跳 *Jian Zhai* (the dance of Jian Zhai) makes much better sense here. But they may have been used interchangeably: a subsidiary dance is called *Tiào si men*

Zhai, wearing a mask with three heads and a costume with six arms.[65] This startling figure was accompanied by masked actors impersonating the Shutting Gods (Jijian shen), deities with the power to close gates and doors against sickness. This group performed three rituals that are of great interest.

First, the four Shutting Gods came on to the temple stage and performed a "Dance of the Four Gates" (or Four Corners). When this ended, one god was standing in each corner of the stage. The Jian Zhai God entered and went to the center of the stage while someone intoned a poem about expelling disease. The Director of the Entertainers offered incense and wine at the front of the stage. (Ceremonies making the stage a sacred space by expelling evil influences are virtually universal in Chinese theater, especially when a ritual opera is to be performed. They must be as old as Chinese opera itself, if not older.) Then the Jian Zhai God led the Shutting Gods off the stage and down to the kitchen, where the food offerings were prepared, paying respects to the Divine

---

跳四門 in one place and *Tiáo si men* 調四門 a little later. Jian Zhai—Inspector of Vegetarian Food—was the name of the god of the kitchen in temples and monasteries.

65. For a picture of Jian Zhai as he appeared in Shanxi *sai*, see Han Sheng et al., eds., *Shangdang nuo wenhua*, pl. 75. This figure has a deep history in East Asian Buddhism. He is one of the Five Great Brilliant Kings, ferocious enemies of demons. In Tendai Buddhism he was called Ususama (Sanskrit Ucchusma); he purified the pollution caused by childbirth and was associated with purification in general (see http://www.onmarkproductions.com/html/myo-o.shtml; Soothill, *A Dictionary of Chinese Buddhist Terms*, p. 330A, gives various combinations of characters for the name). Ucchusma Vajrapala is a guardian god in Indian Buddhism who cleanses or protects against filth (see http://www.tbsn.org/special/ny-6–97/intro.htm). Ucchusma has six arms and three heads, as can be seen from many representations of him (though some have fewer arms and some have more) at http://www.fodian.net/world/ucchusma/ucchusmaa.html. His analogue in Shingon Buddhism is named Kongo Yasha (Sanskrit Vajrayaksha) (see http://www.onmarkproductions.com/html/myo-o.shtml). Kongo Yasha/Vajrayaksha also has three heads and six arms, as can be seen in a fine small thirteenth-century Japanese wood sculpture labeled "Vajrayaksha" in the Freer Gallery (F1909.346). The Jian Zhai god, an inspector of the cleanliness of ritual kitchens, is clearly related to this family of deities. The presence of this figure from esoteric Buddhism in the liturgies of ritual specialists in rural Shanxi is yet another reminder that there is much more to village ritual than meets the uninformed eye. (I ask the reader's indulgence for the citation of Buddhist iconographic material from the web, but it appears to be far richer than what is readily available in print.)

Mother and the other gods on the way. An offering table had been set up, and on it was placed the spirit tablet of the True Lord of the Eastern Kitchen, Master of Fate (Dong Chu Si Ming Zhen Jun)—that is, the Stove God. The Shutting Gods and the Jian Zhai God danced while the Incense Heads made offerings. Then they returned to the stage, the Shutting Gods in the corners and Jian Zhai in the center once again. The Director strode to the front of the stage and chanted the "Jian Zhai Ode," which reads exactly like a section of a traditional popular prosimetric (*shuochang*) narrative.[66] It relates how, in the Yuan dynasty, a kitchen worker successfully led the monk-warriors of the Shaolin Monastery against a besieging army of Red Turban rebels and was enfeoffed as the Jian Zhai God as a reward. So in this interlude with the Jian Zhai God, a clear borrowing from esoteric Buddhism, there was a purification of the stage, an offering to the stove god of the temple kitchen, and an account in popular prosimetric style of the martial exploits that led to the god's current position. After these rituals to purify the stage and honor the Stove God were completed, the *Dui* Operas began, supplemented in this case by Clapper Opera, or *bangzi xi*, a popular type of non-ritual local opera (see Part II).

The Cup Offerings combined with various types of opera dominated the three days of the *sai* proper, which began on the third day after the preparatory activities commenced. Other rituals were also performed—sacrifices to the Sun, Moon, Wind, Well, and so on, but they are not described in our sources and therefore must be passed over. After the final Cup Offering on the last day, it was time to bid the gods farewell. (It was obviously important that they return to their proper abodes; a god who had no place to stay would be quite uncomfortable, reflecting badly on the hospitality of the Divine Mother and resulting in who knows what unpleasant consequences for the village.) An altar was set up at the main gate of the temple, and the Master of Ceremonial drew a giant charm on the ground with bran powder. The Entertainers and other actors assembled in front of it, and incense and wine were offered. After the Master of Ceremonial invited the gods to take their places, he read the "Memorial Seeing Off the Gods," in which he begged pardon

---

66. A version of this can be found in Yang, *Fourteen Manuscripts*, pp. 366–69.

for any inadvertent errors or oversights during the *sai*. The Director of the Entertainers then called out loudly: "We invite the gods to gather at the altar. The men of the participating *shê* are deeply respectful. Today the offerings of incense are finished; let there be gentle breezes and timely rains so we may enjoy great peace!"[67] Then a ram's horn was tossed on the ground to divine what the next year would bring. If its aspect was favorable, the Director called out "A good *sai*! The *sai* is finished!" and his words were echoed by the crowd of spectators. The Director then chanted:

There will be gentle breezes and timely rains, the five grains will be abundant, there will be peace among people and animals, the grain will sprout bountifully, trade will be harmonious, and all affairs will proceed smoothly. Sweep the area in front of the gate[68] and burn a brazier of incense; let all the gods return to their homes and let disasters be driven away and misfortunes averted.[69]

Firecrackers were set off, drums boomed and gongs resounded, those in charge burned sacrificial money and paper images of the gods (and the paper spirit tablets of the gods?), and the divine guests departed in the flames and smoke.

———

Let us pause briefly to consider what we have seen in the *sai* at the Temple of the Divine Mother of the Ninth Heaven. Most obvious is its gigantic scope: the huge procession of over 200 units of all kinds, including the Four-Scene Carts, prodigious contraptions that may have been unique in Shanxi, or even north China. The large scale was made possible because the *sai* was supported by eight villages, not one, and this sponsorship by a village alliance is another notable feature. In fact, all true *sai* had such sponsorship.[70] Also striking is the way in which the entire ritual was grounded in the experience of daily life. There was an offering to the Stove God, the purification of a building, even a

———

67. Yang Mengheng, "Pingshun xian Dongyugou," p. 331.
68. The text has "hall" here, which must be an error.
69. Yang Mengheng, "Pingshun xian Dongyugou," p. 331.
70. Strictly speaking this *sai* was sponsored by a single *shê* in any given year, but since there was a five-year rota, it was in effect joint sponsorship.

narrative in prosimetric form, things very familiar to the villagers. In addition, the gods were clearly imagined to be like human beings: they were invited to a lavish feast and were provided with transportation from their homes to the site of the celebration. Their comfort was a concern—they rode in elaborate palanquins—as was their relative rank. (Recall the Jade Emperor's palanquin being allowed to go ahead of the palanquin of the Nanchui village god in places where the two could not proceed abreast.) The Divine Mother played the role of hostess, and the other gods were her guests. She was considered a native of Nanchui village because her statue was carved from a willow tree that had grown there. In short, the people and their deities were not radically different kinds. True, the gods had great powers, but the people believed, or acted as if they believed, that they could induce the gods to favor them—not surprising considering how much the gods resembled them.

Village leaders organized and supervised the entire *sai* with the assistance of various ritual specialists. Buddhist monks and Daoist priests were nowhere in evidence; the rituals were handled by the Master of Ceremonial and the Director of the Entertainers, who had no religious affiliations.[71] In the eyes of the villagers, the Divine Mother was a local girl who made good, or else a deity who just happened to want a temple on precisely that site west of East River village.[72] In either case she had nothing to do in the popular imagination with the great pantheons of Buddhism and Daoism. Also notable is the absence of any sign of government control or elite guidance. The villagers were left to enact their spectacular rituals—even though they can easily be seen as powerful rivals to state-sponsored rituals—without interference from local officials or the educated elite. Indeed, classically educated villagers and even magistrates participated fully in some *sai*.

---

71. It is important to note that the Director's role in the ritual program appears to have been as important as the Master of Ceremonial's even though the Director was a member of the despised Entertainer (*yuehu*) group.

72. See the folktales about the establishment of the Divine Mother Temple in Cao Zuping and Cao Xinguang, "Pingshun xian Dongyugou," pp. 2–5, in which the Divine Mother and Zhenwu compete for the East River village site.

Dui Operas at the Divine Mother Temple *Sai*

In general there were five types of dramatic performance in a *sai*: mimed and often masked shows that took the form of processions: these were called "Moving *Dui* Operas" (*liu dui xi*) or "Silent *Dui* Operas" (*ya dui xi*). They were something like the performances of the Story Troupes of Sand Hill village we met in Part I. The Mask Opera performed on the second day should probably be placed in this category. There also were what I think of as execution skits, such as *Beheading Han Ba* (the drought demon; *Zhan Han Ba*), *Beheading Hua Xiong* (*Zhan Hua Xiong*), and *Beating the Yellow Consumption Demon* (*Bian da Huang lao gui*)—this last related to the Hebei exorcistic drama *Catching the Yellow Demon* examined at length in Part I. These had little or no dialogue and featured the pursuit of an evil creature or villain off the stage, through the village, and then back on stage, where he was executed. Then there were risqué or obscene comic skits called *yuanben* or "Meat Plays" (*hun xi*), which were performed at night, in the interval(s) between the regular evening operas. Finally there were two types of *Dui* Opera that were tightly integrated with the rituals: the "Supplementary *Dui* Operas" (*chen dui xi*), which were performed in the Offering Pavilion (also called the Incense Pavilion [*xiang ting*]) during the Cup sacrifices, and the "Standard *Dui* Operas" (*zheng dui xi*), also called *Sai* Operas, which were performed on the temple stage in the afternoon and evening.[73] The Supplementary *Dui* Operas must have been very short, since they were interspersed with the Cup Offerings, which, as I have mentioned, came in sets of seven, twelve, or eight depending on the day. The Standard *Dui* Operas were more like conventional operas: they were performed on the temple stage and did not accompany offerings. Zhang Zhennan writes that they lasted between one and two hours.[74] Note that the

---

73. For surveys, see, among many titles, *Zhongguo xiqu zhi: Shanxi juan*, pp. 141–44; Yuan Shuangxi and Li Shoutian, "Shangdang"; Zhang Zhennan, "Yueju yu sai," pp. 235, 241; idem, "Yueju he sai," pp. 8A–B; idem and Ji Guangming, "Zhuan wei yingshen sai-she," pp. 618–22; and Yuan Shuangxi, "Shangdang nuo xi ji qi liubian."

74. Zhang Zhennan, "Yueju he sai," p. 8A; idem and Ji Guangming, "Zhuan wei yingshen saishe," p. 621. We have testimony that a *Dui* Opera entitled *The Great Meeting*

seven part-scripts of the *Dui* Opera *The Great Meeting at Gai* occupy only sixteen pages in Han Sheng's edition. It is not at all clear how many Standard *Dui* Operas (that is, *Sai* Operas) were performed in an evening's program. We have no eyewitness testimony, and our two most important sources, the *Zhou yuexing tu* and the *Tang yuexing tu*, disagree on this issue (although both indicate that multiple *Dui* Operas were performed on a given day).[75] Thus, contextual evidence accords with the textual evidence in suggesting that the Standard *Dui* Operas were probably shorter than the *Za* Operas of southwestern Shanxi, the best-documented village ritual opera genre, and the reason almost certainly has to do with the ritual structure into which they were designed to fit.

One of the main reasons for including the Divine Mother *sai* in this study is that most of the very small number of surviving *Dui* Opera scripts from southeastern Shanxi were originally in the hands of the Wang family, the lineage of Entertainers from West Shê village who performed at the Divine Mother Temple. There is every reason to believe that some of these scripts were performed at the 1938 *sai*. Unfortunately they are not full scripts but the lines spoken by a single character—*jue dan*, or part-scripts.[76] Nevertheless they represent one of the rare cases in which we can connect opera scripts with a specific *sai*.

If Han's transcriptions are accurate,[77] the part-scripts present a character's lines as a single block with no indication of how the lines of

---

at Gai, performed in Nan Shê village, lasted "from right after the noon meal to lamp-lighting time" (Li Yuanxing, "Zhui shu Nan Shê 'Tiao gui,'" p. 461). But Nan Shê's was a single-village *sai* in which villagers, not Entertainers, acted in the operas, and what its residents called "*Dui* Opera" may not have been the same as Standard *Dui* Opera. Nan Shê's so-called *Dui* Operas seem to have had much in common, including length, with the *Za* Operas of southwestern Shanxi, which were also performed by villagers and not Entertainer families.

75. See, e.g., Han Sheng et al., eds., "*Yingshen saishe lijie . . .* zhu shi," p. 94; and Li Tiansheng, "*Tang yuexing tu* jiao zhu," p. 53.

76. They have been published, along with a handful of part-scripts from other families, in Han Sheng et al., eds., *Shangdang nuo wenhua*, pp. 175–302.

77. They appear to be. Plate 23 in the book is a photograph of one page of a manuscript transcribed elsewhere in the volume. I checked the transcription against the photograph and found no mistakes. The caption, however, is mistaken: it is Zhuge Liang's part, not Zhao Yun's.

other characters fit in. Now and then the character's exit is indicated with *xia*, but that is all. In addition, only rarely do we have the lines of more than one or two characters per opera. As a result, it is extremely difficult to get an adequate idea of what the full scripts were like. But even with our limited materials, a number of features are reasonably clear. First, the full scripts must have been quite short—the two longest part-scripts are eighteen and fifteen pages in Han Sheng's edition, and the sole surviving original complete script is only fifteen pages long. Over sixty *Za* Opera scripts are kept in the archives of the Shanxi Opera Research Institute in Taiyuan, the largest collection of local ritual opera scripts in the province. I am very familiar with these scripts, and although a few of them are short, most of them are over seventy pages long and a number top one hundred. But apart from length, *Dui* Operas share many features with the *Za* Operas: almost all are history plays,[78] and they use a character's name rather than role type to indicate who is speaking.[79] The lines were spoken or chanted, never sung, and therefore song-forms were never used. The only accompaniment was drums, gongs, and cymbals. After two or four lines, there were passages of percussion music.[80] Finally, lines almost always were seven characters long, with every other line rhyming.

A few *Dui* Operas were influenced by novels. The opening section of the script for the part of Fan Zeng (dated 1812) in the opera generally known as *The Banquet* [or *Gathering*] *at Hongmen* (*Hongmen yan* [*hui*]) shows clear indebtedness to the novel *Western Han* (*Xi Han yanyi*), to the point that errors in the script can be corrected by reference to the novel.[81] In a number of places, rather than using dialogue to move the

---

78. The only exception appears to be Nazha's part from *Jade Spring Mountain* (*Yuquan shan*), which is a story from the novel *The Investiture of the Gods* (*Feng shen yanyi*). But *Feng shen yanyi*, although it takes place in mythical time, is as full of fighting as history operas.

79. Judging here from the one surviving manuscript of a full script, *The Diagram of the Great Ultimate* (*Tai ji tu*); see Han Sheng et al., eds., *Shangdang nuo wenhua*, pp. 134–49.

80. See *Zhongguo xiqu zhi: Shanxi juan*, p. 142; Zhang Zhennan and Ji Guangming, "Zhuan wei yingshen saishe," pp. 618–19; Zhang Zhennan, "Yueju yu sai," pp. 246–47; and Yang Mengheng, "Lucheng Nan Shê," pp. 21a–b.

81. The part-script is in Han Sheng et al., eds., *Shangdang nuo wenhua*, pp. 175–81; the passages in question here are on p. 176 of the part-script and *hui* 21, pp. 41–42, of the novel.

story ahead, the script has a strong narrative quality, which may well be further evidence of its roots in fiction. One section of the script for Zhang Liang's part in the opera *The Great Meeting at Gai* (*Da hui Gai*) (undated) also shows strong textual echoes of *Western Han*,[82] but the action in the part-script differs from that in the novel. Evidently the author of *The Great Meeting at Gai* had the novel at hand or knew it well but did not simply copy it. This part-script has something of the feel of a solo performance, with a number of effective long songs at the end.

But most of the surviving *Dui* Opera part-scripts show no influence of novels or other sources. The longest is that of Li Shimin (dated 1847)—who would become the great Tang emperor Taizong—in an opera that evidently was called *The Prince of Qin* (*Qin wang*) in the *Dui* Opera repertoire[83] but is known in other genres as *The Temple of Laozi* (*Lao jun tang*). Despite the strong narrative quality of the script (for example, pp. 228–30 present a list of *eighteen* contenders for the Sui throne), I could find no signs of influence from *Shuo Tang, Da Tang Qin wang cihua*, or *Sui Tang yanyi*, the most important long imaginative prose works dealing with the rise of the Tang dynasty. There is a Yuan *zaju* whose plot is roughly the same as the part-script's—*Cheng Yaojin's Axe Cleaves the Temple of Laozi* (*Cheng Yaojin fu pi Lao jun tang*)[84]—but both the plot details and the language are very different from those of the part-script.[85] It is possible that the Yuan opera had a slight influence via many intermediaries, but basically the part-script has to be regarded as an original creation.

There are two part-scripts for the opera *Going After Han Xin* (*Zhui Han Xin*), about Xiao He's efforts to recruit the brilliant strategist Han Xin to the service of Liu Bang in his struggle for supremacy with Xiang Yu after the fall of the Qin. The part-script for Xiao He is dated 1812, and that for Han Xin, which is incomplete, is not dated. Both were in the hands of the Wang family, and it is possible that the two manu-

---

82. Han Sheng et al., eds., *Shangdang nuo wenhua*, pp. 258–59; novel, *hui* 80, p. 182. See also the start of the song, part-script p. 264; and novel, *hui* 82, p. 187.

83. Han Sheng et al., eds., *Shangdang nuo wenhua*, p. 224.

84. Wang Jisi, *Quan Yuan xiqu*, 8: 33–59.

85. There are some *bangzi* operas titled *Lao jun tang*, but I was unable to consult them. My search of the 41 volumes of *Qin qiang* found no text with that title.

scripts are the same age. The script for Xiao He shares a few elements with *Western Han*,[86] but the novel did not have a substantial influence on it. And Han Xin's part-script seems to have no parallels in the novel at all. It does, however, contain a motif present in two Yuan operas but not found in the novel—the construction of a ritual platform where Han Xin receives the title of generalissimo.[87] Here again, the most important novel on the period in which the story in the part-script is set had virtually no influence on it, and although there is a hint of a connection with Yuan drama, it is very faint. So once again the *Dui* Opera version of the story was probably an original creation. This impression is reinforced by an unusual feature of the Xiao He script: it ends with three documents written in formal literary Chinese announcing to the gods that Han Xin has been promoted, which sound almost as if they were taken from a dynastic history. (They were not.) What a village audience would have made of the announcements is difficult to imagine, as is the motive of the author for including them. Needless to say, they cannot be found in either the novel or the surviving Yuan drama.

Finally there is *The Diagram of the Great Ultimate* (*Tai ji tu*) (dated 1915), the only complete original *Dui* Opera to survive in manuscript. It was not in the Wang family's collection, and therefore had no connection with the Divine Mother *sai*, but since it is a full text it offers a particularly good opportunity for source hunting. The general situation can be found in the novel *The Investiture of the Gods*,[88] but the details of the action are very different and the two texts share no language. Nor is there any connection with the *Plain Narrative of King Wu's Assault on Zhou* (*Wu wang fa Zhou pinghua*).[89] In an effort to find an analogue in the local dramatic and performing literature, I searched for the ten titles by which the plot is known, including *Tai ji tu*, in many genres in the catalogue of

---

86. For example, Duke Jing of Qi's description of his dream and Yanzi's explanation of it are almost the same in the novel (p. 75) and the part-script (p. 190).

87. The extant Yuan drama *Xiao He Goes After Han Xin at Night* (*Xiao He yue xia zhui Han Xin*) and a lost Yuan drama called *Han Xin in Poverty Ascends the Platform and Is Anointed General* (*Qiong Han Xin deng tan bai jiang*) have the scene of Han Xin on the ritual platform. See Li Xiusheng, *Guben xiqu jumu*, p. 64; and Zhuang Yibi, *Gudian xiqu cunmu*, p. 235.

88. *Feng shen yanyi*, chap. 61, pp. 607–9.

89. Translated in Liu Cunyan, *Buddhist and Taoist Influences*, pp. 9–75.

popular literature in the Fu Sinian Library of the Academia Sinica (including *Bangzi* opera, *zidi shu*, *ying xi*, *tan ci*, and so on), in the forty-one volumes of *Qin Qiang*, in the thirty-five volumes of *Jingju congkan*, in Berkeley's incomplete set of *Jingju huibian*, and in *Guoju dacheng*, and found nothing. I also consulted the Qing palace opera *Feng shen tianbang* and found that it had almost nothing in common with the *Dui* Opera. There is therefore little doubt that this *Dui* Opera also was an original creation, although it drew on well-known plot material.

Thus most of the *Dui* Operas for which scripts survive were probably original creations. The reasons are not far to seek. The expectations of audiences for *Dui* Operas differed from those of audiences for standard local opera such as Clapper Opera, whose only function was entertainment. *Dui* Opera audiences were probably fairly small because much of the space in the courtyards in front of the temple stages was taken up by the Offering Pavilions, and therefore entry into the temple courtyard during the rituals may have been limited to villagers with a certain status. In addition, the dramas presented by the Entertainers had to mesh with the other parts of the ritual program, such as the Cup Offerings, which almost certainly affected their form. Finally, the Entertainers had very little to do with mainstream local opera, since they performed only with one another and only at *sai*. Therefore they were less likely to be influenced by developments in the wider world of local drama than performers of non-ritual opera.

They also may have maintained their distance from *Za* Opera, *Sai* Opera, and other village ritual opera genres performed by amateurs. Most of the sixty-plus surviving *Za* Operas draw on well-known story lines, and even have familiar titles. Four southwestern Shanxi *Za* Opera titles are also found among the surviving scripts of southeastern Shanxi *Dui* Opera. I carefully compared these and found that there was no sign of mutual influence—they had nothing in common beyond the plot kernel, very broadly construed. In addition, it is fairly clear that in two of the four cases, the *Dui* Opera script has more verse and uses more literary language.[90] This, plus the absence of the Announcer (*dabao zhe*),

---

90. The Zhao Yun part in *Changban* (坂) *po* (Han Sheng et al., eds., *Shangdang nuo wenhua*, pp. 242–49) vs. *Za* Opera ms. no. 38, *Changban* (板) *po*, ca. pp. 79–91; and the Li Shimin part in *Qin wang* (Han Sheng et al., eds., *Shangdang nuo wenhua*, pp. 224–42) vs. *Za*

an archaic feature of *Za* Operas and some other village ritual opera genres, strongly suggests that *Dui* Operas formed a distinct, somewhat more sophisticated subtradition of Shanxi village ritual opera. This might be due to the fact that the Entertainers were professional musicians and actors by birth, whereas the typical village ritual opera was the province of amateurs. But the crude performing style of *Dui* Opera, described above, shows that the form stayed close to its roots in rural ritual drama.

THE ENTERTAINER FAMILIES OF SOUTHEASTERN SHANXI

The Entertainers (*yuehu*), who played a critical role in the *sai*, were a fascinating and little-known social group.[91] I have mentioned them on several occasions; the time has now come to provide a full-scale description of their place in the ritual ecology of southeastern Shanxi.

Entertainers were persons born into families condemned to hereditary Entertainer status. They were *jianmin*, "mean people": they could not marry commoners, could not sit for the examinations, and could not change their status. In some cases they were required to be on call at the local yamen to entertain at banquets and other occasions. (Just what their responsibilities were is never made clear, but they may well have included sexual services.) They were treated with contempt by the general population. And yet the *sai* could not be held without them: "If it does not have Entertainer Opera (*yue ju* [i.e., *Dui* Opera or *Sai* Opera performed by *yuehu*]), it can't be called a great *sai*."[92] And note this definition of a *sai* from the 1710(?) edition of the *Xi zhou zhi*: "A *sai* is when Entertainer families gather in a temple and dance and sing before the

---

Opera ms. no. 9, *Lao jun tang*, ca. pp. 8–39. Since the Li Shimin part-script is by far the longest of the part-scripts, as noted above, and the Zhao Yun part-script is also one of the longer ones, they probably offer the best basis for comparison.

91. *Yuehu* can refer to either individuals or families.

92. A 72-year-old man, probably a native of Zhangzi county, told Zhang Zhennan ("Yueju he sai," p. 16A) that he frequently heard members of the older generation say this when he was young.

god[s]."[93] Although I cannot write at the length the subject deserves, I will give as much information as practicable about the Entertainers, since they were central to the great *sai*.[94]

To begin with a point that is rarely made in published research or interviews, there were two basic types of Entertainers: the coarse (*cu*) and the fine (*xi*).[95] The coarse were instrumentalists who performed at domestic rituals; the fine were both instrumentalists and actors. The "fine" Entertainer families were apparently the same as the Headman (*ketou*) families, who were the only ones who could perform at *sai*. As we have seen, the Wangs of West Shê were one of the eight *ketou* families of Lucheng county, and performed at many *sai*, including the Divine Mother *sai*.[96] One source says that only four Entertainer families could perform at *sai* in Zhangzi county, and another states that Zhangzi county had four Entertainer *ketou* families.[97] Every biography I have seen of an Entertainer who belonged to a *ketou* family mentions the *sai* the family performed at.[98]

Entertainers both "coarse" and "fine" provided the music needed at innumerable occasions in the life of the Shanxi countryside: funerals, weddings, birthdays, full-month and full-year celebrations, and so on.[99]

---

93. This quotation from the *Xi zhou zhi* is given without *juan* or page number or the date of the edition in Han Shuwei, "Shangdang dui xi," p. 322. The only edition of the *Xi zhou zhi* is dated 1710, although there is an 1898 supplement. In the absence of a citation, it was not feasible to confirm the quotation.

94. Two recent Chinese books on the Entertainer households of Shanxi are Qiao Jian et al., *Yuehu*; and Xiang Yang, *Shanxi yuehu yanjiu*. Unfortunately the Qiao compilation is a rather uneven collection of chapters by various hands, and Xiang's book—a published version of a doctoral dissertation—is heavily concerned with music. A truly synthetic social-historical study of this group is still needed.

95. Interview (1988) with two brothers named Li from Wulonghe West village, Jincheng municipality. They were born in 1919 and 1927 into a "coarse" Entertainer family. See Yuan Shuangxi and Li Shoutian, "Jingcheng xian yuehu," p. 633.

96. Li Tiansheng, "Xishe cun," p. 100.

97. Zhang Zhennan, "Yueju he sai," p. 2B; Yuan Shuangxi and Li Shoutian, "Shangdang," p. 479.

98. Found among the manuscript biographies of *sai* specialists by Zhang Zhennan and Bao Haiyan (in the author's collection); published in slightly different form by Yang Mengheng in his "Shanxi saishe yuehu," pp. 224–89.

99. Yuan Shuangxi and Li Shoutian, "Shangdang," p. 479.

I have no evidence on the total number of Entertainer families in southeastern Shanxi in the nineteenth or early twentieth century, but common sense and a few fragments of information suggest that there was probably plenty of work for every family. For example, an inscription of 1698 commemorating the repair of the shrine to the Throat God (Yanhou shen), the patron deity of Entertainers, located in the Jade Emperor Temple of Fucheng village in Yangcheng county, shows that ninety-four men with thirty-three surnames contributed money to the project. Let us assume that the catchment area of the temple was the entire county, and that approximately fifty Entertainer families were represented among the contributors. In Yangcheng county today there are very roughly 1,600 villages (based on an estimate of the number of villages in the 1:200,000 map in the *Shanxi Provincial Atlas*, which shows most of them); there almost certainly were more than 1,000 villages in the late seventeenth century, since the number of villages probably is more stable than the number of people, and in any case, Shanxi's population experienced a major decline after the famines of the late nineteenth and early twentieth century, and the province was also the scene of extensive fighting in the Anti-Japanese War and the Civil War. Even if the number of Entertainer families in Yangcheng county was far larger than fifty, with over 1,000 villages to serve there would have been more than enough to provide a good living for them, since villages probably averaged between 500 and 1,000 people. (We will see that late nineteenth-century contracts frequently specified five or six villages as the Territory of an Entertainer family.)

Most Entertainer families had a monopoly on the performance of ritual music in a specified group of villages. These exclusive territories, called *polu*, *yifan*, and *xiangdao*, among other terms, were the property of the families. Some maintained offices (*guanfang*) in their territories, and it was strictly forbidden for one family to perform in another family's Territory without invitation.[100] We know a good deal about how these territories worked in the nineteenth and early twentieth century

---

100. For general brief discussions of this institution, see Li Tiansheng, "Xishe cun," pp. 100, 105–15, and the contracts in the appendix; and Qiao Jian et al., *Yuehu*, pp. 49, 53–54.

thanks to fieldwork done by Liu Guanwen and contracts collected by him and by Li Tiansheng.[101] Liu is able to trace in some detail the fortunes of one Entertainer family, that of Li Fubao of Upper Sandbank village (Shang Shabicun) of Gaoping county.

In the 1850s Fubao and some of his brothers moved from Upper Sandbank to Lu village, about ten kilometers away in extreme northeastern Jincheng county, where they established a troupe called the Hall of Felicity and Righteousness (Fu yi tang). In 1855, a local Entertainer named Hou Yongning put up three villages of his "ancestral *yishi*"— Huanglu po, Beiyin zhai, and Shujia shan—as security for a ten-year loan of twenty-five ounces of silver from Fubao. In 1861, the Entertainer Dou Gengchen put up a two-village Territory as security for a loan of twenty-three ounces of silver from Fubao for the same term of years. (The villages were Longquan and Wangjia zhuang.) In 1867 four more villages in the Hou family's Territory were used to secure a loan (Yongning sai, Nanzhuang, Dong Zhang hou, and Hedong), this time to Hou Yongming's son, Shuangsong.

Since this was twelve years after Hou Yongning's ten-year loan, clearly he had been unable to repay his debt, and the three villages he had offered as security must have become the property of Fubao. In 1868, Fubao "loaned" Li Jincai 5,000 coins and in return Li "loaned" him a half-share of Wu village. The contract specified that the two families would share equally in the "red and white [i.e., festive and funerary] affairs, large and small," of the village. Finally, in 1876, Fubao obtained a Territory of nine villages as security for a loan of six ounces of silver to an Entertainer named Dou Chouru.[102] What is striking about this transaction is that the villages were in Gaoping county,[103] not Jincheng county where Fubao resided, and that the Territory of Dou

---

101. See Liu Guanwen, "Shangdang diqu," pp. 49–57; and Li Tiansheng, "Xishe cun," pp. 113–17, facsimile on p. 122.

102. The information on loans in this and the preceding paragraph is taken from Liu Guanwen, "Shangdang diqu," p. 53.

103. The farthest was about thirty kilometers from Lu village, the nearest ten kilometers. (The distance given on ibid., p. 54, is incorrect, as is the scale on the map on p. 55.) The villages were Gaoliang, Wangbao, Dongqu zhuang, Xiqu zhuang, Yongyang, Daye zhuang, Gutou zhuang, Zaixiang zhuang, and Shang zhuang.

Chouru was so large. (The low price is also worth noting; something was driving down the value of Entertainer Territories. Could it have been the encroachment of standard drama like *bangzi*? Or the progressive impoverishment of the region?) Thus twenty-one years after Li Fubao arrived in Lu village (not twenty-seven as Liu states), he had amassed a Territory of eighteen and a half villages. The answer to the question of how he accumulated the twenty-five ounces of silver he used to make his first loan remains tantalizingly out of reach. But that is neither here nor there; the point of this brief success (and failure) story is, first, that an Entertainer's Territory was property, just as farmland was, and, second, that the fortunes of individual families could rise and fall quite quickly. This is consistent with what we know of conditions in the north China countryside in the late nineteenth century and reminds me of the rapid change of family fortunes portrayed in some Hebei village operas, such as *Guo Ju Buries His Child*, which date from the same period and come from a nearby region.[104]

We have a number of contracts belonging to the Wang family of West Shê, the family that donated the part-scripts. They provide additional valuable information about the Territories of the Entertainers. As mentioned above, the ancestral home of the Wangs was in Wang Bend village, eighteen kilometers on a direct line north-northeast of West Shê, and for a long time they retained a Territory there.[105] An 1827 agreement settled a dispute between two men named Wang, presumably brothers, occasioned by the complaint of one—which came before the magistrate—that he was not getting a fair share of the family income. Therefore their inherited Territory was divided, with each man receiving nine villages (all near West Shê) as his exclusive Territory. In addition, the agreement specified that when the families "serve according to the old [regulations] at the civil and military yamens of the old capital of

---

104. These operas, which were called Yangge, were performed by village amateurs at New Year's and other festive occasions, and thus had some ritual function, but they do not seem to have been performed at occasions as serious as the *sai*. A number from Ding county are collected in Gamble, trans., *Chinese Village Plays*. For the Chinese texts, see Li Jinghan and Zhang Shiwen, *Ding xian*. My translation of *Guo Ju* can be found in de Bary and Lufrano, eds., *Sources of Chinese Tradition*, 2: 104–17.

105. Li Tiansheng, "Xishe cun," p. 100.

Pingshun, they shall do so on alternate years, but if there is a special celebration both can be summoned."[106]

An agreement of 1889 divided the property of a family in the Wang line into three portions because the younger two of three brothers had come of age. A substantial amount of real estate, including land, houses, timber, and a windmill, was involved. The oldest brother was given the trunk with all the costumes "for the performance of *Sai* Operas" but the agreement permitted his younger brothers to use it when performing "in this Territory." The only Territory specified (four villages in extreme southeastern Lucheng county, three near West Shê) is given to just one brother, and not the oldest.[107] But some villages were withheld from the agreement because a year later (1890) the oldest brother made a settlement with his foster son that included a Territory of seven and a half villages northeast of West Shê in eastern Lucheng county plus other real property (including a number of stage robes). The contract also says this about the family's customary role in two *sai*: "At the annual *sai* in the fourth month at Jia village [in Lucheng county] and the [Lucheng] City-God Temple, [Wang Yongzhen] will supply two men, and [Yanhui, his foster son] will have no part in the fee or negotiations."[108]

Clearly, Territories could vary considerably in size. Some were very large. We are told that north of Changzhi county, Entertainers sometimes rented the right to perform in villages in their Territories to lesser musicians because there were too many for them to service themselves,

---

106. Li Tiansheng, "Xishe cun," p. 114. As noted earlier, Pingshun county had been abolished in 1764 and was not restored until 1911, which explains why the county town is referred to as the "old capital" here. But this means that a nonexistent county had a "yamen" that could command services from Entertainers. One wonders what other activities the "officials" engaged in there. The seeming persistence of the status of the old county seat is extremely interesting and deserves investigation. Did this happen elsewhere when counties were abolished?

107. Ibid., pp. 115–16.

108. Ibid., p. 116. Other documents in this series that give information on dividing Territories are nos. 4, 7, and 8 (although the last appears to be a claim by just one man). Documents that give a sense of the economic circumstances of the better-placed families, in addition to those already cited, are nos. 3 and 9. The last is especially interesting, since it is a contract for a *sai*. (The fee was 39,000 coins.)

a procedure very much like landowners renting land to tenants.[109] Other Territories could shrink to the vanishing point, possibly due to the gambling or opium addiction of their owners. We have evidence of three Entertainers becoming for a time hired laborers working for another Entertainer.[110] There also were Entertainers without performing skills who ended up doing menial jobs for other Entertainers at *sai*— they were called *po xia hu*.[111] Then there is the story told to Li Tiansheng by an informant from Lingchuan county. When he was young, a man of the older generation who was an opium addict used the ten villages of his Territory as security for a loan from an Entertainer family in a neighboring county. All the Entertainers of Lingchuan county later worked together to redeem them.[112] Why did they do this—to protect the addict's family? To save the face of the county's Entertainer families? Either way, it suggests strong group consciousness.

The Entertainer class had a fairly clear hierarchical structure that was probably related in part to differences in economic status: ordinary Entertainer families were subordinate to the Headmen, or *ketou*, as we have already seen.[113] The Entertainer Headmen of a given county were subordinate in turn to the county's Chief of the Headmen (*zong ketou*), who was their officially appointed liaison with local government.[114] Each county also had a sort of council of Entertainer Headmen called the *gongyi hui*. Its leader was appointed by the council and approved by the local magistrate.[115] As already mentioned, only the families of Headmen had the right to perform at the great *sai*. The family within whose Territory the temple was located obviously played a major role, but since no single Entertainer family could put on a *sai* by itself, they

---

109. Qiao Jian et al., *Yuehu*, p. 146.

110. This was during the Japanese occupation, when conditions in Shanxi were very bad. The three eventually regained their status as Entertainers (ibid., p. 54).

111. Yin Gengfu, "Wang Xiaoji," p. 228.

112. Qiao Jian et al., *Yuehu*, p. 125.

113. Ibid.

114. Ibid., p. 124. See also Yuan Shuangxi and Li Shoutian, "Fang lao yiren Cui Luze," p. 547. The Chief of the Headmen for Huguan county was Liu Zhangqiu (the informant's maternal uncle), and that for Lingchuan was Li Xiaoliu. Each had twelve Headmen under him.

115. Qiao Jian et al., *Yuehu*, p. 125.

recruited other *ketou* families to help them.[116] The *Dui* Operas were a special challenge because they required a large number of trained actors, who were scarcer than instrumentalists. And here we return to the part-scripts system.

Only the Chief of the Headmen had the full scripts of the *Dui* Operas.[117] The other Headman families were limited to part-scripts. There is wide agreement in the scholarship that a given family was limited to a given role-type,[118] but this is contradicted by information in the biographies and other sources, which shows clearly that members of one family sometimes performed several role types,[119] and by the fact that the Wang family of West Shê had parts of more than one role-type in its possession. Also, from what we can tell on the basis of the surviving manuscripts, *Dui* Opera, like *Za* Opera, did not use role-types. But our evidence is all quite late, and it is certainly possible that when the *sai* system was at its most flourishing and the Entertainer families were most numerous there was this sort of division of labor among them. It would have been a rational way to deal with the fact that an Entertainer family was just that, a family, and not a troupe. Restricting circulation of the full scripts—which probably contained the stage directions—would also have helped keep them from falling into the hands of lesser Entertainers and thus threatening the profitable monopoly of the Chiefs.

The part-script system had at least one important consequence. Staging a *Dui* Opera involved the collaboration of several families who rehearsed together for only a few days before the performance,[120] and the

---

116. For some of the evidence for this, see Li Tiansheng, "Xishe cun," pp. 100, 109; Bao Haiyan, "Yang Xueren," p. 225; biography of Zun Quncai, draft biographies of *sai* specialists, first unnumbered page after p. 60; and Zhang Zhennan, "Yueju yu sai," p. 234.

117. Yuan Shuangxi and Li Shoutian, "Shangdang," pp. 466, 478; *Zhongguo xiqu zhi: Shanxi juan*, p. 142.

118. For example, Yuan Shuangxi and Li Shoutian, "Shangdang," pp. 478, 479; Han Sheng et al., eds., *Shangdang nuo wenhua*, p. 21; and Zhang Zhennan, "Yueju yu sai," p. 234, which identifies four troupes and their home villages.

119. Li Tiansheng, "Xishe cun," p. 111; Li Shoutian and Yang Mingsheng, "Zhu Zhagen," p. 234.

120. *Zhongguo xiqu zhi: Shanxi juan*, p. 142.

various parts had to fit together seamlessly on the stage. Unless it did not involve cues, a change in any one part would have required changes in the other parts. The ensuing complications would have presented a major obstacle to smooth performance that would have been impossible to overcome in the limited rehearsal time available. In any case the scripts, secular though they were, had substantial ritual significance, and sponsors probably expected or demanded that they not be changed. For all these reasons, *Dui* Opera scripts were likely to have been very conservative.

The social category of "Entertainers" or "Entertainer families" (*yuehu*) was old already in early Qing.[121] In the Northern Wei (probably after the shift of the capital to Luoyang in A.D. 495), women and children in the same population register as a man found guilty of robbery with violence, whether the victim died or not, were entered into the registers of the Entertainers.[122] In Northern Zhou and Sui (mid- to late sixth century) there are examples of men being condemned to Entertainer status as a penalty for their own or their father's disloyalty.[123] This presumably continued right through the Tang, for there is a story of a Song Daoist priest being condemned to Entertainer status.[124] At first, those people registered as entertainers[125] appear to have served mainly in the palace, but eventually they began to serve in prefectural and county yamens as well. Presumably when they served local officials, they also began working for the general population, since the officials had need of their services only on special occasions. It is not possible to be more precise about the timing of this evolution, or to determine when Entertainer status became hereditary. What is clear is that in early Ming the massive purges by the Yongle emperor of those who had opposed his usurpation of the throne created large numbers of Entertainers whose status was intended to be inherited by their descendents

---

121. For sketchy surveys of the history of the Entertainer group, see Qiao Jian et al., *Yuehu*, pp. 107–20; and Xiang Yang, *Shanxi yuehu yanjiu*, pp. 1–40.

122. *Wei shu*, 111.23b–24a; partially quoted in Qiao Jian et al., *Yuehu*, p. 104.

123. Qi Senhua et al., *Zhongguo quxue da cidian*, p. 30A.

124. Morohashi, *Dai Kan-Wa jiten*, s.v. 官妓 (3: 7107.60), quoting *Qun tan cai yu*. Since this is a Ming text, its testimony on Song events should be assessed accordingly.

125. I use lowercase here because they were not just *yuehu*.

in perpetuity.[126] Many Entertainer families in Shanxi who were interviewed in the 1980s believed that they were descended from those exiles.[127]

The newly created Entertainers were not just dispatched to the provinces (especially Shanxi) and left to fend for themselves.[128] Thousands were given to the ever-growing number of major and minor princes (*fan wang, jun wang*), who lived on giant estates bestowed by the Ming founder and his successors.[129] There were three major and seventy-six minor princedoms in Shanxi alone, and they employed thousands of Entertainers.[130] There was a mutual connection between the entertainment and music bureaus at the court and the Entertainers in service to the princes: at times provincial Entertainers were drafted to serve at court (or drifted to the capital of their own accord), and at times individuals trained at court were sent out to the provinces.[131] Of special interest here is the leakage of Entertainers from princely households into the general population, which must have happened when, for example, the women lost their youthful good looks and the skills of the men declined, or after the stipends of the princes were reduced.[132] Such indi-

---

126. For background, see Mote's magisterial *Imperial China*, pp. 584–90, 594–97. An unequivocal statement that the Entertainer status of early Ming "traitors'" families was permanent can be found in *Huangchao tongkao*, quoted in Xiang Yang, *Shanxi yuehu yanjiu*, p. 24. See also the general statements in ibid., pp. 50–51, esp. p. 51 for the Ming period.

127. See Xiang Yang, *Shanxi yuehu yanjiu*, pp. 25–27, for the names of Entertainers from five places in Shanxi who trace their ancestry to Ming exiles.

128. See ibid., p. 50, on Shanxi as a frequent destination for Ming Entertainers.

129. On the Ming princes, see Mote, *Imperial China*, pp. 565–66. On gifts of Entertainers to them, see *Qinding Xu wenxian tongkao*, 104.1b–2a; Xiang Yang, *Shanxi yuehu yanjiu*, pp. 52–54; and Han Shuwei, "Yuanben," p. 18.

130. On the number of fiefs, see Xiang Yang, *Shanxi yuehu yanjiu*, p. 52. On the numbers of Entertainers, note that even in the late stages of the fief system in the early seventeenth century, the household of the Prince of Dai Jian, centered on Datong in northern Shanxi, had over 2,000 Entertainers (ibid., p. 53, *n*1, quoting *Wanli ye huo bian* [1619]). On the relative density of musicians and actors in Shanxi, see Hansson, *Chinese Outcasts*, pp. 63–64.

131. Drafted from province to capital: *Qinding Xu wenxian tongkao*, 104.15b–16a. Drifting: Han Shuwei, "Yuanben," p. 18. Sent out to the provinces: see the story of the Entertainers given to Grand Councilor Du, discussed below.

132. They were cut by 80 percent in 1395 and then in later years declined still further due to the increasing size of the imperial clan (Mote, *Imperial China*, pp. 566, 782).

viduals must have carried with them something of the glamour of their former princely masters.[133]

The same must have been true to a lesser degree of the Entertainers who served at the prefectural and county yamens. There is abundant evidence that Entertainers served at the offices of local officials, although the terms of their service are not entirely clear. Xiang Yang implies that there were some Entertainers who were regular members of the yamen staff (*zai guan yuehu*), whereas others—by far the larger number—had to serve only when summoned.[134] Most of the evidence has to do with Entertainers being summoned to the local yamen. I already noted that in one of the Wang family contracts two brothers agreed to share the responsibility of answering the summons to the yamen. In another case, the eight Entertainer Headman families of Lucheng county took turns being on call at the yamen.[135] I stated earlier that leading Entertainer families—better called lineages—established offices called *guanfang* in their Territories, from which they managed their affairs. It is likely that the term means something like "office for yamen affairs." For example, an old Entertainer named Dou Yinxi (b. 1915)[136] said that his uncle set up an office called a *guanfang* "at the yamen" of Jincheng county. Another informant from the same county, who was born in 1926, said that an Entertainer office was set up "outside the entrance to the yamen."[137] Yuan and Li carried out extensive interviews with old Entertainers in Yangcheng county in 1987. They were told that there was a *guanfang* in the county seat on the north side of a street formerly called Yamen Street where Entertainers were always in residence in case the officials had need of them.[138] They also interviewed an old couple (bicycle-watchers at the county offices) who lived near the site of the former Throat God

---

133. Such a dispersal is suggested by the passage from *Pingyang fu zhi* (no edition or page given) quoted in Han Shuwei, "Yuanben," p. 16.

134. Xiang Yang, *Shanxi yuehu yanjiu*, p. 39. This position seems to be echoed by Zhang Zhengming in "Ming dai de yuehu," p. 208, but he does not cite conclusive evidence.

135. Li Shoutian and Yang Mengheng, "Wang Fuyun," p. 261.

136. Interviewed by Yuan Shuangxi and Li Shoutian in 1988 in Nansai village in Jincheng county.

137. Yuan Shuangxi and Li Shoutian, "Jincheng xian yuehu," pp. 634, 633.

138. Li Shoutian and Yuan Shuangxi, "Yangcheng xian," p. 552.

Temple at the northwest corner of the intersection of City-God Temple *hutong* (alley) and the street that ran past the front of the yamen.[139] (It was in ruins in 1987, its site occupied by the county Grain Bureau.) The couple said that there had been a room (*fang*) on the west side of the outer courtyard of the Throat God Temple where Entertainers who were on call at the yamen stayed.[140] The informants from Yangcheng county are probably referring to the same place. Xiang Yang, citing the draft Shanxi volume of the *Encyclopedia of Chinese Instrumental Music*, says that most Shanxi yamens in the last two centuries of the Qing dynasty had Entertainers in residence or "on call," despite the official "emancipation" of the Entertainers in 1723 and a specific ban on yamen Entertainers in 1725.[141] For example, before 1926 each person in the register of Entertainers in Hejin county was required to spend a month on call at the yamen every year, and in Jishan county as late as the early Republican period there was a house or room constructed by the government at the entrance to the yamen where Entertainers were always in residence, all of whose expenses were borne by the Chief of the Troupe Heads (*zong bantou*, presumably the same as the Chief of the Headmen), in order to serve the needs of officials. Their most important tasks were taking part in the greeting of and bidding farewell to official guests and entertaining at banquets.[142]

The Entertainers did more for local officials than provide entertainment. Just as they did during the *sai*, they assisted at certain government rituals. Dou Yinxi, the old Entertainer quoted earlier, said that Entertainers "on call" were summoned to assist with the *Ding* Sacrifices (*ding sai*) in the second and eighth months. They also accompanied the officials to a temple (not specified) to burn incense after an execu-

---

139. As noted above, the Throat God, Yanhou shen, was the patron saint of Entertainers.

140. Li Shoutian and Yuan Shuangxi, "Si fang Gaoping Yanhou si"; Han Sheng et al., eds., *Shangdang nuo wenhua*, p. 639.

141. Qiao Jian et al., *Yuehu*, 120.

142. Xiang Yang, *Shanxi yuehu yanjiu*, p. 84. I strongly disagree with Matthew Sommer's assumption in *Sex, Law, and Society* that the *yuehu* were prostitutes, which is a fundamental misunderstanding of the situation, at least in Shanxi. It is possible that there was a sexual dimension to the duties of female Entertainers at the yamen, but that is a separate issue, and in any case I have found no evidence for it.

tion.[143] And Entertainer participation in the various ceremonies called "Welcoming the Spring" (*ying chun*) is exhaustively documented. The clearest account of this is in the *Puzhou Prefectural Gazetteer* of 1755:

In times past Shanxi had many first-class female entertainers (*jueji*). Every prefecture had them; they were called "*yuehu*" [i.e., Entertainers]. In Puzhou in Ming times, *yuehu* lived together in the eastern suburb of Puzhou town. When the prefect celebrated the arrival of spring (*xing chun*), they put on heavy makeup and rode horses [in a procession, presumably]. At the drinking party for local gentry and other guests, they were summoned to "assist with the wine." It was like this until the middle of the Kangxi era of this dynasty.[144]

The Puzhou gazetteer editors then quote the 1686 edition of the *Linjin County Gazetteer*:

In the performances at Spring Begins (*li chun*), after the fifteenth day of the twelfth month, skillful Entertainers were selected [to wear] official dress and imitate officials. They were followed by [mock] clerks. They were called "Spring Officials" and "Spring Clerks." [It is not clear how many of each there were.] They went to the yamen, the houses of the eminent, shops, and taverns, and everywhere they went they declaimed encomiums, pouring forth agreeable words. They asked for wine and food and demanded auspicious rewards, calling it "Announcing the Spring." The day before [Spring Begins] the county officials brought together festive processions from the rural districts, indiscriminately using actors and young female entertainers, whom they called "baby girls." With drummers and musicians leading the way and the Spring Ox bringing up the rear, [the magistrate] led his staff, richly dressed and riding in extravagant carriages, to the eastern suburb. This was called "Welcoming the Spring." At the fifth hour, the Ox (which was an effigy made of clay) was beaten to pieces. This was called "Beating the Spring."[145]

---

143. Han Sheng et al., eds., *Shangdang nuo wenhua*, p. 634.

144. Quoted in Yang Mengheng, "Shanxi saishe yuehu," pp. 194–95. Wang Shizhen, a famous early Qing poet and official, described a nearly identical custom that he banned in Yangzhou ca. 1660 in his *Xiang zu biji* (Siku quanshu Wenyuan ge intranet ed.), 7.4a, cited in Meyer-Fong, *Building Culture*, p. 45. In ibid., p. 212, *n*66, Meyer-Fong says that according to the *Yongzheng huidian* the use of musicians and female entertainers by local officials had been banned in 1673. The ban seems not to have had much effect in Shanxi.

145. Ding Shiliang and Zhao Fang, *Zhongguo difangzhi minsu ziliao huibian: Huabei juan*, p. 714, quoting *Linjin xian zhi* (1686). Yang Mengheng, "Shanxi saishe yuehu," pp. 194–

The Spring Ox and related performances to welcome spring are interesting as examples of officially sponsored ceremonies that have a genuinely archaic, pre-Confucian feel—including, once again, a mock killing.
The participation of Entertainers reinforces the sense that we are in the
presence here of a facet of local governance that is all but unknown.

If Entertainers took part in rituals presided over by officials, then
the county or prefectural elites were doing just as the village elites did:
overlooking the Entertainers' degraded status because they were ritually
indispensable. It is difficult not to suspect that at one time their status
was a good deal higher than it eventually came to be. There is a striking
story of the relationship between an eminent Shanxi family and their
Entertainers that suggests this. It was told to Li Shoutian and Yuan
Shuangxi in December 1986 by Cui Luze (b. 1906), an Entertainer who
lived with the Huguan County Yangge Troupe. His maternal uncle was
Liu Zhangqiu, the one-time Chief of the Headmen of the Entertainers
of Huguan county, who presided over something like a school for Entertainers in the Temple of Grand Councilor Du in Maxiang village.
Grand Councilor Du was Du Xiao, an eminent official greatly favored
by Taizu, the Ming founder. When he retired to Maxiang, his native
village, Taizu presented him with a family of Entertainers to enliven
his rustic life. The family was named Liu; Liu Zhangqiu was their
descendant. When Du Xiao died, the villagers built the Grand Councilor Temple in his honor, and the Lius became the hereditary temple keepers, continuing the sacrifices to Du Xiao generation after
generation. Once again we see Entertainers providing ritual services to

---

95, quotes the 1755 (actually 1754) *Puzhou fu zhi*, which claims to be quoting the *Linjin
xian zhi*, but the text Yang gives is greatly condensed from that given in Ding and Zhao.
(I have not been able to check the 1686 *Linjin xian zhi* and therefore have quoted the
text as given by the usually reliable Ding and Zhao.) There are a number of other, similar passages given in the sources: for example, *Yangcheng xian zhi* (1687) and *Yicheng xian
zhi* (1881), quoted in Ding and Zhao, pp. 618 and 649. A good short description of the
ceremony in Fuzhou can be found in Hodous, *Folkways in China*, pp. 19–25. A book I
have not read, but which undoubtedly is full of information on these ceremonies, is
Morgan, *Le tableau du boeuf*. A useful Chinese account is Guo Licheng, *Zhongguo minsu
shihua*, pp. 43–47. A beautiful print of an entire Welcoming the Spring procession (late
nineteenth–early twentieth century) is reproduced in Gao Wen et al., eds., *Mianzhu*, pls.
124–31. The ox is made of paper over a framework of sticks, more common than clay.

the elite. When land reform came, Liu descendants were still living in the temple.[146]

In addition to providing another illustration of just how long-lived certain social arrangements could be in rural China, this story suggests that the relationship between the eminent Du family and their troupe of Entertainers was far deeper than one would have guessed. Why were the Lius, members of a debased caste, chosen to be what amounted to the temple priests? And why was their tenure in that job so enduring? These are questions I cannot answer. But I know that everywhere in China music was more than entertainment; it was an indispensable part of ritual, as was music drama. The people to whom rituals were important naturally resisted any change in them. Those who knew how to perform rituals properly therefore had considerable authority. The actor-singers and musicians who knew how to perform the *sai* and other rituals had that knowledge and the charisma it conferred. They were hereditary "mean people" (*jianmin*), reminded of their inferiority every time they had to make way for a "good person" as they walked down the street, or wait to eat at festival banquets until everyone else had finished. But they were the bearers of the musical and operatic traditions of the *sai* of the Divine Mother of the Ninth Heaven, and all the other *sai* in southeastern Shanxi. With their exclusive Territories, they were functionally integrated into the countryside. They had long-standing relationships with the village, county, and prefectural elites, with the Ming princes, and with the imperial court itself. They governed themselves in the manner of an extremely large and complex guild, and like a guild worked in concert with the local authorities. In late Qing most were debased and despised, like Buddhist monks, perhaps especially after the general crisis of rural north China in the nineteenth century began to destroy the cultural matrix of the countryside. But their forebears—in some cases—had been high officials, who must have

---

146. Yuan Shuangxi, "Shangdang nuo xi ji qi liubian," p. 16, which gives *Lu'an fu zhi*, *juan* 11, as the source for the information about Du Xiao. This story is repeated in Yuan Shuangxi and Li Shoutian, "Shangdang," p. 480; and idem, "Fang lao yiren Cui Luze," p. 546. Other versions of the interview with Cui can be found in Yang Mengheng, "Shanxi saishe yuehu," pp. 288–89; and Han Sheng et al., eds., *Shangdang nuo wenhua*, p. 635.

brought the sophistication of the capital with them into exile. Other ancestors had been in regular contact with local officials and even imperial princes, or went back and forth between the entertainment bureaus in the capital and the provinces. They were formally emancipated in 1723 and were frequently rather well-to-do. They carried on an operatic tradition that they themselves may have invented and a musical tradition that some believe originated in the Tang and Song courts. They shared the low status of all entertainers, made worse because it was hereditary, but in fact the Entertainers were indispensable to the most important communal celebrations in the countryside of southeastern Shanxi, and possibly elsewhere in north China as well. They were a debased elite, one of the many unknown but significant features of the world of the *sai*.

2

The Hou Yi Temple on
Mt. Longquan □ The Masters
of Ceremonial

Entertainers alone could not put on a *sai*. At least as important, though far fewer in number, were the Masters of Ceremonial, the men who knew how and when all the rituals of the multiday *sai* were to be performed. They have not received nearly as much attention from Chinese scholars as the Entertainers, probably because actors and musicians are a safer subject than ritual specialists.[1] Indeed, theater studies is a lively field in China, but religious or ritual studies, except of sects such as those in the so-called White Lotus system, have attracted less interest, especially in north China. No doubt the feeling has been that "feudal superstitions" are best left alone, even though ritual professionals and their special knowledge were obviously of central importance in both town and country. But they are given their due in this chapter, which focuses on the ritual program of the Mt. Longquan *sai* and the ritual specialists called the Masters of Ceremonial.

The temple to Hou Yi, popularly known as the San Zong Temple (San Zong miao), on Mt. Longquan, about ten kilometers north-northwest of Zhangzi town, was built on a hill with a fine view of the surrounding countryside and away from villages—a classic site for a *sai*

---

1. The only substantial scholarly work to take them seriously, at least in Western languages, is Liu Yonghua's dissertation, "The World of Ritual." This is a valuable work, although the author's eagerness to criticize the research of others is unfortunate.

temple.[2] It had two annual *sai* (main days 2/15 and 7/7), no doubt because it was supported by an alliance of eighteen villages, one of the largest I encountered in my research. An alliance of that size could mobilize substantial resources. These *sai* were massive affairs, well known in southeastern Shanxi.

The temple has been completely obliterated—by Japanese troops, I was told—but the site, though surrounded by cultivated fields, has been left unplowed. Wild grasses covered it when I was there, with a few small trees along one side. It was open to the sky, with fine prospects of the cultivated hills all around and the mountains off to the west. Fragments of colorful glazed roof tiles could be found here and there: a peaceful but melancholy place. In several spots, hidden in the long grass, there were tiny shrines perhaps a foot high made from the larger fragments. Small figures, crudely made, had been placed in them by village women praying for sons.[3] It takes a long time for the powers of such places to fade completely.

We do not have a description of the Mt. Longquan *sai* as close-grained as those of the other temples discussed in this part, although we do have an account by Yang Mengheng and Zhang Zhennan apparently based in part on the testimony of local residents. But we have exceptionally important evidence of a quite different sort: a manuscript of the actual ritual program performed there in 1911, 1921, and 1925.

The ritual program of every *sai* was under the direction of a Master of Ceremonial (*zhu li*)—sometimes more than one. These men were the elite of the larger community of *yinyang* masters, who were local specialists consulted by villagers about everything from the best place to build a house to the astrological suitability of a marriage, and who officiated at domestic rituals, especially when the earth was disturbed, as in digging a grave or laying the foundation of a house. They had a place in the rural ritual hierarchy analogous to that of the Entertainers, who supplied music for everyday rituals. Did the Masters of Ceremonial have exclusive Territories like the Entertainers? I have found no evidence that they did.

---

2. Hou Yi was called San Zong in southern Shanxi, where his cult was important. His official title was Nation-Protecting Divinely-Providing King (Hu Guo Ling Kuang Wang).

3. I would have walked right past them had our driver, who lived in the area, not pointed them out.

The reason may be that since they worked on their own, rather than as families, their schedules were more flexible. Why were some *yinyang* masters able to rise to the position of Master of Ceremonial? There must have been a number of factors, but one important reason certainly was the possession of books describing the rituals that made up a *sai* and providing the texts of the many prayers, exhortations, and encomiums that the *zhu li* had to recite. (In this they resembled the Daoist masters of southeastern China, about whom recent scholarship has informed us so copiously.) The rituals were complex and also impossible for outsiders to observe at close range, and so without the handbooks it would have been extremely difficult for a mere *yinyang* master to set up shop as a Master of Ceremonial. The closely held nature of the liturgical manuscripts is also the reason why historians are generally better informed about what happened outside the temple during most *sai* than what took place in front of the altars and within the Offering Pavilion.

THE MASTERS OF CEREMONIAL (*ZHU LI*) AND THE LITURGY OF THE HOU YI *SAI*

We have a Master of Ceremonial's personal summary of the ritual program for the great *sai* held every year on the thirteenth to the seventeenth days of the second lunar month at the Hou Yi temple on Mt. Longquan: *Handbook for Use Before the Gods of the* Sai (*Sai shang za yong shen qian ben*).[4] The *Handbook* is only an outline of the main *sai* rituals. It was compiled in a period when local ritual culture must have been in severe decline, and other, earlier manuscripts provide a more complete picture. But the fact that this text was used at a specific *sai*, one about which we know a great deal, makes it invaluable.

----

4. There are two editions: Yang Mengheng et al., eds., "*Sai shang za yong* . . . jiao zhu"; and Yang, *Fourteen Manuscripts*, pp. 29–60. Proof that this book was a sort of handbook is provided by the various dates that appear in it: not just the 13th to the 17th of the 2nd month (of 1911) that it was originally prepared for, but also "6th month 13th day" on the cover, and "2nd month 26th day" and "10th month, first three days" in the body of the text. That these dates differ from the dates of the traditional *sai* at the Mt. Longquan temple is solid evidence that the manual was used at *sai* elsewhere.

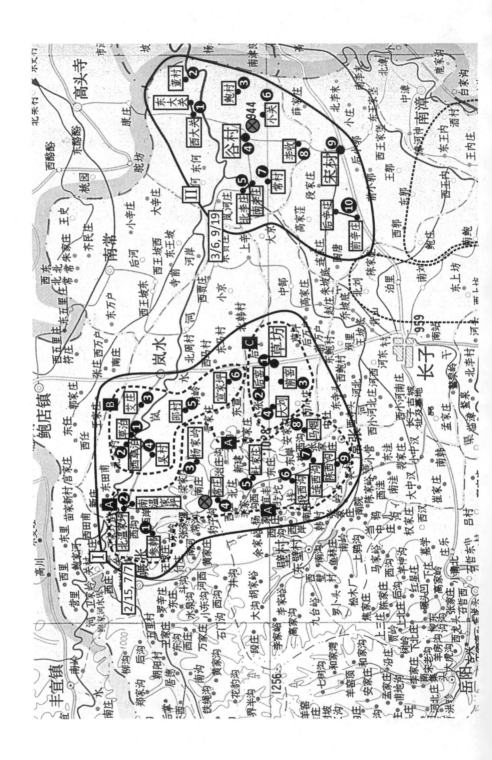

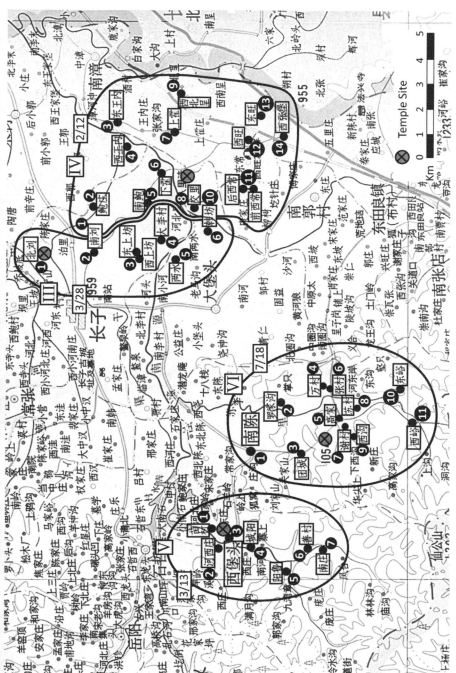

Map 7 Village temple alliances for the sponsorship of *sai* in Zhangzi county

Key to Map 7

Temple alliances were very long-lived, so even though the bulk of the evidence below is of recent date it probably reflects long-established patterns. *Sai* generally were held in the same temple every year. Most *sai* temples were located in the countryside, often on sites with commanding views, but some were in towns, such as Zhangzi. A few were actually located in a village, and the venue of those *sai* sometimes rotated in a set sequence among the member villages. All the listed villages can be located on modern maps, though village names in the written sources occasionally differ slightly from those in the maps.

Name of *sai* or focal temple	Deity	Date of *sai*
I: Mt. Longquan 龍泉山	Hou Yi 后羿	2.15, 7.7

Supporting villages (in three sub-alliances) :

   A: 1) Canhan 參韓, 2) Wenjiaping 溫家坪 [Beiwenjiaping 北溫家坪 and Nanwenjiaping 南溫家坪 of the *Shanxi sheng ditu ji* were probably originally this village], 3) Yangjialing 楊家嶺, 4) Changzhuang 常莊, 5) Dujiazhuang 杜家莊, 6) Duanxigou 段西溝, 7) Lianxigou 連西溝, 8) Mayan 馬煙, 9) Chenxigou 陳西溝;

   B: 1) Dongcaobo 東草泊 [Caopo in the *Shanxi sheng ditu ji*], 2) Xicaobo 西草泊, 3) Aizhuang 艾莊, 4) Wucun 吳村, 5) Shaocun 邵村, 6) Xuanjiaping 宣家坪;

   C: 1) Caofang 草坊, 2) Beiyao 北窯, 3) Nanyao 南窯 [these almost certainly are the Houyao 後窯 and Qianyao 前窯 of the *Shanxi sheng ditu ji*], 4) Daliuzhuang 大劉莊. (Source: *Sai shang za yong shen qian ben* (*jia*) 賽上雜用神前本[甲]. The earliest of several dates in this text is 1911 [p. 29]. Reprinted in Yang, *Fourteen Manuscripts*, pp. 32–33.)

II: Xiaoguan Temple 小關館[觀]	Hou Yi	3.6, 9.19

[I strongly suspect that *guǎn* 館 ("hostel, official residence, etc.") as given in Yang and other recent sources should be *guàn* 觀 ("Daoist temple"). If so, it appears that a Daoist establishment was taken over by a popular cult.]

Supporting villages:

1) Daguan 大關 [Dongdaguan 東大關 and Xidaguan 西大關 of the *Shanxi sheng ditu ji* were probably originally this village], 2) Dongcun 董村, 3) Baocun 鮑村, 4) Gucun 谷村, 5) Lizhuang 李莊 [Beilizhuang 北李莊 and Nanlizhuang 南李莊 of the *Shanxi sheng ditu ji* were probably originally this village], 6) Xiaoguan 小關, 7) Changcun 常村, 8) Lishou 李收, 9) Songcun 宋村, 10) Xincun 辛村 [Houxincun 後辛村 and Qianxincun 前辛村 of the *Shanxi sheng ditu ji* were probably originally this village]. (Source: Yang, *Fourteen Manuscripts*, p. 76, n. 1. Texts 3–5 in this collection relate to the Xiaoguan temple *sai*; no. 3 is dated Yongzheng 3 [1726], while nos. 4 and 5 contain the Qianlong reign title [1736–95]. Nos. 3 and 4 refer to ten supporting villages, but do not name them. The names are supplied by Yang in the cited note.)

III: The Six *Sai* 六賽	Great Lord of the Eastern Peak 東岳大帝	3.28

Supporting villages: 1) Beiliu 北劉, 2) Nanliu 南劉 [this village is also no. 1 in alliance IV], 3) Shangfang 上坊 [This is probably Zhang Zhennan's abbreviated reference to the Dong Shangfang 東上坊 and Xi Shangfang 西上坊 of the *Shanxi sheng ditu ji*], 4) Dali 大李, 5) Liangshui 兩水, 6) Hanfang 韓坊 [this village is also no. 10 in alliance IV]. (Source: Handwritten list of dates and locations of old *sai* in Zhangzi county, prepared by Zhang Zhennan 張振南, in the author's collection.)

IV: Eight-*li* Hollow 八里窪	Hou Yi	2.12

Supporting villages: 1) Nanliu 南劉 [this village is also no. 2 in alliance III], 2) Baozhuang 鮑莊, 3) Dongwangnei 東王内, 4) Xiwangnei 西王内, 5) Nanbao 南鮑, 6) Xiahuo 下霍, 7) Shanghuo

上霍, 8) Jiaoli 交李 [the *Shanxi sheng ditu ji* has Jiaoli 交里], 9) Xibeicheng 西北呈, 10) Hanfang 韓坊 [this village is also no. 6 in alliance III], 11) Xichang 西常 [Houxichang 后西常 and Qianxichang 前西常 of the *Shanxi sheng ditu ji* were probably originally this village], 12) Xiwang 西王 [the *Shanxi sheng ditu ji* has a Xiwang 西旺 in the vicinity, probably the same village], 13) Dongwang 東王 [the *Shanxi sheng ditu ji* has a Dongwang 東旺 in the vicinity, probably the same village], 14) Xizhangbao 西張堡. (Source: Inscription of 1702 commemorating the renovation of the temple. Reprinted in Yang Taikang and Cao Zhanmei, *San Jin xiqu*, pp. 407–9. An inscription dated 1723 refers to the temple as the Mt. Baiyun Temple 白雲山神廟, but the available maps show nothing like a mountain in the neighborhood. Ibid., p. 409.)

V: Southern Seven Villages 南七村　　　Jade Emperor 玉皇大帝　　　3.13

Supporting villages: 1) Miaocun 苗村, 2) Hexi 河西, 3) Xibaotou 西堡頭, 4) Chengyang 城陽, 5) Yanglu 陽魯, 6) Shancun 善村, 7) Nangou 南溝. (Source: Zhang Zhennan, "Yueju he sai," p. 13. In Zhang's handwritten list of Zhangzi *sai*, he states that the deity receiving cult at this *sai* was Grandmother Giver of Sons and Grandsons 子孫奶奶. The *Shanxi sheng ditu ji* has a village named Nanzhuang 南莊 as the southernmost of this cluster, but the 1 : 50,000 Chinese Army map of 1944–45, Zhangzi sheet, shows a village named Nangou 南溝 in that location, confirming Zhang's information.)

VI: Mt. Yongan 永安山　　　Hou Yi　　　7.18

Supporting villages: 1) Nanchen 南陳, 2) Luojiagou 羅家溝, 3) Tuancheng 團城, 4) Wancun 萬村, 5) Gaojia 高家, 6) Zhangcun 張村, 7) Xiecun 解村 [the *Shanxi sheng ditu ji* gives Xiecun 謝村], 8) Sucun 蘇村, 9) Xigou 西溝, 10) Dongyu 東峪, 11) Xiyu 西峪. (Source: Zhang Zhennan, "Yueju yu sai," p. 256a.)

The eighteen villages that supported the Mt. Longquan *sai* are listed in the text in three groups of five *shê* each: West, East, and North (*Xi wu shê, Dong wu shê, Bei wu shê*). Almost all can be found on modern maps. The villages of a particular group of five *shê* shared in the expenses of a given year's *sai*. The responsibility rotated in the order West, East, North, and back to West again.[5] I assume that the gods of the temples of the sponsoring villages were the ones invited to the *sai* in the elaborate ceremony I shall shortly describe.[6]

We know something about the Masters of Ceremonial who owned the *Handbook* and about a number of other men who participated in the Mt. Longquan *sai* at one time or another. I will introduce them before describing the *sai* and its rituals.

The *Handbook* was written down by a man named Niu Zhenguo (1880–1946), who was a native of East Daguan village in extreme north-

---

5. Yang, *Fourteen Manuscripts*, pp. 32–33.

6. The text gives a list of the gods invited to one celebration of the Longquan *sai* but does not indicate the villages they came from (ibid., p. 60.)

eastern Zhangzi county, in the heart of the *sai* culture area. The hereditary occupation of his family was *yinyang* master, and as far back at least
as his great-great-grandfather his ancestors—whose names are known—
had served as Masters of Ceremonial at *sai* in Zhangzi county and elsewhere, including the one celebrated at the Hou Yi Temple on Mt. Longquan.[7] Zhenguo was educated and was a good calligrapher. Late in his
life, when *sai* were performed less and less often, he became a village
schoolteacher. He learned about *sai* rituals during many years under his
father's tutelage. At the age of twenty he began to supervise *sai* himself.
He carefully preserved the *sai* ritual manuscripts handed down in his
family and himself compiled the *Handbook*. On his deathbed, he ordered his two sons to preserve the family's manuscripts, and they did,
even during the Cultural Revolution, when virtually all other manuscripts related to the *sai*, whether ritual manuals or opera scripts, were
handed over by their owners to be destroyed. Almost all the *sai* liturgical manuscripts discovered in the past fifteen years or so were originally
in the hands of the Niu family.

Niu Zhenguo's son, Xixian (1923–94), who was probably the source
of the information about his father, also lived in East Daguan village.[8]
Since he was in his late teens and early twenties when the Japanese invasion, Civil War, and imposition of Communist rule came to southeastern Shanxi, he could not have had many opportunities to put to use
the knowledge gained from his father. Because their father died when
Xixian and his brother were twenty-three and thirteen years old, respectively, they had to survive by farming at first. But gradually, by practicing the family skills of selecting the location of buildings, choosing
grave sites, calculating whether a proposed marriage was astrologically
appropriate, and carrying out the ritual of Thanking the Earth whenever the soil had to be disturbed, they became modestly prosperous.
Because Xixian's son did not wish to carry on his ancestors' profession,
the generations-old family tradition ended with him.

---

7. For Zhenguo's biography, see Zhang Zhennan and Bao Haiyan, "Niu Zhenguo,"
pp. 226–27.

8. For Xixian's biography, see Zhang Zhennan and Yang Mengheng, "Niu Xixian,"
pp. 284–89.

Another Master of Ceremonial who led *sai* at Mt. Longquan was Feng Guiyu (1911–92), who lived in a village in the western suburbs of Zhangzi town that is not on any of my maps.[9] He was renowned for his skill and knowledge, but unlike the Nius, he did not come from a family of *yinyang* masters, instead learning his craft from a childless practitioner in his village named Zhao Guichang.[10] Guichang gave Guiyu five *sai* manuscripts from the Ming Chenghua reign-period (1465–87), one of which was called *Writ of Commands for General Use at Sai* (*Sai shang za yong ting ming wen*). I believe this testimony is accurate; therefore these documents are the earliest dated *sai* manuscripts of which there is a record. They place the tradition firmly in the mid-Ming period. All were destroyed by the Red Guards and Feng's own children during the Cultural Revolution. At that time Feng abandoned the profession of *yinyang* master at the urging of his family, and none of his numerous sons and grandsons wanted to engage in such a dangerous occupation. So a line of local ritual tradition that probably went back to the fifteenth century and certainly to Zhao Renhe, the teacher of Zhao Guichang and one of the most famous *sai* leaders in Zhangzi during the last quarter of the nineteenth century, ended with him.

As for the Entertainers who took part in the Mt. Longquan *sai*, we know the names of four. Yang Xueren (1872–1942) was a Ritual Head and lived in Bi village, about nine kilometers northwest of Zhangzi town. He was literate, and in his youth he copied out part-scripts. Later, when he had his own students, he had them copy part-scripts, too.[11] All his scripts were burned by the Japanese, and the Red Guards destroyed his trunk(s) of costumes and stage properties. The other three were Yang's students: Lu Zhongsuo (1887–1962), Ma Chouxun (1890–1943), and Yan Genzheng (1912–70). Lu was an Entertainer Headman, and Yan, the most eminent of them all, was the Chief of the Headmen in Zhangzi county. The Entertainers of Yan's village, Nanli, were believed

---

9. The information in the following paragraph is from his biography: Zhang Zhennan and Bao Haiyan, "Feng Guiyu," pp. 245–47.

10. A manuscript biography of Feng, in the author's collection, says he was born in 1909, and that his teacher was named 貴長, not 貴常 (the two names are pronounced the same). Guiyu's name suggests that he was the adopted son of Guichang.

11. Bao Haiyan, "Yang Xueren," pp. 224, 225.

to have the oldest traditions and to know more about *sai* ritual and music than anyone else in the county, and of the Nanli Entertainer families the Yans were the most respected.[12]

As it happens, the first section of the *Handbook* is a model contract between Entertainers and the sponsoring villages. It is a fascinating document and provides invaluable authentic information about the performance of the Mt. Longquan *sai*, although some details in it, such as the number of *Dui* Operas to be performed, do not fully conform with the description of the rituals in the body of the text. What follows is a full translation.[13]

[AGREEMENT][14]

Those who have set the terms of this Agreement are the Entertainer Headman, _____, and the Leader [of the participating villages], _____.

Today we have taken full responsibility to offer a *sai* at Mt. Longquan to the honored god, the Nation-Protecting Divinely-Providing King [under the sponsorship of the named] villages. The old rule sets the _____ day of the second month of the third year of the Xuantong era [March 1911] for the Issuing of the Invitation, and the _____ day for Receiving the Gods.[15] There shall be eight musicians for delicate music (*xi yue*), a Director, four civil and four military [stage officials], and Supplementary *Dui* Operas down to the conclusion of the banquet [i.e., the end of the three days of offerings]. There shall be three days on which the invited gods will enjoy the *sai* [offerings and operas], and six days from welcoming to bidding farewell. We take on the responsibility of supplying the set number of thirteen male Entertainers, presenting two *Za* Operas, nine Supplementary *Dui* Operas, and three sets of instrumental opera

---

12. Zhang Zhennan and Bao Haiyan, "Yan Genzheng," p. 248; and idem, "Yan Xiaozheng," p. 239.

13. Yang, *Fourteen Manuscripts*, pp. 29–32. This is the most recent of the Niu family ritual manuscripts. It is dated Min 14.6.13 (2 Aug. 1925) on the cover, but other dates appear in the text: Xuantong 3.2 (March 1911), Min 14.2.26 (20 Mar. 1925), and Min 10.10.1–3 (31 Oct.–2 Nov. 1921). It is said to have been compiled by Niu Zhengguo in 1925 and to have been frequently used by him (Zhang Zhennan and Bao Haiyan, "Niu Zhenguo," p. 227). That the date on the cover of the manuscript is 1925 while three earlier dates in the text suggests that Niu made a fresh cover for the August 1925 *sai*.

14. The original has no title.

15. The text actually says "the ten plus _____ day" (十__ 日) in both cases.

music.[16] In addition, there shall be one Processional *Dui* Opera,[17] one *Dui* Opera at the time when the gods mount their horses, and three comic dialogues. In welcoming the gods to [the temple at] Mt. Longquan, there shall be three Cup Offerings at the Mounting of the Horses, and three at the Dismounting.

The ritual personnel: four civil officials; ten warriors (not counting those standing guard at the offering table); the Director and Subdirector. On the main day of the *sai*: the Director and Subdirector; two Director's staffs (*xi zhu*); an Inspector of Vegetarian Food (*jian zhai*);[18] one of the deities of the twenty-eight Lunar Lodges; two Announcers of Offerings; and eight performers of delicate music. All must wear plain cloth headdresses and light robes. All instruments such as mouth organs (*sheng*), end-blown flutes (*xiao*), tranverse flutes (*di*), double-reed pipes (*guan*), shawms (*suona*), horns (*haotou*), and gongs and drums (*luo gu*), must be clean, bright, and melodious.[19] In events such as the Sacrifice to the Stage (*ji tai*), the Inspection of the Kitchen, the Eight Immortals Welcoming [the Star of] Longevity, the Great Peace flat drum [dances], and the Release of Living Beings, delicate music must always be played, following the directions of the Master of Ceremonial. All male Entertainers must be spirited and robust, and all their costumes must be new. The associated *shê* have agreed to bestow an all-inclusive fee of _____ large coins for the music. Should the directives of the Master of Ceremonial not be followed, minor infractions will be punished before the god, and major ones will be referred to the magistrate for investigation; in no case will there be leniency. Fearing that oral [contracts] are not reliable, the parties have drawn up this Agreement as proof [of their intentions].

Items of middling importance: a lion and tiger shall be emplaced on the stage; there shall be two "inner officials" who will arrange the palanquins; during the three rich offerings [*mao yan*] eight dragon robes and embroidered headbands shall be added, and the accompaniment of one flat drum shall be included.

Items of lesser importance: on the days when the gods are invited and welcomed, the four Entertainers who precede the horses shall wear dragon robes and large red headdresses. There shall be four civil and four military "officials"

---

16. "*Za* Opera" is used here as a synonym for *Dui* Opera.

17. Following Yang's gloss.

18. The stove god of temple kitchens. See above, pp. 207–10.

19. Given the unanimous testimony of the sources that *Dui* Opera, like other Shanxi rural ritual opera, was accompanied almost entirely by gongs and drums, the other instruments mentioned here must have been used in incidental music like the "delicate music."

and one "Emperor"[20] [to lead the] Processional *Dui* [Opera]. On the main day of the *sai*, there shall be six civil and six military officials and one Emperor. On the first and third days of the *sai*, four civil and four military officials shall arrange the palanquins; all their costumes must be clean and fresh. For the three days, a total of _____ feet of red cloth for divination and making name squares shall be provided. The embroidered headdresses, dragon robes, and [costumes of] the Eight Immortals are permitted to be in the current fashion; as for all the rest [of the activities in which the Entertainers participate], the old rules are not to be changed. Let this serve as proof [of the agreement].

This is followed in the manuscript by a list of the villages in the Mt. Longquan *sai* alliance that presumably was part of the contract:

The eighteen godly villages celebrate the Mt. Longquan *sai* in turn. The offerings begin after breakfast, when the third stroke of the bell sounds.

Western Five *Shê*: Canhan [village] and the *shê* of Wenjiaping [*shê* #1] (assessment: 30,000 coins [*wen*]); Yangjialing and the *shê* of Changzhuang [*shê* #2]; the *shê* of the three Xigou [= the villages of Chenxigou, Duanxigou, and Lianxigou: *shê* #3] (assessment: 6,000 coins); the *shê* of Mayan [*shê* #4]; and the *shê* of Dujiazhuang [includes eight unnamed small villages; *shê* #5] (assessment: 13 silver dollars [*dayang*]); then to:

Eastern Five *Shê*: the *shê* of Caofang [*shê* #1] (assessment: 10 silver dollars); the *shê* of Nanyao [*shê* #2]; the Western *shê* of Daliu [*shê* #3]; the Rear *shê* of Daliu [*shê* #4—one village, two *shê*]; and the *shê* of Beiyao [*shê* #5]; then to:

Northern Five *Shê*: the Eastern *shê* of Wu village [*shê* #1] (assessment: [ms. damaged]); the Western *shê* of Wu village [*shê* #2—one village, two *shê*]; the *shê* of East [and] West Caopo [*shê* #3—two villages, one *shê*]; the *shê* of Shao village [*shê* #4] (assessment for the latter [three] is [altogether] 10 silver dollars); and the *shê* of Aizhuang and the *shê* of Xuanjiaping [the last two villages probably formed *shê* #5]. Then [back] to the Western Five *Shê*.[21]

This private transaction, presumably accompanied by a similar contract with the Master of Ceremonial, was followed by a series of public actions.[22] First, the leaders of the sponsoring villages posted announce-

---

20. Following Yang's gloss.

21. The identification of the *shê* is taken from Yang, *Fourteen Manuscripts*, p. 33, *n*1, slightly modified. The text clearly states that there were eighteen villages, though I count at least nineteen.

22. That no model contract for Masters of Ceremonial was included in this manual, which was compiled by a Master of Ceremonial and presumably included the most es-

ments that the time had come to prepare for a *sai*.[23] Men were sent to other villages and even other counties to inform those who might be interested, including merchants. Back at the main temple preparations began: incense and candles were brought in; paper objects and wood-block prints made or purchased; tea, wine, and the ingredients for food offerings prepared; and the many ritual utensils cleaned and made ready.[24] The ritual chefs arrived five days early and began to make the great Flowery Offering—a screen of richly decorated tiles made of deep-fried dough placed between the Offering (or Incense) Pavilion and the main hall of the temple. (This is described in detail in the next section.) The Master of Ceremonial also arrived five days early and at once began to write out the many announcements, couplets, memorials, and prayers that would be needed. (That the ritual texts were written out is notable; among other things, it tells us that the Masters of Ceremonial were literate.) The Entertainers came two days later and began rehearsing.[25] The rooms in which the invited gods would rest during the *sai*, in the arcades (*xiang fang*) along the east and west sides of the main courtyard, were made ready for their distinguished guests: elegant furniture, including beds with hangings, paintings, calligraphy, antique *objets d'art*, plus incense and flowers, were brought in.[26]

PRELIMINARIES, THE "BOOK OF COMMANDS," AND THE ARRIVAL OF THE GODS

On the twelfth of the second month, a spectacular ceremony called "Issuing the Invitations" took place. It began with the ritual of Welcoming the Platters (*ying pan*). (These were the utensils used to carry the all-

---

sential information, suggests that it is far from complete—a conclusion strengthened by further reading in the text. But, to repeat, the fact that this manuscript is directly tied to the Mt. Longquan *sai* outweighs its various inadequacies.

23. Yang Mengheng and Zhang Zhennan, "Shangdang gu sai," pp. 84–85.
24. Ibid., p. 85.
25. Zhang Zhennan and Bao Haiyan, "Shangdang minjian," p. 109.
26. Yang Mengheng and Zhang Zhennan, "Shangdang gu sai," p. 85.

important food offerings from the ritual kitchen to the Offering Hall.) It is described in the *Handbook*:

The pious gentlemen in charge of welcoming the platters go out the main gate of the temple. All carry out their duties, cudgels are grasped, the gong is sounded, the roll is called. They then go [back] into the main hall and bring out the platters, the platter stands, and the mouth-stopping flowers[27] [from their storage places] and proceed to the Pavilion for Welcoming the Gods.[28] The Incense Masters are requested to burn incense, and incense-offering music is played.[29] [All] kneel, making three kowtows every time they kneel. There is a first, second, and third ritual of offering. They make obeisance and rise. They bow. They return to the Incense Pavilion and set down the platters. The Tea Masters and Wine Masters are requested to serve tea and wine; the third cup of wine is poured [on the ground]. The Mouth-Stopping Flowers are laid [on the offering table]. [The participants] retire empty-handed. They are formed into ranks. The Incense and Candle Masters are requested to burn incense. Incense offering music is played. A ritual of four obeisances is performed. There is a first and second ritual of offering, a prayer is read, and then a third ritual of offering. They make obeisance and rise. They bow. That completes it.[30]

So ended the preparations. Then the actual process of inviting the guest deities began. Since it would have taken a great deal of time to visit all the temples in the eighteen villages of the Mt. Longquan alliance, I assume that only temples in the five *shê* sponsoring that year's *sai* were visited.[31] The *Handbook*'s description of the process is very brief:

On the thirteenth day of the second month go to every village of the *shê* [i.e., of the *shê* alliance that is the current sponsor]. First, all the participants are lined up, and the roll called. The screen [of the god's palanquin] is let down. [This implies setting off from the temple at Mt. Longquan.]

[After they arrive in the first village] the Master of Ceremonial is requested to invite the god [of the temple]. The Incense Masters and Candle Masters burn incense. There is incense-offering music. There is a ritual of four obeisances. The Wine Master takes up the wine vessel and pours wine; there are

---

27. Held between the teeth to prevent the officiants from inadvertently speaking.

28. I believe this was a separate, temporary structure.

29. I do not follow Yang's emendation here.

30. Yang, *Fourteen Manuscripts*, p. 33.

31. We do not know how many temples were involved, only that thirty-five gods were guests.

the first and second presentations of wine; a Writ of Invitation is read; there is
the third presentation of wine. They make obeisance and rise. They bow, and it
ends. The participants stand in their places. The *Shê* Head is requested to fetch
the offering platters [for the god of the temple], the platter stands, and the
mouth-stopping flowers. They pick up the platters and depart. [This is
repeated at every temple of the sponsoring villages whose god or goddess
has been invited.] The spirit tablets of the deities of the temples are carried to
Mt. Longquan's Pavilion for Welcoming the Gods, with Hou Yi, the host,
bringing up the rear.[32]

The *Handbook* passes over in silence the huge procession involved in
the issuing of invitations. It could be over a mile in length and have
tens of thousands of spectators.[33] This procession was made up of
smaller processions, one from each *shê*, which must have resembled the
processions described in Part I: there were "floats," some carrying
young people posing in scenes from operas, decorated towers, elaborate parasols, and various sorts of skits performed on foot. There were
the usual troupes of musicians (*bayin hui*, not Entertainers), and at
the very end, any number of "spirit horses." Evidently all these lesser
processions gathered at the San Zong Temple on Mt. Longquan and
accompanied *en masse* the full complement of ritual personnel—Masters
of Ceremonial, *Shê* Heads, Incense Elders, Pavilioners, Attendants, and
all the rest—as they set out with the palanquin carrying the image (or
tablet) of Hou Yi to invite the guest-gods.[34] A young man carrying a
small palanquin of the Way-Opening God (Xing shen) raced ahead to
the next village to give notice that the procession was coming, and then
back and forth between village and procession until it finally arrived.[35]
We do not know which temples were visited. However, we know which
gods were invited thanks to the Diagram for Arranging the Gods at the
end of the *Handbook*, since it was prepared specifically for the Mt. Longquan *sai* sponsored by the Northern Five *Shê*. Further, it appears that
only ten of the thirty-six gods in the Diagram received individual invita-

---

32. Yang, *Fourteen Manuscripts*, p. 34.
33. Yang Mengheng and Zhang Zhennan, "Shangdang gu sai," p. 87.
34. Ibid., pp. 86–87.
35. Ibid., pp. 87–88. For a detailed description of the ritual of invitation, see ibid.,
pp. 89–90.

tions.[36] There were only seven villages in the Northern Five *Shê*, but it would not have been at all unusual for each of those villages to have had a number of temples. The villages were quite close to Mt. Long-quan's Hou Yi Temple—the most distant was only four kilometers away—so all could have been visited in one day.

As the procession went from temple to temple, the gods that were added took their positions according to the order of precedence defined by the Diagram for Arranging the Gods—with Hou Yi (San Zong), the host, always bringing up the rear. When all the invited gods had been collected, the great procession headed back to the temple on Mt. Longquan along a route lined with masses of people. It was this spectacle, rather than the rituals that took place in the temples, that most people saw and that must have seemed to them the main point of the *sai*. (And this is another reason we know more about the processions than the rituals.) When the procession reached the San Zong Temple, most of the marchers, with their parasols and their floats, their spirit horses and their towers, went home. But the ritual personnel and the Entertainers still had much to do. The *Handbook* outlines their tasks:

The participants line up, burn incense, and incense-offering music is played. There is a ritual of four obeisances. After the fourth, the participants do not rise. The Wine Master pours out the wine. There are the first, second, and third presentations of wine. They make obeisance and rise. They bow and leave. They go to the Offering Pavilion.[37] The Report ("Zou bing wen") is read to put the gods at ease. It ends. The participants line up, the Incense and Candle Masters burn incense, incense-offering music is played, they make obeisance, and there is a ritual of four obeisances. The Wine Master takes up the wine vessel and pours wine. There are three presentations of wine. They make obeisance and rise. They bow. It ends. The Master of Ceremonial is re-

---

36. The twenty-three who were not "seen off" at the end of the *sai*, plus Hou Yi, the host, and the two guardian gods of the temple, the Earth God and the God of the Five Ways, probably did not receive individual invitations. This is discussed below, p. 277 and n. 123.

37. The *Handbook* is silent about where the tablets of the gods were placed, and when Yang Mengheng and Zhang Zhennan ("Shangdang gu sai," p. 90) state that they were brought into the main hall as soon as the procession returned to the San Zong Temple, and were set down in proper order after the Writ of Invitation was "read" by the Earth God and the God of the Five Ways.

quested to invite the spirit tablets of the Earth God and the General of the Five Ways into the Pavilion for Welcoming the Gods. The [Writ of] Invitation [is read].[38]

The Pavilioners[39] are set in order, and the roll is called. There is a Processional *Dui* Opera. The costumes are examined. The director recites [congratulatory verses].[40] The Pavilioners line up and perform a ritual of four obeisances, not rising after the fourth. Grasping the wine vessel, the Wine Master rises, proceeds to the [spirit tablet of the] Earth God and kneels, salutes him, pours wine, and rises. He goes to the Sun [the Sun's spirit tablet?] and kneels. There is the first presentation of wine, a wine serenade, and the second presentation of wine. He [presumably the Master of Ceremonial] grasps the vessel and reads the "Writ to the Sun." There is the third presentation of wine, the Master of Ceremonial Drenches the Sun,[41] and concluding music is played three times. He [the Master of Ceremonial] kneels in front of the Earth God, respectfully offers wine three times, speaks of wine three times [a reference to the recitation of an Ode to Wine], reads the Writ of Invitation, rises, and stands in place. They[42] divide into ranks, and the Director begins a Processional *Dui* Opera. It ends. They do a ritual of four obeisances, respectfully offer wine three times, and a wine serenade is played three times. They make obeisance, rise, and stand in place. They divide into ranks, the Director begins a Processional *Dui* Opera, and it ends. They do the ritual of four obeisances, respectfully offer wine three times, play a wine serenade three times, make obeisance, rise, and stand in place. A melody is played. The participants go into the [main hall of the] temple and set down their implements. There is a ritual of four obeisances, three respectful offerings of wine, a melody, and it ends.[43]

That is, the rituals ended. But that evening the Entertainers performed a Standard *Dui* Opera on the temple stage. Food offerings,

---

38. It was read on behalf of the Earth God and the General of the Five Ways, gods of the temple and spokesmen for San Zong (Yang Mengheng and Zhang Zhennan, "Shangdang gu sai," p. 90). It was called the "Xia qing wen" (Yang, *Fourteen Manuscripts*, p. 35, *n9*).

39. *Ting zhi* 亭只 = *ting zi* 亭子.

40. Yang Mengheng and Zhang Zhennan, "Shangdang gu sai," p. 91. Such verses were known as *zan ci*. Many have survived in the three Niu manuscripts called *Saichang gu zan*, as well as in *Zhou yuexing tu* and *Tang yuexing tu*.

41. *Pao taiyang*; the sources are silent on what this involved.

42. It is not clear which ritual personnel are involved here.

43. Yang, *Fourteen Manuscripts*, pp. 34–35.

which sound a bit like snacks, were prepared for the gods watching the operas, as prescribed in the *Handbook*:

On the thirteenth day of the second month: Issuing the Invitations. There must be a god's palanquin and three platters of sesame candy.[44] (The stage crew receives them [at the end of the day].)[45] There are three incense platters [taken with] the invitations made at the base and the peak of the mountain[?]. (The stage crew receives them.) There are three sesame candy platters placed before Heaven and Earth. (The monks receive them.) In the performance of [Standard] *Dui* Operas at night, when the Way-Opening God enters, one table with ten bowls of vegetarian food is offered. (Not divided; given to the *shê* [personnel].) A feast is presented to the gods: platters of dough rolls, fruit, and dried meat, [decorated with?] flowers and grasses.[46]

Thus ended the first of the two preparatory days of the *sai*. The following day, the fourteenth, was devoted to formally welcoming the gods, and then came the three main days of offerings, prayers, and opera, followed by the day on which the gods were bade farewell. The reader, who may already feel somewhat overwhelmed, should bear in mind that this account of the San Zong Temple *sai*, based as it is on a Master of Ceremonial's highly abbreviated handbook, presents only a small part of the total experience. And in any case it will not do to summarize or abbreviate the ritual program, at least until something like an authentic impression of the *sai* has been created. In many of the rituals, repetition was central. Although there was an overarching narrative logic that arose from the central metaphor of the birthday celebration, this was not visible in the individual day-long segments. In those segments one specific action—such as inviting guests and getting them settled into their quarters—was encrusted with layer upon layer of ritual modules.[47] This slowed all actions led by the Master of Ceremonial—greeting, entering, feasting—to the majestic tempo of the gods.

---

44. Yang says these were made of deep-fried dough, but the text clearly says "candy."

45. The text specifies which group of ritual officiants receives each food offering at the end of the ritual.

46. Yang, *Fourteen Manuscripts*, p. 36.

47. For modularity in Chinese culture, see Ledderose, *Ten Thousand Things*. I have had interesting conversations about such elements in Chinese symbolic culture, not just ritual life, with my former colleague William S-Y. Wang, who calls them "pre-fabs."

As noted above, the *Handbook* says nothing about what happened to the tablets of the gods after they reached the San Zong Temple. Evidently they were placed in the temple's main hall in the order dictated by the Diagram for Arranging the Gods shortly after the great procession dispersed.[48] Either while they were still being reverently held by the Pavilioners, or just after they were placed on their individual tables in the main sanctuary, what the *Handbook* calls a Report ("Zou bing wen") was read by the Master of Ceremonial. There is no text with this title in the *Handbook*, but Yang says the "Zou bing wen" was quite similar to the "Book of Commands" ("Ting ming ben"), which *is* in the *Handbook*.[49]

In contrast to what we have read so far, the "Book of Commands" is a text that was intended to be recited, not a summary of actions to be performed. It gets us as close as we can get to the intellectual and symbolic world of the Mt. Longquan *sai* in the early twentieth century.[50]

BOOK OF COMMANDS
FOR THE FIRST DAY

I [the Master of Ceremonial] announce to the honored god, the Supreme Thearch, the Jade Emperor: Today all those with responsibilities in the *sai*, including the greater and lesser *Shê* Heads, the Incense Elders of the Left and Right, the Chefs, and the Entertainers, make obeisance at the foot of the steps [of the temple's main hall]. They wait in their places, attending to your commands; they dare not act on their own authority. The honored god, the Jade Emperor, issues his directions: you may venture to bow and attend to his commands—bow and attend to his commands!

---

48. It is barely possible that they were first placed in the elaborately decorated rooms on the east and west sides of the courtyard, which were the symbolic residences of the great gods, and moved to their proper places later. See Yang Mengheng and Zhang Zhennan, "Shangdang gu sai," p. 85.

49. Yang, *Fourteen Manuscripts*, p. 46, *n*.

50. I follow the text as edited by Yang Mengheng (ibid., pp. 45–54) but have frequently disagreed with his editorial decisions. There are two analogous texts in earlier manuscripts: a section in the *Tang yuexing tu* (1818) called "Writ of Commands" (Yang, *Fourteen Manuscripts*, pp. 419–28), an extremely important text, part of which I use below; and the "Writ of Commands and Report" ("Ting ming zou bing wen"), in *Saichang gu zan (bing)* (1797) (Yang, *Fourteen Manuscripts*, pp. 334–39).

The Director [the leader of the Entertainers] replies: The two ranks of Incense Elders, bow and attend to his commands!

Prayers in the spring and recompense in the autumn, *sai* in the summer and sacrifices in the winter, are the same today as they were in ancient times.[51] Today we rejoice over the moistening rains. It is our good fortune to have encountered the birthday of the honored god.[52] The sagely host of August Heaven has been respectfully invited to draw near the precious hall; all the gods of Sovereign Earth have descended to the incense altar. The chief *Shê* Head stands respectfully in front; all the Incense Elders are deeply reverent. Now listen to the Commands with decorum and propriety.

I have heard that of the awesome ceremonies that are the spirit [*qi*] that harmonizes Heaven and Earth, ritual is the greatest. Confucius the sage, humaneness, righteousness, ritual propriety, and wisdom.[53] Bees have their lord and master, geese [in flight] have their order of precedence—how much more is this the case with men! The state takes the people as fundamental; the people regard food as their Heaven. I say: today the *Shê* Heads respectfully express their piety by making offerings in recompense for the favor of Heaven's gentle breezes and timely rains. [You] bestow the clouds and send the rain and the winds that blow across all the land. The rain moistens the cultivated fields, the five kinds of soil bring forth the five grains, the grasses and trees of the hills and streams flourish, and the gardens and groves are lush, all because the wind and rain have been timely [and the *yin* and *yang* have been in balance].[54] [Therefore] the people have hope for a good harvest, on which their lives depend. Without selfishness, without [discord],[55] and with sincere hearts, they requite the immense beneficence of Heaven and Earth; they make this *sai* of recompense for the beneficence of Heaven's rain and dew. We respectfully invite all the gods under your jurisdiction to come and smell the incense and lis-

---

51. Note that this *sai* was held in the second month, not the summer.

52. Most sources give the sixth day of the sixth lunar month as Hou Yi's birthday.

53. There obviously is a problem with the text here. Compare the "Writ of Commands" in *Tang yuexing tu* (Yang, *Fourteen Manuscripts*), p. 420: "The writings of Confucius the sage first established humaneness, righteousness, ritual propriety, and wisdom."

54. There is a problem with the text after 時 (p. 45, para. 3, l. 4), and I have emended it on the basis of the "Writ of Commands" in *Tang yuexing tu*, p. 420, which has many parallel passages.

55. Comparison with the *Tang yuexing tu* text shows that there is a problem here. The simplest way to emend it is to assume that *so* 所 is a mistake for a word denoting a negative quality, such as the homophone *so* 唆 "discord," which I have done. Accordingly I have not followed Yang's punctuation.

ten to the music. The *Analects* says: "The gentleman treasures three ways: his every gesture must show that he is a stranger to violence; he must compose his countenance so as to appear trustworthy; his manner of speaking must show that he is a stranger to impropriety."[56] These three are the foundation of self-cultivation, the center of the Way. Receive instruction from superiors, provide instruction for inferiors, then all will respect the relationships between ruler and minister, superior and subordinate, father and son, older and younger brother. He whose speech does not prayerfully inform the gods, neither near nor far, neither reverent nor respectful, such is the petty man. . . .[57] It is like birds and beasts: parrots can speak.[58] Look at nothing contrary to ritual, listen to nothing contrary to ritual, say nothing contrary to ritual, do nothing contrary to ritual.[59] These four are the rituals of men.

Wine is first [among offerings?]: it is presented to kinfolk and nourishes[60] the aged, is offered to the spirits, welcomes visitors, and entertains guests—how can one not understand this?[61] Warm it and clarify it [but do not drink it] to excess. [In the villages and hamlets virtuous men and women remain separate. As to gambling and bringing lawsuits, reject evil and accumulate virtue. Whether poor or rich, whether old or young, travelers give way to others on the roads, the lowly withdraw before the mighty, the young make way for the old. Gaze at nothing that is contrary to ritual, and your behavior will be admirable and you will not take up what is evil. If virtuous literati set up schools in the *shê* and explain (the Classics?) to gentlemen from all around,][62] how can

---

56. *Analects* 8.4. I have drawn on the translations of both Waley and Lau.

57. Something has clearly dropped from this sentence, and the text continues with the obviously corrupt 尊即以分明. "Writ of Commands," p. 420, gives some idea of the correct reading, but it, too, is corrupt. In my article "'Confucian' Elements in the Great Temple Festivals" (p. 143, *n*38), I discuss at length the deviations of the "Writ of Commands" from *Li ji, juan* 1, its source here, and their significance.

58. Yang's transcription is incorrect; the manuscript actually reads: 比似禽獸, 鸚鵡 能以言語, which is what I have translated, correcting the punctuation. Yang also proposes a very large emendation based on the "Writ of Commands." I do not give it since it is completely speculative; the interested reader can consult the "Writ of Commands," which as I mentioned in the preceding note was influenced directly or indirectly by *Li ji* here. Our text is radically faulty; evidently the author was unaware of the classical references in the text he was copying. This is a valuable hint as to his educational level.

59. An unacknowledged quotation from *Analects* 12.1.

60. Yang's transcription is incorrect: the ms. has *yang* 養, not *shan* 善.

61. Yang's emendation here is unnecessary.

62. The long section in brackets is almost completely illegible in my photocopy of the ms.; perhaps Yang had access to a better copy. He made emendations to it, how-

they not know their own hearts and bear all the things that life may bring? If you misbehave in even the slightest way, lose [your sense of] proper measure and do evil, the punishment that the gods will send down will not be trivial.

Sai are given to repay Heaven and Earth's power of birth and fruition, and to celebrate the blessings of a bountiful harvest. From the time when Jiao Liang plowed,[63] people offered *sai* of recompense. This happiest of the affairs of the fields was passed on from generation to generation and continues even today. The state takes the people as fundamental, the people regard food as their Heaven. What is basic to food is nothing more than the five grains; what brings grain to fruition is nothing more than cultivating and ripening. Cultivating is done with nothing more than human labor; [but] ripening truly is the gift of the gods. Thus if we take pleasure in the benefit of a bumper crop, we must look for the cause in the descent of blessings. So we [play] the zithers and beat the drums, invite all the gods and hold a *sai* of recompense.

The *Analects* says: "Sacrifice to the gods as if they are present."[64] The *Odes* says: "A visit from the Spirits / Can never be foreseen; / The better reason for not disgusting them."[65] Of rituals, none is greater than sacrifice, and in sacrificing nothing is more important than reverence. With reverence the gods rejoice, without respect the gods spit out [the offering food]. Therefore take care not to be negligent [in the sacrifices]. Now I invite . . . and announce it.[66] You all must listen section by section. Observe my regulations, let each of you demonstrate your sincerity.[67]

There follows what should be the central part of this text, the "commands" that set out the responsibilities of the participants. But the longer entries simply write about the object involved—its history or other characteristics—rather than describing the actions expected of the participants. Moreover, much of the prose is extremely ornate, quite different from the rest of the text. For example, a number of the longer entries end with a rhymed quatrain on the subject at hand, making it even less like a set of instructions. A parallel passage in the "Writ of

---

ever, that closely resemble those in the parallel passage in the "Writ of Commands" in his edition of *Tang yuexing tu*. See Yang, *Fourteen Manuscripts*, p. 420.

63. 自芟糧邦. The translation is tentative.

64. *Analects* 3.12.

65. *Classic of Poetry*, no. 256, Arthur Waley's translation (*The Book of Songs*, p. 302).

66. I do not understand 一予等 and have not attempted a translation.

67. Yang, *Fourteen Manuscripts*, pp. 45–46.

Commands" in *Tang yuexing tu*, which clearly is closely related to the "Book of Commands," uses much simpler language, has more detailed instructions, and in addition lists many more roles, including some that are of central importance, such as the *Shê* Heads, the Incense Elders, and the Director.[68] Accordingly, for the balance of this text I translate from the "Writ of Commands" in *Tang yuexing tu*. Our copy—the only copy—dates at least in part from 1818, but it must have been based on an older exemplar.[69]

—To the *Shê* Heads who make offerings to the gods: from now until the end of the *sai* practice abstinence and bathe, keep in perfect order your gowns and headdresses. During the day you must be sincerely respectful [of the rituals], at night go to the temple and sleep in front of the gods. Then make a sincere vow that the members of the *shê* will repay and congratulate Dragon Heaven [for its beneficence].[70]

Offer a *sai* to the gods for three days, burning incense, presenting wine, and offering feasts. Every day go out to welcome the Offering Platters and then retire. Early and late invite and see off the Two Immortal [Girls], and make offerings to the Sun and the Wind. On the main day of the *sai*, invite and see off the Star of Long Life. During the entire program of offerings, you must hold the incense burners and make obeisance in front of the gods.

In the morning, put on your clothes and shoes, which must be in perfect order; in the evening, take them off in a place far removed from the gods. Every day as the incense smoke rises continuously, you must be careful and grave. You must not drink wine to excess, or allow your robes and headdresses to be disheveled, or fail to be present for the offering of incense and the presentation of wine because you are enjoying yourself outside the temple, or drink and pursue pleasures during the day, or go about with the licentious and consort with prostitutes at night, or insult the sagely ones at the banquet, or treat

---

68. Ibid., pp. 420–25.

69. Both texts were in the hands of the Niu family from at least the 1930s on. The surviving manuscript of *Tang yuexing tu* was prepared for use at an unnamed *sai* in Tunliu county, which borders Zhangzi county on the north. There are published versions of this important text in *Xiyou* 1990, special number on *Tang yuexing tu*, and in *Zhonghua xiqu* 13 (1998.8), both edited by Li Tiansheng; and in Yang, *Fourteen Manuscripts*. I have used Yang's edition but also consulted Li's in *Zhonghua xiqu*.

70. Dragon Heaven (Long Tian) is seemingly the deity to which the *sai* was dedicated.

perfunctorily the saints and worthies who have descended to the festival. Great good fortune will descend on the reverent, great blame on those who are careless. If you offer sacrifice with sincere hearts, year after year there will be a favorable response: the rain will be gentle and the breezes refreshing, the produce of fields and silkworms will be superabundant. All will be well with every family; every baby, boy or girl, will be well formed.

The members of the *shê* have discussed it [and have decided to hold] a three-day *sai* with music and activities. Gold, silver, and pictures of the deities will be burned before the gods, there will be a great offering (*jiao*) in thanks for the protection provided by Dragon Heaven.

—To the Incense Elders who make offerings to the gods: from now to the end of the *sai* practice abstinence and bathe, and let your robes, headdresses, and shoes be new and fresh; do not insult the gods or be careless; listen intently for the cock's crow at the fifth watch, then come all together to burn incense before the gods and pray to Dragon Heaven, and great blessings without limit will appear.

Every day at the *yin* [3–5 A.M.] and *you* [5–7 P.M.] hours, incense must be offered to the gods. Those who do not come will have their punishment decided after their case is discussed if their offense is slight, but those whose offense is heavy will be fined one *jin* of candles. The members of the *shê* will decide on the punishment of those who do not observe the prohibitions, who cause disturbances, or drink wine, or engage in violence, or reject the gods.

—To the Pavilioners: from now until the end of the *sai*, when walking attend to your steps, when speaking keep your voices low. When presenting the dishes, lift them high; when taking them away, be reverent. You must change your clothes and bathe, you must be respectful, you must practice abstinence sincerely and reverently. If you are insulting or careless, the divine gods will secretly send down the Star of Disaster; it will summon misfortune and call up calamities, it will be accounted a great evil. You must be cautious when serving the honored gods.

—To the Attendants: from now until the end of the *sai*, you must wear brocade robes, embroidered jackets, and knee-length outer robes. When you dance to greet the gods, you should always maintain the proper posture. When the food offerings are being carried back and forth, chase away the flies to keep them from falling into the food, for the divine gods cannot enjoy that which is unclean. Consider the directives again and again: you must be careful, you all must be sincere and respectful!

—To those in the Food [Bureau]: in ancient times there was no cooking with fire, and so when the animals were sacrificed, they were cut up and the pieces placed in the ritual vessels; when they used the flesh of animals and fowl, they ate it raw. In the offerings at the ancestral hall and the banquets at the palace, they adjusted the five flavors in accord with the season and the hour.

In summer there are flies and midges; so wash your hands in the kitchen. Keep everything clean, and use new dishes. In transforming the raw into the cooked [to make] delicacies of all kinds, in cutting up meat to make dishes, the sacrifice is foremost. Therefore act in accordance with the great rituals in making offerings to the revered gods.

—To those in the Incense Bureau: [incense was] invented by sages and worthies; it penetrates Heaven and Earth and moves the gods and spirits. Harmony is created by its bright fragrance. Thickly the auspicious clouds [arise from] the precious tripod and golden brazier, changing to clouds, changing to mist, offerings to the revered gods.

—To the cooks: from now until the end of the *sai*, make a complete set of godly platters. Keep the flies and mosquitoes away. If you speak near the godly platters, keep your voice low and turn away from them. Always wear your [schedule of] work and rest on your belt [?], do not sneeze near the kitchen. Cook with the most meticulous cleanliness; the food and fruits must be fresh. If through negligence you do not provide the gods with what they should receive, do not complain when disaster befalls you.

—To the men responsible for [providing] the godly platters: from now until the end of the *sai*, collect the godly money and purchase oil and flour for the making of the godly platters. Keep the financial records in good order, make an account of income and expenses. Do not drink wine; wash yourselves. Practice abstinence and be pure; be neat and clean. Do not do evil things or create disturbances, do not drink or say outrageous things. To taste the dishes before they are offered is to be disrespectful in making offerings to the saintly ones and to waste the gods' money. In buying foodstuffs, keep careful accounts; to cheat the members of the *shê* is to show contempt for Dragon Heaven. If there are those who disobey these rules, [remember that] the eyes of the gods are everywhere. Good fortune will descend on the sincere, whereas the careless and disrespectful will invite blame. The gods will have their revenge, and then it will be too late for remorse.

—To those who purchase supplies: from now until the end of the *sai*, buy supplies for the feasts offered [to the gods]. Purchase all sorts of fruit, star anise, tea, salt, pepper, ginger, [soy] sauce, flour, and rice, all in the proper amounts. Also bamboo shoots, wood-ear fungus, ten-flavor tobacco, combs coarse and fine, new toothbrushes, handkerchiefs, woodblock prints, decorated mirrors, powder and rouge, wooden ladles, spoons, and chopsticks.

Prepare accounts for these purchases. Make purchases for the feast that is offered to the gods according to the funds available.

Do not do one thing and speak of two [i.e., do not buy one thing and say you bought two]. In the expenditure of funds, do not buy luxuries or pile up cheap stuff. If there are shortages of materials or items, so that there are insufficiencies, if the spoons are old and the combs are broken or dirty, if you divert money to yourself and explain it with plausible words, you may be able to deceive the members of the *shê*, but you will not be able to deceive the saints and worthies at the banquet. Then if flying disasters and grievous harms descend on you, it will be too late for you to repent. Starting today, attend to the orders and know them thoroughly, always reform the evil and follow the worthy.

—To those in the Tea Bureau: select Dragon Sprout tea and prepare it skillfully. Steam rises from the amber fluid in the pure white cup; tea in a "pure peak cup" can be offered to august Heaven and Earth and can be used to honor the gods here below. You must be sincere and pure of heart; do not allow a negligent attitude to take root, or you will suffer the calamities that come to those who disdain the gods.

—To those in the Wine Bureau: Yi Di invented it, Du Kang comprehended the immortals.[71] Use the rice and yeast of the Tian family and water from Dongting Lake, brew wine jade-green and rich, heat it so that it is fragrant and delicious.[72] When it is offered to the gods of heaven and earth, there will be a response; offered before the throne of the [Heavenly] Emperor, all the gods can partake of it. The writings of Confucius have three thousand words [devoted to wine]; Li Bo has a hundred poems devoted to jugs of wine. You also must be pure of heart. Do not blend in old wine or be disrespectful.

—To the Libationers of tea and wine: from now until the end of the *sai*, practice abstinence and bathe. When you stand before the gods and serve the tea and wine, pour the golden flagons again and again; when the Cups come to you, fill them full. Be careful what you say, serve the gods respectfully.

—To those in the Woodblock Print Bureau: Cai Lun was the first [to make paper]; his renown has lasted since ancient times. Print pictures of the gods, transient splendors. Write the banners for the pious with great skill, spread

---

71. Yi Di is Yang's (and others') emendation. Both Yi Di and Du Kang were the legendary creators of wine. I do not understand the function of the phrase "comprehended the immortals" (*tong xian*) here; no doubt there is a problem with the text.

72. There is a problem with this sentence also, and the translation is tentative.

abroad the events of the myriad regions of the realm.[73] Honor Heaven, honor Earth, respond to and requite the divine gods.

—To those in the [Bureau of] Fruit: at the time of the Three Emperors, Shen Nong rejoiced in his flowers and fruits. Red peach [blossoms] and white plum [blossoms], Immortals' peaches and golden fruit, fruits of all kinds are to be new-picked and fresh in color. Do not be disrespectful, and your sincerity will be praised.

—To those in the Lantern Bureau: make a full display of silver lanterns on lotus stands and respectfully present wax candles, all of which must be kept constantly burning.[74] Respect the revered gods, and do not let them go out.

—As for decorating the main hall: hang curtains from the ridgepole, cover the floor with flowered carpets. Set out the tables and chairs, place colored curtains around them. Do not use old furniture, it is your duty to use new.

—To those in the Accommodations Bureau: Set up beds with curtains appropriate to the season. Completely prepare pillows and sleeping mats. Be careful and meticulous.

—To those in charge of the Mountain Matshed: you should devote all your energy to the preparation of . . . ,[75] dark mountains with green cypresses, strange stones and gnarled pines, the majestic peaks of Diecui,[76] the high-soaring Kunlun. Make the mountains and the trees like this. Do not shirk the work, the eyes of the gods see [what you do] as clearly as if in a mirror.

—To those in charge of the Flowery Matshed: from now until the end of the *sai*, prepare nails, hemp twine, and flour paste. Go all together beforehand to the altar and take care of [writing] the inscriptions and collecting the flower . . . ,[77] and hang them all up. Make your offerings to the gods and sages with sincere hearts, thus protecting the peace of the people of the *shê*. You must clearly understand that if you do not provide an encampment[?] and

---

73. This passage is obscure. I have punctuated after 馬. I assume that 樓修五鳳 is a garbled version of 五鳳樓, an allusion implying literary skill.

74. Reading 蓮 for 連, as in Li Tiansheng's edition in "*Tang yuexing tu* jiao zhu."

75. The text reads 綵絑結, which makes no sense here and little enough anywhere.

76. To the best of my knowledge there is no mountain named Diecui; the term refers to the color of distant mountains. But the phrase is intended to be parallel to the following one; I suspect that the author mistakenly believed *diecui* to be the name of a notable mountain and have translated accordingly.

77. 棚 must be an error.

make an excuse for not appearing before the altar, if there is a deficiency in the hemp twine, nails, and cordage, or if you misappropriate the fabric for memorials or the spirit money, although it is seen by the people of the *shê* as being inconsequential, it is cheating the sages and worthies. If thereafter you experience catastrophes and disasters, do not blame Dragon Heaven. If you are sincere, many blessings will be sent down, but if you are greedy, a myriad crimes will be imputed to you. You must understand the commands fully in advance, correct what is evil, and follow what is worthy.

—To all those who make offerings to the gods: from now until the end of the *sai*, when you carry out the sacrifices to the gods, you must practice abstinence and bathe. Sincerity and purity should be your sole concern. In presenting the offerings to the sages and worthies at the banquet, in the morning you should put on your robes and shoes taking care that they are in good order, and in the evening take them off far from the altar. Even in the burning heat of summer, it is not permitted to let your clothes hang open or to one side. Your heads must not be uncovered, nor your feet bare. Do not do evil by drinking and talking wildly. If your body is stinking and filthy, it is an insult to the sages and worthies of this *shê*. Even if your brothers-in-law are there, you must not joke or talk boisterously with them. If you maintain great ceremoniousness and great integrity, the gods will be highly delighted. Sincerity will call down blessings and happiness; remissness will provoke disaster and call down disease. Now you know our instructions fully; you all must be cautious and sincere.

—To the Announcers of the [Sacrificial] Dishes: from now until the end of the *sai*, you must practice abstinence and bathe. Your robes and shoes must be in good order. Hold the spirit tablets high, go back and forth attentively. When food is presented, announce the quantities; when wine is poured, make clear [the sequence]. Respect Heaven and respect Earth when you make your announcements to the gods.

—To the Equalizers [of financial burdens?]: from now until the end of the *sai*, put up the announcements and busy yourselves with urging the people of the *shê* [to fulfill their responsibilities]. Insert [the names of] the recalcitrant [in the announcements] and check off all the people of the *shê* [as they pay?]. Urge on the musicians and fully prepare the list of contributors (*cai zhi*)[?]. Lead in an orderly manner the followers of the Way to make a joint pledge regarding the sacrifices, each observing the utmost sincerity. Await the time with reverence; then offer sacrifice to the honored gods.

—To the Supervisors of Food: from now until the end of the *sai*, the three streets will jointly [provide][78] provisions for the Entertainers. You must make a general announcement at the outset to all families, large and small. You must take account of whether their standing is high or low and [arrange for them to] send [their contributions] at the [agreed-upon] time, without mistake or tardiness. The things that are used must be complete and in good order. Keep an accurate account of the money and other things [given to the Entertainers]. The property [i.e., the contributions] of the people of the *shê* must not be misappropriated. If there are those with greedy hearts who under the pretext of sacrificing to the gods in fact scheme [to get] the wine and food of the Entertainers; who have no regard for the good order of the people of the *shê* but instead drink and misbehave when they come to the temple; whose speech does not distinguish between the respected and the lowly; who, when they move, use wild and obscene language and, when they stand still, look about angrily; who do not follow the rules for making offerings to the gods and try to scare people by flaunting their power and lack of scruple—such men, although they may frighten everyone in the *shê*, how could the gods abide them? Before evil men have even thought up their schemes, the gods will already know about them. If they then encounter flying disasters and terrible catastrophes, it will be too late to repent. Since we fear that [some of you] may be harboring improper intentions before the *sai* begins, we are making known this warning ahead of time.

—To those who take care of the sheep: from now until the end of the *sai*, those who have already purchased sheep should honestly declare how much they cost and should not be dishonest. First, the sheep must be led [into the temple]; [the "head sheep"] is to be killed before the altar. Then cut it up to make dishes, which must be prepared reverently for the gods' feast. Do not say you have done two things when you have only done one, recklessly inflate the prices [you claim to have paid], take funds for your own use, or say what is not true. If you make offerings disrespectfully, eat before the sacrifices have been carried out, cheat the people of the *shê*, or insult the gods, flying disasters and terrible catastrophes will descend on you, but it will be too late to repent. It is well to make this known beforehand so there will be no offenses and crimes.

—To the Masters of the Gods [i.e., the Masters of Ceremonial]: from the time King Yao established . . . , rituals have been used to make offerings to the gods. The musical asterisms were set up in the Zhou, Tang, and Song dynasties, Masters of the Gods were selected who wrote books for the managing of sacrifices

---

78. I suspect the 祀 in the text is an error.

and *sai* to August Heaven and Empress Earth. The Hanlin Academy completely composed the Five [musical] Notes, and Xuan Yuan harmonized the scale. These together made both the *yin* and *yang* melodies, which were arranged according to the sequence of the musical asterisms. The essence of the arrangement was transmitted in writings.[79] What you write and do should fully accord with the books, you should speak truly and properly with nothing omitted. When you come and go before the gods, follow the order [of the asterisms]; when you burn the incense and serve the wine, when you recite the sagely odes and documents, you must be single-minded and attentive and not be careless. If you have the protection of the gods and Heaven and fully comprehend the rituals of the sages above, you are worthy to act as Masters of the Gods.[80]

The orders for the Entertainers:

—To the ancient order of Headmen: you should select both major and minor Entertainers, then don your costume and headdress and wear them as you pass back and forth while making offerings to the gods. Every type of musical instrument must be on hand. Note accurately on an invoice the number of major and minor members of the troupe. You must share out fairly the food sent to the troupe every day. The money and goods that the people of the *shê* have already given you should be apportioned fairly according to each person's proper share. Do not try to deceive the people of the *shê* by cunningly misappropriating any funds you have received or by taking food or tea intended for the troupe or by cheating all or any troupe members. Even if members of the troupe are unwilling to speak up about it, it will eventually be discovered in the investigations of the gods.

—To the ancient order of the Training Bureau for Major Music: when Fu Xi created the zither (*qin*) and the large zither (*se*), the former was 7 feet 2 inches long. When Shen Nong created the five-string zither, he made it 2 feet 6.6 inches long. King Wen of Zhou added two strings and called it a seven-string zither. King Shun played a five-string zither. Since [he felt that] the added strings [on an instrument of the old] length produced an inharmonious sound, he made the zither 3 feet 6.6 inches long. The king of Shang created the single-string zither. The large zither originally had fifty strings, but in the time of the Yellow Emperor, they were reduced to twenty-five.

In the time of Xuan Yuan, they investigated the eight tones and adjusted the eight airs, creating the standard pitches. Emperor Wu of the Han created the

---

79. The present text is one of the writings referred to.
80. This section is unusually problematic, with questions in every sentence.

Music Bureau (*Yue fu*), and in the second year of the Kaiyuan era [A.D. 714], Emperor Ming of the Tang established the Music Training Academy (*Jiao fang*) next to the Penglai Palace. King Jie of the Xia established female musicians by his authority. In the Xia dynasty Yao was responsible for the flourishing of singing and dancing, Huang Fanchuo authorized the use of clappers, and Emperor Ku created large and small drums. Emperor Ming of the Tang created the *jie* drum and honored all the kinds of music. Nüwa created the *sheng* and *huang* reed mouth organs. Qiu Zhong of the Han invented the transverse flute (*di*), making it 2 feet 4 inches long, with seven holes and five tones. King Shun created the two-foot flute (*xiao*), later shortening it to 1 foot 5 inches to harmonize with the Zhonglü mode. In the Han dynasty the Wusun princess married the khan.[81] Because the journey was so long and she was homesick for the Han court, she invented the lute (*pipa*). Embracing it, she sang on her horse, plucking it as accompaniment. Meng Tian invented the *zheng* zither. It was in the form of the Three Powers[?], was six inches [*sic*] long, and had thirteen strings. . . .[82] Zhong Rong created the *ruan* lute. It had thirteen frets and four strings. Emperor Zhongzong of the Tang re-invented it, changing it in accord with popular taste and calling it moon lute. All musical instruments were created by sages and have come down to us to use as offerings to the gods in celebrating the *sai*.

—To the ancient order of the troupe: from now until the end of the *sai*, you will perform as ordered knave-and-butt *yuanben* and *Dui* Operas and *Za* Operas as offerings during the gods' banquets. Lyrics should be in accord with the old traditions of the *Taiping* [*yuefu*, a Yuan dynasty collection of melodies], songs with the [traditions of the] Music Bureau and the Pear Garden. There are forty major melodies for men, 3,000 minor songs for women. Your work must be carried out in an orderly manner, your costumes must be new, and you must have all the instruments you need. When the Platters are being offered in order, you must not fail to follow the commands, wearing your costumes and displaying a joyous countenance serving the gods. In offering congratulatory odes and songs before the gods, you must not cover your heads or hide your faces. The Headman-leader must be careful, the sound of gongs and drums should fill the air without ceasing, reed mouth organs should be loud and resonant. In offering the gods their dharma feast, do not swindle them by being remiss. If you use intimidation to cheat the gods, it will summon the Star of Calamity, who will investigate thoroughly.

---

81. The Wusun princess was Chinese, the daughter of the prince of Jiangdu. Her marriage to the Wusun khan was part of Han's foreign relations strategy.
82. The meaning of the rest of this sentence and the next is obscure.

—To the ancient order of the Leaders for the Three Days: from now until the end of the *sai*, in . . . setting out the Platters, all must be kept clearly in order. From ancient times to the present, the music of the asterisms was bequeathed by the sages of old, the rites and ceremonies were determined by our forebears. In this morning's saintly assembly, invite the honored gods and seat them in the main hall. Acting as Leader, lead the participants in making music for three days in accordance with the season. As the *Diagrams of the Musical Asterisms* has it, in spring use the seventh *gong* note, in summer the seventh *shang* note, in autumn the seventh *jiao* note, and in winter the seventh *yu* note. The high notes should be like the song of the phoenix, in the middle are the tones of the scales, incorporating the forty major melodies (*da qu*) and the six keys and eleven modes. Offer up music from the eight types of instrument: those made of metal, stone, silk, bamboo, gourd, clay, and wood. All the melodies of Heaven, Earth, the Year, the Month, the Day, and the Hour should be in accord with the twenty-eight Lunar Mansions and the five notes of the scale. Your decorated headdresses must be immaculate and your costumes new. For songs and dances presented during the offering of the Platters, winds and percussion should adopt the *gong* and *shang* notes. For the first meeting, which belongs to the civil side, use the following wind and stringed instruments: *xun* ocarina, *zhi* flute, dragon flute, *zheng* zither, [*gu*]*qin* seven-string zither, lute, and iron chime. For the later meeting, which belongs to the martial side, there are the "hundred acts" such as rope dancing, barbarian dancing, and stave drumming. Let every tone be presented to the gods with care and respect. Do not give in to dishonest impulses; if you do, you will be guilty of deception.

—To those who play stringed and wind instruments and pluck . . . :[83] from now until the end of the *sai*, in your offerings of songs to the gods, you must wear new clothes and always keep your instruments with you. When the congratulatory odes are offered early and late, there must be gorgeous melodies to accompany them.

—To the onlookers: the men [should be] worthy, the women virtuous. Distinguished people may enter the temple and stand together in ranks to watch. There must be no disturbances or jostling for position. Men should be on the left, women on the right. There must be no drinking or impropriety whatsoever in the audience. Rude behavior and disturbances will offend Dragon Heaven; there will certainly be retribution, but then it will be too late to repent.

Listen to the commands and understand what you hear: every person must

---

83. The text has 彈色 here, which must be an error.

be reverent, obey the regulations, and make offerings to the gods with a sincere heart. After you have enjoyed the *sai*, every day your hidden desires will receive the silent aid of the gods, there will be a myriad of blessings and great protection. May the emperor live a myriad years, and his ministers a thousand autumns; let there be tranquility throughout the world and the myriad people be employed contentedly at their work. Let the rains be gentle and the breezes refreshing, buying and selling be harmonious, the five grains grow abundantly, and all affairs enjoy great good fortune. All must be sincere and always refrain from stealing. The gods will respond [to misdeeds], and all those they pursue will wish [they had not done wrong]. Year after year sacrifice at the *sai*, and all will enjoy peace. Be guided by our former practices, and you will give rise to none of the myriad crimes. If you break the prohibitions, your crime will be great. Beware, beware! Remember, remember!

This ends the recitation of the commands; you may rise.[84]

The "Book of Commands" and the "Writ of Commands" are exceptionally valuable documents. First of all, they show us just how many people were involved in the production of a *sai*, an amazing number considering that the venue was a rural village. Second, resources both human and material were mobilized on a lavish scale, to put it mildly. It is not surprising that such celebrations tended to earn the disapproval of local officials, who saw their tax quotas going up in (incense) smoke and being frittered away on banquets for the gods. In terms of ideology, the Writ is completely Confucian, or Neo-Confucian: the only quotations are from the *Analects* and the *Odes*, and there is no hagiography, no emotionally charged language. But the values being preached are what we might call sub-Confucian. They are conventional popular ideas about the human and divine worlds: respect for social distinctions, reverence for the gods, emphasis on the importance of showing gratitude for their beneficence, and constant insistence on good order, both ritual and social. Since the audience for this recitation was probably limited to the men who had roles to play in the *sai* rituals and other members of

---

84. As mentioned earlier, the long part beginning with "To the *Shê* Heads" (above, p. 256), and ending here is taken from the "Writ of Commands," found in *Tang yuexing tu* (Yang, *Fourteen Manuscripts*, pp. 420–25). I used this text to supplement the closely related "Book of Commands," part of the *Handbook for Use Before the Gods of the* Sai, which is defective. The following descriptions are taken once again from the *Handbook*.

the village elite,[85] perhaps this is not surprising. But even villagers who were not part of the local elite would not have objected to the emphasis on good order and respect for divine and human hierarchy.

The absence of Daoist or Buddhist elements shows that we are dealing with a ritual regime very different from that of Fujian, Taiwan, southern Guangdong, and the Hakka regions that have received so much scholarly attention in the past couple of decades. But in addition there is a complete absence of anything like religious excitement or even exorcism. There is no sense of encountering the Powers, any moments of awe or mystery. This may be where the values of the local elite, to which the ritual masters belonged, are most clearly visible.

On the fourteenth, the gods were formally welcomed. Indeed, the central rituals of that day suggest that it was the day of their arrival. The *Handbook* has a very brief description of the day's activities, and then several pages later, a detailed description of the rituals of mounting and dismounting.

The fourteenth day: Greeting the Gods. Seal-script incense procession.[86] Processional *Dui* Opera. Three Heaven and Earth platters. (The monks receive them.) Three Incense Table platters. (The stage crew receives them.) There are thirty-six God-Settling Platters and thirty-six Honey Towers.[87] (The Pavilioners receive them.) Thirty-six cups of tea and thirty-six cups of wine are offered.[88] There is one Director; three feet of red cloth [are given to] the opera staff.

In the afternoon [of the fourteenth], there is the Mounting-up Banquet. A *Dui* Opera is performed. Vegetarian food.

First Cup: dates and Inches-of-Gold [gold-colored deep-fried inch-long pieces of dough with date paste, representing ingots of gold].

---

85. The "Writ" specifically states that "distinguished people" could enter the temple, where the rituals were performed.

86. This was the name given to an elaborate procession of all the ritual principals during which they walked once around the temple courtyard and then crisscrossed in the middle, thus appearing to trace out a character in seal script. They seem to have ended in front of the Offering Hall, where they bowed and offered incense (Yang Mengheng and Zhang Zhennan, "Shangdang gu sai," p. 92; Yang, *Fourteen Manuscripts*, p. 58, *n*3).

87. Made of paper with pieces of carved deep-fried dough stuck in the top.

88. There were in fact thirty-six gods, counting Hou Yi / San Zong, the host.

Second Cup: dried lychee and large buns. (All given to the *shê* personnel.)
Third Cup: pears and rice.

At night there is the Dismounting Banquet. Non-vegetarian food. A *Dui* Opera and three Cups, according to the [form of the] Mounting-up Banquet.[89]

The Mounting-up and Dismounting Banquets are described in much greater detail later in the text, as I just mentioned.[90] They seem to have prefigured the Cup Offerings of the three main days. In the Mounting-up Banquet, the Pavilioners, accompanied by the Attendants and Parasol-Bearers, brought out food offerings on their platters. Each offering was called a *hui*. (As we saw in Part II, *hui* was also used in *Za* Opera scripts to mean "act," though the terms in mainstream opera are *chang* or *zhe*. This is yet another sign of the close relationship between village ritual and drama.) Each *hui* had two parts, the first consisting of fruit, the second of things like sesame candy and buns. Two *hui* were called a Cup. A total of three Cups, that is, six *hui*, were offered, plus a seventh, concluding *hui*.[91] There were also sacrifices to the Sun. It was probably after this that the gods were invited to get on their horses and the entire company processed around and through the courtyard and out the main gate.[92] The tablets of the San Zong God, the Earth God, and the General of the Five Ways were placed outside the gate to await the gods. When they arrived (or returned), everyone went back into the temple, with the tablets of the gods carried in the proper order, and three more Cups were offered, along with a *Dui* Opera, all concluding with further offerings of food and wine.[93] This may indeed have been intended to symbolize the actual arrival of the gods' invisible essences, while the ceremonies on the thirteenth were just a courtesy due to the gods' material forms, their tablets. (Note that statues do not seem to have played much of a role in this *sai*, another indicator of how "Confucian" it was.)

----

89. Yang, *Fourteen Manuscripts*, pp. 36–37. My glosses on the names of certain dishes are taken from Yang's notes.

90. Ibid., pp. 42–44.

91. Ibid., p. 43.

92. I suspect that the spirit tablets were left in place in the main hall, ready to be inhabited (or re-inhabited) by the gods on their arrival (or return).

93. Yang Menghang and Zhang Zhennan, "Shangdang gu sai," p. 93.

THE MAIN *SAI* RITUALS AND
THE DIAGRAMS FOR ARRANGING
THE GODS

The Mounting and Dismounting Banquets took place on the four-teenth. The fifteenth was the first of the three main days of the *sai*. The *Handbook* continues:

Fifteenth day [of the second month]. The two Immortal [Girls] are invited.[94] Seal-script incense procession. Leading the Sheep longevity noodles.[95]

Offering to the Sun: three platters of sesame cakes. (The Master of Cere-monial receives them.)

Sacrifice to the Stage [an exorcism]. There is a banquet table in the kitchen with fifteen sesame cakes, fifteen *gebiao*, fifteen dough rolls, and a platter of pork. (One-half *jin* per participant; the Entertainers receive it.)[96]

Sacrifice to the Stove. A banquet table with fifteen sesame cakes, fifteen *ge-biao*, fifteen dough rolls, and a platter of pork. (The Overseer of Lodgings [for the gods] receives it.) There is the ceremony of the "Leading the Sheep."[97] There are the rituals of Writing Characters and Bowing to Felicity. They cross the courtyard in the village[?].

After noon, sacrifice to the Wind: three platters of sesame candy. (The En-tertainers receive them.)

In the afternoon, entertainment. Non-vegetarian offerings. *Dui* Operas are performed during three [*mao yan*] Cups.[98]

First Cup: dates and Inches-of-Gold.
Second Cup: dried lychee and large buns.

------

94. Er xian nainai. They were young sisters who fell sick and died due to the labor of picking medicinal herbs in the mountains for the villagers. Their cult was widespread in southeastern Shanxi. For a brief account see *Shanxi tongzhi* (Siku quanshu Wenyuan ge intranet edition), 165.9b. A similar passage is quoted in Yang, *Fourteen Manuscripts*, p. 40, *n*12.

95. See below for "Leading the Sheep" (*ling yang*).

96. This and the following may be abbreviated references to the purification of the stage and kitchen by the Jian Zhai God and the four Shutting Gods that was part of the *sai* at the Temple of the Divine Mother (see pp. 209–10).

97. This served to select the village or alliance that would sponsor the next *sai*, or to ratify the selection if there was a fixed rota (ibid., p. 41, *n*19).

98. These are almost certainly the *mao yan* Cups listed in the programs for the six-teenth and the seventeenth, although that label is not used here.

Third Cup: pears and rice. (*Shê* personnel receive them.)

Night Cups: perform musical *yuanben*.

First Cup: dates and Inches-of-Gold. (The *Shê* Heads [receive them].)
Second Cup: ginkgo buns. (Pavilioners.)
Third Cup: persimmon cakes and *budiao*[?]. (Master of Ceremonial.)
Fourth Cup: dried lychee and Crescent Moons [a kind of dumpling].
    (Buyers.)
Fifth Cup: red cakes with black dates. (Overseer of the Gods' Lodgings.)
Sixth Cup: green bean hairy turtles.[99] (Entertainers.)
Seventh Cup: pears and rice. (*Shê* personnel.)

Send off the Two Immortals to conclude.[100]

The sequence of seven, twelve, and eight Cup Offerings on the three
main days of a *sai* is already fixed in the oldest of all the *sai* manuscripts,
the *Tang Musical Asterisms with Diagram of Seven at the Start, Eight at the
End (Tang yuexing zao qi wan ba tu)*, which has an internal date of 1522
and was written for use in Changzhi county.[101] That sequence seems to
have been shared by all *sai* and was in fact one of their few defining
characteristics. Since the Cup Offerings were so important, I will supplement the *Handbook*'s rather meager account with a much fuller description written by Yang Mengheng and Zhang Zhennan.[102] We know
from internal evidence in their article that they sometimes relied on
local informants. They may also have drawn on Zhang's own memories,
since he was born in 1912, was a native of the county in which the
Mt. Longquan Hou Yi Temple was located, and had witnessed a number of *sai* in his youth. He also devoted years to studying *sai* after
retirement.

The food offerings were prepared in a ritual kitchen in the temple
set up especially for the *sai*. (A sacrifice to the stove god of the ritual
kitchen took place on the fifteenth, as we have seen; all aspects of the
sai were caught in the web of ritual.) They were eventually placed on

---

99. Reading 龜 for 主.
100. Yang, *Fourteen Manuscripts*, p. 37.
101. Ibid., pp. 401–4. It is puzzling that the ms. is dated 1522, since Changzhi county
did not officially come into existence until 1528 (Zhang Jizhong, *Shanxi lishi zhengqu dili*,
p. 218).
102. Yang Mengheng and Zhang Zhennan, "Shangdang gu sai," pp. 94–96.

tables in the Offering Pavilion (also called the Incense Pavilion), which, as mentioned, was a permanent structure on the central axis of the temple, between the main gate and the main hall. At the end of the day, the offerings were given to various ritual personnel, who were carefully specified in the *Handbook*. The location of the spirit tablets of the gods during the start of the Cup Offerings is not entirely clear. Either they remained in ordered ranks in the main hall, where they had been placed on the very first day, or they were moved to the gods' quarters on the east and west sides of the courtyard. This last would make sense, but there is no evidence for it—except that according to Yang and Zhang, the gods' tablets were brought into the "sacrificial area"—either the main hall or the Offering Pavilion—at the start of each day there were Cup Offerings, which means that they resided elsewhere. But in any case, the central action of the three main days was the transfer of food offerings from the kitchen to the Offering Pavilion. This process was extremely elaborate.

The Pavilioners picked up the tablets of their assigned gods, and a large procession assembled, marched around the temple courtyard, and then wound about within it, ending at the Offering Pavilion. Entertainers playing instrumental music and dressed in their characteristic costumes led the procession, followed by the Masters of Ceremonial. Then came the *Shê* Head, wearing a long gown, mandarin jacket, and a velvet ceremonial hat, holding a dragon-headed staff and carrying a brazier filled with burning incense. He was followed by four Incense Masters carrying long sticks of incense wrapped in special cloth, four Candle Masters carrying lanterns, a number of Incense Elders holding slender sticks of incense, and several youths with unbound hair called the Water Officials. Then came the Pavilioners, each with a "mouth-stopping flower" clenched in his teeth and carrying his god's spirit tablet. They were accompanied by their Attendants and Parasol-Bearers. Bringing up the rear was a crowd of Ushers carrying cudgels. Some or all of the men came to a halt in the Offering Pavilion—I suspect only the Pavilioners, since it is hard to imagine that everyone could have fit into the space under the Pavilion's roof (and this would explain their titles)—and the music stopped. The Pavilioners put down the gods' tablets (probably in the Offering Pavilion), and a long series of obeisances, incense offerings, invocations, and the like were performed.[103]

The food offerings came in two parts. First, there was a set of three especially rich Cup Offerings called the *mao yan* Cups. During these offerings, Supplementary *Dui* Opera was performed and the Director of the Entertainers walked around the offering tables reciting various encomiums to the gods.[104] Then in the evening, there was the offering of Seven Cups, accompanied at Mt. Longquan by *yuanben*.[105] When the Cup Offerings were finished, the two Immortal Girls were seen off (it would not do for the maidens to stay overnight in a temple filled with male gods), and the day's activities were done.

The Cup offerings were repeated with slight variations on the sixteenth and seventeenth, the second and third of the three main days of the *sai*. They are described in the *Handbook*:

Sixteenth [day of the second month]. Invite the two Immortal [Girls]. Receive [the Star of] Longevity at the Palace of Longevity [a temporary structure made of paper].[106] Seal-script incense procession. Settle the Star of Longevity [in his palace]. [Supply] four feet of both red and white cloth [to be used by the Master of Ceremonial]. One small cloth for the presentation of the memorial [to the Star of Longevity]. (To be used by [the Director of] the Entertainers.) *Eight Immortals* is presented on stage. Entertainers [costume themselves as] the Eight Immortals.[107] (The Master of Ceremonial presides.) *The Monkey Sheds His Husk* [is performed]. One rooster. One pigeon, for use in the Release of Living

---

103. The *Handbook* appears to give a different sequence on p. 43, but it is so condensed that it is of little use.

104. Yang Mengheng and Zhang Zhennan, "Shangdang gu sai," p. 96. Note that here we have an Entertainer, a member of a debased group, addressing the gods directly.

105. Yang, *Fourteen Manuscripts*, p. 37. It is hard to imagine why the bawdy *yuanben* were used to accompany these important offerings, and I find it difficult to believe that this was a customary procedure. I have a good deal of evidence that the Seven Cups were presented in the afternoon elsewhere: Duan Youwen, "Jin dongnan," pp. 4–6, 12–13; and Li Tiansheng, "*Tang yuexing tu* jiao zhu," pp. 122–23. Yang's reconstruction may be in error here.

106. This ritual, which is said to have been quite important, is described in Yang Mengheng and Zhang Zhennan, "Shangdang gu sai," p. 97.

107. The meaning here is obscure.

Creatures.[108] On returning from receiving the Star of Longevity, the Eight Immortals present wine and the memorial.

The Jade Emperor, the Star of Longevity, and the San Zong God [Hou Yi] eat at three tables. [Each has] fifteen sesame candies, one portion of pork, fifteen dough rolls, fifteen *gebiao*, and one chicken.

Sacrifice to the Sun: three platters of sesame candy.

Handing over the Spirit Tablets: fifteen sesame candies, fifteen *gebiao*, fifteen dough rolls, one Honey Tower, three platters of sesame candy.

During the afternoon Cups, there are three *mao yan* Cups, and three *Dui* Operas are performed.

Sacrifice to the Wind: three sesame candy platters.

> First Cup: dates and Inches-of-Gold.
> Second Cup: dried lychee and large buns.
> Third Cup: pears and rice.

Night Cups: *Za* Opera, *yuanben*.[109]

Sacrifice to the Moon: three platters of sesame candy.

> First Cup: dates and Inches-of-Gold. (*Shê* Heads.)
> Second Cup: dried lychee and large buns. (Pavilioners.)
> Third Cup: millet "Crescent Moons." (Master of Ceremonial.)
> Fourth Cup: persimmon cakes and *budiao*. (Buyers.)
> Fifth Cup: walnut cakes. (Accountant.)
> Sixth Cup: red cakes with black dates. (Storehouse guard[s].)
> Seventh Cup: persimmon cakes and *luan* cakes. (Monks.)
> Ninth Cup:[110] red grape cakes. (Attendants.)

---

108. A text to accompany the Release of Living Creatures can be found in another of the Niu manuscripts, "Old *Zan* for the *Sai* Arena [I]" (*Saichang gu zan* [*jia*]), Yang, *Fourteen Manuscripts*, pp. 279–81. It tells two parallel stories of men who saved injured animals and were rewarded for it. In one a certain Yang Bao was rewarded by the Jade Emperor for rescuing an injured bird. A character of the same name gains a supernatural reward for rescuing an injured bird in the prologue story to the Ming tale, "The Foxes' Revenge," from *Xing shi heng yan*, translated by Yang Xianyi and Gladys Yang in *The Courtesan's Jewel Box*, pp. 65–66. All the details are different, but still the coincidence is striking. In fact, I doubt it is a coincidence; somehow the narrative element of a man named Yang Bao receiving a supernatural reward for rescuing an injured bird entered the common fund of story. Patrick Hanan (*The Chinese Short Story*, p. 242, *sub* "HY6.") dates the prologue to the late sixteenth century or later.

109. It is not clear how *Za* Operas differed from *Dui* Operas. Also, I do not understand why no human recipients of the preceding offerings are named.

110. There is no Eighth Cup in the manuscript.

Tenth Cup: sugar kernel cakes. (Tea and Wine Bureaus.)
Eleventh Cup: ginkgo Turtle[111] Heads. (Entertainers.)
Twelfth Cup: pears and rice. (*Shê* personnel.)

Sending off the Two Immortals: three platters each of sesame candy and dough rolls. (Master of Ceremonial.)

Last Act [the third of the three main days, the seventeenth of the second month]. Great Peace drumming. The two Immortal [Girls] are invited. Seal-script incense procession.

Offering to the Sun: three platters of sesame candy.
Afternoon Cups: three *mao yan* Cups, non-vegetarian food offerings.
Sacrifice to the Wind: three platters of sesame candy.

First Cup: dates and Inches-of-Gold.
Second Cup: ginkgo buns.
Third Cup: pears and rice.

Night Cups: *Za* Opera, *yuanben*, *Dui* Opera.
Sacrifice to the Moon: three platters of sesame candy.

First Cup: dates and Inches-of-Gold. (*Shê* Heads.)
Second Cup: dried lychee and large buns. (Pavilioners.)
Third Cup: white millet cakes. (Master of Ceremonial.)
Fourth Cup: persimmon cakes and Crescent Moons. (Buyers.)
Fifth Cup: red ginkgo cakes. (Chief Manager.)
Sixth Cup: walnut cakes. (Overseer of the Gods' Lodgings.)
Seventh Cup: persimmon [cakes] and *luan* cakes. (Entertainers.)
Eighth Cup: pears and rice. (*Shê* personnel.)[112]

The *Handbook* clearly omits many activities during the sixteenth and seventeenth (the second and third main days, the fourth and fifth over-all), but there is no way to reconstruct them, and I will go on to the final day. The text's treatment is extremely brief, and instead of trans-lating it, I summarize Yang and Zhang's more substantial account, since it includes a number of interesting items.[113]

---

111. Again reading 龜 for 主.

112. Yang, *Fourteen Manuscripts*, pp. 37–39.

113. Yang Mengheng and Zhang Zhennan, "Shangdang gu sai," pp. 98–100. As usual, they do not indicate their sources, but it is noteworthy that they quote three short verses that were spoken during the proceedings—just the sort of thing that we know from other cases was remembered by participants or even onlookers for decades.

The last of the six days of the Mt. Longquan *sai* took place on the eighteenth of the second month. It began with the Master of Ceremonial using wheat bran powder to draw a giant charm in the temple courtyard while reciting incantations to bring good fortune and keep calamities away. After burning incense in paying his respects in the Offering Pavilion, he dipped his fingers in basins of water held by the youths with unbound hair who were called the Water Officials and spattered droplets in the four directions, appealing for good weather in the coming year. The participants then provided a farewell meal for the gods with food brought from their own homes,[114] during which the various *Shê* Heads and other men with managerial responsibilities knelt before the gods to declare that they had acted with sincere reverence for the gods and to vow that they had not personally benefited, inviting the gods to examine the truth of what they were saying. (This sort of public accounting was common at the end of large communal festivals; in the Southern Seven Villages' *sai*, it took place late at night with all lamps put out and the Entertainers playing music that sounded like wailing.)[115]

The Entertainers then performed a skit called *Hopping* Tanzi (*Tiao tanzi*)[116] and other dances. This was concluded by the firing of a blunderbuss, the detonation of many firecrackers, and loud drumming. Then the Director began to take apart the beautiful screen of carved dough tiles called the Flowery Offering and distribute the pieces to the onlookers.[117] All the paper josses and offering "ingots" were gathered and burned, and the Master of Ceremonial[118] chanted:

---

114. Yang, *Fourteen Manuscripts*, p. 39.

115. Zhang Zhennan, "Yueju yu sai," p. 256. The solemnity of this public accounting and the evident sincerity of the denial of self-interest provides an interesting contrast with William Hinton's (*Fanshen*, p. 30) flat assertion that the landlord Sheng Jinghe skimmed off money from the *sai* of Long Bow village, which is only about thirty-five kilometers northeast of Mt. Longquan. After reading the liturgical texts and descriptions of eye-witnesses, one wants more than ever to know just how reliable Hinton's account is.

116. *Tanzi* can mean "scout" or "spy," but I have no idea what it denotes in this case.

117. This was partly confirmed by interviews with villagers at Xiaozhang village, about four kilometers east of the temple, on Oct. 15, 1993 (Interview transcript, p. 20).

118. Yang Mengheng and Zhang Zhennan have the Director chanting this and performing the final divination, which must be a slip.

We invite the gods to gather at the altar;
All the men of the united *shê* have been devout and sincere.
On this day the incense will cease;[119]
Let there be gentle breezes and timely rains.[120]

The Master of Ceremonial then divined by tossing a ram's horn on the ground. If there was a good result, the spectators all shouted "A good *sai*! The *sai* is over!" The Master of Ceremonial repeated their words and recited the following verse:

There will be gentle breezes and timely rains, the five grains
    will produce abundantly,
Men and horses will be untroubled, the fields will give a
    rich harvest.
Trade will be harmonious and all affairs will enjoy success.
Sweep clean the courtyard, burn a full brazier of incense;
Let the gods return to their places and keep all misfortunes away!

Then the supplementary food offerings provided by the sponsoring villages were divided equally in front of the gods, and everyone went home.[121]

Not only do we have an unprecedented amount of detail about the rituals of the Mt. Longquan *sai*, we also know exactly which gods were the honored guests, information that is very rare. The *Handbook* contains three Diagrams for Arranging the Gods (*pai shen bu*). They show which gods were present and how their tablets were to be arranged during the *sai* at three different temples, one of which was the Hou Yi temple on Mt. Longquan. It begins with a note:

Shao village *shê* Diagram for Arranging the Gods.[122] The god is at Mt. Longquan. In the eastern ranks there are eighteen pavilions. [Their gods are] not seen off. In the western ranks, the [gods of the] eleventh, twelfth, thirteenth,

---

119. Emending 绛 to 將.

120. Yang Mengheng and Zhang Zhennan, "Shangdang gu sai," p. 99.

121. Ibid., pp. 99–100. The concluding words and actions closely resemble those at the Divine Mother *sai*.

122. Shao village *shê* was one of the North Five *Shê*, presumably the most important of them, although it is not listed first in the roster of that village alliance given earlier in the *Handbook*.

fourteenth, and fifteenth pavilions [are not seen off].[123] In the western[124] ranks there are seventeen pavilions.[125] Libationers: three men. Cudgel holders: three men. Sounding metal [staff bearers]: two men. Tea Masters: two men. Wine Masters: two men. Attendants: four men. Incense and Candle Masters: two men. Brazier bearers: two men. Pavilioners: two men.[126]

The note is followed by the actual diagram. It is in the form of two chevrons or inverted "Vs." I first name all the gods on the right leg of the upper chevron, beginning with the central and most senior god, then all on the left leg, and similarly for the lower chevron. Gods that are well known I merely name; the others I identify briefly, except for several about whom I could find no information. The word "tea" in parentheses after the god's name means he (or she) was to be served tea (and vegetarian food) rather than wine (and meat dishes).

[*Top chevron, right leg*:]

The Jade Emperor

Cheng Tang [founder of the Shang dynasty]

The reigning emperor

Tai Qing (tea) [Laozi in his role as one of the Three Pure Ones of Daoism][127]

Confucius

Qing Yuan Miao Dao Zhen Jun [Zhao Yu, disciple of the Sui Daoist master Li Jue and killer of a flood dragon][128]

Guan Di

---

123. Yang, *Fourteen Manuscripts*, p. 60. I see no other way to make sense of this sentence. The gods who were not "seen off" in all probability were not included in the elaborate rituals of welcoming, either. As mentioned earlier, this suggests that on the day of the great procession the palanquin of the San Zong god invited only ten gods (thirty-six minus the twenty-three not seen off, the host god, and the gods of the host temple, the Earth God and the General of the Five Ways).

124. Emending 兩 to 西.

125. The thirty-sixth pavilion was the Jade Emperor's, which was located in the middle and hence was in neither the eastern nor the western ranks.

126. The preface and the diagram can both be found in Yang, *Fourteen Manuscripts*, p. 60. The comment about two Pavilioners is puzzling, since we know that each god had his or her own Pavilioner.

127. Zong Li and Liu Qun, *Zhongguo minjian zhu shen*, p. 6.

128. *Huitu Sanjiao yuanliu soushen daquan*, p. 113.

Hu Guo Ling Qi Wang (Nation-Protecting Divinely-Ordering King) [unidentified]

Taihua Long Wang [a dragon king]

Zhaoze Long Wang [a dragon king]

Daxiu Long Wang [a dragon king]

[Top chevron, left leg.]

Shen Nong

Shakyamuni (tea) [the characters of the name have been partly reversed: "Mo ni shi jia" rather than "Shi jia mo ni"]

Tang Taizong [the first great emperor of the Tang, whose power base was in Shanxi]

The God of the Eastern Peak (Dong Yue Tian Qi Ren Sheng Di Jun)

Wu Tu [the five kinds of soil]

Wu Gu [the five kinds of grain]

The Immortal Oldster, Chief of the Sages (Zong sheng xian weng) (tea) [unidentified]

Hou Yi [the host; mythical archer who shot down nine suns when all ten came out together, scorching the earth]

Qi Sheng Guang You Wang [Cui Ziyu, also known as Cui Fujun, widely worshipped in the Changzhi region, according to one tradition magistrate of Zhangzi in the Tang][129]

Guang De Ling Ze Wang [unidentified]

Great Sage of the Divine Pool (Ling Qiu Da Sheng) (tea) [unidentified]

Third Sage of the Divine Pool (Ling Qiu San Sheng) (tea) [unidentified]

[Lower chevron, right leg.]

Baiyun Long Wang [a dragon king]

Yeming Long Wang [a dragon king]

Wind Earl (Feng Bo)

Rain Master (Yu Shi)

Chi Ci Guang Chan Hou [the god of cattle]

General of the Five Ways (Wu Dao Jiangjun) [one of the gods of the temple]

The Lady of This Hall (Ben Dian Niangniang) [wife of the host god]

[Lower chevron, left leg.]

Second Sage of the Divine Pool (Ling Qiu Er Sheng) (tea)

Daluo Chong Shu Zhenren (tea) [see next]

---

129. Zong Li and Liu Qun, *Zhongguo minjian zhu shen*, p. 592.

Daluo Chong Hui Zhenren (tea) [divine sisters, extremely popular in the
    Changzhi region, commonly called Er xian nainai, the Immortal Girls]
God of Thunder and Goddess of Lightning (Lei Gong and Dian Mu)
The Earth God of This Place (Dang Chu Tudi) [i.e., the host temple]
The Way-Opening God (Xing Shen).

According to notes on the diagram itself, the chevrons were placed
pointing north, that is with the Jade Emperor occupying the position farthest from the Offering Pavilion and in the deepest part of the main hall.
The two ranks on the east have a total of seventeen gods, and the two on
the west eighteen,[130] which is the reverse of the count given in the note
prefacing the diagram. There is a total of thirty-six gods, which accords
with the number of platters and other implements given in the text.

Of the deities who can be identified, fourteen are directly related to
weather or farming (including here all the Dragon Kings plus Hou Yi
and Shen Nong), five are classical or part of state orthodoxy (Cheng
Tang, the reigning emperor, Confucius, Guan Di, and the Eastern
Peak), four are Shanxi gods (Tang Taizong, Qi Sheng Guang You
Wang, Daluo Chong Shu Zhenren, and Daluo Chong Hui Zhenren),
four are what we can call "generic local deities" (General of the Five
Ways, the temple's Earth God, the Lady of This Hall, and the Way-
Opening God), two are Daoist (Tai Qing and Qing Yuan Miao Dao
Zhen Jun), one is Buddhist, and one—the Jade Emperor—is beyond
classification. Weather/farming gods, classical/orthodox gods, and
Shanxi/generic local gods account for twenty-seven of the thirty-one. I
do not know if the preponderance of deities relating to agriculture (and
weather) is typical of pantheons elsewhere in rural China. Certainly the
emphasis on weather gods in the pantheon is what we would expect in
a region where drought was always a concern. That classical/orthodox
deities had a larger role than Buddhist and Daoist deities fits with the
ideological tenor of the *Handbook*, with its heavy emphasis on the importance of ritual and use of quotations from the *Analects* and the *Odes*.

The main purpose of the Diagram was to establish the precedence
of the various gods, and the results are conventional but worth noting.

---

130. As mentioned, the Jade Emperor was in the center and was not counted with
either east or west.

The top nine gods are, in order (assuming that east [left] is superior to west):[131] the Jade Emperor; Cheng Tang, founder of the Shang dynasty; Shen Nong; the reigning emperor; Shakyamuni Buddha; Tai Qing, i.e., Laozi; Tang Taizong (the greatest of the early Tang emperors); Confucius; and the God of the Eastern Peak. The only one of them that can be classified as a local or regional deity is Tang Taizong, whom Shanxi claimed as its own. And only Shen Nong has a direct connection with agriculture (although I cannot recall seeing a rain prayer or similar plea for a good harvest being directed to him). Gods with lower places in the first rank and all the gods in the second rank are far more likely to have connections with weather and crops, and with the site of the *sai* (when they can be identified).

———

We know a great deal about the rituals of the Mt. Longquan *sai* because we can read the handbook used by a Master of Ceremonial while leading them. The ceremonies described in it are long and complex, extraordinarily so when one considers that they were, after all, for use in villages where most of the people had little or no education and, even more important, that they were created by village ritual specialists. These men were not Daoist or Buddhist clerics, nor were they local officials or literati. Their surviving work from southeastern Shanxi shows virtually no influence of Daoist or Buddhist or Neo-Confucian ideas. Yet what they created was neither primitive nor crude. On the contrary, it was in performative terms highly sophisticated. The Masters of Ceremonial are not to be underestimated. Nor are the Entertainers. The *Handbook* makes clear that their Director worked in close coordination with the Master of Ceremonial and as an equal, not a subordinate. He was not a ragamuffin impresario but had a central role in the direction of the rituals of sacrifice.

The Masters of Ceremonial had little to do with the seasonal rituals studied in Part I. Their proper sphere was the celebrations honoring village gods. Using written liturgical manuals that in some cases were centuries old, they performed rituals on the gods' birthdays that were hu-

———

131. See McDermott, "Emperors, Elites, and Commoners," p. 330, *n*20, on the question of whether left is superior to right in Chinese custom.

mane and pragmatic, based on the belief that only with their blessings would crops ripen and people and animals thrive; that divine beneficence deserved the most sincere gratitude; and that the best way to express this gratitude was through reverent rituals replete with processions, prayers, music, opera, and food. The handbook studied in this chapter shows that the teachings embedded in the *sai* did not go beyond the perennial philosophy of the Chinese common people: the centrality of ritual; veneration of the gods; filial piety; courtesy to guests; deference to hierarchy; respect for community norms. These values were not said to reflect the will of the gods; they were expressed in rituals that had been created by the ritual masters. The gods were present to receive the thank-offerings of the people; the only demands they made had to do with the behavior of the ritual personnel. In a monotheistic regime this would be called ethics or community values, consonant with but subordinate to larger religious truths. But for the non-Buddhist, non-Daoist religion of rural north China, for which we have no proper name, these values and attitudes (plus beliefs and stories about the gods and the Other World) constituted the entire discursive content. It was ritual that was fundamental, not doctrine, and the rituals were understood to have been made by the same men who for most of the year advised villagers on when to hold funerals and where to build houses. Those men, the Masters of Ceremonial, who had sole authority over *sai* ritual, told people how to behave, not what to believe.

3

The Hou Yi
Temple of Big West Gate
□
The Ritual Chefs

THE TEMPLE AND THE
ORGANIZATION OF THE *SAI*

The three foundational elements of Chinese festival culture were ritual, opera, and banqueting. In temple festivals one never was present without the other two. Zhangzi people had a saying: "In the great *sai* there are three professions: Wang Eights [Entertainers], chefs, and the ghostly *yinyang*s [the Masters of Ceremonial]."[1] I focused on the Entertainers in the chapter on the Divine Mother *sai* and on the Masters of Ceremonial in the chapter on the Mt. Longquan *sai*. In this chapter I pay special attention to the ritual chefs and the remarkable food offerings they created: the banquet for the gods and the edible sculptures that were a standard feature of all *sai*.

Of the *sai* I have studied, the one most vividly described from the villager's point of view was held during the sixth month at a large temple outside the West Gate of the county seat of Zhangzi in honor of Hou Yi, or San Zong. It was called the Big West Gate *sai* (Da xi guan sai).[2] It

---

1. Zhang Zhennan, "Yueju yu sai," p. 239. It sounds considerably better in Chinese: "*Da sai sai san hang—wang ba, chuzi, gui yinyang.*"

2. The main sources for the *sai* of Big West Gate are three articles by Zhang Zhennan, all quite similar: "Yueju yu sai," "Yueju he sai," and "Zhongguo Shanxi." Zhang's

was supported by an alliance of five neighborhoods, called "streets" (*jie*), in Zhangzi town—East Street, South Street, Little West Street, Big West Gate, and North Gate.[3] Each was responsible for one year in a five-year rota. According to Zhang Zhennan, these five streets had eight temples capable of holding *sai*, and they may well have actually done so. Think of one small town having eight festivals on the scale of a *sai* in one year, with numbers of others, equally large—such as that at Mt. Longquan—only ten to fifteen kilometers away![4] The people who lived in southeastern Shanxi had an extraordinarily rich festival life, even in the dark days at the turn of the twentieth century and after the anti-superstition campaigns of the early Republic. We know that before the Japanese war there still were at least three *sai* in Zhangzi town every year: one at the City-God Temple and one at the Guan Di Temple, plus the one at Big West Gate. (Both the City-God Temple and the Guan Di Temple were in Little West Street, which may well have been the main commercial area.)[5] Feng Guiyu, an experienced Master of Ceremonial, said that each had its own character: the *sai* at the City-God

---

descriptions in many places are clearly those of an eyewitness. Moreover, he sometimes speaks of himself as an observer. For example, "I was born in 1912, and from what I remember and what I have been told, in [Zhangzi town] alone there were eight temples that could host great *sai* . . ." ("Yueju yu sai," p. 238); "I do not understand the ritual details of the offering of Cups. At first I just watched the excitement and spectacle. When I began to gather material, most of the old musicians had died and the other elders did not really understand [the rituals] either" (ibid., p. 234). I regard Zhang's testimony as highly reliable, although by no means infallible. Other important sources are an interview with Feng Guiyu, an old Master of Ceremonial who lived in West Street of Zhangzi town (Li Tiansheng, "Saishe shikuang"), and the biography of the ritual chef Song Changshan (Zhang Zhennan and Bao Haiyan, "Song Changshan," pp. 281–83).

3. That five "streets" were sponsors is clear from Zhang Zhennan, "Yueju yu sai," p. 237. Their names can be inferred from ibid., p. 238, and are explicitly identified in a manuscript note by Yang Mengheng in the author's collection. The 1 : 50,000 Chinese Army maps of Shanxi, based on surveys done in 1924, show Zhangzi as a walled city divided neatly into four quadrants by one east–west and one north–south street. There is a tiny "suburb" outside the main west gate, probably the site of the temple, and an even tinier one outside the north gate. There is another important street just inside the west wall and parallel to it, running south from the northern wall to the main east–west street—quite possibly Little West Street.

4. See map of village *sai* alliances around Zhangzi, pp. 238–41.

5. Zhang Zhennan, "Yueju yu sai," p. 238.

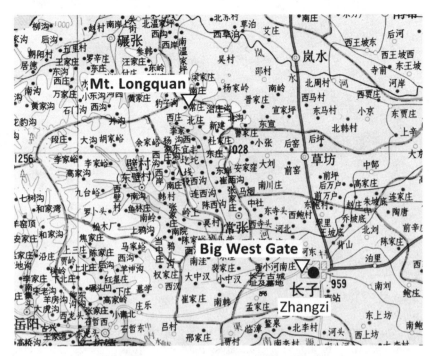

Map 8 Sites of Hou Yi temples at Mt. Longquan and Big West Gate and environs. (Both temples have been destroyed.) 1 cm = 1.7 km (SOURCE: *Shanxi sheng ditu ji*).

Temple had an official aura (*guan qi*), that at the Guan Di Temple had a mercantile aura (*cai qi*), and that at the Hou Yi (or San Zong) Temple at West Gate had a popular aura (*tu qi*). The City-God *sai* was run by the yamen, and the magistrate and all his staff marched in the procession to invite the guest-gods. The *sai* at the Guan Di Temple was run by the town's businessmen and was characterized by a procession with very lavish decorations (although it is hard to imagine anything more lavish than the Hou Yi procession, which I will describe shortly).[6] One wonders if this was typical for unremarkable county capitals in southeastern Shanxi.[7] Only the Guan Di Temple is still standing; it is used for housing and storage. The Hou Yi Temple was destroyed after 1949.

---

6. Zhang Zhennan and Bao Haiyan, "Feng Guiyu," p. 245, quoting Feng.

7. The current population of Zhangzi is estimated at nearly 40,000 by Falling Rain Genomics (www.fallingrain.com/world/), and is marked with a symbol used for places whose population falls between 20,000 and 50,000 in the 1995 *Shanxi Provincial Atlas*,

The Hou Yi Temple of Big West Gate was already in existence in the late thirteenth century, since there is an inscription commemorating its repair by a Mongol local official in 1319.[8] An inscription from the Ming Hongzhi reign period (1488–1505) mentions that there is a five-bay stage in the temple,[9] and in rural southeastern Shanxi a temple with a stage that large almost certainly hosted *sai*. An inscription from 1577 says there have been "sacrifices in the temple for generations . . . [and] the villagers have made solemn offerings there for a long time." In the final poem of that inscription are the lines "When the villagers come to make their sacrifices, / there is the clangor of bells and drums."[10] The 1734 *Shanxi Provincial Gazetteer* also says: "In the present dynasty every year on the sixth day of the sixth month local officials make offerings [at the San Zong Temple of Zhangzi's West Gate]. Some say the god has authority over hail, and so the *sai* of entreaty (*dao sai*) is very rich."[11] The 1778 edition of the Zhangzi county gazetteer mentions that "villagers vie to present offerings of animals [on the sixth day of the sixth month] at the San Zong Temple(s)."[12]

The temple was from all accounts very impressive. Even the record from the Ming Hongzhi period says that "its gold and jasper were dazzling, [its appearance] surpassing all other temples."[13] In the third and fourth decades of the twentieth century, the period from which Zhang Zhennan's memories must date, it still was an imposing place, even though by that time many temples had already fallen into disrepair or been turned to other uses, thanks to Republican anti-superstition campaigns. On a 1993 visit to the site, which was then mostly bare ground surrounded by nondescript one-story buildings, Zhang pointed out

---

p. 32. (The Falling Rain website does not indicate the source of its population estimates.) Zhangzi was probably a good deal smaller in the late nineteenth century, in the aftermath of the famine—perhaps 10,000?

8. *Shanxi tongzhi* (Siku quanshu Wenyuan ge intranet edition), 165.5a.

9. Ibid.

10. "Chong xiu San Zong miao ji" (Wanli 5); text in Yang Taikang and Cao Zhanmei, *San Jin xiqu*, pp. 398, 399.

11. *Shanxi tongzhi* (Siku quanshu Wenyuan ge intranet edition), 165.5a.

12. Quoted in Ding Shiliang and Zhao Fang, *Zhongguo difangzhi . . . Huabei juan*, p. 622. It is not clear if one or more San Zong temples are being referred to here.

13. *Shanxi tongzhi* (Siku quanshu Wenyuan ge intranet edition), 165.5a.

Fig. 11 Zhang Zhennan showing the dimensions of the
Flowery Offering in the Guandi Temple, Zhangzi town
(SOURCE: photograph David Johnson).

where various parts of the temple had once stood. When the dimensions were paced off, they were roughly 120 by 195 feet.[14] According to
Zhang, the main hall of the temple was five bays wide and very lofty. A
seated image of Hou Yi was in the middle, flanked on one side by a local rain god not known elsewhere, and on the other by a goddess whom
Zhang speculates may have been Hou Yi's wife, Chang E, the goddess
of the moon. The tile roof had upturned eaves, and the ridge was decorated with glazed figures of auspicious animals. All the flying brackets
and the interior rafters and purlins were carved and painted. There were
"moon gates" on either side of the main hall, and directly in front of it

---

14. That is, 40 by 65 paces. Interview transcripts, p. 3 (with reconstructed plan).

was a large open hexagonal structure with a colorfully decorated ceiling called the Incense Pavilion (*xiang ting*), where all the offering rituals took place. (We have encountered similar structures, though not hexagonal, in both the Divine Mother and Mt. Longquan temples; it appears to have been a feature of all *sai* temples and many other large temples in southern Shanxi.) To the east and west of the main hall were three-bay halls, one dedicated to Guan Di, the other to the Dragon King. Beyond those halls were two smaller three-bay rooms that faced each other across the courtyard: the eastern one was the Libation Master's Room and the western one the Master of Ceremonial's Room—the offices of the men who presided over the *sai*.

Extending to the south of these rooms, completing the eastern and western sides of the courtyard, were two long buildings, each of thirteen bays. The northernmost five bays in the eastern building formed the Chamber for Receiving Officials, and its counterpart on the west side was called the Chamber for Welcoming Guests. The next five bays in the eastern building were made into a room called the Chamber of Timely Rains, and its counterpart on the west was called the Chamber of Towering Clouds. According to Zhang, these two rooms were decorated with antique porcelains and bronzes, jade carvings, and other *objets d'art*, while calligraphy and paintings by famous masters hung on the walls. The rooms were so beautiful that visitors would just stand gazing in silence, reluctant to move on.[15] The southernmost three bays of the eastern building formed the Room for Overseeing Food, and its counterpart on the west was called the Accounts Room.

The courtyard was bounded on the south by a two-story brick structure through which the main entrance ran, like a gate in a city wall. Directly above that, facing the courtyard, was the stage. On each side of the stage was a three-bay room, the one on the east called the Abbot's Room, the one on the west the Great Kitchen. The rafters and brackets of the stage were decorated with carvings of flowers, trees, birds, animals, and characters from opera, and further embellished with large plaques. One that hung from the front eave said "Building for Entertain-

---

15. Zhang Zhennan, "Yueju yu sai," p. 241. As mentioned in the preceding chapter, there was a similar room in the Hou Yi Temple on Mt. Longquan.

ing the Gods" (*wu shen lou*), and another in the middle of the back wall
had large gold characters reading "Building for Dancing for Rain" (*wu yu
lou*). Large clay statues of seated guardian gods flanked the temple's entrance. They were about twelve feet tall and dressed in armor, "with glar-
ing eyes, angry expressions, and magnificent appearance, so that when
people looked at them they were scared to death."[16] Just south of the
main entrance was a single-arch stone bridge, called the Bridge of Rising
Clouds. About fifty yards south of the bridge and facing north (and thus
facing the main altar of the temple) was a large, beautifully decorated
seven-bay stage. It was there that the *bangzi* operas, or "big operas"—
extremely popular with the people, but with no ritual significance—were
performed, both during the *sai* and at other times. (The temple stage was
reserved for the operas performed by the Entertainers.)[17]

A month before the *sai* was to begin, a respected and powerful elder
was chosen by the villagers to have overall control. His formal title was
Master of Sacrificial Wine (*zhu chang*), but he was popularly called "Old
Shê Head" (*lao shêshou*).[18] According to Zhang Zhennan, the *zhu chang*
selected the Entertainers, the Master of Ceremonial, the chefs, and the
standard opera troupe or troupes in addition to the villagers who would
take part, such as the Pavilioners, Incense Elders, and skilled craftsmen
like carpenters and painters.[19]

As we have seen, *sai* were imagined as gods' birthday celebrations—
in this case Hou Yi's. Invitations were sent to gods of neighboring "streets" and villages, presumably those more or less of Hou Yi's
class.[20] On the third day of the sixth month, after a ritual called "Greeting the Water" (*jie shui*), whose function is unclear, all the high *sai*

---

16. Zhang Zhennan, "Yueju he sai," p. 3B.

17. This description combines Zhang Zhennan's accounts in "Yueju he sai," pp. 3B–
4A, and "Yueju yu sai," pp. 238–39.

18. Zhang Zhennan, "Yueju he sai," p. 4A.

19. It seems unlikely that all the organizational work fell on the *zhu chang*'s shoulders,
as Zhang says. I expect that there was some sort of committee or board to manage
what was after all an extremely complex undertaking, and that the *zhu chang* was the
head of it.

20. The details of how the guest lists were worked out, like the history of the various village alliances, would provide invaluable information about local society in the
region, but I have found virtually no evidence bearing on these questions.

officials went to the Earth God Temple, where the Director of the Entertainers recited several verses and the Earth God was requested to inform the gods invited to the *sai* that they should gather at the temple of
the Flame Emperor (Yan Di)—Shen Nong—also called the High
North Temple (Bei gao miao), in Zhangzi.[21] A ritual called "Running to
the Sun" was performed, and the musicians played *qupo*.[22] They returned to the main temple, and the Pavilioners drew lots to see which
god they would have responsibility for.[23] Then each set about arranging
on his god's table, probably in the main hall, an incense burner and a
screen. (The screen probably was behind the tablet, the incense burner
certainly in front.) Each god also had two Table Bearers (*han tai zhuo*)
and one Moonshade Handler (*da yue zhao*) in attendance.[24]

THE PROCESSION AND THE
FLOWERY OFFERING SCULPTURE

On the morning of the fourth day of the sixth month, the traveling
image of Hou Yi, carried in his palanquin by eight men and accompanied by musicians, was taken from his temple to the temple of the
Flame Emperor. There he awaited the spirit tablets or palanquins of
the gods of the surrounding villages who were responding to his invita-

---

21. Zhang Zhennan, "Yueju yu sai," p. 237.

22. Interview with Feng Guiyu, p. 121. What was called "Drenching the Sun" (*paò* 泡
taiyang) by the Longquan *sai* informants is here called "Running to the Sun" (*paǒ* 跑 *taiyang*). Since I have been unable to discover what happened during this ritual, I do not
know which is the correct word, although "running" makes a good deal more sense.
Qupo was the name for a combination of music and dance in Tang times, but after
Northern Song it came to be synonymous with "Grand Melodies" (*da qu*). *Qupo* were
also used in the Ming and Qing opera genres *Kunqu* and *Chuanqi*. How the term happens to crop up in Shanxi village rituals is a mystery. See Qi Senhua et al., *Zhongguo
quxue da cidian*, p. 31A–B.

23. This is one of several passages in the description of the Big West Gate *sai* that
closely resemble passages in the description of the Mt. Longquan *sai*. Since Zhang
Zhennan was an important source for both, it is possible that one of the accounts was
padded with material from the other. If so, I believe that the West Gate description
should be considered the primary one. (Of course, the two *sai* may simply have been
similar.)

24. Zhang Zhennan and Bao Haiyan, "Feng Guiyu," p. 122.

tion.[25] In the mid-afternoon, all of them processed to Hou Yi's temple. This procession was much longer and more impressive than the morning one, since it included the palanquins of the invited gods and dozens of "acts." People came from twenty *li* around to see the spectacle, wearing new clothes and "as excited as at New Year's." They lined the route of the procession; from time to time someone would say it was coming, and everyone would rush to get close to the road. When the procession finally came (at around 3 P.M.), "it wound through the streets and alleys like a blue-green dragon," accompanied by the booming drums and wailing shawms of many bands. "The crowds undulated like waves" as they tried to see the spectacle.

Because all the young parents on the street wanted their toddlers [to see, they] lifted them up. So above the crowd there appeared a layer of children's caps, with [colorful] new patterns . . . setting off [the babies'] smiling faces. Add to that the glorious sun and fragrant breezes of the early sixth month, so gentle and comfortable, and one couldn't help but feel an exhilarating happiness.[26]

The procession began with an honor guard of old musicians. The first pair carried red placards with the words "Stand Aside!" and "Silence!"; the second pair carried banners on which were written "Pure Way" and "Flying Tiger." The rest carried implements with fanciful names such as "Golden Melons" and "Big Marsh Fans." All this ritual paraphernalia came from the Laozi Temple in Nanzhuang village, about a mile and a half away. This honor guard was an old custom, and it led the procession no matter which street was the sponsor of the *sai*.

After the honor guard came martial arts troupes led by strong men brandishing rope whips who walked in single file to clear the way; they were followed by men naked from the waist up dueling with short spears, "boxing," and brandishing swords, "making people's blood run

---

25. As above, the description that follows combines Zhang's accounts in "Yueju he sai" and "Yueju yu sai." Most is close paraphrase, but passages I feel are especially important are translated, set off by quotation marks, and an exact citation given.

26. Dragon: Zhang Zhennan, "Yueju yu sai," p. 249; babies: idem, "Yueju he sai," p. 5B. These comments are precious evidence of the impact a *sai* had on ordinary people—including Zhang Zhennan, whose memories were still vivid after fifty years.

cold."[27] They were followed by the palanquins of the Five Honored Gods, known locally as the "Little Framework Lords," led by Dharma Cymbals and Altar Drums. The gods had clay heads with faces painted red, white, blue, black, and yellow, and wore hats and robes over wooden framework bodies.

Then came a troupe of flute players whose music "sounded like the wind," leading the "Springy Four-Man Palanquin." This was made of folded padded satin quilts and padded satin mattresses, and was about a yard square. In the middle of the palanquin were seated two porcelain dolls, secured with cords made of colored silk floss. Antique vases, jade mirrors, and other old objects carved from wood or stone were attached to the sides. The palanquin was supported by flexible wooden poles wrapped with colored silk. The young men carrying it wore white gowns open to the waist, exposing their decorated undershirts. Taking such high steps that they looked like they were going to lose their balance, they rhythmically bounced the palanquin up and down so that the tassels on its corners flew about.

Next came the "Stiff Four-Man Palanquin," which also was preceded by a troupe of musicians playing softly. The stiff palanquin was made of wood and was shaped like a square pagoda. It had brightly painted designs on each side and was decorated with silk, flowers, and mirrors. At the top was attached an object like a feather duster, made of the tail feathers of roosters, over a yard long, to symbolize the palanquin's cloud-brushing height. Strips of colored cloth hung down all around, tangling and fluttering.[28] Before each palanquin came a band, and after it several "spirit horses," fully saddled and bridled, with flowers on their heads, which were provided for the gods to ride.

There were any number of "Lifted Characters." In these, an iron frame with a long iron rod extending above it was tied securely to a strong young man and hidden under his clothes. Then a boy or girl in costume was tied to the rod in such a way that he or she could freely sing, gesture, and speak in midair, six feet or more above the ground.

---

27. Zhang Zhennan, "Yueju yu sai," p. 250.

28. This is very reminiscent of the Four-Scene Carts at the Divine Mother *sai*, although of course on a smaller scale.

(They first put on their makeup, then were secured to the rod, and finally put on their costumes.)[29] There also were "Shouldered Characters." These were square platforms like tables that were about a yard on a side and were carried by two men. A specially shaped iron rod was fixed securely in the platform, and a girl was tied to its upper end while a boy stood on the table beneath her, the costumes of both concealing the rod. Each platform presented a well-known acrobatic scene from a popular opera, and apparently the scenes came in sets of four.[30] All the performers were youths of about fifteen years of age.

In addition, many "little stories" were crowded in between the more elaborate regular "stories." These included "Golden Buildings," "Silver Sunshades," "Solitary Dragon Colts," "Stilt Walkers," "Double Stilt Walkers," "The Son Pulls the Basket,"[31] "Boats on Dry Land," "Two Demons Fight Over a Bushel Basket," and so on. The Golden Buildings and Silver Sunshades had all sorts of women's and children's gold and silver jewelry hanging on them. As they were carried along, the natural movements of the bearers made the jewelry tinkle, creating, according to Zhang, an extraordinarily attractive effect.

Just ahead of the palanquin of Hou Yi came a troupe of ten or more musicians and a group of actors dressed as generals. There was one generalissimo wearing a commander's helmet, green armor, a long beard, and court boots, accompanied by four lesser generals holding aloft fluttering banners. They rode five of the large horses used by the opera troupe to pull the carts containing their costume and prop trunks. Behind these "generals" came the Golden Drum Banner, which had

---

29. We have already encountered this type of float in the Divine Mother *sai*.

30. Zhang mentions four operas from which scenes were presented in this way; all were martial or mythological romances, as one would expect given the presence of female characters. Incidentally, these were not *sai* operas. A beautiful New Year's print from Mianzhu, about sixty kilometers north of Chengdu in Sichuan, mentioned earlier, shows a procession with displays that look almost exactly like the "shouldered characters" (see Gao Wen et al., eds., *Mianzhu nianhua*, pls. 126, 130).

31. A traditional didactic story in which a man pulls his bedridden father out into the fields in a basket, planning to abandon him. The man's son, who has come along, reminds his father not to forget to bring the basket back. When the man asks why, his son replies that he will need it when the time comes to abandon *him*. The man then sees that it is an evil thing and brings his father back home.

been sent by the yamen. Two yamen runners went before it carrying a big banner and a hanging gong, and some of the others carried lictor boards.[32]

The Master of Ceremonial and all the other officiants came next, followed by the great carriage of Hou Yi, the San Zong god, whose formal title was "Brilliance-Manifesting Nation-Protecting Divinely-Providing King." The god's head was of clay, which made possible fine modeling of his features, and he wore a gold headdress and dragon robes. He was seated in an eight-man palanquin on a throne covered with real tiger skin. He had a red face and a long beard and held a plaque of office in his hands. Bringing up the rear of the procession was a man carrying a yellow silk sunshade and another carrying a six-foot-long banner, red with black edges, on which were the words "Arbiter of Destiny of the Three Armies."

When the procession reached the Big West Gate Temple, most of the "story" troupes took off their costumes and left. Only the musicians and other ritual personnel entered the temple grounds, presumably with the palanquins of Hou Yi and the other gods.[33]

There were eight or twelve offering tables in the Offering Pavilion. The "permanent offerings," which remained in place for all three days of the festival proper, were placed on the inner section of the tables, and the Cup offerings, which were regularly replenished, were placed on the outer sections, along with an incense burner and candle stands.[34] The permanent offerings were also called the Complete Manchu-Chinese Banquet (*Man Han quan xi*).[35] There were thirty-six dishes in each part of the banquet.[36] For the Chinese banquet, local dishes such

---

32. Baoban. I have not been able to discover a description of these and the translation is tentative.

33. Zhang says nothing about how the tablets (or statues) of the invited gods got from the Flame Emperor Temple to the Hou Yi Temple. Nor, for that matter, does he say how the guest gods traveled to the Flame Emperor Temple from their home temples.

34. Zhang Zhennan, "Yueju yu sai," p. 241.

35. According to the ritual chef Song Changshan, this was also called the *mao yan*, a term we saw used to denote an especially rich three-Cup offering in the Longquan *sai* (Zhang Zhennan and Bao Haiyan, "Song Changshan," p. 283).

36. Zhang Zhennan says thirty-two in "Yueju yu sai," p. 241; the number thirty-six comes from Song Changshan's biography by Zhang and Bao Haiyan, p. 282.

as "red and white ham" and "crisp meatballs" were prepared,[37] but the Manchu banquet featured exotic fare—a villager's idea of imperial cuisine, perhaps. For example, there was a "tortoise platter" (pork and pork fat in the shape of a tortoise), a "snake platter" (an entire pig's intestine made to look like a snake), and a "man platter" (a plucked chicken, sans head and feet, with a small clay head of an old man stuck in the neck).[38] The serving dishes used for the permanent offerings were of earthenware or porcelain; the others (the "platters") were made of wood.[39]

All this obviously called for a high degree of skill in the chefs, as did the many other dishes they had to prepare, which are described below, but the triumph of their art was a great screen called the Flowery Offering (*hua ji*).[40] According to the ritual chef Song Changshan (b. 1922), the chefs arrived over ten days before the *sai* was to begin. On the first day, they built the stove and lit it, and then mixed the flour for the *hua ji* and other sculptures. Each batch consisted of sixty *jin* of wheat flour with the proper amount of water. Turmeric, which produced a golden color, and malt sugar, which made the finished objects hard, were added, and everything mixed and kneaded together. This would be repeated three or four times for a great *sai*, so nearly 250 *jin* or approximately 275 lbs of flour might be used. The mixture was rolled out into sheets, which were cut into squares.[41] Various designs were carved into the tiles with small sharp knives; where the cuts were deepest, the tiles became translucent. The tiles were deep-fried until they were hard and golden-

---

37. Song Changshan's biography names a few familiar Chinese restaurant dishes for the Chinese banquet, including sweet and sour fish(!).

38. Manuscript biography of Song Changshan, pp. 36–37, in the author's collection. The parallel section of the printed biography, Zhang Zhennan and Bao Haiyan, "Song Changshan," p. 283, differs in some details.

39. Manuscript biography, p. 39.

40. The description of the *hua ji* is taken from Zhang Zhennan, "Yueju yu sai," pp. 239–40, and the biography of Song Changshan by Zhang Zhennan and Bao Haiyan, "Song Changshan," p. 283. Much of my language is a very close paraphrase of the Chinese.

41. One source says they were six inches square, but I suspect they were often somewhat larger than that. See the interview with Mr. Zhang Zhiqun, Oct. 17, 1993 (interview transcripts, p. 45).

colored. After they cooled, they were attached one by one to a framework. When completed, it was nearly ten feet high and over sixteen feet wide. It was set up between the Offering Pavilion and the main hall of the temple. In effect, it served to demarcate the inner and outer altars or sacred spaces. It was further decorated with blossoms and leaves made of colored paper. To quote Zhang Zhennan, who certainly had seen the *hua ji* at the Big West Gate temple, it looked like "level upon level of mansions and pavilions, with terraces and verandas everywhere. It was superbly beautiful, dazzling and overwhelming the onlookers."[42]

The chefs also fashioned many small figures no more than eight inches high, with clay heads and paper bodies made with great skill, representing characters from operas. They were attached to the *hua ji* about six feet from the ground. There were seven or eight scenes, each with three to five characters.[43] This spectacle attracted crowds of onlookers: "they examined every part with great care and discussed the high points with one another."[44]

That such elaborate works of art were created for the great *sai* tells us all we need to know about the talent and creativity of village artisans. Using everyday materials, they gave brilliant expression to the imaginative universe of the townsmen and farmers. Opera was a big part of it, and those ordinary people engaged in intense discussions of the fine points of the *hua ji* are the best possible illustration of the process by which key scenes from famous operas became deeply embedded in popular consciousness.[45] But quite apart from their iconographic content, the *hua ji* allowed villagers and townsmen to directly experience what we would call art. They could examine the skillfully carved scenes at leisure and if they were lucky, take a tile home at the end of the festival. It is deeply moving to imagine unlettered, work-worn farmers and their families looking intently at the tableaux on the *hua ji* (or for that

---

42. Zhang Zhennan, "Yueju yu sai," p. 240.

43. Zhang mentions six titles in "Yueju yu sai," and more titles in other versions of the essay. All those I can identify are historical operas.

44. Zhang Zhennan, "Yueju he sai," p. 4B.

45. See Johnson, "Actions Speak Louder Than Words," p. 32, where such scenes are called "tableaux."

matter gazing into the gorgeously decorated Chambers of Timely Rains and Towering Clouds). They may have been the most beautiful things those people ever saw. This is why, to me, the *hua ji* are the central symbol of the *sai*.[46]

THE RITUAL BANQUET

The Cup offerings were just as important at Big West Gate as at other *sai*, but since I described them in detail earlier, I will not describe them here. However, Zhang Zhennan offers some valuable details not found in other accounts. The musicians played in the Offering Pavilion while the food was being presented. They wore flat headdresses with golden bands and a pheasant feather at the right temple, and long, green-trimmed red robes with collars. The Director wore a black gauze official's hat and high court shoes, and had a long beard hanging down from his mouth. (This sounds very much like a stage costume.) When a Cup was offered, the musicians entered first, led by the Director. They were followed by the Old *Shê* Head carrying an incense burner, and by the Masters of Incense and Candles, the Incense Elders, the Water Officials, the Pavilioners, and the Ushers, immaculate and silent. The Pavilioners were carrying the gods' tablets and had flowers clenched in their teeth. All the officiants went around and across the courtyard, ending in the center. As the Master of Ceremonial read hymns (*ci*) to Hou Yi, wine and tea were offered to the gods' tablets, which were being held by the Pavilioners. The Director intoned a prayer, and then as the entire company processed around the Offering Pavilion, the Master of Ceremonial read the following sacrificial writ.

Take thought: men are not gods and are unable to assist in their own protection. Gods are not men and are always able to help people live in peace. Therefore those who in gratitude sacrifice to the god with sincere hearts are able

---

46. As noted in Chapter 1 of Part I, elaborate dough sculptures, although not on the scale of the *hua ji*, played an important role in establishing the ritual space in the Fandrum ceremony celebrating the New Year in Renzhuang village in southwestern Shanxi. Shanxi dough sculptures should not be imagined as lumpy or heavy; they could be remarkably intricate and delicate, truly an impressive folk art form. See references, Part I, Chapter 1, *n*38.

to request and receive the descent of good fortune[47] and the bestowal of blessings.

The West Gate quarter of the county town of Zhangzi has a temple to the [San] Zong god, where the four streets and five *shê* of the city take it in turns to put on a *sai* and make offerings.[48]

Standing before the honored god, Brilliance-Manifesting, Nation-Protecting, Divinely-Providing, we say: Your merit [was established] during the Xia dynasty when you assisted the rule of Yao. You controlled the lightning and pacified the thunder, the great virtue of which has not diminished over a thousand years. You speared the wind and shot [arrows at] the suns, the mighty merit of which is still fresh after a hundred generations. All beings with blood and breath honor and love you.

At this time it is the sixth day of the sixth lunar month, the birthday of the revered spirit. According to principle, we ought to abstain [from that which should be abstained from] and cleanse ourselves, and sincerely sacrifice. We respectfully offer for the god's enjoyment one troupe performing [ritual] *yue*[*hu*] opera [i.e., *Dui* Opera] and one troupe, the Yue Yi Troupe, performing [non-ritual] grand opera [i.e., Shanxi *bangzi*], and also the Incense Assembly [the procession] and the *Shê* Displays [the "floats" and the like in the procession], to requite the great virtue of the honored god's eternal and universal bestowal of timely rains and the merit of his making people and livestock secure. We humbly entreat the god to bestow his great favor without limit on later generations, and to let the myriad people feel his virtue for thousands and tens of thousands of years without end.[49]

Granted that this text does not have the important function of the "Writ of Commands" recited at the start of the Longquan *sai* (and, probably, at every *sai*), I still think the difference in tone is significant. The "Writ of Commands" was written in what was evidently intended to be elevated prose and was laden with Confucian sentiments and classical references. This address to the same god is a straightforward declaration of the gratitude of the people for the god's protection, praise for his powers, and a description of what people are doing to thank him. It is plainspoken, without tensions or anxiety. This might be

---

47. Reading 祥 for 詳.

48. As we have seen, Zhang Zhennan speaks of *five* streets as the organizing units; it may be that he used "street" as this text uses *shê*.

49. Zhang Zhennan, "Yueju yu sai," p. 242. No source is given for the text.

because its function in the ritual was more routine than the "Writ of Commands"; but it might also be because townspeople, not farmers, were the primary audience, and townsfolk are unlikely to be quite as anxious about the weather, and the mood of the weather gods, as farmers.

After the address to the god was read, the Master of Ceremonial ordered that the offerings begin. There were a large number of these, as we have seen in the other *sai*. But whereas the dishes offered in the Mt. Longquan *sai*, according to the ritual manual, were fairly simple, the ones offered at the Big West Gate *sai*, according to the testimony of one of the chefs, were extremely elaborate. We have already encountered the Manchu-Chinese banquet with its seventy-two dishes. If this served the function of the triple *mao yan* Cups, as seems possible, it may even have been presented on each of the three days of the *sai* proper. In addition to that, hundreds and hundreds of something like snacks were prepared, plus seventy-two platters for the Mounting and Dismounting Feasts and twenty platters of "dry" and "wet" dishes. Song Changshan, a former ritual chef, listed the following dishes and their amounts:[50]

800 Golden Inches (each about two inches long and half an inch thick, made of dough first steamed and then deep-fried, representing ingots of gold);
400 Connected Buns (steamed in pairs);
120 Preserved Egg Cakes;
120 Sun-and-Moon Cakes;
120 White Tip Cakes;
80 Small Long Life Peaches (steamed, with the ends colored red);
40 Green Hairy Turtles (steamed in the shape of a turtle and colored green);
160 Fish of Two Colors (80 red and 80 yellow);
40 Three-cornered Candies (wrapped and sealed with a hot iron);
120 Plum Blossom Cakes (steamed in the shape of plum blossoms and colored red);
100 Large Sesame Candies (deep fried, one inch by two inches);
2,500 Small Sesame Candies (half the size of the preceding);

----

50. He was describing what he had cooked for a *sai* at West Baotou village, but since he had worked at nearly every *sai* in Zhangzi county, the food offerings at Big West Gate were probably similar, although I expect there were more of them.

500 Hydrangea Frycakes (deep fried, with a hydrangea design pressed into the top);

100 Long Frycakes (bar-shaped, one inch by two inches);

5 platters of Five-Color Frycakes (like the preceding, but with five colors);

100 Linked Rings (made of deep-fried noodles);

10 platters of "Dry Offerings" (vegetarian);

10 platters of "Wet Offerings" (non-vegetarian);

36 platters for the Mounting Feast (vegetarian); and

36 platters for the Dismounting Feast (vegetarian).

In addition there were large quantities of steamed bread, rice, red dates, a kind of orange, lychees, and yellow pears, plus large amounts of tea and wine.[51]

Few things can bring home the scale of the great *sai* more powerfully than this list. Zhang Zhennan describes the scene:

With the offering of every Cup, there were many elaborate and diverse rituals. . . . When the reading of the prayer was over, the food offerings were presented. The musicians played, and the food was sent out from the kitchen, vegetarian and non-vegetarian dishes carefully separated. . . . There were boiled, oil-fried, smoked, and steamed dishes, glasses of tea and cups of wine, platter upon platter, dish upon dish, oranges and gingko, pears and dates.[52]

There were, of course, also operas, but I have already described *Sai* operas in considerable detail, and Zhang has nothing new to add. He also mentions a series of rituals or ritual skits, such as the Release of Living Beings, the Inspection of the Kitchen, the Mounting and Dismounting rituals, the drawing of a gigantic charm with wheat bran, the flicking of water in the four directions by the Master of Ceremonial, the skit called *The Monkey Sheds His Husk*, the Hopping *Tanzi*, the sending off of the gods, and the final divination with a ram's horn, all of which have already been described in the section on the Longquan *sai*.[53]

---

51. Manuscript biography of Song Changshan, pp. 38–39.

52. Zhang Zhennan, "Yueju yu sai," p. 242, supplemented by Zhang's manuscript, "Gu Shangdang," p. 10. The words translated as "oranges," "pears," and "dates" are 枳元, 交梨, and 火棗. I am not sure of the exact meaning of these words and have given approximations.

53. Zhang Zhennan obviously had experienced the Big West Gate *sai* personally. Even fifty years later he was able to point out where the temple had been, the location

What is unique about the evidence for the Big West Gate *sai*, in addition to the vivid descriptions of the temple and the procession, is the detailed information about the food offerings. If the operas and processions had an overwhelming impact in the realm of the imagination, the symbolic world, the sight of the fantastic array of food offerings must have had a powerful physical, indeed visceral, impact on the village audience. The people who squeezed into the temple courtyard were accustomed to a simple diet. They feasted at New Year's and at important family events such as weddings and funerals, but never did they see the kinds of dishes served at the *sai* (with some exceptions in the Chinese part of the Manchu-Chinese Banquet), or the quantities. Probably only a few people understood the words of the Master of Ceremonial, and most are likely to have preferred the Shanxi *bangzi* operas performed outside the temple to the unsophisticated operas performed on the temple stage. But everyone could relate directly to the food offerings; this was a symbolic form people intuitively understood. And because the dishes offered to the gods were ones they themselves could (and did) eat, the celebration of the god's birthday ceased to be metaphorical and came to life. This was one more way in which the gods were brought into the human world, and people were enabled to directly engage with them, in the villages of southeastern Shanxi.

---

of the *hua ji* in the Guan Di Temple (the site of the merchants' *sai*—it is still standing), and other details. He probably witnessed the Mt. Longquan *sai* as well, since it was not far from Zhangzi.

Conclusion

The chapters on the Divine Mother, Mt. Longquan, and Big West Gate *sai* provide thick descriptions of both spectacle and sacrifice—the processions, the operas, and the food offerings of the great temple festivals of southeastern Shanxi—together with detailed information on the specialists without whom a *sai* was not a *sai*: the Entertainers, the Masters of Ceremonial, and the chefs. All this should make permanently untenable the assumptions (conscious or unconscious) on which so many theories of Chinese history and society have been based, that "Chinese peasants" lived in a simple world where they labored only to stay alive, were powerless to act in their own interest (except when unbearable conditions drove them to rebel), were uneducated and thus incapable of managing complex undertakings, and were so beaten down by life that they did not have the imaginative energy to create their own symbolic world but had to make do with customs inherited from their ancestors and what they were taught by their betters; that they were faceless, voiceless, passive, unknowable, and irrelevant, and therefore could be ignored.

But once one stops ignoring the country folk and begins to pay close attention to their world, questions begin to arise. There are many, but the one that seems most in need of an answer is as follows. The most notable characteristics of the *sai* are their scope, complexity, and historical depth. Now, given independence from ideological or religious authority, a certain amount of disposable income, a foundational belief that the gods can affect people's lives and are responsive to generous and respectful treatment, a rich tradition of story and song, and plenty of time, villagers in many places could probably have created the sort of extravagant displays that we saw in the *sai* processions; indeed, we know they did. But the *rituals* of the *sai* are a different matter. They were not the natural products of an exuberant folk imagination but rather were created by the Masters of Ceremonial. We have only a few of the liturgical manuscripts on which the *sai* were based, but it is clear that the ones we do have were related to one another and were part of some sort of ritual tradition, although it is very poorly understood. How did that system (if it was a system) originate? Where did this complex ritual repertoire of, by, and for north Chinese villagers come from? The more fully one is persuaded of the importance of the *sai*, the more pressing this question becomes.

In an earlier publication,[1] I suggested that a given ritual handbook could have been created by an educated resident of a village "on the basis of liturgical texts intended for other purposes, or in imitation of important public or domestic ceremonies."[2] Possible textual models were the *Xingli daquan*, an official Qing dynasty ritual compendium, and, at the other end of the textual spectrum, Zhu Xi's *Family Rituals*. Likely candidates among public ceremonies were the Community Libation ritual (*xiang yinjiu li*), the Community Compact (*xiang yue*), and sacrifices to the ancestors. Further research made it clear that the opposition between texts that were read and ceremonies that were observed was overly schematic. There was a fairly broad range of texts, from the complex to the simplified, and an extremely broad range of rituals that could have been observed by one segment or another of the population. In what follows I will discuss briefly three rituals that were the province of the socio-educational elite, and two that were performed by and for villagers. It will be seen that they all have elements in common and could easily have had some role in the formation of *sai* rituals.

---

1. Johnson, "'Confucian' Elements in the Great Temple Festivals," pp. 160–61.

2. For examples of such works, not necessarily created by villagers but certainly aimed at a popular audience, see Hayes, "Specialists and Written Materials," pp. 81–82, 100–103; and Brokaw, *Commerce in Culture*, p. 622, index entry "Ritual handbooks."

In Zhu Xi's *Family Rituals* the most elaborate form of ancestral sacrifice is called the "Sacrifices for the Four Seasons."[3] Note the main headings of the rite:

1. Sacrifice in the second month; divine to choose the day.
2. "Three days before the event, practice purification."
3. "One day before the event, set the places and arrange the utensils."
4. "Inspect the animal offerings, clean the utensils, and prepare the food."
5. On the day, set out the food offerings early in the morning.
6. "When the sun is fully out, take the spirit tablets to their places."
7. "Greet the spirits" (*can shen*).
8. "Invoke the spirits" (*jiang shen*).
9. "Present the food" (*jin zhuan*).
10. "Make the first offering" (*chu xian*).
11. "Make the second offering" (*ya xian*).
12. "Make the final offering" (*zhong xian*).
13. "Urge the spirits to eat."
14. "Close the door."
15. "Open the door."
16. "Receive the sacrificial foods."
17. "Take leave of the spirits" (*ci shen*).
18. "Put the tablets back."
19. "Clear away the remains."
20. "Eat the leftovers."[4]

In later centuries, dozens of versions of Zhu Xi's book were produced that were intended to be easier to use than the original.[5] One very influential late fifteenth-century popularization provided "a list of

---

3. For general background see Ebrey, trans., *Chu Hsi's* Family Rituals; idem, *Confucianism and Family Rituals*.

4. Ebrey, trans., *Chu Hsi's* Family Rituals, pp. 155–66. In the interest of brevity, I have used a combination of quotation from and paraphrase of Ebrey's translation.

5. This is a perfect example, by the way, of how an important intellectual or religious or even technical system could come to exist in a number of versions, each produced by or for an important social-cultural group, a process I describe in "Communication, Class, and Consciousness," pp. 71–72.

people and equipment to secure in advance" of each ritual, together with what amounted to a script to be used by the Master(s) of Ceremony (*li sheng*).[6] Another important early modification of Zhu Xi's model, the use of ritual experts who called out commands to the participants, may have been inspired by local performances of state sacrifices.[7] This is analogous to my suggestion that some aspects of *sai* ritual could have been inspired by village public ceremonies. Other changes included burning paper "spirit money" and omitting the opening and closing of the door to the ancestors' "room" while they ate.[8] These were added to (or subtracted from) "the core elements," which, according to Ebrey, were "purification, invoking the spirits, . . . pouring libations of wine to them, the triple offering with a woman making the second offering, use of written prayers, [and] the offering of a varied meal including cooked meat, grain, and vegetables."[9]

Rituals of the Qing state cult celebrated by officials in county and prefectural capitals are fairly well known because local gazetteers frequently provide liturgies for them. In the Guangxu edition of the *Shanxi Provincial Gazetteer*, there are many such, including one for the annual sacrifice to Guan Yu.[10] It begins by saying that the participants should purify themselves for two days, and everything should be put in order on the day before the ritual. It lists the three sacrificial animals and the many sacrificial utensils to be used. This is followed by a series of commands from the Sacrificer (*cheng ji guan*), the Ritualist (*dian yi*), and the two Cantors (*zan li lang*)—who presumably speak alternately—which I translate below.[11]

Early on the day of the ritual the officiants assembled in the temple and the ceremony began:

---

6. Ebrey, *Confucianism and Family Rituals*, p. 174. For the term *li sheng*, see below, *n*19.
7. Ibid., pp. 172–73.
8. Ibid., p. 189.
9. Ibid., p. 184.
10. *Shanxi tongzhi* (1892 ed.). The Guan Yu liturgy can be found in *juan* 41, pp. 5040–41.
11. The connecting "stage directions" are either translated, paraphrased, or omitted in the interest of brevity. The language outside the parentheses is translated from the text. The words in parentheses are summaries, based directly on the text. I have added the material in square brackets.

RITUALIST: Singers and dancers, perform the song of the *sheng deng*.[12] All participating officials, singly and jointly take your places.

CANTOR: Take your places! Welcome the god! Offer up music to greet the god! Ascend to the incense position! (*He leads the Sacrificer up the eastern steps to his place before the incense altar.*) Present the incense! (*The Incense Master* [si xiang] *gives it to the Sacrificer, who presents incense three times.*) Resume your places! Make obeisances and arise!

RITUALIST: Present the silk and wine, proceed with the first sacrifice. (*There is a prayer, a dance, and the wine vessel is filled with wine.*)

CANTOR (*after leading the Sacrificer up the eastern steps*): Go before the spirit tablet! Bow! (*The Master of Silk and Master of Wine place a basket of silk and the wine vessel on the altar with appropriate obeisances and withdraw. Then the Master of Prayers approaches the altar and offers the prayer tablet on the left of the altar. The Sacrificer is ordered by the Cantor to bow. The Master of Prayers is ordered to read the prayers, does so, places the prayer tablet on the altar, makes obeisance, and withdraws.*) [*To the Sacrificer:*] Prostrate yourself and arise!

RITUALIST: Proceed with the second offering. (*There is a dance, music is played, and wine is offered at the left of the altar, as in the first offering.*)

Ritualist: Proceed with the final offering! (*There is a dance, music is played, and wine is offered at the right of the altar, as in the second offering. The music stops and the dancers withdraw.*)

RITUALIST: Drink the [Wine of] Blessings and receive the meat.

CANTOR: Go to the place for receiving the [Wine of] Blessings and the meat! (*He leads the Sacrificer to the place of obeisance in the middle of the hall. The wine and meat are brought to the altar and the Cantor commands the Sacrificer:*) Bow! Drink the Wine of Blessings! (*An assistant on the right gives him the wine, he offers it, then gives it to an assistant on the left, who receives it and rises. The same is done with the meat.*)

CANTOR [*to the Sacrificer*]: Prostrate yourself and arise! Resume your place! (*After three prostrations and nine head knockings by the Sacrificer and his assistants, the Ritualist says:*) Remove the food. (*A text is read, music is played, and the food is removed.*)

RITUALIST: Bid farewell to the god (*song shen*). (*Another text is read, more music is played, more obeisances are made.*) Present the prayers, silk, and food and send

---

12. A *deng* was a round, covered container with a foot. I have not been able to identify the *sheng deng*. Note that Incense Master (just below) was also a *sai* officer.

them to be burned. (*Preparations are made, and then he says:*) Watch the burning. (*The Cantor leads the Sacrificer to watch the burning of the sacrifices.*)

This ended the sacrifice to Guan Yu ritual.

Official Ming and Qing sacrifices to Confucius have been well described by Thomas Wilson. Here is his "schematic account":

[There was] a preparatory fast two or three days before the rite, then, in the first two hours after midnight on the morning of the ceremony, the ritual instructors, officers, and assistants arranged the vessels and offerings in front of the altar. Drums were sounded, the gates opened, and the blood and fur of the victims buried outside the main gate. The musicians, dancers, and consecration officers then assumed their assigned positions in the temple grounds. Music was played, the novices danced on the front platform, and hymns were chanted while the spirit was escorted to the temple (*yingshen*). The consecration officer . . . moved in front of the altar, performed a sequence of a bow, prostration, rising, prostration, rising, stood erect to present silk, incense, and libation, and then resumed his position at the foot of the stairs. A prayer (*zhu*) was then sung, and the silk, libation, and prayer were placed on the altar. . . . The consecration officer . . . repeated his libation offering . . . a total of three times (*sanxian*). [He] drank some of the blessed wine and received a portion of the sacrificial meat. The assisting consecration officers proceeded to the altar in front of each of the spirit tablets to move the sacrificial vessels slightly, indicating completion of the ceremony. The spirit was bidden farewell (*songshen*), all processed out of the temple through the main gate following behind the spirit, and prayer and silk . . . were burned.[13]

The twelfth-century model for the major annual ancestral sacrifice and its later popularizations, the Qing liturgy for the annual sacrifice to Guan Yu, and the Ming-Qing official sacrifices to Confucius have a strong family resemblance and almost certainly were based on a common template, which I have not felt it necessary to trace. They also have a number of elements that are clearly present—although much transformed, given different names, and not always in the same sequence—in the ritual summarized in the *Handbook for Use Before the Gods of the Sai*. The *sai* and these elite rituals are all structured around the offering of food,

---

13. Wilson, "Sacrifice and the Imperial Cult of Confucius," pp. 270–71. I have put the passage in the past tense.

and in the programs of all there is the emplacing of spirit tablets, greeting the spirits, presenting the food, making offerings in sets of three, taking leave of the spirits, and putting away the spirit tablets.

But there is one fundamental difference: the ancestors were offered a full meal of food that had been cooked, but the gods and sages got uncooked meat and grain, together with silk; indeed, higher-ranking deities received entire carcasses of the sacrificial animals.[14] This seemingly small difference is actually very important, for one of the defining characteristics of the *sai* is that they were giant banquets. Spiritual beings who were offered cooked food, especially in the form of familiar dishes, which included the ancestors as well as gods of the *sai*, would have seemed less alien to ordinary people than the august divinities and sages who were expected to enjoy raw food, and even whole carcasses. I suspect that sacrifices devised by or for ordinary people always included food that the observers could imagine eating, whereas those devised by the political and intellectual elites carefully avoided that, just as statues were used to represent the gods in popular worship while the elite preferred to use wooden tablets on which the name and titles of the god were written. I return to this below.[15]

According to Wilson

Virtually every degree holder in the Empire was familiar with the sacrifices to Confucius . . . because they would have participated in the ceremony at local schools from the early years of their formal education. This is perhaps the

---

14. For a vivid description of the offerings during the official sacrifices to Confucius, see Doolittle, *The Social Life of the Chinese*, 1: 364. A large stone altar stood in front of the tablet of Confucius, and in front of the altar were three stone tables. "On the large table, which was placed between the other two, was the carcass of a yearling bullock. On one of the small tables was the carcass of a small hog, and on the other that of a very poor goat. The hair of these animals had been carefully removed, and the bodies, uncooked, were placed in a kneeling position, with their heads toward the tablet of Confucius, as though they were devoutly contemplating the virtues of the sage." Doolittle also states that there were "several dishes of food," but does not say whether it was cooked or not. Wilson ("Sacrifice and the Imperial Cult of Confucius," pp. 259, 260 *n*29) says that minor sacrifices used cooked meat, and that in early(?) Ming cooked meat was specified.

15. It has not escaped my attention that the logic of the food offerings of the *sai* as they are described in my sources differs significantly from the model put forward by Arthur Wolf in his influential article "Gods, Ghosts, and Ancestors," pp. 176–78.

only [official] sacrifice that they would have participated in more than once and perhaps many times, even if they never received a bureaucratic appointment.[16]

In addition, all serving officials must have observed the state sacrifices to Guan Yu frequently during their careers. So here we have one ritual familiar to virtually all the educated elite and another, very similar, that was experienced by all past and present members of the corps of officials; both would have contributed to their idea of what a formal sacrifice should be. If former students or retired officials returned to their native villages and towns, and many of them did, they would have taken their knowledge of these rituals with them. In addition, any educated man, even one who had never left his village, would very likely have studied one version or another of the *Family Rituals* and would have been familiar with Zhu Xi's prescriptions for the chief annual sacrifice to the ancestors. And, as we have seen, that ritual had much in common with the sacrifices to Guan Yu and Confucius. Thus if former officials or local literati were called on by their neighbors to create a ritual for the village, or wished to reform local customs through ritual, they would have had models ready to hand. It is entirely possible that the ancestors of the *sai*, and other local rituals, were created in this way.

Another of the possible sources of *sai* rituals mentioned above was the imitation of officially sponsored rituals performed in villages and towns. Many people witnessed such ceremonies, not just degree-holders and former officials. A case in point is the "Community Compact."[17] In 1529 the court approved a proposal that Community Compacts be established across the country. It was mandated that Ming Taizu's "Six Maxims" be read at community meetings to be held every two months. In villages, those who gathered were to consider "the tutelary gods" as their hosts. (This notion of a god as "host" has clear parallels in the *sai*, although there, of course, the guests were other gods,

---

16. Wilson, "Sacrifice and the Imperial Cult of Confucius," p. 269. Wilson must be referring to official rites, since all educated men would have participated frequently in sacrifices to their ancestors.

17. The information on the Community Compact that follows is taken from McDermott, "Emperors, Elites, and Commoners," pp. 336–37. The language in quotation marks is McDermott's translation of an official document of 1529.

not mere villagers. The idea of local gods acting as hosts to the villagers could only have occurred to someone who had no understanding of the religious mentality of villagers.) At the appropriate time, "a position for the god and an incense table are to be set up. The [*shê*] head and manager are to lead all [the community] members to pay respects in front of [the god's] spirit tablet [*shenzhu*], offer up incense, present liquor, and perform the Two Bows ritual."[18] When this was finished, all the participants lined up according to age on either side of the spirit tablet, and the deputy head of the *shê* moved to the center and read the "Six Maxims."

This very simple, officially sanctioned ritual, devised by the educated elite and led by the local *shê* head, was performed in villages across China and thus must have been witnessed by any number of young *yin-yang* masters with ambitions to lead important, and lucrative, local rituals. They could have used it as the basis of more elaborate rituals of their own devising that eventually were written down in manuals and passed on to heirs or disciples. Is it merely a coincidence that the earliest of the *sai* manuals is dated 1522 and the Community Compacts were inaugurated in 1529? Here local specialists, not the educated elite, would have been the vector by which the official sacrificial model was spread.

Local specialists such as *yinyang* masters may also have imitated rituals they encountered in books. They could, for example, have learned about the structure of the ancestral sacrifices by reading one of the many simplified versions of the *Family Rituals* in circulation. Indeed, Yonghua Liu has discovered that sections of a ritual manual used by a village Master of Ceremony (*li sheng*) in Sibao, Fujian, and almost certainly written by him or another *li sheng*, were copied from an inexpensive popular version of the *Family Rituals* published in Sibao.[19] Another Sibao village ritual manual is a liturgy of a Sacrifice to the Saints.[20] It

---

18. This appears to contradict the idea of the god as host.

19. Liu Yonghua, "The World of Rituals," p. 175. Sibao was the source of the popular imprints that are the subject of Cynthia Brokaw's magisterial monograph, cited above. I have followed Liu (and most other scholars) in translating *li sheng* as "Master of Ceremony," reserving "Master of Ceremonial" for the *zhu li* of southeastern Shanxi, although functionally they seem identical.

20. Liu's translation is at ibid., pp. 139–42. See also pp. 163–70. The occasion on which the sacrifice to the saints was performed is not made clear.

was probably based on a written exemplar, although the source could have been official local rituals that the author witnessed. Liu stresses the similarities of this ritual, taken from a manual owned by a village Master of Ceremony, to state rituals, and they are clear: purification and preparation (which are not mentioned but can be presumed); greeting the spirit; making three offerings, including silk; taking leave of the spirit; and burning the offerings.

But the Sibao Sacrifice to the Saints resembles even more closely the major seasonal sacrifice to the ancestors in Zhu Xi's *Family Rituals*, especially in the modified versions popular in Ming and Qing times. Above all, both Zhu Xi's sacrifice to the ancestors and the village Sacrifice to the Saints feature food offerings resembling a full meal, which the spirits are urged to eat. As I have already said, this is a crucial difference from the state-sponsored rituals.[21] I think we are justified in assuming that the village manual of the Sacrifice to the Saints, written by a rural ritual specialist and printed in a small town in interior Fujian, was in fact, like the other Sibao ritual manual, modeled on one version or another of Zhu Xi's *Family Rituals*, although it is possible that it also imitated certain features of official rituals that could have been seen in villages or towns.

Thus there was something like a basic model or template of state-sponsored sacrifice that could have been spread to the countryside by officially designed public rituals like the Community Compact, which was performed before an audience of villagers, or by school rituals like the sacrifice to Confucius that would have been familiar to all former government students, or by official sacrifices to Guan Yu that were witnessed many times by all officials. And local ritual specialists could have created their own liturgies on the basis of Zhu Xi's *Family Rituals* or other orthodox texts, as we have seen in the case of the Sibao ritual manuals.

Nevertheless, any given *sai*, considered as a whole, including the activities both inside and outside the temples, had many, many elements

---

21. Even though one of the ritual manuals Liu collected contains sections copied from a local popular edition of the *Family Rituals*, he does not seem to have noticed how close the resemblance is between the Sacrifice to the Saints liturgy and the *Family Rituals* (see ibid., p. 175).

not found in the sacrifices to Guan Yu, Confucius, or the ancestors, or the Community Compact, or the Sacrifice to the Saints. The *sai* may indeed have originally been modeled on rituals such as the grand ancestral sacrifice or the sacrifice to Confucius and been brought into local culture in ways similar to those suggested above, or have originated in part in village rituals such as the Community Compact or the Sacrifice to the Saints—but *sai* were orders of magnitude larger and more complex. And, above all, they were sharply *different* from other rituals both official and popular: opera and elaborate mimed performances were fully integrated into the ritual, with the Master of Ceremonial and the Director of the Entertainers working in close coordination; the gods who were to be guests at the *sai* received invitations from the host god that were delivered in person; the objects that symbolized the gods were treated like individuals, whether they were tablets, as in the Mt. Longquan *sai*, or statues, as in other *sai*—further evidence that people felt the gods were really present; the food offerings were far more lavish, with seven, twelve, and eight Cups added to the triple offering that characterized official sacrifices; no Daoist or Buddhist teachings were in evidence; there was a hint of exorcism during the sacrifice to the stage in the Mt. Longquan *sai*, and much more than a hint in other *sai*; there were a large number of sacrifices—to the wind, the stage, the sun, the moon, the stove god, and so on—that were not part of the main program at all but appear to have accreted to it over time; and there were the elaborate public exhortations by the Master of Ceremonial to all the many participants in the ceremonies, down to those with quite menial tasks, which served to draw the community more deeply into the proceedings.

The *sai* certainly had elements in common with official or orthodox rituals. Whether one chooses to emphasize the similarities or the differences depends on one's tolerance for generalization at the expense of detail, or perhaps one's preference for structure over texture. To me, the similarities between the ancestral sacrifices, the official sacrifices, and even popular rites derived from them such as the Sacrifice to the Saints are patent; but the *sai*, although clearly related to those rituals, are in the end profoundly different from them. The Master of Ceremonial, the Entertainers, and the villagers jointly created a unique blend of elements from many sources: classical ritual and its popularizations, to be sure, but also local customs, ancient beliefs, and the needs and tastes of the people at large.

Scale mattered: the non-*sai* rituals we have looked at—all of them presided over by local officials or *li sheng*—were fairly small, either because they involved only a lineage or lineage segment, or because the people in general did not care much about them or were not allowed to participate. The *sai* by contrast mobilized entire villages whose residents participated heart and soul in them. If we look at a *sai* as a total event, ignoring for the moment its ritual-theological core, the closest analogue in the universe of Chinese ritual is probably the Daoist *jiao*. Daoist ritual has, of course, been minutely described by many scholars. Merely reading the brief chapter called "The Basic Program" in John Lagerwey's monumental *Taoist Ritual in Chinese Society and History*[22] brings us at once into a world of opera, processions from village to village, prodigious food offerings, temporary structures built just for the *jiao*, and total community engagement that is very reminiscent of the *sai*. What is different, profoundly different, is the ritual program itself and the ritual specialists who performed it. Daoist priests had a monopoly on the *jiao*, and, as we have seen, the Masters of Ceremonial had a monopoly on the *sai*. Their rituals may have some superficial structural similarities, but to try to fit *sai* and *jiao* into a common mold is to falsify both. The theology or cosmology of the *jiao* was much deeper and more complex than that of the *sai*—even if we give full attention to the role of the twenty-eight lunar lodges and associated astrological elements in the classic *sai*, which I have said little about because they did not figure in the Mt. Longquan liturgy. In addition, Daoist priests underwent a far more complete and demanding training than did the Masters of Ceremonial. They were the inheritors of a religious tradition that had been developing for two millennia and possessed a canon of nearly 1,500 scriptures, whereas the Shanxi Master of Ceremonial cannot be said to have been part of a fully developed religion at all.[23] In short, the similarities between *sai* and *jiao* lay in those things,

---

22. Lagerwey, *Taoist Ritual.*

23. The number of works in the Daoist canon is taken from the list of scriptures in Schipper, *Concordance du Tao-tsang,* pp. 1–28.

such as processions, theatricals, and feasting, that were in the hands of the people at large; the features that were controlled by the ritual specialists—Daoist priests or Masters of Ceremonial—were utterly different. *Jiao* as giant communal rituals seem not to have been common in Shanxi, and perhaps not anywhere in north China. If it was in fact the case that *sai* played in north China the role *jiao* played in south China, then, given the profound differences in their theological/ritual cores, that would mark a cultural difference between the two regions of the greatest importance.

The *sai* were not the creation of a highly trained clerical or liturgical elite, but of local ritual specialists—also an elite, it is true, but of a very different kind—who must have been highly sensitive to the needs and standards of their audiences, just as the Entertainers were. *Sai* rituals drew on classical ritual forms that were familiar to and respected by the people, but they made use of much nonclassical content and forms as well, creating in the end a unique amalgam that was genuinely of the people, which we must assume expressed their view of the world and the universe. This sacrificial tradition seems to have evolved pretty much independently of China's sacerdotal religions, Daoism and Buddhism, just as the ritual opera tradition developed outside the mainstream of Chinese opera. The *sai* were not controlled by educated clerical elites but by local specialists who had independent sources of income. This is a central point. Even though there was considerable resemblance between one *sai* and another thanks to the central role of the Masters of Ceremonial and the Entertainers, who worked from written manuals and scripts, and they were not creations of individual communities to the extent that the New Year festivals were; still, each had its own special features. ("Of ten *sai*, nine are different.") Taken as a whole, they formed a genuinely popular ritual tradition in which both the "priests" and the gods were not radically separate from the people, and the central concern was communal well-being, not individual salvation or purification.

————

Very early in the morning of the sacrifice to Confucius, many food offerings were placed on tables in front of the altar: three goblets (*jue*) of wine; three soups—an unsalted beef broth in a covered pot and two tureens of mixed beef and salted pork soup; nuts, grasses, and condiments in covered baskets and bowls; salt, dried fish, dates, chestnuts, hazelnuts, water caltrops, water lilies, and dried venison in baskets of woven bamboo; bowls of pickled leeks, turnips, celery grass, minced venison, rabbit, and fish, bamboo shoots, sweet breads, and "pork blades"; uncooked glutinous and plain millet, uncooked "rice stalks" and sorghum, and white silk. Also in front of the altar, somewhat farther away, were tables on which were placed the whole carcasses of an ox, a pig, and a goat.[24] As we have seen, three offerings were made during the ritual, but evidently there was little actual movement of the food.[25] The food was not intended to be delicious: "Utmost reverence lies not in the flavor of the sacrifice. . . . What is revered is the smell of the ethers."[26] The word Wilson translates as "ethers" is *qi*: literally, "air," "vapor," "breath." One might suppose that the text is saying it is the aroma of the food that is important, not its taste. But few if any of the offerings to Confucius were cooked; their aromas were barely detectable, or if detectable, as with the sacrificial animals, far from appealing. That was intentional: "The offerings of the former kings are edible, not pleasurable to eat."[27]

In short, in the view of the classicists, offerings to the spirits were to be pure and austere; they were prepared according to the dictates of tradition, not human preferences. Their fragrance came from their imperceptible essences, not their all-too-physical aromas. But the food offerings in the *sai*, especially the so-called permanent offerings of the Manchu-Chinese Banquet (or at least the Chinese part), were very appetizing. This disparity can stand for all the differences between the great official sacrifices and the sacrifices of the *sai*: the creators of the *sai* assumed that the preferences of gods and the preferences of people were very similar. This opened a way for the development of a ritual that people would find both familiar and overwhelming. This was also true of the decorations in the temple—the awesome Flowery Offering, cov-

---

24. Wilson, "Sacrifice and the Imperial Cult of Confucius," pp. 277–78. My description of the sacrifice is taken directly from Wilson's article.

25. Ibid., pp. 270–71.

26. Ibid., p. 278.

27. Ibid.

ered with level upon level of skillfully carved pavilions and terraces, and the two lavishly decorated rooms called the Chamber of Timely Rains and the Chamber of Towering Clouds. And it was true of the procession, with its richly embellished "palanquins" made of fine fabrics, its Golden Buildings and Silver Sunshades festooned with jewelry, its music, and its scenes from opera, with heroines magically suspended in midair.

The classical and the vernacular ritual programs did not, as one might expect, simply co-exist, each in its own sphere, vernacular deferring to classical. Zhangzi, to take a case about which we know a good deal, was a walled town, a county capital with a yamen, a magistrate, and his civilian and military staff. This meant that numerous rituals of the state cult were celebrated there, including sacrifices to the city god and Guan Di. But in Zhangzi the magistrate also organized and led a *sai* to the city god, and the merchants presented a lavish *sai* to Guan Di.[28] So the two ritual regimes were somehow simultaneously active there. Furthermore, ordinary people resident in the town and the surrounding area may well have found the Guan Di *sai* superior in every respect, including spiritual efficacy, to the official sacrifices to him. And, strikingly, even the magistrates appear to have conceded the superiority of the *sai* as a ritual form—what other reason could they have had for sponsoring a *sai* to the city god when they also celebrated an official ritual to him? In any case, there was little in the *sai* we have studied that an official would have found subversive or morally suspect: the attitudes and values expressed were supportive of conventional ethics and the political-social status quo.

This has important implications. Many people in Zhangzi, especially members of the town's educated elite, would have had the opportunity to compare, for example, official rituals honoring Guan Di with the *sai* celebrating his birthday.[29] How did the comparison affect their opinion of the official rituals? The magistrate honored the city god with a *sai*,

---

28. And there was the Hou Yi Temple just west of the town, whose *sai* was entirely supported by residents of the town, and whose procession went through its streets.

29. This assumes that the audience for official sacrifices was limited to degree holders, government students, and, probably, nontitled members of the local economic and social elites.

even though there were official sacrifices to him twice a year, along with the wind, clouds, thunder, rain, and mountains and rivers.[30] How did this affect popular attitudes toward the state cult? I think it is obvious that if the rituals of the state cult and the *sai* were accorded approximately equal legitimacy, which seems to have been the case in Zhangzi and a number of other county towns in southeastern Shanxi, the *sai* would have appeared superior in every way. That is, a ritual created by the people (to be sure, at least partially on a foundation of classical ritual forms) would have been considered more appropriate or efficacious than a ritual sanctioned by the state and long tradition. This amounted to the state losing at least some of its monopoly on ritual legitimacy. But if it lost that, what did it have left? Was perhaps the officials' *sai* a peculiarity of a few counties in southeastern Shanxi? But why should it have been? There may have been analogues all over north China.

Thus we can conclude that the state exerted virtually no control over popular symbolic resources unless they threatened the established order; that village temple festival rituals were not a reflex of more sophisticated systems but an original creation; that the officially approved system of rituals was irrelevant to the vast majority of the population; and that local ritual had more weight than state ritual for ordinary people, and perhaps even officials, with local ritual seen as really efficacious, and state ritual as a sort of charade. Readers may be reluctant to accept these propositions, but consider: virtually none of the material in Part III came from the sorts of older sources normally used to write Chinese history, whose authors knew next to nothing about village life, or from surveys and fieldwork by Japanese researchers in the 1930s and 1940s, and European and American researchers after the war, whose theoretical

---

30. The information on official sacrifices comes from Taylor, "Calendar of [Official] Sacrifices: Late Ming." There were also city god *sai* in the county seats of Lucheng and Yangcheng (Duan Youwen, "Jin dongnan," pp. 4–7; Li Shoutian, "Yangcheng xian"). There was in fact a category of *sai* called "officials' *sai*," which presumably was characterized by official sponsorship and must have commonly involved the city god, but I do not know how common such *sai* were. According to Li Shoutian, in the Yangcheng Officials' *Sai* the magistrate forced the Master of Ceremonial and the Entertainers to donate their services.

commitments or ideological agendas often obscured the realities of what they were studying. Those realities were in any case so complex that only local people could understand them, and they would have been reluctant to share that understanding with outsiders even if they could have articulated it. But precisely such local knowledge, oral and written, is the basic material out of which this book was made.

Concluding Observations

TEMPLE FESTIVALS
AND THE RURAL ORDER

The focus of this book is the symbolic life of farmers, not the attitudes and values of the cultural elite. And I have limited my research to the "spectacle and sacrifice" of a few village rituals rather than attempt a broad survey of traditional festival culture. The closer you look, the more you see, and the less familiar the topic, the more surprises it will have in store. Both the Entertainers and the Masters of Ceremonial can count as surprises. The Masters of Ceremonial were related to the ubiquitous "masters of ceremony" (*li sheng*) or *yinyang* masters (*yinyang xiansheng*) who advised ordinary people on matters ranging from funeral ritual to the siting of houses, but they were far more important, since (at least in southeastern Shanxi) they had the responsibility of leading giant communal rituals organized by village alliances. For the common people and the local elite, and quite possibly officials as well, they had the final word on the most important ceremonies; there was no higher authority. But their rituals show no trace of Daoist influence, which suggests that statements such as "Taoist ritual functions as the main structuring element in the vast liturgical framework that supports the festival of the local gods" and "'The modern popular religion' [in China] . . . in reality . . . is Taoism asserting itself . . . as the *national religion*," which are representative of a widely shared position, probably apply only to southern

China.[1] By the same token, the Daoist *jiao* ritual, nearly universal in southern China, was not important in southeastern Shanxi, where the *sai* reigned supreme.[2]

The Entertainers initially caught my attention because they were a hereditary caste of ritual actors and musicians, uncommon in China, but the discovery that they owned Territories in which they had exclusive rights to perform domestic rituals and which they could mortgage or bequeath to heirs was truly surprising, as was the fact that the Director functioned virtually as an equal of the Master of Ceremonial during the *sai* rituals. This plus the Entertainers' close association with local officials, which I was unable to investigate as thoroughly as I would have liked, showed that they were far more deeply integrated into local society than one would have thought possible, given their supposedly degraded social and juridical status. This in turn suggests that we should assume that local social hierarchies were a good deal more intricate than the conventional wisdom suggests.

We are able to reconstruct the rituals of the *sai* only because a dozen or so liturgical manuscripts survived the Cultural Revolution. If those texts had been destroyed, the tradition, rich as it was, would for all intents and purposes have been unrecoverable. It is obvious that if the literate elite did not value a tradition it will not have made much of an impression on the written record, and so the survival of traditions is heavily dependent on the prejudices and preferences of that class. But even though we are aware of this, still there is a tendency to feel that if a tradition was lost, it did not deserve to survive. Only when we encounter a situation like this does the reality sink in that a tradition may have been extraordinarily interesting and important even if the record-keeping class ignored it.

The idea of a lost tradition reappeared when I was studying the history of village ritual opera. The operas performed on temple stages

---

1. Dean, *Taoist Ritual and Popular Cults of Southeast China*, p. 3; Schipper, *The Taoist Body*, p. 14. That these statements are true for southern, or more precisely southeastern, China, is shown in many publications, e.g., Lagerwey, "Popular Ritual Specialists in West-Central Fujian."

2. There is an immense literature on the *jiao*; Lagerwey is the main authority. A detailed comparison of *jiao* vs. *sai* would be of the greatest interest.

during village festivals in southern Shanxi obviously had many archaic features, and their stagecraft and music were much less sophisticated than those of the regional opera genres that arose in the Qing, which had no ritual function. Although it was impossible to reconstruct the evolution of the ritual opera genre—over many centuries no one had considered it worthwhile to describe operas performed in temples in any detail—there were enough hints to suggest strongly that village ritual opera, conservative and intensely local, had developed on its own track, separate from regional opera. This came to stand in my mind for the entire spectrum of village traditions, all of them invisible in the standard sources, hidden from all but the most persistent (and lucky) investigators.

Two other things became clear as a result of my research into Shanxi ritual opera, most of which I was unable to use in this book.[3] First, the sharp distinction we tend to draw between (serious) ritual and (entertaining) opera is a category error as far as rural north China is concerned. Ritual and opera were simply two facets of a single festival performance complex. Second, although I expected that the scripts would reveal a common body of attitudes and values, since they were performed in the same kind of settings before people who came from more or less the same economic and educational strata, in fact they did not. The "messages" ranged from straight Confucian orthodoxy to complete ethical nihilism. I hope to deal with this disconcerting finding in a future study.

Although some ritual opera scripts showed what appeared to be the influence of chantefable, which could be construed as evidence of a connection with the earliest period in the history of opera, others clearly had drawn directly or indirectly on Ming novels, especially *The Romance of the Three Kingdoms*. The influence of historical fiction on the symbolic world of villagers was also demonstrated in the New Year festivities of Sand Hill village, when eighteen villagers dressed as characters from the novel *Shui hu zhuan* (known in English by several titles, including *All Men Are Brothers* and *Water Margin*) paraded through the streets seven times a day for three days. Obviously villages were not

---

3. I hope to publish this material separately, and in the near term put it on a website.

sealed off from the world of letters; any number of intermediating agents—storytellers, opera troupes, cheap books, woodblock prints, residents returned from distant parts, educated men in retirement— helped bring the culture of the literate elite to the farmers. It is particularly important to stress that we have *virtually no idea* of village literacy rates region by region and century by century and hence have no reliable way to gauge the connections between villagers and the classically educated, between hamlet and metropolis, that so often depended on the written word. Nor do we have any systematic regional data on another vector for the transmission of elite culture to the countryside, the educated men who for one reason or another returned to live in their home villages. This is a major impediment to our understanding of the way late imperial Chinese society worked.

Early in my research, I became aware that the *sai*, the largest temple festivals, were sponsored by groups of villages. Epigraphic evidence suggests that membership in these alliances was very stable, and hence it must have been an important part of a village's identity. This is confirmed by the fact that Renzhuang's withdrawal from the group of villages that sponsored the annual festival at the Pengzu temple, which had taken place many years earlier, was still noted in recent accounts of the village's rituals. My research turned up six village alliances in eastern Zhangzi county alone, an area less than twenty-five by thirty kilometers; a serious research campaign using Ming and Qing temple inscriptions would almost certainly uncover many more in southeastern Shanxi and elsewhere in north China. This is an important new element in our picture of the north China countryside. (See Map 7.)

Since the villages in an alliance were accustomed to cooperating in the complex undertaking that was a large-scale temple festival, it would have been natural for them to act jointly in other matters, such as self-defense. Those festival activities with a military character, such as maneuvers by squads of armed young men, were perhaps not as out of place as the casual observer might suppose. As mentioned in the Introduction, the village alliances of southeastern Shanxi offer an interesting contrast to G. William Skinner's standard marketing areas and Philip Kuhn's *tuanlian*, two influential models of rural social organization in late imperial times. Skinner's nodal points are market towns, whereas

Kuhn's are villages he calls "bureaus," the headquarters of powerful local lineages, and more specifically schools in those villages.[4] My focus is on ritual rather than trade or militarization, and the village alliances I found were centered on temples; they operated below the level of market towns and were not controlled by the local gentry.[5] Thus three important areas of rural life—commerce, self-defense, and ritual—each produced its own type of village alliance. This suggests that the structure of local society in late imperial times was far more complex than has hitherto been assumed. We need to have a much better understanding of the interrelationship of these local systems.

I have been speaking of village alliances, but it would be more accurate to say *shê* alliances, since *shê* rather than *cun*, *zhuang*, *li*, or any of the more familiar Chinese words for "village" is constantly used in the sources to name the units that sponsored *sai*. Local ritual units called *shê* had existed in the Chinese countryside since time out of mind, and in a recent study Kenneth Dean has traced their evolution in coastal Fujian from the Song period on. One of his conclusions is that in late Ming they evolved from their original status as government shrines into "fundamental building block[s] of the local temple system," which sounds rather similar to their function in southern Shanxi, as we have seen.[6]

The resources that could be mobilized by the *shê* alliances were on display in the temples they built and the annual festivals celebrated in them. As one might expect of temples sponsored by a group of villages, many *sai* temples were constructed in the countryside, thus avoiding identification with a specific village. It is difficult to be sure since it is not easy to identify them, and so many temples have been destroyed,

---

4. See Skinner, "Marketing and Social Structure in Rural China"; and Kuhn, *Rebellion and Its Enemies*. The ongoing project of Kenneth Dean and Zheng Zhenman on the historical development of irrigation and ritual systems of the Xinghua region of Fujian is providing yet another perspective on intervillage alliances; see their *Ritual Alliances*.

5. The village alliances may have had something in common with the rural units called *xiang* that interested the eighteenth-century reforming official Chen Hongmou; see Rowe, *Saving the World*, pp. 381–82.

6. Dean, "Transformations of the *Shê*," p. 45. Dean's work also uses ritual rather than economic networks to study local society and politics, although irrigation systems, which have both ritual and economic aspects, enter heavily into his models.

but *sai* temples were probably a good deal larger than the average village temple, and some were very imposing indeed. Those I have seen embody a more austere aesthetic than temples in southeastern China, with an occasional echo of Ming-Qing imperial architecture. Some were founded in the Jin or Yuan dynasties, or even earlier, and were reconstructed and enlarged many times thereafter. These temples are emblems of the deep devotion that local cults inspired, a devotion systematically ignored or denigrated in the standard sources.

Both the processions and the offering rituals give further evidence of the resources villagers lavished on the *sai*. One of the most striking documents that I encountered was Zhang Zhennan's minutely detailed description of the great procession during the festival at the Hou Yi Temple in Big West Gate, with its martial arts troupes, bands, palanquins of the Five Honored Gods, Springy Four-man Palanquins, Lifted Characters, Golden Buildings, Silver Sunshades, Golden Melons, Solitary Dragon Colts, and on and on.[7] Then again there were the spectacular Four-Scene Carts of the Divine Mother Temple of the Ninth Heaven, four of which made their appearance every year in the great festival procession. It is fascinating to note that at about forty-five feet in height they were comparable to the Balinese funeral towers called *badé* central to Clifford Geertz's *Negara*.[8] The immense banquets offered to the gods are yet another way of illustrating the resources that people poured into their festivals. Thus the multivillage alliances that sponsored the *sai* had the ability to mobilize very substantial resources, both financial and political. Villagers would not be the automatic losers in any local test of ideological authority or even armed conflict. We will have occasion again to point out that on an everyday basis the villages were in many ways more than a match for the imperium.

The *sai* and other village festivals were not just sites for the display of political and economic power. They also mobilized people's emo-

---

7. See Zhang Zhennan, "Yueju yu sai," among other versions; and Part III, Chapter 3, above.

8. Geertz (*Negara*, p. 119) notes that a *badé* "could get up to sixty or seventy feet," implying that some were less tall. The paperback edition of his book features a painting of a *badé* on the cover. The sheer number of temple festivals and other ritual activities in the Chinese countryside often seems positively Balinesian.

tions on many levels, and what is political power without an emotional core? Beauty arouses emotion, and objects in the festivals were sometimes very beautiful. One example of this is the Bends of the Yellow River, an array of 19 × 19 rows of lanterns on shoulder-high stakes set up in a large open space during the New Year festivities. The great grid of 361 lamps, stretching across fields that were usually completely dark at night, must have been strikingly beautiful. Walking the Nine Bends had a protective magical function, but surely the aesthetic effect created by the lantern array added to its imagined potency. Even more impressive to my mind were the wall-sized screens called the Flowery Offerings, which the reader will recall were constructed of intricately carved tiles made of deep-fried dough. These are described in great detail by those who saw them in their youth; clearly they never forgot them. Here the very simplest materials and techniques were carried into the realm of high decorative art. Objects this extraordinary could have been inspired only by occasions felt to be extraordinary, and in turn their very existence helped reinforce the impression that the *sai* were events of the highest importance.

In addition to the purely aesthetic impact of creations like the Nine Bends and the Flowery Offerings, there were performances that aroused audience emotions by being shocking or frightening. These belonged more to the world of seasonal festivals of Part I than to the temple festivals we studied in Part III. There were, for example, the Mask Tableaux of Guyi, in which actors wore full-head masks of gods, some of them quite grotesque, and played the parts of gods—one of several occasions when a god apparently left his usual place in the main hall of his temple and walked through the village, in this case on the way to a temporary stage. If the villagers had any awe of the gods at all, this must have been a disturbing experience. Still, in the Mask Tableaux the gods were integrated into a show that was presented on a stage, and hence to that extent controlled. There was another type of performance, one in which a demonic figure jumped off the stage and went on a rampage through the streets of the village, bursting out of the world of make-believe and into the realm of the real. These unnerving displays were frequently connected with the beheading of an evil creature such as the drought demon Han Ba or the ancient monster Chi

You. In northeastern Shanxi the actor playing Han Ba, wearing a fresh sheep's stomach over his head, leaped off the stage and ran through the audience, splattering them with sheep's blood. He dashed through the streets pursued by stage gods and real villagers until he finally was captured and brought back to the stage for execution. Such performances were fairly common. They often involved the use of real or imitation blood and bloody props like a raw animal's stomach or intestines, which would have intensified the dread that the performance aroused.

The most memorable of all such shows was the trial and execution of the Yellow Demon, a truly remarkable creation of the Chinese popular imagination. The Yellow Demon was an evil creature who was intended to excite fear and loathing in the audience. He did not even have the benefit of a mythical pedigree. His was a drama not of escape and recapture but of trial and punishment. We have videos of this event, and the near hysteria of the mob of spectators is obvious. The Demon is dragged before the King of Hell, who condemns him to be skinned alive and gutted, and then is taken to an open platform where the sentence is carried out, using bloody offal, imitation blood, and thick smoke as props. Watching this, it is easy to imagine a time when scapegoat figures like Han Ba or the Yellow Demon were actually set upon and torn apart by the villagers. Here we arrive at the most primitive levels of the villagers' symbolic world, the wellsprings of violence rightly feared by both clerical and secular elites.[9]

As we have seen, however, the Yellow Demon performance is about more than primitive fears and violence. The most remarkable aspect of the whole show is the interpretation that accompanies it in the lines spoken by the Staff-holder, who explicitly refers to the production as an opera and tells members of the audience that if they are unfilial they will be "taken to the Southern Stage, where you will be gutted and flayed"—the Southern Stage, not the torture chambers of Hell. Here divine punishment is conflated with operatic performance and the dis-

---

9. There are echoes here of public punishments of enemies of the state during the worst of the Maoist terror; they, too, were posed on platforms before crowds of people and then abused or killed. This is probably not a coincidence.

tinction between gods and actors, between the genuinely supernatural and the artificially theatrical, is intentionally effaced. This is not simple pandering to people's baser instincts in order to drive home the importance of filial piety. The deeper message is that human sacrifice is wrong and, even more important, unnecessary, since it is just as effective to make the whole thing into a play.

The intellectual and moral sophistication of the Yellow Demon performance will be a surprise to anyone who expects village ritual and drama to be artless and uncomplicated. Another segment of Guyi's New Year festivities provides an even bigger challenge to those who are inclined to underestimate the intellectual complexity of the village world. In the Mask Tableau called *Levying Demon Soldiers*, the narrator states that when Third Master White Eyebrows, the main god of Guyi, was still a mortal, he was chased from Shanxi to a village in southwestern Hebei by enemy soldiers.[10] Just then the villagers were celebrating a temple festival, and Third Master escaped his pursuers by putting on a mask and joining the procession. In Guyi this Mask Tableau was staged as an offering to Third Master White Eyebrows, who was there to watch it, in the person of a villager impersonating him—that is, wearing his mask. This figure sat on stage in the posture of the Third Master in his temple, listening to the story of the long-ago temple festival in which the Third Master took part by putting on a mask and marching in the procession. Here the distinctions between ritual and opera, between secular and sacred, between naïve representation and self-conscious awareness of the act of representation, simply collapse. And this little skit was prepared for a village audience in a tiny out-of-the way hamlet deep in the north China countryside. All this suggests that there may be something quite unexpectedly formidable in village symbolic culture if we know where to look for it.

Each of the foregoing topics is a reminder of how rich village culture was and how little we know about it. Each will amply repay further study. Beyond these are two themes that seem especially important, and I end with an exploration of them.

---

10. This is perhaps a refiguring of the forcible resettlement of tens of thousands of Shanxi villagers to southwestern Hebei in the early Ming.

THE STAGE IN THE TEMPLE

When opera first appears in the Chinese historical record, it has already been taken into village temples. There is some reason to believe that village audiences were watching opera in China before it moved to the cities. But I am not interested in quibbling about where exactly opera first appeared, since there is too little evidence to make a conclusive argument either way. The really important point is that the earliest known stages for which there is epigraphic evidence, which date to the eleventh and twelfth centuries, were constructed in village temples. Since stages did not *have* to be built in temples, this means that opera had been integrated into the liturgies of temple festivals virtually as soon as it appeared. What explains this? It is possible that by Song times the rituals of village cults had become routinized and lost their symbolic potency, and that opera brought to them new energy and life that were highly attractive. Rituals themselves were performances, but performances that were under the control of the educated elite and had come to be heavily structured, intensely hierarchical, nearly immobile, and symmetrical. Opera was in the hands of ordinary people and was characterized by movement, asymmetry, (scripted) spontaneity, and conflict, and hence it offered precisely what traditional ritual lacked.

What were those early temple operas *about*? The little evidence we have concerning the content of pre-Yuan operas points toward comedy; we know nothing about dramas with other themes. But it seems unlikely that villagers in eleventh- and twelfth-century Shanxi spent large sums of money to add stages to their temples merely to provide a venue for slapstick routines. So it is possible that in this early period exorcisms were moved onto temple stages and thus given a more imposing setting. Note the tradition that the ancestor of Shanxi's *Za* Opera, a form that was used for temple festivals, was *Lord Guan Beheads Chi You*, which certainly was exorcistic. There is some reason to believe that the earliest temple stages were simple raised platforms rather than the roofed and partially walled structures of later times, and thus similar to the raised platform on which the Yellow Demon met his fate.[11] The

---

11. Liao Ben, *Zhongguo gudai juchang shi*, pp. 13–20.

Staff-holder's insistence in *Catching the Yellow Demon* that it was all only a show, that no real killing had taken place, might be similar to what happened on those very early temple platform-stages. Or, looking at the matter from a different perspective, the educated elite, who had been campaigning for centuries against inhuman ritual practices, including the sacrifice of living people, may have supported opera in the hope that it would displace blood sacrifices and violent exorcisms. It is interesting to note that the rise of village ritual opera took place in precisely the same period—roughly the eleventh to thirteenth centuries—that important segments of the educated elite were identifying more and more strongly with their native places, which could have made them more sensitive to or aware of what happened during village rituals.[12]

But the open platforms were soon given roofs, and there is no sign whatsoever that exorcistic operas ever were commonly performed on Shanxi temple stages during the festivals celebrating gods' birthdays in late imperial times. Even the few operas with overtly religious subjects, such as the Mulian and Miaoshan stories, did not find a place in the repertoire. This perhaps is not surprising, considering that those stories had nothing to do with the gods being honored at the annual festivals. Yet there were no operas about *them*, either; hagiographic or cultic opera never became a significant part of the ritual opera repertoire.[13] When we finally get substantial evidence concerning the content of Shanxi rural ritual opera, in the sixteenth century, the subjects are heavily historical-military, and I suspect that was true almost from the very beginning. If so, what explains the absence of exorcistic or cultic operas?

------

12. On this important social change, see Hymes, *Statesmen and Gentlemen.*

13. Exorcistic dramas featuring masked performers, often mimed to the words of a narrator and performed on the ground before an altar, were very common in most areas of China south of the Huai River (dozens of examples are documented in the volumes of the *Minsu quyi congshu*). They could be performed in a home, an ancestral temple, or an open space in the village. They are often called *nuo* opera (*nuoxi*), but would better be called *nuo* drama, since they do not fit my definition of ritual opera. By contrast, the ritual operas in Shanxi and environs that I have studied were performed on temple stages by actors who rarely wore masks, and were almost never overtly exorcistic or hagiographic. There seems to have been little *nuo* drama north of the Yellow River.

When opera was brought into the village temples, it must have functioned as an *offering*, if not immediately, then before very many decades had passed; and it never lost that function. Operas were part of the offerings that were the central business of the *sai* and presumably all temple festivals. (We see this in Daoist *jiao* also, although they are far more complex and thus are difficult to compare with the *sai* and their analogues.) But note that there was in the Chinese ritual universe a basic opposition between offering and exorcism. Offerings took place in a temple as part of a carefully scripted ceremony; they were provided by people whose attitude toward the Powers was respectful, submissive, and conciliatory. Exorcisms took place mostly outside the temples, in forecourts or streets or fields;[14] the attitude of exorcists toward the Powers was often hostile, aggressive, and violent. Offerings assumed that people and the Powers were akin; the Powers were just higher in a hierarchy that also included humans and indeed all living things. Exorcisms assumed that the Powers were profoundly alien, dangerous antagonists to be engaged and destroyed. Fear of demonic powers called forth extreme, even violent, countermeasures; we see this in the Yellow Demon performance, the beheading skits, even in the procession of villagers wearing their big-headed god masks. Indeed, almost all masked performances evoked a sense of the alienness of the Powers, which is probably why operas performed on temple stages as offerings to the gods seldom used masks. Some operas, such as "Mulian," did indeed function as exorcisms, but the vast majority of ritual operas known to us were performed as offerings. Bringing opera into the ritual realm extended the humanizing effect that was ritual's classical justification.

If kinship between people and the Powers was implicit in the popular conception of offerings, then it follows that offerings to the gods would consist of things similar to what people enjoyed. This was true of food offerings, and evidently was true of drama offerings as well. But would people not have enjoyed seeing operas about the local gods,

---

14. Of course there were exceptions, since exorcistic activities took place everywhere, including at the start of opera performances in temples. I am not trying to account for the entire range of religious performance here but to construct two ideal types that I believe accurately represent lived realities.

the events of their lives and the miracles they performed after becoming deities? Probably; after all, virtually every god had his or her own hagiography, which often circulated in written form and sometimes was even the subject of temple murals. Everyone knew myths and legends about the gods. Yet there were no operas about them, and that meant people did not want operas of that sort. Perhaps a typical hagiography simply was not good theater, and to make it entertaining would have required the sacrilegious falsification of the god's true story. Or perhaps people felt that a good host would never allow him or herself to be glorified before invited guests, some of whom were his superiors. Whatever the reason, there were no operas about the gods of the *sai*. Yet opera was indispensable to the festival. Romances and farces did not suit the solemnity of the occasion (though farces could be performed late at night, as a sort of counterpart to proper operas). This left historical-military operas, which treated serious subjects in an exciting yet (usually) morally uplifting way. They would not offend the gods in the audience, and the villagers could identify with the heroes and heroines. Indeed, some of the characters in the most popular operas had lived in Shanxi, and a few were even adopted as ancestors by people of the same surname (as with the Yang family generals). So military-historical operas made the ideal dramatic offering: acceptable to both gods and people, serious but still entertaining.

THE COMPETENT VILLAGE

Very early in my research, one thing became obvious: the festivals and rituals I was studying varied greatly from village to village. Of course, certain general features were widely shared—processions, welcoming and sending off the gods, offerings in the temple—but these were far less impressive than the differences. Such a degree of ritual autarky could exist only in the absence of an ecclesiastical authority with the power to regulate local ritual activity, and also only if the government took no interest in ordinary village cults. The striking variation in local ritual repertoires meant quite simply that in the realm of ritual, and also opera, villages were left alone. This was true in other spheres as well. H. B. Morse, a member of the Chinese Imperial Maritime Customs

Service with long experience in China, wrote in 1913 that "it is doubtful if the actual existence of a government [apart from tax-collection] is brought tangibly to the notice of a tenth, certainly not to a fifth, of the population. The remaining eighty or more per cent live their daily life under their customs . . . interpreted and executed by themselves. Each village is the unit for this common-law government."[15] Another astute observer of the pre-revolutionary scene in China, R. F. Johnston, said that the villages of the British concession of Weihaiwei "are somewhat like so many little self-contained republics."[16] The Eurocentric vocabulary in these assessments should not obscure their essential accuracy. Even today a well-informed student of southern Fujian can speak of village temple committees as "China's second government."[17] And I have already quoted Philip Huang's comment that "even in the 1930s, all but the most highly commercialized villages of the North China plain were still relatively insular communities."[18] Note that there is a positive feedback loop here: autonomy would in turn have encouraged the development of administrative and even legal competencies.

A few statistics will show why the relative independence of Chinese villages noted by Morse and Johnston, and implicit in the ritual heterogeneity I found in my research, was unavoidable. The lowest level at which the field administration of the central government functioned was the *xian*, or county. Each county in theory was run by a magistrate and two deputies, but John Watt says that in fact there were only 1,660 such officials in 1785.[19] Whatever the actual numbers, it is obvious that "the magistrate [was] a one-man government."[20] What did this one man have to govern? In 1800, China's population was at least 300 million,[21]

---

15. Quoted from Morse's *Trade and Administration of China* in Kung-chuan Hsiao, *Rural China*, p. 262.

16. Johnston, *Lion and Dragon in Northern China*, p. 155.

17. See Dean, "China's Second Government."

18. Huang, *The Peasant Economy*, p. 224.

19. Nominal number: Ch'ü, *Local Government in China*, p. 8; actual number: Watt, *The District Magistrate*, p. 15.

20. Ch'ü, *Local Government in China*, p. 13.

21. Peterson, *Cambridge History of China*, vol. 9, pt. 1, p. 570, citing the census of 1786. But the adjacent text suggests that it could actually have been as high as 400 million. Mote (*Imperial China, 900–1800*, p. 906) proposes a total of 360 million for 1800.

and there were approximately 1,280 counties.[22] If villages had an average population of 250, there would have been, on average, 940 villages per county; if the average population of a village was 500, then 470 per county. But this assumes that the total population was 300 million; it probably was higher. What could three men, or perhaps only two, or one, even allowing that they had at their disposal many clerks and runners, do with 500 or 1,000 villages? Virtually nothing. The magistrate is unlikely to have even visited more than a few during his limited term in office. People came to him; he did not go to them. For most people the function of the county magistrates was therefore largely symbolic. Village autonomy was the necessary result.[23]

This autonomy must have worked to strengthen the identification of villagers with their villages. Not only the houses and temples but also everything that made the village unique was the creation of their ancestors and perhaps also of they themselves; how could they not be deeply attached to them? This identification must have become a central part of a villager's self-image; living in that particular village made him or her different from other people. Note the comment by Sidney Gamble at the beginning of his extensive survey of villages in north China: "No two villages were alike in the sample groups we studied in Hopei, Shansi, Shantung, and Honan."[24] This sense of uniqueness must in turn have powerfully encouraged residents to contribute generously toward village activities and projects, the results of which can be seen in the lavish processions we have studied and the grand temples constructed in their hundreds of thousands throughout rural China.

The contributions were not merely material; creative energies were also channeled into village work: we can recall the dedication of the village actors and musicians who began learning their skills when they were children and practiced them during leisure moments in the fields, products of loving craftsmanship like the Four-Scene Carts or the Flowery Offerings, and so on. People behave like this when they are

---

22. Ch'ü, *Local Government in China*, p. 2.

23. Autonomous though the villages may have been, the residents understood that they were bound to pay their taxes and looked to the magistrate to punish serious criminal behavior.

24. Gamble, *North China Villages*, p. 1.

committed to something bigger than themselves, something that lifts them out of their ordinary concerns. And this sort of devotion, which was probably felt by almost everyone in the village, reinforced the sense that the village and its residents were special. The self-referential quality of *Levying Demon Soldiers* becomes completely comprehensible when seen from this perspective. Such devotion also would have led naturally to intense conservatism.

The absence of ecclesiastical or governmental domination of temple ritual, local opera, festival processions, and every other means by which symbolic resources were deployed in the villages allowed local variants to thrive, eventually rivaling or even surpassing what the imperium and, in the areas I am familiar with, the great religions had to offer. The officially approved system of rituals almost certainly was irrelevant to the vast majority of the population, and perhaps even to local officials. This is not to say that the attitudes, beliefs, and values of the country folk did not have many elements in common all across China, because they did. But those elements were embodied in a remarkable array of forms; and who is to say whether the medium or the message is more important?[25]

These arguments are unlikely to apply to the smallest and poorest villages. And for large, prosperous villages that resembled towns, the situation was also different, since they were more likely to have attracted the attention of officials and to have had more residents with superior positions in the hierarchies of dominance and education. I suspect also that much of what I have proposed will not fit villages in southern and southeastern China, especially those in regions where lineages dominated social life. There, as writers like James Watson and David Faure have shown, other issues come into play. The same can be said of regions where Daoist ritual and ritual masters played the leading role in local cult activity. But for southern Shanxi, and quite possibly

---

25. I have argued strongly in a number of publications that late imperial Chinese culture was highly integrated, and that is still my position. But I have also insisted that actually identifying the common elements is an intellectual challenge of the first order. I have suggested that we should look to nonverbal "tableaux," derived from opera and ritual, as a possible way of approaching this problem. Here I am in the same conceptual territory.

also southern Hebei, northern Henan, and eastern Shaanxi, and perhaps for many other areas in north China, the independent, creative, self-conscious village—the competent village—was probably the norm. This was the stage on which the spectacles and sacrifices to which this book is devoted were played out, and which they helped to create.

Reference Matter

Bibliography

Primary Sources, Including Unpublished Material

All the important rural liturgical manuscripts discovered in Shanxi since the mid-1980s can now be found in two volumes: Yang Mengheng, ed., *Shangdang gu sai xiejuan shisi zhong jian zhu*, and Han Sheng et al., eds., *Shangdang nuo wenhua yu jisi xiju*. Yang's book contains the fourteen manuscripts contributed by the Niu family of Eastern Daguan village, Zhangzi county; Han's a number of manuscripts from the Cao family of Nan Shê village, Lucheng county, two previously published, the others appearing for the first time.[1] Although it would appear at first glance that since relatively few texts are involved their usefulness is limited, they are in fact so rich that they will occupy scholars for many years to come. I believe such work will lead to a change in prevailing ideas (such as they are) about village religion in north China as radical as that which has already taken place regarding southern and southeastern China.

Other liturgical manuscripts have been published unsystematically. One example is the book devoted to the Fan-drum ritual of Xinzhuang village in southwestern Shanxi: Huang Zhusan and Wang Fucai, *Shanxi sheng Quwo xian Renzhuang cun* Shangu shenpu *diaocha baogao*. Harder to find are the thirteen

---

1. Bibliographic details and Chinese characters for all titles in this section can be found in the body of the Bibliography. An account of the discovery of the Cao and Niu manuscripts is given above near the start of Part III; the two previously published Cao manuscripts are identified there. There are numerous earlier editions of the most important manuscripts, particularly the two commonly known as *Tang yuexing tu* 唐樂星圖 and *Zhou yuexing tu* 周樂星圖.

brief invocations and other ritual texts from a manuscript in the hands of Zhang Peijin 張培金 of Zhangzi, which are printed in an appendix to his biography, published in *Minsu quyi* 107/108 (1997.5), pp. 276–81; the manuscript list of food offerings made at a single-village *sai* in Miao village, Zhangzi, reprinted in the same issue of *Minsu quyi* (pp. 292–97); and the invocation used at the *sai* at the Sanzong Temple of Zhangzi's West Gate, printed in *Xiju ziliao* 8 (1984.1), p. 7.

In addition to the original liturgical sources just mentioned, there is an abundance of inscriptions on stone that can provide invaluable historical and contextual information. Much of this material has not been collected, much less analyzed, since epigraphers have tended to ignore Ming and Qing inscriptions in favor of earlier and rarer ones. But publications focusing on inscriptions related to temple stages have begun to appear, such as two compilations by Feng Junjie: *Shanxi xiqu beike jikao* and *Taihang shenmiao ji saishe yanju yanjiu*. A recent book that contains many inscription texts, as well as hundreds of rare photographs of Shanxi temples, temple murals, and other material remains together with detailed field notes made over several decades is Yang Taikang and Cao Zhanmei, *San Jin xiqu wenwu kao* (2 vols.). This work is the starting point for any serious work on temple theaters in Shanxi.

This project has benefited from unusually rich information on individual ritual specialists who lived in southeastern Shanxi villages from the late nineteenth to the late twentieth century. Much of this material was published in *Minsu quyi* 107/108, but I have also used handwritten drafts of biographies by Zhang Zhennan and Bao Haiyan that include additional information, plus an autograph autobiography of Mr. Zhang (61 + 16 pages, plus cover letters, dated 1991). These are referred to in the notes as "draft biographies" or "manuscript biographies."

I recorded the interviews in which I participated during a trip to southeastern Shansi in October 1993, and the tapes were later transcribed by Mr. Li Tiansheng. This resulted in a 67-page handwritten transcript, which also includes plans of temples visited. References in the notes are to the page numbers in this manuscript. I also interviewed Mr. Li Yuanxing during that trip; those notes are separate, as are the notes of my interviews with Xu Cheng and other old performers in Renzhuang in June 1992.

I must also acknowledge access to some unpublished notes kindly granted to me by Mr. Han Sheng in Taiyuan in October 1993.

Videotapes of villagers walking the Nine Bends of the Yellow River and of the "Capturing the Yellow Demon" ritual in Guyi, neither with production data, apparently made during the 1990s, were made available to me by Professor Wang Ch'iu-kuei. Another videotape of portions of the Yellow Demon ritual was given to me by Dr. Sarah Jessup. This visual documentation was crucial to my understanding of the Yellow Demon ritual.

Anyone concerned with Chinese local society knows the importance of detailed maps. I relied heavily on the 1995 *Shanxi sheng ditu ji*, which has excellent county-level maps at 1:200,000. Also important are the 1:50,000 Chinese Army maps of southeastern Shanxi, based on surveys made in 1924 but not printed until 1944 and 1945, held in the Fu Sinian Library, Academia Sinica, Taiwan. Although the latter have to be considered drafts, the large scale and early date make them invaluable.

Books and Articles Consulted

Bai Tian 白天 and Chen Liping 陳麗萍. "Huangtu gaoyuan nuo wenhua de xin faxian: Shouyang Goubei nuo wu 'Ai shê' diaocha" 黃土高原儺文化的新發現—壽陽溝北儺舞"愛社"調查. *Zhonghua xiqu* 12 (1992.3): 368–74.

Bao Haiyan 暴海燕. "Yang Xueren" 楊雪仁 (1872–1942) [entertainer]. In Yang Mengheng, ed., "Shanxi saishe yuehu yinyangshi chuhu zhuanji" (q.v.).

Bo Songnian 薄松年 and Duan Gaifang 段改芳, eds. *Zhongguo minjian meishu quanji* 中國民間美術全集, vol. 4, *Shanxi* 山西. Beijing: Renmin meishu chubanshe, 1993.

Bodde, Dirk. *Festivals in Ancient China*. Princeton: Princeton University Press, 1975.

Bohr, Paul Richard. *Famine in China and the Missionary*. Harvard East Asian Monographs 48. Cambridge: East Asian Research Center, Harvard University, 1972.

Brandt, Nat. *Massacre in Shansi*. Syracuse, NY: Syracuse University Press, 1994.

Brokaw, Cynthia. *Commerce in Culture: The Sibao Book Trade in the Qing and Republican Periods*. Cambridge: Harvard University Asia Center, 2007.

Cao Zupeng 曹祖彭. "Si jing che jianjie" 四景車簡介. Manuscript in the author's collection.

Cao Zupeng and Cao Xinguang 曹新廣. "Pingshun xian Dongyugou Donghe cun Jiutian shengmu miao" 平順縣東峪溝東河村九天聖母廟. Manuscript in the author's collection.

Chai Jiguang 柴繼光 et al. *Jin yan wenhua shuyao* 晉鹽文化述要. Taiyuan: Shanxi renmin chubanshe, 1993.

Chau, Adam Yuet. *Miraculous Response: Doing Popular Religion in Contemporary China*. Stanford: Stanford University Press, 2006.

Chen Gaoyong 陳高傭. *Zhongguo lidai tianzai renhuo biao* 中國歷代天災人禍表. Shanghai: Shanghai shudian, 1986.

Christian, William A., Jr. *Local Religion in Sixteenth-Century Spain*. Princeton: Princeton University Press, 1981.

Ch'ü T'ung-tsu. *Local Government in China Under the Ch'ing*. Stanford: Stanford University Press, 1969.

Dean, Kenneth. "China's Second Government: Regional Ritual Systems in Southeast China." In Wang Ch'iu-kuei 王秋桂 et al., eds., *Shehui, minzu yu wenhua zhanyan guoji yantaohui lunwen ji* 社會, 民族與文化展演國際研討會論文集. Taipei: Center for Chinese Studies, 2001.

―――. "Lineage and Territorial Cults: Transformations and Interactions in the Irrigated Putian Plains." In Lin Meirong, ed., *Belief, Ritual, and Society: Papers from the Third International Conference on Sinology*. Taipei: Institute of Ethnology, Academia Sinica, 2003.

―――. *Taoist Ritual and Popular Cults of Southeast China*. Princeton: Princeton University Press, 1993.

―――. "Transformations of the *Shê* (Altars of the Soil) in Fujian." *Cahiers d'Extrême-Asie* 10 (1998): 19–75.

Dean, Kenneth, and Zheng Zhenman. *Ritual Alliances: A Survey of Village Temples and Ritual Activities on the Irrigated Alluvial Plain of Putian, Fujian*. Leiden: E. J. Brill, forthcoming.

Ding Shiliang 丁世良 and Zhao Fang 趙放, eds. *Zhongguo difangzhi minsu ziliao huibian: Huabei juan* 中國地方志民俗資料匯編: 華北卷. Beijing: Shumu wenxian chubanshe, 1989.

Dolby, A. W. E. *A History of Chinese Drama*. London: P. Elek, 1976.

Doleželová-Velingerová, Milena, and J. I. Crump. *The Ballad of the Hidden Dragon*. Oxford: Clarendon Press, 1971.

Doolittle, Justus. *The Social Life of the Chinese*, vol. 1. New York: Harper and Brothers, 1865.

Dou Kai 竇楷. "Luogu za xi: yi zhong secai danhua le de nuo xi" 鑼鼓雜戲——一種色彩淡化了的儺戲. *Zhonghua xiqu* 12 (1992.3): 231–46.

―――. "Shi lun 'Ya dui xi'" 試論"啞隊戲." *Zhonghua xiqu* 3 (1987.4): 168–78.

Dou Kai and Yuan Hongxuan 袁宏軒. "Shilun Shanxi luogu za xi" 試論山西鑼鼓雜戲. *Xiqu yishu* 1983.4: 73–79.

Dou Kai and Zhao Bingsheng 趙炳晟. "Shanxi Pingding 'Yu ji' huodong chu tan" 山西評定"雩祭"活動初探. *Zhonghua xiqu* 14 (1998.8): 211–30.

Du Lifang 杜立芳. "Lun Longyan za xi" 論龍岩雜戲. In *Puju shinian* 蒲劇十年. Linfen: n.p., 1959.

Du Xuede 杜學德. "Guyi daxing nuo xi 'Zhuo Huang gui' kaoshu" 固義大型儺戲"捉黃鬼"考述. *Zhonghua xiqu* 18 (1996.5): 146–74.

———. "Hebei sheng Wu'an shi Guyi cun de ji shen yishi he dui xi sai xi yan-chu" 河北省武安市固義村的祭神儀式和對戲賽戲演出. *Minsu quyi* 125 (2000): 153–94.

———. *Yan Zhao nuo wenhua chu tan* 燕趙儺文化初探. Lanzhou: Gansu ren-min chubanshe, 1998.

Duan Shipu 段士朴 and Xu Cheng 許誠. "*Shangu shenpu* chu tan" "扇鼓神譜"初探. *Zhonghua xiqu* 6 (1988.2): 88–100.

Duan Youwen 段友文. "Jin dongnan Lucheng yingshen saishe xisu kaoshu" 晉東南潞城迎神賽社習俗考述. *Minsu quyi* 110 (1997): 1–20.

Duara, Prasenjit. *Culture, Power, and the State*. Stanford: Stanford University Press, 1988.

Dudbridge, Glen. *The Hsi-yu Chi: A Study of Antecedents to the Sixteenth-Century Chinese Novel*. Cambridge: Cambridge University Press, 1970.

Dundes, Alan, and Alessandro Falassi. *La Terra in Piazza*. Berkeley: University of California Press, 1975.

Ebrey, Patricia Buckley. *Confucianism and Family Rituals in Imperial China*. Prince-ton: Princeton University Press, 1991.

Ebrey, Patricia Buckley, trans. *Chu Hsi's* Family Rituals. Princeton: Princeton University Press, 1991.

Edgerton-Tarpley, Kathryn. "Family and Gender in Famine: Cultural Re-sponses to Disaster in North China, 1876–1879." *Journal of Women's History* 16.4 (2004): 119–47.

Fan Tang Nüwa jing 反唐女媧鏡. Wei jing tang 維經堂 edition, preface dated 1753.

Fan Xiaoping 范小平. *Mianzhu muban nianhua* 綿竹木版年畫. Chengdu: Si-chuan renmin chubanshe, 2007.

Faure, David. "Lineage Development in North China, a Case from Shansi Province." Paper presented to the Workshop on the Comparative Study of Chinese Local Society, Academia Sinica, Taiwan, Sept. 2005.

———. *The Structure of Chinese Rural Society: Lineage and Village in the Eastern New Territories, Hong Kong*. Hong Kong and New York: Oxford University Press, 1986.

Feng Junjie 馮俊杰. *Shanxi xiqu beike jikao* 山西戲曲碑刻輯考. Beijing: Zhonghua shuju, 2002.

———. *Taihang shenmiao ji saishe yanju yanjiu* 太行神廟及賽社演劇研究. Taipei: Minsu quyi congshu, 2000.

Feng shen yanyi 封神演義. Taipei: Sanmin shuju, 1998.

Feuchtwang, Stephan. *Popular Religion in China: The Imperial Metaphor*. Richmond, Eng.: Curzon, 2001.

Frend, W. H. C. *The Rise of Christianity*. Philadelphia: Fortress Press, 1984.

Fu Xihua 傅惜華. *Beijing chuantong quyi zonglu* 北京傳統曲藝總錄. Beijing: Zhonghua shuju, 1962.

Gamble, Sidney D. *North China Villages: Social, Political, and Economic Activities Before 1933*. Berkeley: University of California Press, 1963.

———. *Ting Hsien: A North China Rural Community*. Stanford: Stanford University Press, 1968 (1954).

Gamble, Sidney D., trans. *Chinese Village Plays*. Amsterdam: Philo Press, 1970.

Gao Wen 高文, Hou Shiwu 侯世武, and Ning Zhiqi 寧志奇. *Mianzhu nianhua* 綿竹年畫. Beijing: Wenwu chubanshe, 1990.

Geertz, Clifford. *Negara: The Theatre State in Nineteenth-Century Bali*. Princeton: Princeton University Press, 1980.

Goodrich, Anne S. *Peking Paper Gods: A Look at Home Worship*. Monumenta Serica Monographs 23. Nettetal, Ger.: Steyler, 1991.

Graham, D. C. *Folk Religion in Southwest China*. Smithsonian Miscellaneous Collections 142, no. 2. Washington, D.C.: Smithsonian Institution, 1961.

Grootaers, Willem. "The Hagiography of the Chinese God Chen-wu (The Transmission of Rural Traditions in Chahar)." *Folklore Studies* 11.2 (1952): 139–89. Reprinted in idem, *The Sanctuaries in a North-China City* (q.v.).

———. "Rural Temples Around Hsüan-hua (South Chahar), Their Iconography and Their History." *Folklore Studies* 10.2 (1951): 1–125.

———. *The Sanctuaries in a North-China City: A Complete Survey of the Cultic Buildings in the City of Hsüan-hua (Chahar)*. Brussels: Institut Belge des Hautes Études Chinoises, 1995.

———. "Temples and History of Wanch'üan 萬全 (Chahar): The Geographical Method Applied To Folklore." *Monumenta Serica* 13 (1948): 209–315.

———. "Les temples villageois de le région au sudest de Tat'ong (Chansi Nord), leurs inscriptions et leur histoire." *Folklore Studies* 4 (1945): 161–212.

Guo Jingrui 郭精銳. *Che wang fu quben tiyao* 車王府曲本提要. Guangzhou: Zhongshan daxue chubanshe, 1989.

Guo Licheng 郭立誠. *Zhongguo minsu shihua* 中國民俗史話. Taipei: Hanguang wenhua shiye, 1983.

Guojia wenwuju 國家文物局. *Zhongguo wenwu ditu ji: Shanxi fence* 中國文物地圖集: 山西分冊. Beijing: Zhongguo ditu chubanshe, 2006.

Han Sheng 寒聲. "'Dui xi,' bei xiju shi yiwang le de bianzhang" "隊戲," 被戲劇史遺忘了的篇章. In *Nuo xi, Zhongguo xiqu zhi huo huashi* 儺戲, 中國戲曲之活化石. Hefei: Huangshan shushe, 1992.

———. "Qian yan" 前言. In idem et al., eds., "*Yingshen saishe lijie chuan bu sishi qu gongdiao zhu shi*" (q.v.), pp. 51–55.

Han Sheng and Chang Zhitan 常之坦. "*Yingshen saishe lijie chuan bu sishi qu gong-diao* chu tan" "迎神賽社禮節傳簿四十曲宮調"初探. *Zhonghua xiqu* 3 (1987.4): 118–36.

Han Sheng, Yuan Shuangxi 原雙喜, and Li Shoutian 粟守田. "Cong Song Jin yuewu dui xi xianketu kan San Jin wenhua" 從宋晉樂舞隊戲綫刻圖看三晉文化. *Zhonghua xiqu* 10 (1991): 96–107.

Han Sheng, Li Shoutian, and Yuan Shuangxi, eds. *Shangdang nuo wenhua yu jisi xiju* 上黨儺文化與祭祀戲劇. Beijing: Zhongguo xiju chubanshe, 1999.

———. "*Yingshen saishe jisi wenfan ji gong zhan qumu* de shiliao jiazhi" "迎神賽社祭祀文範及供盞曲目"的史料價值. *Zhonghua xiqu* 11 (1991.12): 63–71.

———. "*Yingshen saishe jisi wenfan ji gong zhan qumu* zhushi" "迎神賽社祭祀文範及供盞曲目"注釋. *Zhonghua xiqu* 11 (1991.12): 1–62.

———. "*Yingshen saishe lijie chuan bu sishi qu gongdiao* zhu shi" "迎神賽社禮節傳簿四十曲宮調"注釋. *Zhonghua xiqu* 3 (1987.4): 51–117.

Han Shuwei 韓樹偉. "Shangdang dui xi yu sai he nuo" 上黨隊戲與賽和儺. *Zhonghua xiqu* 12 (1992.3): 311–25.

———. "Yuanben de liuzhuan yu yuehu: Shangdang yuehu yuanben zhe" 院本的流傳與樂戶—上黨樂戶院本折. Conference paper in the author's collection, probably from the 1990s.

Hanan, Patrick. *The Chinese Short Story*. Cambridge: Harvard University Press, 1973.

Hansson, Anders. *Chinese Outcasts: Discrimination and Emancipation in Late Imperial China*. Leiden: Brill, 1996.

Hao He 郝赫. *Shu qu zan fu xuan* 書曲贊賦選. N.p., n.d. Restricted circulation publication in the author's collection, preface and postface dated 1983.

Harrison, Henrietta. *The Man Awakened from Dreams: One Man's Life in a North China Village, 1857–1942*. Stanford: Stanford University Press, 2005.

Hayes, James. "Specialists and Written Materials in the Village World." In David Johnson, Andrew Nathan, and Evelyn Rawski, eds., *Popular Culture in Late Imperial China*. Berkeley: University of California Press, 1985.

Hinton, William. *Fanshen*. New York: Monthly Review Press, 1966.

Hodous, Lewis. *Folkways in China*. London: Probsthain, 1929.

Holm, David. *Art and Ideology in Revolutionary China*. Oxford: Clarendon Press, 1991.

———. "The Death of *Tiaoxi* (the 'Leaping Play'): Ritual Theatre in the Northwest of China." *Modern Asian Studies* 37.4 (2003): 863–84.

Homans, George C. *English Villagers of the Thirteenth Century*. New York: Harper Torchbooks, 1970 (1941).

Hsiao, Kung-chuan. *Rural China: Imperial Control in the Nineteenth Century*. Seattle: University of Washington Press, 1960.

Hu Ji 胡忌. "Jin Yuan yuanben de liuzhuan" 金元院本的流傳. *Yishu yanjiu* 9 (1988): 68–104.

———. "'Yuanben' zhi gainian ji qi yanchu fengmao" "院本"之概念及其演出風貌. *Zhonghua xiqu* 8 (1989.5): 1–28.

Huang and Wang, *"Shangu shenpu" diaocha baogao*: see Huang Zhusan and Wang Fucai, *Shanxi sheng Quwo xian Renzhuang cun* Shangu shenpu *diaocha baogao*.

Huang, Philip C. C. *The Peasant Economy and Social Change in North China*. Stanford: Stanford University Press, 1985.

Huang Youquan 黃有泉 et al. *Hongdong da huaishu yimin* 洪洞大槐樹移民. Taiyuan: Shanxi guji chubanshe, 1993.

Huang Zhusan 黃竹三. "Nuo xi de jieding he Shanxi nuo xi bianxi" 儺戲的界定和山西儺戲辨析. Unpublished paper dated 1992 in the author's collection.

———. "Shanxi Hongdong xian Huoshan Shuishen miao ji Shuishen miao jidian wenbei jisi yanju kaoshu" 山西洪洞縣霍山水神廟及水神廟祭典文碑祭祀演劇考述. *Minsu quyi* 109 (1997): 1–58.

———. "Tan dui xi" 談隊戲. 1997 conference paper in the author's collection.

———. "Wo guo xiqu shiliao de zhongda faxian" 我國戲曲史料的重大發現. *Zhonghua xiqu* 3 (1987.4): 137–52.

Huang Zhusan and Jing Lihu 景李虎. *"Shangu shenpu* yuanliu zai tan" "扇鼓神譜"源流再探. *Zhonghua xiqu* 13 (1993.8): 190–206.

Huang Zhusan and Wang Fucai 王福才. *Shanxi sheng Quwo xian Renzhuang cun* Shangu shenpu *diaocha baogao* 山西省曲沃縣任莊村"扇鼓神譜"調查報告. Taipei: Minsu quyi congshu, 1994.

Huang Zhusan, Wang Fucai, and Jing Lihu. "Shanxi Quwo Renzhuang *Shangu shenpu* he shangu nuoji diaocha baogao" 山西曲沃任莊"扇鼓神譜"和扇鼓儺祭調查報告. *Minsu quyi* 85 (1993): 241–71.

Huang Zhusan, Zhang Shouzhong 張守中, and Yang Taikang 楊太康. "Cong Bei Song wulou de chuxian kan Zhongguo xiqu de fazhan" 從北宋舞樓的出現看中國戲曲的發展. *Minsu quyi* 35 (1985): 25–38.

Huguan xian Wenwu bowuguan 壺關縣文物博物館. "Zhenze gong ji qi shenhua chuanshuo" 眞澤宮及其神話傳説. Mimeograph copy in the author's collection (possibly mid-1980s).

Huitu Sanjiao yuanliu soushen daquan 繪圖三教源流搜神大全. Shanghai: Shanghai guji chubanshe, 1990.

Hymes, Robert. *Statesmen and Gentlemen: The Elite of Fu-chou, Chiang-hsi, in Northern and Southern Sung*. Cambridge: Cambridge University Press, 1986.

Idema, Wilt, and Stephen West. *Chinese Theater, 1100–1450: A Source Book*. Wiesbaden, Ger.: Franz Steiner, 1982.

Jing, Anning. *The Water God's Temple of the Guangsheng Monastery: Cosmic Function of Art, Ritual, and Theater.* Leiden: Brill, 2002.

Jingju cong kan 京劇叢刊. 35 vols. in 7. Shanghai: Xin wenyi chubanshe, 1953–55.

Jingju huibian 京劇匯編. Beijing: Beijing chubanshe, 1957– .

Johnson, David. "Actions Speak Louder Than Words: The Cultural Significance of Chinese Ritual Opera." In idem, ed., *Ritual Opera, Operatic Ritual: Mu-lien Rescues His Mother in Chinese Popular Culture.* Berkeley: Chinese Popular Culture Project, 1989.

———. "Communication, Class, and Consciousness in Late Imperial China." In David Johnson, Andrew Nathan, and Evelyn Rawski, eds., *Popular Culture in Late Imperial China.* Berkeley: University of California Press, 1985.

———. "'Confucian' Elements in the Great Temple Festivals of Southeastern Shansi in Late Imperial Times." *T'oung Pao* 83 (1997): 126–61.

———. "Mu-lien in *Pao-chüan*: The Performance Context and Religious Meaning of the *Yu-ming pao-ch'uan.*" In idem, ed., *Ritual and Scripture in Chinese Popular Religion, Five Studies.* Berkeley: Chinese Popular Culture Project, 1995.

———. "Report on 堯山聖母廟與神社, by Qin Jianming 秦建明 and Marianne Bujard." Paper presented at the International Conference on Water Control and Social Organization in Northern China, Paris, June 2004.

———. "Scripted Performances in Chinese Culture: An Approach to the Analysis of Popular Literature." *Hanxue yanjiu / Chinese Studies* 8.1 (June 1990): 37–43.

Johnson, David, trans. "Kuo Chü Buries His Son." In Wm. Theodore de Bary and Richard Lufrano, eds., *Sources of Chinese Tradition,* 2nd ed., vol. 2. New York: Columbia University Press, 2000.

Johnston, R. F. *Lion and Dragon in Northern China.* London: John Murray, 1910.

Keene, Donald. *Seeds in the Heart: Japanese Literature from Earliest Times to the Late Sixteenth Century.* New York: Henry Holt, 1993.

Kikkawa Yoshikazu 吉川良和. "Guan yu zai Riben faxian de Yuan kan *Fo shuo Mulian jiu mu jing*" 關於在日本發現的元刊"佛説目蓮救母經." *Xiqu yanjiu* 37 (1991): 177–206.

Kuhn, Philip. *Rebellion and Its Enemies in Late Imperial China: Militarization and Social Structure, 1796–1864.* Cambridge: Harvard University Press, 1970.

Lagerwey, John. "Popular Ritual Specialists in West-Central Fujian." In Wang Ch'iu-kuei et al., eds., *Proceedings of the International Conference on Society, Ethnicity and Cultural Performance,* vol. 2. Taipei: Center for Chinese Studies, 2001.

———. *Taoist Ritual in Chinese Society and History.* New York: Macmillan, 1987.

Laufer, Berthold. "Zur kulturhistorischen Stellung der chinesischen Provinz Shansi." *Anthropos* 5.1 (Jan.–Feb. 1910): 181–203.

Ledderose, Lothar. *The Ten Thousand Things*. Princeton: Princeton University Press, 2000.

Li Huaisun 李懷蓀. "Chenhe xi 'Mulian' chutan" 辰河戲"目蓮"初探. In *Mulian xi xueshu zuotanhui lunwen xuan* 目蓮戲學術座談會論文選. Changsha[?], 1985.

Li Jinghan 李景漢 and Zhang Shiwen 張世文. *Ding xian yangge xuan* 定縣秧歌選. Taipei: Minsu congshu, 1971 (1933), vols. 37–40.

Li Shoutian 栗守田. "Yangcheng xian de chenghuang jisi" 陽城縣的城隍祭祀. Manuscript dated 1993.4.12 in the author's collection.

Li Shoutian and Yang Mengheng 楊孟衡. "Wang Fuyun" 王福雲 (1914–1986) [entertainer]. In Yang Mengheng, ed., "Shanxi saishe yuehu yinyangshi chuhu zhuanji" (q.v.).

———. "Zhu Zhagen" 朱紮根 (1886–1951) [entertainer]. In Yang Mengheng, ed., "Shanxi saishe yuehu yinyangshi chuhu zhuanji" (q.v.).

Li Shoutian and Yang Shuangxi. "Yangcheng xian yingshen saishe ji yuehu yanchu huodong" 陽城縣迎神賽社及樂戶演出活動. In Shanxi sheng Shangdang xijuyuan, ed., *Xiju ziliao* 15 下 (1987.1): 551–55.

Li Tiansheng 李天生. "Nan Shê Cao Manjin [Cao Zhan'ao] caifang ji" 南社曹滿金[曹占鰲]采訪記. *Zhonghua xiqu* 13 (1993.8): 124–25.

———. "Saishe shikuang caifang jilu" 賽社實況采訪記錄. *Zhonghua xiqu* 13 (1993.8): 121–23.

———. "*Tang yuexing tu* jiao zhu" "唐樂星圖"校注. *Zhonghua xiqu* 13 (1993.8): 1–130.

———. "*Tang yuexing tu* san lun" "唐樂星圖"散論. *Xi you* 1990, special issue, pp. 49–75.

———. "Xishe cun Wang xing yuehu kao" 西社村王姓樂戶考. *Minsu quyi* 133 (2001): 99–124.

———. "You 'Shanxi saishe zhuan ji' yin chu de hua" 由"山西賽社專輯"引出的話. *Minsu quyi* 110 (1997): 179–98.

Li Tiansheng and Tian Sulan 田素蘭. "Saishe jili yu yuehu jiyue" 賽社祭禮與樂戶伎樂. *Minsu quyi* 115 (1998): 211–46.

Li Xiusheng 李修生, ed. *Guben xiqu jumu tiyao* 古本戲曲劇目提要. Beijing: Wenhua yishu chubanshe, 1997.

Li Yi 李一. "Quwo Shangu nuo xi jumu kaoxi" 曲沃扇鼓儺戲劇目考析. Paper presented at the International Conference on Nuo Opera Studies, Linfen, Shanxi, 1990.

———. "*Shangu shenpu* zhushi" "扇鼓神譜"注釋. *Zhongguo xiqu* 6 (1988.2): 60–87.

Li Yuanxing 李元興. "Zhui shu Nan Shê 'Tiao gui'" 追述南舍"調龜." In Shanxi sheng Shangdang xijuyuan, ed., *Xiju ziliao* 15 下 (1987.1): 458–63.

Li Yuming 李玉明. *Shanxi minjian yishu* 山西民間藝術. Taiyuan: Shanxi renmin chubanshe, 1991.

Liang Fangzhong 梁方仲. *Zhongguo lidai hukou, tiandi, tianfu tongji* 中國歷代戶口, 田地, 田賦統計. Shanghai: Shanghai renmin chubanshe, 1980.

Liang Zuoteng 梁祚騰. "Shanyin xian de 'Sai-sai' qingkuang" 山陰縣的"賽賽"情況. *Zhonghua xiqu* 8 (1989.5): 147–51.

Liao Ben 廖奔. "Jin dongnan ji shen yishi chaoben de xiqu shiliao jiazhi" 晉東南祭神儀式抄本的戲曲史料價值. *Zhonghua xiqu* 13 (1993.8): 131–57.

———. *Song Yuan xiqu wenwu yu minsu* 宋元戲曲文物與民俗. Beijing: Wenwu yishu chubanshe, 1989.

———. *Zhongguo gudai juchang shi* 中國古代劇場史. Zhengzhou: Zhonghua guji chubanshe, 1997.

———. *Zhongguo xiqu shengqiang yuanliu shi* 中國戲曲聲腔源流史. Taipei: Guanya wenhua, 1991.

Liu Cunyan. *Buddhist and Taoist Influences on Chinese Novels*, vol. 1, *The Authorship of the Feng Shen Yen I*. Wiesbaden, Ger.: Otto Harrassowitz, 1962.

Liu Fu 劉復 and Li Jiarui 李家瑞. *Zhongguo suqu zongmu gao* 中國俗曲總目稿. Beiping: Guoli zhongyang yanjiuyuan, Lishi yuyan yanjiusuo, 1932.

Liu Guanwen 劉貫文. "Shangdang diqu yuehu fenbu yu qianxi" 上黨地區樂戶分布與遷徙. In Qiao Jian et al., *Yuehu: Tianye diaocha yu lishi zhuizong* (q.v.).

Liu Tong 劉侗. *Di jing jing wu lue* 帝京景物略. Beijing: Beijing guji chubanshe, 2000.

Liu, Yonghua. "The World of Rituals: Masters of Ceremonies (*Lisheng*), Ancestral Cults, Community Compacts, and Local Temples in Late Imperial Sibao, Fujian." Ph.D. diss., McGill University, 2003.

"Liu Xuande san gu cao lu ji" 劉玄德三顧草廬記 (Ming *chuanqi*). *Guben xiqu congkan chuji* edition. Shanghai: Shangwu yinshuguan, 1954.

Loewe, Michael, and Edward Shaughnessy, eds. *The Cambridge History of Ancient China*. Cambridge: Cambridge University Press, 1999.

Long Pide 龍彼得 (Piet van der Loon) and Shi Binghua 施炳華, eds. *Quanqiang Mulian jiu mu* 泉腔目蓮救母. Taipei: Minsu quyi congshu, 2001.

Lu Chengwen 路成文. *Shanxi fengsu minqing* 山西風俗民情. Taiyuan: Shanxi sheng difangzhi bianzuan weiyuanhui, 1987.

Lu Keyi 魯克義 and Guo Shixing 郭士星, eds. *Shanxi juzhong gaishuo* 山西劇種概說. Taiyuan: Shanxi renmin chubanshe, 1984.

Mao Gengru 茆耕茹. *Mulian ziliao bianmu gailue* 目蓮資料編目概略. Taipei: Minsu quyi congshu, 1993.

Maspero, Henri. "The Mythology of Modern China." In J. Hackin et al., eds., *Asiatic Mythology*. New York: Crescent Books, 1963.

McDermott, Joseph. "Emperors, Elites, and Commoners." In idem, ed., *State and Court Ritual in China*. Cambridge: Cambridge University Press, 1999.

Meng Yuanlao 孟元老. *Dong jing meng hua lu* 東京夢華錄 (1147). In *Dong jing meng hua lu (wai si zhong)* 東京孟華錄 (外四種). Shanghai: Shanghai gudian wenxue chubanshe, 1956.

Meyer-Fong, Tobie. *Building Culture in Early Qing Yangzhou*. Stanford: Stanford University Press, 2003.

Mo Yiping 墨遺萍. *Puju shihun* 蒲劇史魂. N.p., n.d. [1981?].

Morgan, Carol E. *Le tableau du boeuf du printemps*. Paris: Collège de France, 1980.

Mote, F. W. *Imperial China, 900–1800*. Cambridge: Harvard University Press, 1999.

Muir, Edward. *Civic Ritual in Renaissance Venice*. Princeton: Princeton University Press, 1981.

Mulian baojuan quan ji 目蓮寶眷全集. Hangzhou, 1877. Copy in the collection of Wu Xiaoling.

Nienhauser, William, ed. *The Indiana Companion to Traditional Chinese Literature*. Bloomington: Indiana University Press, 1986.

Ortolani, Benito. "Shamanism in the Origins of the Nô Theatre." *Asian Theatre Journal* 1.2 (Autumn 1984): 166–90.

Ouyang Youhui 歐陽友徽. "Song Yuan yi zhu: du naogu za xi 'Bai yuan kai lu' zha ji" 宋元遺珠—讀鐃鼓雜戲"白猿開路"札記. *Zhonghua xiqu* 15 (1993.8): 192–202.

Overmyer, Daniel, ed. *Ethnography in China Today*. Taipei: Yuan-Liou Publishing, 2002.

Peterson, Willard J., ed. *The Cambridge History of China*, vol. 9, pt. 1, *The Ch'ing Empire to 1800*. Cambridge: Cambridge University Press, 2002.

Po Sung-nien and David Johnson. *Domesticated Deities and Auspicious Emblems: The Iconography of Everyday Life in Village China*. Berkeley and Los Angeles: Chinese Popular Culture Project, 1992.

Prip-Møller, J. *Chinese Buddhist Monasteries*. Hong Kong: Hong Kong University Press, 1982 (1937).

Qi Senhua 齊森華 et al., eds. *Zhongguo quxue da cidian* 中國曲學大辭典. Zhejiang jiaoyu chubanshe, 1997.

Qiao Jian 喬健, Liu Guanwen 劉貫文, and Li Tiansheng 李天生. *Yuehu: tianye diaocha yu lishi zhuizong* 樂戶: 田野調查與歷史追踪. Taipei: Tangshan chubanshe, 2001.

Qin Jianming 秦建明 and Marianne Bujard. *Yao shan shengmu miao yu shen shê* 堯山聖母廟與神社. Beijing: Zhonghua shuju, 2002.

Qinding Xu wenxian tongkao 欽定續文獻通考. Qing. Siku quanshu Wenyuan ge intranet edition.

Qing Menggu Che wang fu cang qu ben 清蒙古車王府藏曲本. 1,662 vols. Beijing: Shoudu tushuguan, 1991.

Qin qiang 秦腔. 41 vols. Xi'an: Shanxi sheng wenhua chubanshe, 1958–59, 1980–86.

Qu Liuyi 曲六乙. "*Shangu shenpu* de lishi xinxi jiazhi" "扇鼓神譜"的歷史信息價值. *Zhonghua xiqu* 6 (1988.2): 101–23.

Quan Tang shi 全唐詩. Siku quanshu Wenyuan ge intranet edition.

Qu hai zongmu tiyao 曲海總目提要. Qing. Beijing: Renmin wenxue chubanshe, 1959.

Ren Guangwei 任光偉. "Sai xi, naogu za xi chu tan" 賽戲, 鐃鼓雜戲初探. *Zhonghua xiqu* 3 (1987.4): 195–210.

———. "Sai xi, naogu za xi er tan" 賽戲, 鐃鼓雜戲二探. *Zhonghua xiqu* 13 (1993.8): 260–69.

Roberts, Moss, trans. *Three Kingdoms*. Berkeley: University of California Press, 1991.

Rowe, William. *Saving the World: Chen Hongmou and Elite Consciousness in Eighteenth-Century China*. Stanford: Stanford University Press, 2001.

San Guo yanyi 三國演義. Hong Kong: Xingzhou shijie shuju, n.d.

Schipper, Kristofer. *Concordance du Tao-tsang: titres des ouvrages*. Paris: École française d'Extrême Orient, 1975.

———. *The Taoist Body*. Berkeley: University of California Press, 1993.

Seaman, Gary. *Journey to the North: An Ethnohistorical Analysis and Annotated Translation of the Chinese Folk Novel* Pei-yu-chi. Berkeley: University of California Press, 1987.

Shanxi difang xiqu huibian di yi ji: naogu za xi zhuanji yi 山西地方戲曲匯編第一集: 鐃鼓雜戲專輯一. Taiyuan: Shanxi renmin chubanshe, 1981.

"Shanxi Ji shan Jin mu fajue jianbao" 山西稷山金墓發掘簡報. *Wenwu* 1983.1: 45–63.

Shanxi sheng ditu ji 山西省地圖集. Taiyuan: Shanxi sheng cehui ju, 1995.

Shanxi sheng ge juzhong jumu diaocha 山西省各劇種劇目調查. Taiyuan: Shanxi sheng di er jie xiqu guanmo yanchu da hui, 1957.

Shanxi shifan daxue xiqu wenwu yanjiusuo 山西師範大學戲曲文物研究所, ed. *Song Jin Yuan xiqu wenwu tu lun* 宋金元戲曲文物圖論. Taiyuan: Shanxi renmin chubanshe, 1987.

Shanxi tongzhi 山西通志. 1734. Siku quanshu Wenyuan ge intranet edition.

Shanxi tongzhi 山西通志. 1892. Reprinted—Beijing: Zhonghua shuju, 1991–2002.

Shanxi xiancun difang xiqu mulu 山西現存地方戲曲目錄. N.p., 1980. Mimeograph copy in the author's collection.

"Shanxi Xinjiang Nanfan zhuang, Wuling zhuang Jin Yuan mu fajue jian bao" 山西新絳南范庄, 吳嶺庄金元墓發掘簡報. *Wenwu* 1983.1: 64–72.

Shen Bojun 沈伯俊 et al., eds. *San Guo yanyi cidian* 三國演義辭典. Chengdu: Ba Shu shushe, 1989.

Shen Defu 沈德符. *Gu qu za yan* 顧曲雜言. Ming. Siku quanshu Wenyuan ge intranet edition.

Shi Yaozeng 史耀增. "Heyang tiaoxi ji qi shehui huanjing" 合陽跳戲及其社會環境. *Minsu quyi* 117 (1999): 217–32.

Shi, Zhongwen. *The Golden Age of Chinese Drama: Yuan Tsa-Chü.* Princeton: Princeton University Press, 1976.

Skinner, G. William. "Marketing and Social Structure in Rural China." 3 pts. *Journal of Asian Studies* 24.1–3 (Nov. 1964–May 1965).

Sommer, Matthew. *Sex, Law, and Society in Late Imperial China.* Stanford: Stanford University Press, 2000.

Soothill, William. *A Dictionary of Chinese Buddhist Terms.* Taipei: Buddhist Culture Service, 1962 (1937).

Spence, Jonathan. *The Search for Modern China.* New York: Norton, 1990.

Su wenxue congkan 俗文學叢刊. 500 vols. Taipei: Zhongyang yanjiuyuan, Lishi yuyan yanjiusuo, 2001–5.

Taiping guangji 太平廣記. Siku quanshu Wenyuan ge intranet edition.

Tao Junqi 陶君起. *Jingju jumu chutan* 京劇劇目初探. Beijing: Zhongguo xiju chubanshe, 1980.

Tao Zongyi 陶宗儀. *Chuogeng lu* 輟耕錄. Ming. Siku quanshu Wenyuan ge intranet edition.

Taylor, Romeyn. "Calendar of [Official] Sacrifices: Late Ming." Undated photocopy of typescript in the author's collection.

"Tong que tai" 銅雀臺 (Shanxi *Za* opera). In *Shanxi difang xiqu huibian* 山西地方戲曲匯編, vol. 1, *Luogu za xi* 鑼鼓雜戲. Taiyuan: Shanxi renmin chubanshe, 1981.

Twitchett, Denis, ed. *Cambridge History of China*, vol. 3, pt. 1, *Sui and T'ang China, 589–906.* Cambridge: Cambridge University Press, 1979.

Waley, Arthur, trans. *The Book of Songs.* New York: Grove Press, 1960.

Wang Ch'iu-kuei 王秋桂. "Yuanxiao jie bukao" 元宵節補考. *Minsu quyi* 65 (1990): 5–33.

Wang Ch'iu-kuei et al., eds. *Proceedings of the International Conference on Society, Ethnicity and Cultural Performance.* 2 vols. Taipei: Center for Chinese Studies, 2001.

Wang Fucai 王福才. "Hunyuan minjian shehuo—'Shua gushi'" 渾源民間社火—耍故事. 1991 conference paper in the author's collection.

———. "Shanxi zhongnan bu shenmiao beike zhong de xiqu minsu ziliao jilu" 山西中南部神廟碑刻中的戲曲民俗資料輯錄. *Minsu quyi* 127 (2000): 23–56.

Wang Jiaju 王家駒. "Zhangzi Baodian hui" 長子鮑店會. *Shanxi wenshi ziliao* 山西文史資料 11 (1981): 174–77.

Wang Jisi 王季思, ed. *Quan Yuan xiqu* 全元戲曲. Beijing: Renmin wenxue chubanshe, 1999.

Wang Liang 王亮. "Luogu za xi de yanchu tizhi yu lishi yuanyuan" 鑼鼓雜戲的演出體制與歷史淵源. *Minsu quyi* 116 (1998): 209–22.

Wang Liqi 王利器. *Yuan Ming Qing san dai jinhui xiaoshuo xiqu shiliao* 元明清三代禁毀小説戲曲史料. Shanghai: Shanghai guji chubanshe, 1981.

Wang Shucun. *Paper Joss: Deity Worship Through Folk Prints*. Beijing: New World Press, 1992.

Wang Shucun 王樹村, ed. *Zhongguo meishu quanji* 中國美術全集, vol. 21, *Minjian nianhua* 民間年畫. Beijing: Xinhua shudian, 1985.

Wang Xiaju 王遐舉. "Jianjie Jinnan de 'Luogu za xi'" 簡介晉南的"鑼鼓雜戲." *Xiqu yanjiu* 6 (1958.2): 118–20, plus illustrations.

Wang Zhijun 王止峻. "Tan sai xi" 談賽戲. *Shanxi wenxian* 山西文獻 13 (1979): 100–101.

Watson, James L., and Rubie S. Watson. *Village Life in Hong Kong: Politics, Gender, and Ritual in the New Territories*. Hong Kong: Chinese University Press, 2004.

Watt, John R. *The District Magistrate in Late Imperial China*. New York: Columbia University Press, 1972.

Wei shu 魏書. Beijing: Zhonghua shuju, 1974.

Wen Xing 溫幸 and Xue Maixi 薛麥喜. *Shanxi minsu* 山西民俗. Taiyuan: Shanxi renmin chubanshe, 1991.

Will, Pierre-Étienne. *Bureaucracy and Famine in Eighteenth-Century China*. Stanford: Stanford University Press, 1990.

Wilson, Thomas. "Sacrifice and the Imperial Cult of Confucius." *History of Religions* 41 (Feb. 2002): 251–87.

Wolf, Arthur. "Gods, Ghosts, and Ancestors." In idem, ed., *Religion and Ritual in Chinese Society* (q.v.).

Wolf, Arthur, ed. *Religion and Ritual in Chinese Society*. Stanford: Stanford University Press, 1974.

Wu Cheng-han. "The Temple Fairs in Late Imperial China." Ph.D. diss., Princeton, 1988.

Wurm, S. A., and Li Rong, eds. *Language Atlas of China*. Hong Kong: Longmans, 1987.

Wutai xian wenhua ju 五台縣文化局. "'Sai xi' shilue" "賽戲"史略. *Xi you* 1984.2: 59–60.

Xiang Yang 項陽. *Shanxi yuehu yanjiu* 山西樂戶研究. Beijing: Wenwu chubanshe, 2001.

Xi Han yanyi 西漢演義. Shanghai: Guangyi shuju, 1948.

Xu Hongtu 徐宏圖. *Zhejiang sheng Pan'an xian Shenze cun de lianhuo yishi* 浙江省 磐安縣深澤村的煉火儀式. Taipei: Minsu quyi congshu, 1995.

———. *Zhejiang sheng Pan'an xian Yangtou cun de Xifang le* 浙江省磐安縣仰頭 村的西方樂. Taipei: Minsu quyi congshu, 1995.

Yang, *Fourteen Manuscripts*, see Yang Mengheng, ed., *Shangdang gu sai xiejuan shisi zhong jian zhu.*

Yang Mengheng 楊孟衡. "Gu ju zheguang" 古劇折光. *Xi you* 1987.3: 23–27.

———. "Lucheng Nan Shê 'Tiao jia gui'—Shangdang gu sai kaocha zhi yi" 潞城南舍"調家龜"—上黨古賽考察之一. Mimeograph dated 1997.1 in the author's collection.

———. "Luogu za xi kaolue" 羅鼓雜戲考略. 2 pts. *Puju yishu* 蒲劇藝術 62 (1996.1): 17–24; 63 (1996.2): 27–32.

———. "Pingshun xian Dongyugou Jiutian shengmu miao sai" 平順縣東峪 沟九天聖母廟賽. In Feng Junjie, *Taihang shenmiao ji saishe yanju yanjiu* (q.v.).

———. "Song Jin gu ju zai Shanxi zhi liubian" 宋晉古劇在山西之流變. *Xiqu yanjiu* 26 (1988): 45–61.

———. "You 'nuo' ru 'sai' shuo" 由"儺"入"賽"說. *Zhonghua xiqu* 12 (1992.3): 180–92.

———. "Zhang Zhennan" 張振南. In idem, ed., "Shanxi saishe yuehu yin-yangshi chuhu zhuanji" (q.v.).

Yang Mengheng, ed. *Shangdang gu sai xiejuan shisi zhong jian zhu* 上黨古賽寫卷 十四種箋注. Taipei: Minsu quyi congshu, 2000.

———. "Shanxi saishe yuehu yinyangshi chuhu zhuanji" 山西賽社樂戶陰陽 師廚戶傳記." *Minsu quyi* 107/108 (1997.5): 161–289.

Yang Mengheng and Xie Yuhui 謝玉輝. "Shanxi sheng Linyi xian Sanguan xiang Xinzhuang Luogu za xi" 山西省臨猗縣三管鄉新莊鑼鼓雜戲. *Minsu quyi* 89 (1994): 133–60.

Yang Mengheng and Zhang Zhennan 張振南. "Shangdang gu sai jiyi kaoshu" 上黨古賽祭儀考述. *Zhonghua xiqu* 16 (1995.12): 82–100.

Yang Mengheng, Zhang Zhennan, and Bao Haiyan 暴海燕, eds. "*Sai shang za yong shen qian ben* jiao zhu" "賽上雜用神前本"校注. *Zhonghua xiqu* 16 (1995.12): 32–81.

Yang Mengheng et al., eds. *Zhongguo bangzi xi jumu da cidian* 中國梆子戲劇目 大辭典. Taiyuan: Shanxi renmin chubanshe, 1991.

Yang Taikang 楊太康 and Cao Zhanmei 曹占梅. *San Jin xiqu wenwu kao* 三晉戲曲文物考. 2 vols. Taipei: Minsu quyi congshu, 2006.

Yang Xianyi and Gladys Yang, trans. *The Courtesan's Jewel Box*. Beijing: Foreign Languages Press, 1981.

Ye Mingsheng 葉明生. *Fujian Shouning siping kuilei xi Nainiang zhuan* 福建壽寧四平傀儡戲奶娘傳. Taipei: Minsu quyi congshu, 1997.

———. "Yu ji ji qi yishu xingtai chu tan" 雩祭及其藝術形態初探. *Zhonghua xiqu* 11 (1991.12): 129–47.

Yin Gengfu 尹耕夫. "Wang Xiaoji" 王小雞 (1885–1965) [entertainer]. In Yang Mengheng, ed., "Shanxi saishe yuehu yinyangshi chuhu zhuanji" (q.v.).

Yu Daxi 余大喜 and Liu Zhifan 劉之凡. *Jiangxi sheng Nanfeng xian Sanxi xiang Shiyou cun de tiao nuo* 江西省南豐縣三溪鄉石郵村的跳儺. Taipei: Minsu quyi congshu, 1995.

Yuan Ke 袁珂. *Zhongguo shenhua chuanshuo cidian* 中國神話傳說詞典. Shanghai: Shanghai cishu chubanshe, 1985.

Yuan Shuangxi 原雙喜. "Dui xi juese hangdang tizhi" 隊戲角色行當體制. In Shanxi sheng Shangdang xijuyuan, ed., *Xiju ziliao* 戲劇資料 15 下 (1987.1): 367–68.

———. "Shangdang nuo xi ji qi liubian" 上黨儺戲及其流變. 1990 conference paper in the author's collection.

Yuan Shuangxi and Li Shoutian 栗守田. "Fang laoyiren Cui Luze" 訪老藝人崔路則. In Shanxi sheng Shangdang xijuyuan, ed., *Xiju ziliao* 15 下 (1987.1): 546–47. Reprinted with slight revisions in Yang Mengheng, ed., "Shanxi saishe yuehu yinyangshi chuhu zhuanji" (q.v.).

———. "Fang Lingchuan xian Dong Chenquangou 'Yanhou shi' miao" 訪陵川縣東陳犬溝"咽喉師"廟. In Shanxi sheng Shangdang xijuyuan, ed., *Xiju ziliao* 15 下 (1987.1): 545–46.

———. "Jincheng xian yuehu huodong fangwen xiao ji" 晉城縣樂戶活動訪問小記. In Han Sheng et al., eds., *Shangdang nuo wenhua yu jisi xiju* (q.v.).

———. "Shangdang yuehuxi gaishuo" 上黨樂戶戲概説. In Shanxi sheng Shangdang xijuyuan, ed., *Xiju ziliao* 15 下 (1987.1): 464–80.

———. "Si fang Gaoping Yanhou si" 四訪高平咽喉司. In Han Sheng et al., eds., *Shangdang nuo wenhua yu jisi xiju* (q.v.).

Zeng Bairong 曾白融. *Jingju jumu cidian* 京劇劇目辭典. Beijing: Zhongguo xiju chubanshe, 1989.

Zhang Geng 張庚. "Xu yan" 序言. In *Zhongguo xiqu zhi: Shanxi juan* (q.v.).

Zhang Geng et al., eds. *Zhongguo dabaike quanshu: xiqu, quyi* 中國大百科全書: 戲曲, 曲藝. Beijing: Zhongguo dabaike quanshu chubanshe, 1983.

Zhang Jizhong 張紀仲. *Shanxi lishi zhengqu dili* 山西歷史政區地理. Taiyuan: Shanxi guji chubanshe, 2005.

Zhang Zhengming 張正明. "Ming dai de yuehu" 明代的樂戶. *Ming shi yanjiu* 1991.1: 208–13.

Zhang Zhennan 張振南. "Ji Lucheng *Lijie chuan bu* zhi hou Zhangzi you caide yi chu yanjiu xiqu guibao" 繼潞城"禮節傳簿"之后長子又采得一處研究戲曲瑰寶. *Zhangzi wenshi ziliao* 4 (1989): 145–49.

———. "Pingshun xian de pao che hui" 平順縣的跑車會. Manuscript dated 1993 in the author's collection.

———. "Yueju he sai" 樂劇和賽. In Shanxi sheng Shangdang xijuyuan, ed., *Xiju ziliao* 8 (1984.1): 1–16.

———. "Yueju yu sai" 樂劇與賽. *Zhonghua xiqu* 13 (1993.8): 230–59.

———. "Zhangzi xiqu yanjiu gaikuang" 長子戲曲研究概況. *Zhangzi wenshi ziliao* 2 (1986): 127–53.

———. "Zhongguo Shanxi gu Shangdang minjian 'Yingshen saishe' si shen su gui" 中國山西古上黨民間"迎神賽社"祀神俗規. Manuscript dated 1993.4 in the author's collection.

Zhang Zhennan and Bao Haiyan 暴海燕. "Feng Guiyu" 馮貴玉 (1911–1992) [master of ceremonial]. In Yang Mengheng, ed., "Shanxi saishe yuehu yinyangshi chuhu zhuanji" (q.v.).

———. "Niu Zhenguo" 牛振國 (1880–1946) [master of ceremonial]. In Yang Mengheng, ed., "Shanxi saishe yuehu yinyangshi chuhu zhuanji" (q.v.).

———. "Shangdang minjian de 'Yingshen saishe' zai tan" 上黨民間的"迎神賽社"再探. *Zhonghua xiqu* 18 (1996.5): 103–23.

———. "Shangdang Xi Nancheng miao sai" 上黨西南呈廟賽. *Minsu quyi* 107/108 (1997.5): 353–56.

———. "Song Changshan" 宋長山 (1922–) [ritual chef]. In Yang Mengheng, ed., "Shanxi saishe yuehu yinyangshi chuhu zhuanji" (q.v.).

———. "Yan Genzheng" 閻根正 (1912–1943) [entertainer]. In Yang Mengheng, ed., "Shanxi saishe yuehu yinyangshi chuhu zhuanji" (q.v.)

———. "Yan Xiaozheng" 閻小正 (1906–1940) [entertainer]. In Yang Mengheng, ed., "Shanxi saishe yuehu yinyangshi chuhu zhuanji" (q.v.).

Zhang Zhennan and Ji Guangming 冀光明. "Zhuan wei yingshen saishe yanchu de duizi xi" 專爲迎神賽社演出的對子戲. In Lu Keyi and Guo Shixing, eds., *Shanxi juzhong gaishuo* (q.v.).

Zhang Zhennan and Yang Mengheng 楊孟衡. "Niu Xixian" 牛希賢 (1923–1994) [master of ceremonial]. In Yang Mengheng, ed., "Shanxi saishe yuehu yinyangshi chuhu zhuanji" (q.v.).

Zhang Zhizhong 張之中. "Dui xi, yuanben yu za ju de xingqi" 隊戲, 院本與雜劇的興起. *Zhonghua xiqu* 3 (1987.4): 153–67.

———. "Shanxi nuo xi gaishuo" 山西儺戲概說. *Zhonghua xiqu* 12 (1992.3): 132–47.

Zhang Zhizhong et al. "*Shangu nuo xi* luxiangpian wenben" '扇鼓儺戲'錄像片
文本. Linfen, 1989. 29 pages. Transcript of videotape of 1989 performance
of *Shangu shenpu*, with introduction and notes. Restricted circulation text in
the author's collection.

Zhao Kuifu 趙逵夫. "Bei Song nuo xi 'Zuo Houtu' yanjiu" 北宋儺戲"坐后
土"研究. *Zhonghua xiqu* 20 (1997.4): 96–117.

———. "Fenyin shangu nuo xi de xingcheng shidai yu wenhua yunxu" 汾陰
扇鼓儺戲的形成時代與文化蘊蓄. *Zhonghua xiqu* 13 (1993.8): 207–29.

Zheng Zhizhen 鄭之珍. *Mulian jiu mu quan shan xiwen* 目蓮救母勸善戲文.
Ming. *Guben xiqu zongkan chu ji* edition.

Zhongguo dabaike quanshu: xiqu, quyi 中國大百科全書: 戲曲曲藝. Beijing:
Zhongguo dabaike quanshu, 1983.

Zhongguo lishi ditu, xia 中國歷史地圖, 下. Taipei: Chinese Culture University
Press, 1984.

Zhongguo meishujia xiehui, Shanxi fenhui 中國美術家協會山西分會 et al.,
eds. *Jinnan muban nianhua ziliao* 晉南木版年畫資料. N.p., 1980.

Zhongguo tongsu xiaoshuo zongmu tiyao 中國通俗小説總目提要. Beijing: Zhongguo wenlian chuban gongsi, 1990.

Zhongguo xiqu quyi cidian 中國戲曲曲藝辭典. Shanghai: Shanghai cishu chubanshe, 1981.

Zhongguo xiqu zhi: Shanxi juan 中國戲曲志: 山西卷. Beijing: Wenhua yishu
chubanshe, 1990.

"Zhongyang yanjiu yuan Lishi yuyan yanjiusuo suozang Suqu zongmu mulu"
中央研究院歷史語言研究所所藏俗曲總目目錄. N.p., n.d. Manuscript.

Zhou Mi 周密. *Wu lin jiu shi* 武林舊事. Ca. 1280. In *Dong jing meng hua lu (wai si
zhong)* 東京孟華錄 (外四種). Shanghai: Shanghai gudian wenxue chubanshe, 1956.

Zhuang Yibi 莊一拂. *Gudian xiqu cunmu huikao* 古典戲曲存目匯考. Shanghai:
Shanghai guji chubanshe, 1982.

Zong Li 宗力 and Liu Qun 劉群. *Zhongguo minjian zhu shen* 中國民間諸神.
Shijiazhuang: Hebei renmin chubanshe, 1986.

Glossary-Index

Harvard East Asian Monographs
(*out-of-print)

Harvard East Asian Monographs

Harvard East Asian Monographs

Harvard East Asian Monographs

Harvard East Asian Monographs

Harvard East Asian Monographs